Revolution and Political Violence in Central Europe

In the wake of World War I and the Russian revolutions, Central Europeans in 1919 faced a world of possibilities, threats, and extreme contrasts. Dramatic events since the end of the war seemed poised to transform the world, but the form of that transformation was unclear and violently contested in the streets and societies of Munich and Budapest in 1919. The political perceptions of contemporaries, framed by gender stereotypes and antisemitism, reveal the sense of living history, of "fighting the world revolution," which was shared by residents of the two cities. In 1919, both revolutionaries and counter-revolutionaries were focused on shaping the emerging order according to their own worldview. By examining the narratives of these Central European revolutions in their transnational context, Eliza Ablovatski helps answer the question of why so many Germans and Hungarians chose to use their new political power for violence and repression.

Eliza Ablovatski is Associate Professor and Chair of the Department of History at Kenyon College. Ablovatski is a historian of Central and Eastern Europe interested in gender and Jewish history. She is the coauthor of three books of oral histories of Jews from Czernowitz, including *Zwischen Pruth und Jordan: Lebenserinnerungen Czernowitzer Juden* (2003) and *". . . und das Herz wird mir schwer dabei": Czernowitzer Juden erinnern sich* (2009).

Studies in the Social and Cultural History of Modern Warfare

General Editors
Robert Gerwarth, *University College Dublin*
Jay Winter, *Yale University*

Advisory Editors
Heather Jones, *University College London*
Rana Mitter, *University of Oxford*
Michelle Moyd, *Indiana University Bloomington*
Martin Thomas, *University of Exeter*

In recent years the field of modern history has been enriched by the exploration of two parallel histories. These are the social and cultural history of armed conflict, and the impact of military events on social and cultural history.

Studies in the Social and Cultural History of Modern Warfare presents the fruits of this growing area of research, reflecting both the colonization of military history by cultural historians and the reciprocal interest of military historians in social and cultural history, to the benefit of both. The series offers the latest scholarship in European and non-European events from the 1850s to the present day.

A full list of titles in the series can be found at:
www.cambridge.org/modernwarfare

Revolution and Political Violence in Central Europe

The Deluge of 1919

Eliza Ablovatski

Kenyon College

CAMBRIDGE
UNIVERSITY PRESS

CAMBRIDGE
UNIVERSITY PRESS

Shaftesbury Road, Cambridge CB2 8EA, United Kingdom

One Liberty Plaza, 20th Floor, New York, NY 10006, USA

477 Williamstown Road, Port Melbourne, VIC 3207, Australia

314–321, 3rd Floor, Plot 3, Splendor Forum, Jasola District Centre, New Delhi – 110025, India

103 Penang Road, #05–06/07, Visioncrest Commercial, Singapore 238467

Cambridge University Press is part of Cambridge University Press & Assessment, a department of the University of Cambridge.

We share the University's mission to contribute to society through the pursuit of education, learning and research at the highest international levels of excellence.

www.cambridge.org
Information on this title: www.cambridge.org/9781108978781

DOI: 10.1017/9781139049535

First published 2021
First paperback edition 2023

A catalogue record for this publication is available from the British Library

Library of Congress Cataloging-in-Publication data
Names: Ablovatski, Eliza, author.
Title: Revolution and political violence in Central Europe : the deluge of 1919 /
Eliza Ablovatski, Kenyon College, Ohio.
Other titles: Deluge of 1919
Description: Cambridge, United Kingdom ; New York, NY : Cambridge
University Press, 2021. | Series: Studies in the social and cultural history of
modern warfare | Includes bibliographical references and index.
Identifiers: LCCN 2021000636 (print) | LCCN 2021000637 (ebook) |
ISBN 9780521768306 (hardback) | ISBN 9781108978781 (paperback) |
ISBN 9781139049535 (ebook)
Subjects: LCSH: Revolutions – Europe, Central – History – 20th century. |
Hungary – History – Revolution, 1918-1919 – Influence. | Germany – History –
Revolution, 1918 – Influence. | Soviet Union – History – Revolution, 1917-1921 –
Influence. | Budapest (Hungary) – History – 1872-1945. | Munich (Germany) –
History – 20th century. | Europe, Central – Politics and government – 20th century. |
Hungary – Politics and government – 1918-1945. | Germany – Politics and
government – 1918-1933.
Classification: LCC DAW1049 .A25 2021 (print) | LCC DAW1049 (ebook) | DDC
943.0009/041–dc23
LC record available at https://lccn.loc.gov/2021000636
LC ebook record available at https://lccn.loc.gov/2021000637

ISBN   978-0-521-76830-6   Hardback
ISBN   978-1-108-97878-1   Paperback

For my father, Lyman L. Johnson, for showing me the way.

And for my children, Rada, Kazik, and Stas, I can't wait to see what you do.

Contents

Tables

Figures

Acknowledgments

This book studies the way that narratives develop and the communities in which memories are shared and elaborated. My own ideas have similarly developed through my participation in a variety of communities of scholars and friends over the years of this book's gestation. My topic is at the nexus of German history, Hungarian history, Habsburg history, comparative history, women's history, Jewish history, the history of World War I, and the histories of the Russian Revolution and the Soviet Union, as well as histories of memory, revolution, and trauma. My work has benefitted from intellectual exchange and conversation with scholars in all of these fields, and I hope that they will recognize the sparks of their influence in my work.

I am grateful for the financial and intellectual support of several foundations and institutions that enabled research in four countries, including the Council on European Studies, the Columbia University History Department, the International Research & Exchanges Board, the Friedrich-Ebert-Stiftung, the American Council of Learned Societies, the Volkswagen-Stiftung, the National Endowment for the Humanities, and my wonderful employer, Kenyon College. In Berlin, I found a home at the Zentrum für Vergleichende Geschichte Europas (ZVGE) under the direction of Jürgen Kocka and Holm Sundhaussen. Jürgen Kocka also invited me to participate as a fellow in the stimulating research group on civil society that he formed at the Wissenschaftszentrum Berlin (WZB). I am indebted to both the ZVGE and the WZB for intellectual as well as financial support, and particularly the research support of the librarians at the WZB.

At Columbia University, I was lucky to learn to write history from the examples of my advisor, István Deák, and the late Fritz Stern. Their love of a good story and appreciation for both the ironies of history and the dangers of illiberalism continue to inspire me. Volker Berghahn and the late Mark von Hagen introduced me to compelling debates and issues in historical scholarship and generously guided me into the profession. Isser Woloch's course on the French Revolution sparked my interest in the lived experience in revolutionary cities. In and out of the classroom, my cohort of graduate students at Columbia formed a stimulating community: Paul and Jessie Cheney, Michael Ebner,

Anna Fishzon, Edna Friedberg, Christina Gehlsen, Eagle Glassheim, Michael
L. Miller, Annie Polland, Iris Rachamimov, David Tompkins, Wendy Urban-
Mead, and Max Voegler. And the New York years were more delightful thanks
to friends like Fausto Espinosa, Lesley Porcelli, and Tina Truman.

In Berlin, David, Max, Christina, and I joined Ari Sammartino, Winson Chu,
and Karolina May-Chu for stimulating discussions, archival tips, and support.
The hospitality and generosity of Christina and Max, as well as Anke Gliesche
and Violeta Mićić, made it hard to leave Berlin and always easy to return. I have
had two academic homes at the Freie Universität in Berlin, the ZVGE and the
Osteuropa-Institut, and my friends there have supported this project through
the years as well: Malte Fuhrmann, Jörn Grünewald, and the whole of the
KolČern collective: Marianna Hausleitner, Stefan Gehrke, Gertrud Ranner,
Anja Fiedler, Nils Kreimeier, Gaby Coldeway (for the sake of the "Belgian
women's movement"), and especially Axel Halling, who has been a friend and
colleague over decades in both Berlin and Budapest. Thanks to Axel, I met the
Csordás family who made me feel at home in Budapest. Robert Nemes, David
Frey, and Árpád von Klimó, another displaced "Berliner," helped introduce me
to the archives in Budapest. It was a pleasure to live and work in the city along
with Hilary Lackey, Mišel Vasiljević, Chris Medalis, Michael L. Miller, and
Mara Bodis-Wollner. I am grateful to Michael Brenner for welcoming me to
Munich and inviting me to his seminar on German Jewish history, and to
Marcus Khoury for his excellent company there. In Vienna many years ago,
Maureen Healy and Daniel Unowsky welcomed me to the city and to the world
of research; they have remained friends and model historians.

A formative event for me and for my work on this project was the women's
history conference organized in 1999 by Elena Gapova and the European
Humanities University in Minsk. That conference was the seed of a brilliant
intellectual and support network: Lisa Kirschenbaum, Cynthia Paces, and
Nancy Wingfield, who made me feel welcome in the historical profession,
introduced me to other historians, read my work, and encouraged me. Nancy
read through this entire manuscript with eagle eyes and inciteful comments,
and offered (along with my daughter, Rada) the final encouragements to bring
the book to fruition. In supporting me to finish the book, thanks are also in order
for my friends and colleagues at Kenyon College, particularly my fellow
historians, and my writing teammate, Katherine Elkins.

My father, Lyman L. Johnson, a historian of Latin America, has always taken
my work seriously, has treated me as a colleague from the start, and has read
and reread every word of this book. He and my mother, Susan Johnson,
supported me in every way during this project, and my mother's feminism
and her personal and professional engagement for women inspired my interest
in women's history. My debts to my parents are immeasurable and it is thanks
to them that I am a historian. Finally, I want to thank my own family. My

husband, Alexandr Ablovatski, has been a partner in years of conversations about central and eastern Europe, revolution, and the world. A child of perestroika, his curiosity, sensitivity, and humor show me daily the best of humanity's ability to adapt and to live through historically unsettled times. My children, Radmila, Kazimir, and Stanislav, keep me focused on the present and optimistic about the future.

Introduction

It was the best of times, it was the worst of times, it was the age of wisdom, it was the age of foolishness, it was the epoch of belief, it was the epoch of incredulity, it was the season of Light, it was the season of Darkness, it was the spring of hope, it was the winter of despair, we had everything before us, we had nothing before us, we were all going direct to heaven, we were all going direct the other way – in short, the period was so far like the present period, that some of its noisiest authorities insisted on its being received, for good or for evil, in the superlative degree of comparison only.

Charles Dickens, *A Tale of Two Cities* (1859)

Like Dickens' novel of the French Revolution, this book is a tale of two revolutionary cities – Munich and Budapest – at a time of great uncertainty and upheaval. In the wake of World War I and the Russian revolutions, Central Europeans in 1919 faced a world of possibilities, threats, and extreme contrasts. The war and revolutions had caused the deaths of millions of people worldwide and the injury and displacement of millions more, and seen the overthrow of centuries-old ruling dynasties and the birth of brand new states defined by the ideas of nationalism and socialism. The world-historical transformations affected the lives of Central Europeans on every level, interlocking individual experiences and observations with the grand narratives of history. Most Central Europeans were acutely aware of how their lives had been elevated or hijacked into a world-historical struggle or moment of change. As they struggled in difficult circumstances with the daily business of their lives, they were pulled voluntarily and involuntarily into the politics and violence of their postwar societies. Political leaders made proclamations in their names and shouted slogans at demonstrations and on posters; city streets became the sites of shooting and lynchings. Their wallets filled with successive, competing, and often worthless currencies as they tried to provision their families. They found their public and private identities as teachers, students, workers, mothers, writers, Jews, Christians, women, and soldiers politicized by the ideological narratives of the time. Lives disrupted by the war were set even further adrift as it became clear that there was no way back to the familiar prewar world. As much as that world had been stifling or difficult, the world of 1919 was, like

Dickens' evocation of the French Revolution, one which could be seen as many things, but always "in the superlative degree of comparison only."

Dickens' novel famously begins with the paradox, "It was the best of times, it was the worst of times"; the 1919 revolutions in Central Europe evoked similarly dichotomous interpretations. Dramatic events since the end of the world war seemed poised to transform the world, but the form of that transformation was unclear and violently contested. The political perceptions of contemporaries, framed by gender stereotypes and antisemitism, reveal the sense of living history, of "fighting the world revolution," that was shared by residents of the two cities. By examining how contemporaries experienced the contradictory "best of times" and "worst of times," we uncover important information about the worldview and intellectual milieu that came to predominate in both interwar Germany and Hungary, playing an important role in their later national histories of antisemitism and fascism.

In 1919, it seemed to many observers not only that the "old world" could be remade, reimagined, and reformed, but also that it must be. Both revolutionaries and counterrevolutionaries were focused on shaping this emerging new order according to their own worldview. All of the political conflicts of nineteenth-century Central Europe, the struggles over suffrage, nationalism, and socialism, which had mostly remained in the realm of politics and ideas, suddenly seemed to burst into violent physical reality in the streets and societies of Munich and Budapest in 1919. The possibilities of 1919 were liberating and terrifying at once – ordinary people as well as elites found themselves empowered by the atmosphere of uncertainty and hope. By examining the narratives of these Central European revolutions, this book helps answer the question of why so many Hungarians and Germans chose to employ their new political power for violence and repression.

The idea of world revolution profoundly shaped events in Central Europe in 1919. Revolution is naturally a liminal moment – the old order has been torn down, is in ruins (or so it seems), and the new is still uncertain. In such moments, images of a "topsy-turvy" world fly to the forefront, and it is not primarily the topics of economic or political transformation that serve as fodder for the imagination but rather the breaking of taboos – gender hierarchies overturned, ritual sacrifices, iconoclasm. In these liminal moments, the language of race and gender was tremendously important for symbolizing the breakdown of "normality." Revolutionary archetypes of a world overturned helped to determine the behavior of participants and the perceptions of observers on both sides of the revolutionary divide. Revolutionary leaders telegrammed to Moscow about their victories and legislated for a new world order. At the same time, conservatives saw even the proclamation of democratic republican governments at the end of the war in autumn 1918 as "the deluge." Their memoirs and letters bemoan a total social and moral breakdown and describe the "filthy" and "dangerous" reality that they observed on the streets around them. Even the German author Thomas Mann – a moderate bourgeois observer, caught in the middle of the Munich revolution in March 1919 – described how "news from the world has really shaken me," after reading of the revolution in Budapest and communist demonstrations in Vienna and Italy.[1] Angry at the Entente and the terms of the Paris peace treaties, Mann found the news of world revolution and the revolt against the Paris Peace Conference exhilarating, "even if in the form of communism." He felt "ready to take to the streets and shout 'Down with the western liar-democracies! Long live Germany and Russia! Long live communism!'"[2] During the 1919 revolutions in Munich and Budapest, many people experienced the desire to demonstrate, revolt, and shock, and what they observed around them was shocking.

In 1919 Central Europe came close to hosting the world revolution hoped for and predicted by Vladimir Lenin and Lev Trotsky, yet the revolutions in Budapest and Munich were historical ephemera. Following the defeat of the Habsburg Monarchy and its German imperial ally at the end of World War I, the cities of Budapest and Munich underwent the only successful – if only temporarily – soviet revolutions outside of Russia. Both revolutionary governments fell quickly in the face of armed counterrevolution in the spring and summer of 1919. Nonetheless, these brief revolutions had lasting effects on the politics and culture of postwar society. This book examines the Central European revolutionary moment in 1919 that followed World War I, placing local events in Munich and Budapest into a larger, transnational, European revolutionary tradition. This is a "tale of two cities," so to speak and, like Dickens' novel, we are concerned with the histories of two cities during a time of revolutionary upheaval and violence. Through this transnational comparison we see the power of preexisting motifs of revolution, race, and gender in shaping both the actions of revolutionaries and counterrevolutionaries and the narratives that explain them.

The Revolutionary Idea

Even before the French Revolution, Europeans had begun to think of society as an object to be shaped and created through human thought and action rather than passively received or experienced. Revolution was the act of radically transforming the given social order, and the French revolutionaries had shown that this was possible. This initial assumption of revolutionary possibility shaped all modern European politics after 1789. Along with the inspiration or

---

[1] Diary entry for Monday, March 24, 1919. Thomas Mann, *Tagebücher 1918–1921*, edited by Peter de Mendelssohn (Frankfurt a.M.: S. Fischer Verlag, 1979), 177–8. Unless otherwise noted, all translations from German and Hungarian are my own.

[2] Ibid.

temptation of revolution came its twin or mirror, fear and the desire to prevent revolution, to protect the social order from radical transformation.

Between the French Revolution and World War I there were many European revolutions, and most of them failed. These were stagings of the revolutionary idea, even farces, according to Karl Marx. The Paris Commune, 1848, 1830 – in all of these cases, 1789 was both evoked and condemned – the story of the French Revolution provided the narrative frame for observers and participants in later events.[3] With each staging, the revolutionary narrative and drama was honed by participants and opponents, adding new dramatic elements and vocabulary. These reoccurring upheavals, however infrequent and localized they seem with hindsight, kept the question of revolution at the center of political discourse all over Europe in the nineteenth century, both for those who hoped for and those who feared the next uprising.

Parallel to this chronology of acute political uprisings, nineteenth-century politicians developed a ritualized language of revolution. In particular, the new and growing working-class political parties adopted platforms calling for revolutionary change, mostly along Marxist lines. The language of revolution, tied to the possibility of remaking the social order, played a central role in the education and recruitment of working-class supporters and in creating a positive identification of their economic interests with the political platform of socialist parties. The radical language of most of these parties was usually far more revolutionary than the actual political program the parties pursued in parliamentary politics.

The radical language that drew workers to the parties raised their expectation of revolution and a radical transformation of society in their favor. It also had a mirror effect in the increasingly hyperbolic fear of revolution and the working class among the middle and upper classes and their refusal in many cases to accept even moderate demands made by representatives of the workers. The experience of the German Sozialdemokratische Partei Deutschlands (SPD), Europe's largest working-class party by far, provides an excellent example of this. Solidly reformist and committed to change from within the parliamentary system, the party retained radical revolutionary rhetoric in its platform. Despite its reformist actions and its mass membership, the party was outlawed for over a decade (1878–90) in the German Empire under the conservative Chancellor Otto von Bismarck. Owing to universal manhood suffrage in the German Empire, the SPD maintained its influence despite the ban. Although the party was illegal, SPD politicians continued to be voted into the German Reichstag.

[3] Some recent works have used a similar perspective on the power of revolutionary events to create violent counterrevolutionary terror, see Adam Zamoyski, *Phantom Terror: Political Paranoia and the Creation of the Modern State, 1789–1848* (New York: Basic Books, 2014); and on the Paris Commune, John Merriman, *Massacre: The Life and Death of the Paris Commune* (New York: Basic Books, 2014).

Once it became legal again after 1890, the SPD become the largest party in the Reichstag by the outbreak of World War I. Its revolutionary rhetoric, however, prevented the bourgeois parties from joining it in a governing coalition. Thus, even the European socialist party with the greatest parliamentary representation remained outside of parliamentary governance in Imperial Germany.

Other Central European socialist parties found themselves even more politically isolated, with no incentive to moderate their revolutionary platforms. In the Habsburg Monarchy, Hungarian conservatives desperately fought any attempt to widen suffrage through the end of World War I. Lack of suffrage reform meant that the Hungarian socialists had no chance of winning elections and having representation in parliament. With its main membership outside the electorate and no likelihood of suffrage reform, the Hungarian socialists hewed to their calls for political revolution, enhancing conservative fears. This cycle of exclusion and radicalization marked the prewar history of socialist politics in Hungary.

Along with failed revolutions and radical rhetoric, the decades before World War I saw concrete changes in Europe. The nineteenth century was a time of radical transformation of society, though almost none of it was brought about by political revolution. The transformation of economy, society, and politics that is lumped by historians, not inappropriately, under the umbrella of industrial revolution was at least as radical as the changes desired or feared in the failed political revolutions of the century. Some of the conflicts seen in Central Europe in 1919 had to do with transformations that had already occurred and that were merely sanctioned after the fact by the revolutionaries. The widening of suffrage, the emancipation of women, workers, and Jews, the central role of urban populations in national politics, and the expansion of industrial production were all supported by laws and actions of the revolutionary governments in 1918 and 1919, but they were hardly brought about by the declaration of a republic or a soviet republic. These were the products of long-term developments in Central Europe, developments that conservatives and imperial governments sought to ignore or cover over in the decades before World War I. But the suffering of the long war brought the deep crises of society to the surface, forcing them onto the political agenda.

The outbreak of World War I seemed to change everything for Central Europeans. In the first flush of patriotism, governments and their opponents offered messianic visions of national (and nationalist) unity and ideas about the redemptive power of violence and sacrifice. Many observers noted how hatred of foreign foes suddenly trumped hatred of enemies at home. Over the course of the war, mass conscription, rationing, and war provisioning integrated the masses into the state bureaucracy to an unprecedented degree. This integration and sacrifice on behalf of the state during the war led to an emotional identification with the state and nation and to demands for compensation and representation on a political level. In the midst of this situation, the Russian revolutions of February and October 1917 relocated "revolution" back into the realm of active rather than merely rhetorical politics.[4] In the midst of the violence of the world war and waves of mass strikes across Europe, Lenin and the leaders of the Bolshevik Party proclaimed that the October Revolution would be the herald of the world revolution.

Historians have often described Europe in 1917 using explosive metaphors of tinderbox or powder keg, a situation ready for ignition by the acts and words of revolutionaries.[5] That ignition famously happened in Russia, where, in early March, protests on the socialist International Women's Day in the capital, St. Petersburg, eventually resulted in the abdication of the tsar and the end of the Romanov monarchy. Parliamentary leaders established a provisional government and, at the same time, across the country workers, soldiers, students, peasants, and others formed councils or soviets. The provisional government and the councils struggled for power and for control of the country. Yet, in truth, by the summer of 1917, neither the councils nor the provisional government was in control of the country. Russia seemed to be falling into chaos when, on November 7, Lenin and his Bolshevik Party overthrew the provisional government, employing the popular slogan of "all power to the soviets!" This revolutionary seizure of power sent shock waves into a war-weary Europe that was still reeling from the news of the first Russian Revolution.

The new Soviet leadership believed that its only chance of survival was in the further spread of revolution. A Soviet-led but backward and agrarian Russia could not endure with hostile neighbors and the strike waves in 1918 in Central Europe and the mutinies of troops on various fronts seemed to suggest that the revolution might spread. What was hoped for in Moscow and St. Petersburg was desperately feared in the other European capitals. Therefore, when revolution broke out in Central Europe at the end of the war, the region sat at the nexus of all these forces. Was this another performance of the well-worn tragicomic drama as in 1830 or 1871, or was this the real thing? The revolution that had been awaited and dreaded since at least 1789 could have been happening. Would the crises of the nineteenth century finally be resolved through political transformation and violence?

The threat of world revolution was a dominant concern of the ministers and governmental representatives who gathered in Paris in January 1919 to

---

[4] The revolutions actually occurred in March and November by the European calendar but are usually referred to by February and October, the months of the Russian Orthodox calendar then in use in the Russian Empire (in 1917 the two calendars were about two weeks different).

[5] My favorite metaphor of the revolutions has always been Eric Hobsbawm's "like mushrooms after the rains" for the spontaneous creation of soviets all over the Russian Empire. Eric Hobsbawm, *Age of Extremes: The Short Twentieth Century, 1914–1991* (New York: Penguin, 1994), 61.

conclude the peace treaties. The work of the thousands of experts and delegates of the Entente powers at the Paris Peace Conference took not just months but years and was not complete until the final treaty with Turkey was signed in 1923. The conference addressed not only contentious questions of reparations and territorial adjustments but also establishing a new international order in the wake of the dissolution of the German, Habsburg, Ottoman, and Russian empires. The example of Russia, where the fall of empire had led to communist rule loomed especially large in their considerations.

The revolutions in Munich and Budapest occurred in the spring of 1919, following the armistice that officially ended World War I.[6] Their location, Central Europe, situated them both geographically and ideologically between Paris and Moscow. The Soviets and the Entente, these contending constituencies, served as audience, suitors, enemies, and historical models. The French Revolution and the Paris Commune as well as the 1905 and ongoing revolutions in Russia offered positive and negative examples for understanding the whirl of events. Revolutionaries and counterrevolutionaries in Munich and Budapest understood that events in their cities were part of a larger political drama unfolding across Europe and the world. The Russian Revolution and the Paris Peace Conference were the international contexts in which the Bavarian and Hungarian revolutions first succeeded and then failed, and in which events were remembered and compared.

A World Revolution in Central Europe?

May Day 1919 was an auspicious occasion. It was the first time Europeans were able to celebrate the workers' holiday since the end of the terrible "Great War" in which millions had lost their lives and millions more had been maimed or displaced. It was also only the second May Day celebrated since the October Revolution of 1917 had brought the Bolshevik Party to power in Russia and proclaimed the world's first workers' state. Bolshevik leader Vladimir Ilych Lenin greeted the cheering crowds assembled on Red Square for the May Day demonstrations. According to the official report in the party paper *Izvestia*, "After greeting the Moscow and world proletariat, Lenin compared the May Day celebrations of the previous year with the present celebrations."[7] His comparison with 1918 reflected positive changes in both the security of communist power in Russia and the progress of the world revolution.

Lenin's speech used the narrative of the Central European revolutions to tell a powerfully optimistic tale of world revolution. Though small and embattled,

---

[6] Of course, despite the ongoing Peace Conference, the fighting was not over everywhere, especially not in Central and Eastern Europe and the former Russian Empire.

[7] *Izvestia* 93, May 3, 1919, in V. I. Lenin, *Collected Works*, vol. 29, 4th edition (Moscow: Progress Publishers, 1972), 328–31 (accessed via marxists.org).

the allied revolutions in Bavaria and Hungary offered proof that the Bolsheviks in Russia were not isolated radicals but rather the vanguard of a wave of successful European revolutions. This narrative could reassure his embattled supporters in Russia as they faced the ongoing civil war. It could also inspire communist revolutionaries both in the former Russian Empire and further afield that their cause was not only just but ascendant. Along these lines, Lenin assured his listeners that Soviet power in Russia was more secure since the November armistice had ended World War I and that the terms of the peace obliged German troops to withdraw from the Russian territories they had occupied as a result of the punitive Treaty of Brest-Litovsk that they had imposed on the new Soviet state in March 1918. *Izvestia* contrasted May 1919 to 1918: "On May the First the year before, [the Soviets] had been threatened by German imperialism, [now] it had been routed and dispersed." In the spring of 1919, the historical tide seemed to have turned in socialism's favor and a wave of revolution swept across Europe. In his speech, Lenin reminded the demonstrators in Moscow that "the emancipated working class was triumphantly celebrating its festival freely and openly not only in Soviet Russia, but also in Soviet Hungary, and in Soviet Bavaria."[8] Lenin connected the workers in Moscow to their comrades in "Red Petrograd and in Budapest" and announced the liberation by the Soviet Red Army of Sevastopol in the Crimea to a lengthy ovation. Such Red Army victories against the forces of what he called "Anglo-French imperialism" showed that the enemies of Soviet power "would certainly be unable to resist the united forces of Soviet Russia, Hungary, and Bavaria." In closing, *Izvestia* reported, "Lenin expressed his confidence in the final victory of Soviet power all over the world and exclaimed, 'Long live the world Soviet republic! Long live communism!'"[9] For the crowds cheering Lenin in Moscow, as well as for those who desperately feared the spread of communist revolution, May Day 1919 seemed to mark a new era in world history, signaled in part by the revolutions in Budapest and Munich.

Yet while Lenin confidently addressed the crowd on Red Square and spoke of workers' victories, the Bavarian Soviet collapsed, along with the hopes of Lenin and the Bolshevik leadership that this German revolution was a sign of a turning tide for world revolution.[10] Armed forces of the German central government and volunteer counterrevolutionary militias marched into "Red

---

[8] Ibid.   [9] Ibid.

[10] The Russian word "soviet" means "council" in English. The German is "Rat" and the Hungarian "tanács." The 1919 revolutionary governments, following the example of the Russian revolutions and the usage of the new Soviet Union, called themselves council governments (*Räteregierung, Tanácsköztársaság*). I will use soviet (lower case) as a synonym for council and the German and Hungarian equivalents in English, and Soviet (capitalized) for the USSR, or, as here, when part of a proper or colloquial name for the Central European revolutionary governments.

Munich" on May 1, and by midday, the city had fallen. While Lenin boasted to the crowds in Moscow that German imperialism had been "routed and dispersed," German counterrevolutionary forces were busy defeating the Bavarian revolutionary government and its Red Army. Far from Lenin's May Day vision of the workers of Central Europe "demonstrat[ing] their strength," the communist-led soviet government in Munich was easily overwhelmed. Counterrevolutionary forces killed more than 600 people in the first week of May in Munich, most of them workers or "red" soldiers, including fifty-three Russian prisoners of war. The defeat of the Bavarian council government brought an end to the postwar revolutions in Germany; the progress of the world revolution suffered a serious defeat.

In his speech, Lenin had optimistically talked about the allied military force of the three socialist states of Bavaria, Hungary, and Russia. In truth, the Hungarian Revolution was more important for the Bolshevik leadership ideologically, as a symbol of the spread of world revolution, than it ever could be militarily or strategically. The example of the Hungarian Revolution proved to the world that their victory in Russia was not a fluke of history. Soviet-style government could also succeed in more industrially advanced European countries such as Hungary, where, Lenin claimed in an article in *Pravda*, "the general cultural level of the population is higher" and "the proportion of industrial workers to the total population is immeasurably greater" than in Russia.[11] Another historically important aspect of the spring 1919 revolutions in Hungary and the southern German province of Bavaria, according to Lenin, was that they had been largely peaceful, with no violence in the transfer of power to the soviets. This was important, he argued in *Pravda*, because the ongoing civil war in Russia made many observers associate revolution and soviet power with violence. In his words, "blind people, fettered by bourgeois prejudices . . . confused certain specific features of Russian soviet government, of the history of its development in Russia, with Soviet government as an international phenomenon. The Hungarian proletarian revolution is helping the blind to see."[12] In other words, the Central European revolutions were important to the idea of world revolution because they showed that soviet government could be established in places very different from tsarist Russia, without the violence of the Russian example.

In fact, the soviet revolution had been both popular and bloodless in Hungary, with the exception of the murder of the conservative Prime Minister István Tisza, which leaders of the revolutionary government had neither organized nor ordered. In March 1919, the provisional government in Budapest collapsed when the terms of the Treaty of Trianon, prepared in Paris, with its huge territorial losses for Hungary, were announced. Governing in the

---

[11] *Pravda* 115, May 29, 1919, in Lenin, *Collected Works*, vol. 29, 387.   [12] Ibid.

name of the workers' and soldiers' councils, and riding a wave of popular outrage at the Entente, a new soviet government of communists and socialists, led by the journalist and former prisoner of war in Russia, Béla Kun, took over power. As Lenin announced in a radio speech at the time of the Hungarian soviet revolution in late March, "The bourgeoisie voluntarily surrendered power to the Communists of Hungary." In a comment which could also be seen as justification for his own party's October Revolution, Lenin said that the Hungarian example proved "to the whole world that when a grave crisis supervenes, when the nation is in danger, the bourgeoisie is unable to govern. And there is only one government that is really a popular government," a soviet government.[13]

Although the Bavarian revolutionary government had already collapsed by May Day 1919, the soviet government in Hungary, embattled and fighting on several fronts, survived through the summer. Writing later in May 1919, after the Bavarian revolution's defeat, Lenin praised Soviet Russia's remaining ally: "Hungarian Workers! Comrades! You have set the world an even better example than Soviet Russia." Acknowledging the struggle of the fledgling Hungarian soviet government against counterrevolutionary forces, who were fighting with the approval (if not the actual assistance) of the French-led Entente, Lenin called on Hungary's workers to "be firm" in "[your] most gratifying and most difficult task of holding your own in a rigorous war against the Entente."[14] Because of the civil war in his own country, Lenin could offer no military support from the Russian Red Army, but he offered the Hungarians moral and ideological support, telling them, "You are waging the only legitimate, just and truly revolutionary war ... a war for the victory of socialism. All honest members of the working class all over the world are on your side. Every month brings the world proletarian revolution nearer."[15] But instead of world revolution, the summer months of 1919 brought the defeat of the Hungarian revolution. In late June the soviet government withstood an attempted counterrevolution in Budapest during the meeting of the national Congress of Soviets, but by August the forces of the counterrevolution had "routed and dispersed" the Red Army all over the country and the revolutionary government fled from the capital, ending for good the brief moment of international soviet revolution proclaimed by Lenin in his May Day speech.

In Moscow there has long been a commemorative plaque on the building from which Lenin announced his greetings to revolutionaries in Hungary at the end of the world war. No similar plaque adorns a wall in Budapest to commemorate this moment of seeming world revolution. In fact, after the end of

[13] "Communication on the Wireless Negotiation with Béla Kun," speeches on gramophone records, in ibid., 242–3.
[14] *Pravda* 115, May 29, 1919, in ibid., 391.   [15] Ibid.

postwar state socialism in 1989, all statues of Kun were taken down, along with all the other public socialist monuments, and moved outside of Budapest to the Statue Park museum, to form a crowded cluster of yesterday's idols.[16] But even the historical figure of Kun who was relegated to this statuary exile after 1989 was a different, post-World War II, version of himself, not the recipient of Lenin's telegram. The early Cold War socialist regime in Hungary did not want to remind its friends in Stalinist Moscow of the details of the failed 1919 revolution, of the fact that Lenin only sent telegrams, not troops or arms that might have aided the fledging revolutionary neighbor, or the fact that Kun himself was a victim of Stalin's terror after fleeing to the Soviet Union in 1919. Because Bavaria was a part of post-1945 West Germany, the Cold War similarly provided an ideological framework for commemorating the failed 1919 revolution in Munich. There are public markings in Munich for some of the events of 1919, but no plaque which makes this link between the Bavarian revolution and the Russian Revolution, though the Soviet leader, Lenin, also sent a telegram of greetings to the Bavarian soviet republic. Those greetings arrived on April 27, 1919, just as the forces that defeated the soviet government were surrounding the revolutionary city.[17]

A broad and international counterrevolutionary effort, including both new socialist-led democratic governments and radical right-wing militias, defeated the Central European experiments with soviet-style government. The places Lenin had praised for their nonviolent revolutionary examples were pushed into violent civil war and counterrevolution. This book analyzes the new world created by those defeats. Central Europe after the defeats of 1919 obviously did not experience the hoped for "new dawn" of world revolution and the building of a new socialist society. But despite some of the trappings of restoration, Central Europe also could not and did not experience a return to prewar, prerevolutionary society, politics, or culture. When we look back at how the 1917 revolutions transformed Russian society and culture, the transformation seems self-explanatory – a new state was formed with a powerful new historical framework, centered on the revolutionary narrative. Because the 1919 revolutions in Central Europe failed to create new revolutionary states, their roles in shaping interwar society and culture have not been viewed in the same transformative way. Yet in Central Europe as well, new founding narratives were developed for the postwar states, and though these often harkened back to symbols and mythic representations of the past, they were most often centered

---

[16] See Maya Nadkarni, "The Death of Socialism and the Afterlife of its Monuments: Making and Marketing the Past in Budapest's Statue Park Museum," in Katharine Hodgkin and Susannah Radstone, eds., *Contested Pasts: The Politics of Memory* (New York: Routledge, 2003), 193–207.

[17] "Message of Greetings to the Bavarian Soviet Republic," delivered April 27, 1919, first published in *Pravda* 111, April 22, 1930; Lenin, *Collected Works*, 325–6.

on the recent heroic counterrevolutionary struggle. And most dangerously and corrosively for interwar politics and culture, this counterrevolutionary struggle centered on the antisemitic narrative of a struggle against so-called Judeo-Bolshevism.[18] The two cities analyzed here, Munich and Budapest, are both examples of the extremes of the 1919 revolutions and counterrevolutions and of the role of antisemitism in counterrevolutionary political violence and in counterrevolutionary culture in general.

Central European Revolutionary Narratives

In his wonderful study of the 1892 cholera epidemic in Hamburg, Germany, historian Richard J. Evans writes that each plague story has its own narrative. A plague sets up a narrative of missed chances, possible clues, suspense, and "cathartic stock-taking."[19] The history of revolutions is much the same. The fact of a revolution, like the fact of an epidemic, sets up a series of questions. Was it inevitable? Could it have been avoided? If so, when and in what circumstances was avoidance possible? Was it the result of long-term social processes or immediate events? Was it caused by a relatively small group of fanatics or was it supported by a majority of the population? What were the intellectual trends that fed its ideologies? What were the social structures and experiences that caused mass dissatisfaction? The answers to these questions determine the way that the story of the revolution is told. Does the history of the French Revolution begin with the agrarian structures of medieval France, with the philosophers of the Enlightenment, or with the American Revolution and the fiscal crises of the 1780s? The background we choose to focus on frames the narrative of the revolution.

In this book I analyze the revolutionary narratives created in Central Europe during and immediately following the violent events of 1919. These narratives were proclaimed on posters, offered as arguments in court, published in newspapers and academic journals, written in letters to friends, and even sent on photo postcards to acquaintances elsewhere in Europe. Later, explanations for the revolutions continued to be debated and contested, offered in memoirs, histories, and legislative battles of the interwar period. These narratives demonstrate how contemporaries gave meaning to the traumatic political events of

---

[18] See Eliza Ablovatski, "The 1919 Central European Revolutions and the Myth of Judeo-Bolshevism," in Michael L. Miller and Scott Ury, eds., *Cosmopolitanism, Nationalism and the Jews of East Central Europe* (New York: Routledge, 2014); and, more recently, Paul Hanebrink, *A Specter Haunting Europe*: (Cambridge, MA: Harvard University Press, 2018).

[19] Richard J. Evans, *Death in Hamburg: Society and Politics in the Cholera Years, 1830–1910* (Oxford: Clarendon Press, 1987), vii–viii. The structure he describes for "plague literature" can be employed as a model for many of the writings on the failed revolutions of 1919.

the immediate post-World War I era and also show how the 1919 events were assimilated into the broader European revolutionary trajectory.

In the century since the 1919 revolutions, they have been the subject of research and publications, both official and private, some polemical, some scholarly. Interest in the events has waxed and waned with the political transformations of the region. The stories of the Budapest and Munich revolutions have been woven tightly into the European revolutionary narrative, but they no longer dominate that tapestry. By reexamining these two failed revolutions in the context of the ongoing world revolutionary moment of 1919, we regain a sense of their significance. Importantly, this transnational study combines and compares the results of research into both the Bavarian and the Hungarian experiences of revolution and counterrevolution in 1919, moving beyond national explanations and narratives of the time to a broader understanding of the culture of counterrevolution in early twentieth-century Central Europe.

The collapse of the Soviet bloc and the political changes in Europe since 1989 forced us to reevaluate many events of European history as well as widely held assumptions about "Central Europe" and "Eastern Europe" in particular. Not only are far more archives open to historians but there has been renewed debate over the last three decades and more about what "Central Europe" might mean as a culturally or politically distinct region or idea, as the European Union has expanded to include many former Soviet bloc countries.[20] These changes tore down the barriers of Cold War geography that had seemed to separate the histories of Hungary and Germany. Now, the rise of a new generation of populist, nationalist, and often openly racist political parties and movements in Central Europe (and Europe more generally) evokes parallels to the rise of the interwar Right in the region. In 1919, revolutionaries, counterrevolutionaries, and the citizens of Munich and Budapest were aware that they were part of the same Central Europe. Germans and Hungarians had been bound by a military alliance for the four years of war and both experienced the ignominy of defeat. Munich and Budapest were part of a common turn-of-the-century literary and cultural heritage of coffeehouses and artistic modernism. They also shared a history of anti-emancipatory political movements and increasing antisemitism, although this was stronger in Vienna than in Munich or

---

[20] In the initial decade or so after 1989, it seemed the dominant narrative was one of a region with a resurrected and historically resonant civil society and interwar Central Europe as a liberal oasis between Germany and Russia, as in works by Timothy Garton Ash and others. More recently, the resurgence of nationalist and right-wing politics, especially in Hungary and Poland, has brought another narrative to the fore, one that emphasizes the continuities between the interwar Right and current politics. This echoes earlier perceptions of Central and Eastern Europe as a region defined by nationalism.

especially Budapest. These cultural traditions, with all their positive and negative aspects, were similar in the two cities. In our own era, following another meaningful turn of the century, it is this idea of a cultural "Central Europe" that most often provides the answer to the politically and geographically contentious question of "where is Central Europe?" By comparing the counterrevolutions in these two cosmopolitan, Central European capitals, we put these political events into the broader context in which their contemporaries viewed them.

The role of memory in shaping a collective sense of history is a particularly important issue for historians of regime changes or political transitions. Over the last decades, in Central and Eastern Europe and unified Germany historians, politicians, and citizens have had to reevaluate the post-1945 socialist governments and societies and reconcile these historical moments with the larger narratives of European and national histories. This book examines how an earlier regime change and historical caesura, the revolution and counterrevolution of 1918 and 1919, were comprehended and historicized by contemporaries, and how these events were fitted into the self-perception of these cities and into both historical narratives and collective memory.

This study reveals important facets of the contemporary understanding of the events of 1919 in both cities. The consensus view was that these were "alien" events initiated and carried out by foreigners ("Russians" and "Prussians") and Jews. I focus on antisemitism, anti-Jewish violence, and political activity as the main themes of this investigation. Antisemitism was paired with other anti-emancipatory and anti-modernist views, and the defense of "traditional" or national gender roles was an important part of the counterrevolutionary movement. The study of these two cases reminds us of the importance of anti-urbanism and anti-cosmopolitanism in the counterrevolutionary ideology and culture that shaped interwar Central Europe.

In Germany and Hungary counterrevolutionaries mobilized support and recruited for their militias in similar ways, portraying the revolutionary governments as alien and not representing the interests of the native population. On April 16, 1919 Johannes Hoffmann, the Social Democratic prime minister of Bavaria, issued an appeal to the public from the government's exile in Bamberg, calling for volunteers to join militias to fight the revolutionary soviet government in Munich. The poster boldly addressed its audience as "Bavarians! Compatriots!" and asked the "men of the Bavarian mountains, Bavarian highland, Bavarian forests, [to]rise up as one." The proclamation urged its audience, "Step forward! Now! The Munich disgrace must be wiped out!"[21] Two days

---

[21] Bayrische Hauptstaatsarchiv (BHSA) IV, Kriegsarchiv, Höhere Stäbe, Bund 1, Akt 3; 1c, "Aufruf! Bayern! Landsleute!" April 16, 1919.

later, the exiled Hoffmann government issued another proclamation reassuring the citizens of Munich that the government was coming to their aid: "Help is on its way to free you from the Russian terror and all the horrors of Bolshevism."[22] In Hungary, Miklós Horthy, leader of the counterrevolutionary National Army, appealed in similar terms to Hungarians as he prepared to enter Budapest. In an announcement delivered to the city's newspapers, Horthy declared that the "Hungarian military might has been reawakened and is on its way to Budapest, thanks to the noble people of Transdanubia [Hungary's rural plains or *Puszta*]." He told the citizens of the capital city, "over which red rags and foreign flags had waved for months," that "international adventurers and corrupt Hungarians" were responsible for the city's "disgrace."[23] Not only in the echoed idea of the "disgrace" of soviet rule but more broadly in both of these cases, we see the struggle and appeal of counterrevolution framed within the above-mentioned conflict. There was a battle between natives, "Bavarians" or "Hungarians," and "alien elements" (the "Russian" Jews in the government); between the village, the "mountains ... highlands ... forests," and the urban center, the "disgrace." This battle also defined the gendered roles of the "Bavarian men" and the "sons of the *Puszta*" as defenders of the social order.

The conflict between alien and native is particularly noteworthy in the case of Munich, where the aspect of Bavarian "nationalism" or particularism has often been obscured in studies that treat the "German revolutions" as a single phenomenon. This is particularly true in general histories of Weimar Germany, which often devote much more attention to the failed Spartacus uprising in Berlin than to Munich, where two successive soviet governments actually ruled for almost a month. While the revolutionaries and counterrevolutionaries in Munich certainly looked to events in Kiel or Berlin as the vanguard of the German revolution, their perspective was not only "German" but rather at once more international and more local. Events in the Russian Civil War and in Hungary were the background for a battle for Bavaria and its future. Even counterrevolutionaries in 1919 were more likely to view their allies as being the Catholic Habsburg legitimists in Hungary and Austria than Protestant conservatives in the north of Germany. In fact, in 1919 a web of plots and connections linked Munich, Budapest, and Vienna in a triangle of counterrevolutionary intrigues, as well as military and financial connections.[24]

---

[22] BHSA IV, Kriegsarchiv, Höhere Stäbe, Bund 1, Akt 3; 1c, "An die Bevölkerung Münchens," April 18, 1919.

[23] "Ein Aufruf des Oberkommandanten Nikolaus Horthy," *Pester Lloyd*, November 14, 1919.

[24] A classic work on the conspiratorial circles around Erich Ludendorff in Bavaria is Bruno Thoss, *Der Ludendorff-Kreis 1919–1923* (Munich: Kommissionsbuchhandlung R. Woelfle, 1978); for Bavarian monarchist circles, Robert S. Garnett, *Lion, Eagle, and Swastika: Bavarian Monarchism in Weimar Germany, 1918–1933* (New York: Garland, 1991); for the Habsburg restoration attempts in Hungary and their regional connections, Bela Menczer, "The Habsburg Restoration: Hungary in 1921," *History Today* 22 (1972): 128–35; there is a transnational

Examining the 1919 counterrevolutions in Munich and Budapest together as part of a shared historical episode puts the violence and political rhetoric into a wider Central European context and demonstrates the importance of the failed revolutions for the cultural and political climate of the two countries in the interwar years. We can observe the complicated roles of antisemitism and gender perception in framing contemporaries' understanding of these political and social events, particularly the role of antisemitism in the violent reaction to revolution. While both the revolutions and their downfalls have been the objects of historical inquiry as well as polemical writing, the two have never been studied together, as part of a broader counterrevolutionary culture and movement in Central Europe. Since Adolf Hitler himself described the Munich revolutions in *Mein Kampf* as the "beginning of my political activity," studies of the cultural and political ramifications of each of these revolutionary episodes have tended to remain within separate national historical narratives, used to explain the rise of Nazism in Germany, antisemitic politics, or the postwar socialist regime in Hungary.[25]

This book examines the way the 1919 revolutions were represented both before and after their failures. It demonstrates the double vision that many contemporaries had about the events, believing multiple and even conflicting narratives of the revolutions' viability, danger, and importance. Both on the Left and the Right there was uncertainty if the revolutions were doomed or had a chance to succeed, if they were "poor copies" of the Russian Revolution or part of the same world revolutionary context. In political histories of the revolutions of 1918 and 1919, citizens become simply "support bases" for one or the other political faction. This book attempts to examine what people thought about the momentous and sometimes preposterous events unfolding in their city, as well as what they knew about the larger political drama. Human beings have the wonderful and horrible quality of adjusting to any circumstances and the ability to think critically about events even as they adjust; these two "cities under siege" offer us many such examples. They show that contemporaries, both supporters and opponents of the revolution, often held contradictory views of things: they believed at the same time that the revolution wouldn't last long and that it would last forever; that the leaders were charlatans and that they were truly dangerous; that the whole thing was a charade of a revolution and that they were living in terror. Even on the Left, supporters seemed to be unable to decide if they were building a socialist society or holding out some

comparison of some of the paramilitary connections in Robert Gerwarth and John Horne, eds., *War in Peace: Paramilitary Violence in Europe after the Great War* (Oxford: Oxford University Press, 2012).

[25] Adolf Hitler, *Mein Kampf*, translated by Ralph Manheim (Boston: Houghton Mifflin, 1971), 207–8.

sort of symbolic last stand. The historical models of the Paris Commune and the Russian Revolution both seemed relevant, but no one was sure which one they were reliving. Most importantly, people were trying to figure out "was this the world revolution?"

Chapter 1 looks back at the prewar history of Munich and Budapest. Nostalgic ideas about the world before "the deluge" of war and revolution played an important role in how people came to understand the revolutions, particularly the idea that they were foreign or unnatural. I offer a brief critical examination of the roots of some of the myths that later developed about the character of the cities and their residents, in particular beliefs about the two cities' Jews and industrial workers. From the outbreak of war in 1914 through the defeat of the revolutions in 1919, residents in Budapest and Munich lived in the heightened realm of dramatic historical events, trying at the same time to make sense of how these events fit into their own life stories and the histories of their cities and countries. In Chapter 2, I present the major storylines of these crisis years and show not only how hard it was for people in Munich and Budapest at the time to know what was going on in their own cities but how difficult it is even today to determine what actually happened. Together, these histories or perceived histories formed the building blocks for the narratives of 1919 that developed during the revolutions and counter-revolutions. Beginning in Chapter 3, I analyze more closely the process of narrative formation, focusing on the role of revolutionary scripts and rumors in instigating terror and political violence in Budapest and Munich. We see how people reacted as much to the phantoms of rumor and fear as to the real situations around them, particularly the counterrevolutionaries who created the terror they feared would come with revolution. Then, in Chapter 4, I look at the postrevolutionary courts that determined the guilt of individuals charged with crimes to do with the 1919 revolutions. The trials of both prominent and minor revolutionary figures served as important sites for forging a consensus about what had happened and who was responsible. They offer a dynamic vista onto this process, as competing versions of events were offered to the courts. The different versions heard in court vied to persuade the judges about the guilt or innocence of individual defendants. As the narratives about the revolution circulated in popular culture, gender and race served as primary explanatory frameworks, structured around the ideas of "Judeo-Bolshevism" and a "topsy-turvy" gender order, examined in Chapter 5. Chapter 6 follows this process into the immediate interwar years, looking at the uses and consequences of the narratives that people told about the 1919 Bavarian and Hungarian revolutions. The experiences of war and revolution gave residents of Budapest and Munich the sense of living in world-historical times, and this book unearths the stories they told to explain their experiences and the way that those stories functioned in inspiring and justifying political violence. I analyze many narratives spun from 1919: of "Judeo-Bolshevism," of World Revolution, of socialist intrigue, of gender turned over, and of Jewish martyrdom. From their opposing perspectives, the tale tellers insisted on a dramatic role for the Central European revolutions, on their, in Dickens' words, "being received, for good or for evil, in the superlative degree of comparison only."

1 Central European Roots of Revolution

From the time of their occurrence, the inhabitants of Munich and Budapest tried to find an explanation for the Soviet-style revolutions of 1919 that had taken place in their cities. In both places, many within the population believed foreign interlopers had caused the revolutions, and thus they were alien to the social and political development of their nations. In contemporary narratives and in historical scholarship, authors treat the revolutions as violent parentheticals, not as part of the main national narrative. On the Right, conservatives took the revolutions to be the result of criminal manipulations carried out by communist leaders with support from Moscow – an international plot, often framed as "Judeo-Bolshevism."[1] Yet we know that huge crowds of residents of the two cities had enthusiastically greeted the revolutions and many people who had no affiliation with the communist party initially supported the new regimes. On the Left, supporters of the revolutions claimed that they had fulfilled the desires of the working class, yet neither city had a large industrial proletariat. How can these conflicting analyses be reconciled? We must examine the urban fabric of Budapest and Munich before the events of 1919 and explore how these societies dissolved into civil war. Although contemporaries considered them to be dramatic breaks with the past (for better or worse), the revolutions and related societal rifts were part of a process of historical development with roots in the long nineteenth century, in the strange mixture of anti-urbanism and anti-modernism that had become embedded in these major Central European urban centers and the general antisemitism of the population, as well as in the increased level of violence and toleration for industrial-level violence caused by the mass brutality of World War I.

A brief history of each city shows us the roots of both the hopes and the fears of the world revolution that convulsed Europe after World War I, linking prewar debates on the "Jewish Question" to the later, widespread conviction that Jews were at the center of the era's revolutionary action. The topsy-turvy world of revolution shocked conservatives such as the right-wing Hungarian

---

[1] I talk in detail about the idea of Judeo-Bolshevism as a frame for reactions to the revolutions in Chapter 5.

novelist Cecile Tormay: "It was as though the city had for years devoured countless Galician immigrants and now vomited them forth in sickness. How sick it was! Syrian faces and bodies, red posters and red hammers whirled around in it. And Freemasons, feminists, editorial offices ... night cafes came to the surface – and the ghetto sported cockades of national colors and chrysanthemums."[2] For observers such as Tormay, political restoration after 1919 was inextricably tied up with, and depended upon, the restoration of the social, racial, and gender order that had been threatened by the revolutions.

Following the defeat of the spring 1919 revolutions, the vocabulary and grammar of gender and antisemitism played a powerful role for contemporaries in identifying the authors of the revolutionary events as well as in distributing punishment and blame for the revolution. Polemical assignments of racial and gendered responsibility for revolutionary excesses and ambitions became inextricably connected to contested interpretations of national identity and a national historical trajectory. In both Munich and Budapest, witnesses and, later, postrevolutionary authorities tended to blame the revolutions on "foreign," especially Jewish, influence. A comparison between these two cities therefore allows us to examine critically both the actual role played by Jews in the two 1919 revolutions and the singular role of antisemitism in framing and giving direction to counterrevolutionary agitation and physical violence. Although both cities experienced a wave of anti-Jewish agitation and even attacks during the counterrevolution, only in the Hungarian case did the strength of anti-urbanism and other aspects of antisemitic ideology lead to both mass anti-Jewish violence and a stronger political consensus for anti-Jewish political action, such as the *numerus clausus* law of 1921 that drastically limited Jewish access to higher education in Hungary. In Bavaria, violent anti-Jewish actions were far less numerous and official sanctions were limited to the expulsion in 1923 of a few hundred Jewish families with Polish citizenship.

Both historians and politicians have sought to use the failed Central European revolutions for their own ends, asserting connections between political crises that afflicted Munich and Budapest in the brief revolutionary period and the social and cultural problems that were associated with prewar economic change and social dislocation.[3] For some writers, such as the Hungarian Oszkár Jászi and the German Oskar Maria Graf, looking backwards to the nineteenth century in the wake of the two revolutions seemed to reveal a range of unresolved problems and systemic injustices, which lurked beneath the surface of rapid modernization or had been there all along but were underestimated. Later historians and critics argued that the political extremism and violence that

---

[2] Cecile Tormay, *An Outlaw's Diary* (London: Philip Allan & Co., 1923), vol. 1, 9. I discuss Tormay's political and literary work in detail in Chapter 5.

[3] Chapter 6 details the historiography of the 1919 revolutions and the commemorative practices surrounding them.

followed the two failed revolutions anticipated and perhaps signaled the rise of fascism, World War II, and even the later development of state socialism.

The dramatic and tragic events in Munich and Budapest in 1919 – revolution, counterrevolution, and civil war – can be viewed as indicative of a much wider conflict between the modern or modernizing elements within each state and the forces that opposed them, and antisemitic politics and even violence served as important vocabulary and framing expressions of these tensions in society. This was true in both Germany and Hungary, before and especially after the revolutions of 1919. Antisemitism and the question of the role of Jews in the revolutions have played important interpretative roles in the understanding of what caused both revolution and counterrevolution to erupt in Munich and Budapest. Even before 1918, many contemporaries claimed that the question of revolutionary politics was, in effect, a version of the so-called Jewish Question in modern European society. In fact, the question of Jewish emancipation and assimilation across the region was tied to other revolutionary and emancipatory ideologies such as socialism, feminism, and democracy. European historians have often looked at the widespread participation of Jews in the revolutions of this era to explain the spread of anti-Jewish violence and antisemitic politics that followed, echoing the worries of Jewish leaders at the time, who wrote pleading editorials trying to dissociate the revolutions from their Jewish communities and even hoping Jewish revolutionaries might think of the possible harm their political actions could have on coreligionists. This easy association between Jewish revolutionaries and antisemitic counterrevolutionary violence obscures the actual nature of antisemitism during this period: antisemitism had a chameleon-like character. The so-called Jewish Question was linked in people's minds to all the major problems of the day. In Germany and the Habsburg lands, antisemitism was actually a symbol – perhaps *the* symbol – of wider cultural divisions within society. The language of political antisemitism was attached to a whole range of conservative, anti-modernist, anti-urban beliefs. As a result, the "Jewish Question" was conflated with other troubling "questions" of the day: the "woman question," the social question. Antisemitism, by the end of the nineteenth century, was no longer a "sincere" political platform, an economic backlash, or a populist political strategy; it had become, as historian Shulamit Volkov has argued for Imperial Germany, "a cultural code."[4]

Volkov's idea of a cultural code helps to explain some of the seemingly contradictory manifestations of antisemitism in Imperial German and Habsburg Hungarian society, as well as to highlight its generally anti-emancipatory and anti-modern aspects. Her reminder of the ties between antisemitism and anti-feminism in the nineteenth century also has great explanatory power for both German and

---

[4] Shulamit Volkov, "Antisemitism as Cultural Code: Reflections on the History and Historiography of Antisemitism in Imperial Germany," *Leo Baeck Yearbook* 23 (1978): 34–5.

Hungarian society after World War I. Analysis of contemporary discussions of women and gender roles reveals the significant role that fears of female emancipation played in anti-revolutionary ideology. Among the numerous societal norms and structures that the revolution threatened to change, none seemed so primal, nor were so likely to ignite hostility, as gender roles and the structures of the family. This meant that the behavior of women during the revolution and their roles as supporters or victims had immense symbolic importance for contemporaries. In the image of revolutionary "womanhood" people believed they could discern an entire worldview; a woman with a certain short haircut or a cigarette could stand in for the "world revolution" and all it sought to overturn. In addition to providing a better understanding of the Right in interwar Central Europe, this perspective also helps to move past a persistent and pernicious historical myth: the idea that Jewish revolutionaries, in Russia and in the 1919 Central European revolutions, sparked an antisemitic reaction. By examining the related roles of antisemitism and anti-feminism in the 1919 counterrevolutions, I break this illusion of causality that often points to Jewish revolutionaries in explaining interwar antisemitism or the anti-Jewish violence of the Hungarian counterrevolution. Just as anti-feminism and fears of gender disruption were not caused by women's large-scale participation in the revolutions (in fact, aside from Rosa Luxemburg, the prominent revolutionary martyr, markedly few women had visible roles in the revolutionary leaderships), so too the antisemitism of the counterrevolution was not caused by Jewish revolutionaries. The Jewish revolutionaries fit with a preexisting narrative and illustrated it for its supporters, but the narrative did not originate with their activities.

Race and gender function differently, and threatened changes to traditional gender and racial or ethnic hierarchies excite different reactions. For all the counterrevolutionary attention to gender disruption and to female revolutionaries, women were not a major focus of counterrevolutionary violence, whereas Jews, particularly in Hungary, were victimized in massive numbers. Studying gender and race together in the context of the 1919 counterrevolutions does not suggest equivalence between anti-feminism and antisemitism. Instead, an analysis of counterrevolutionary attitudes to women and ideologies of gender can help us to better understand postrevolutionary antisemitism. By looking at antisemitism in combination with anti-feminism and the entire anti-emancipatory worldview that came to prominence in the wake of the two revolutions, we can see past an oversimplified connection between Jewish revolutionaries and antisemitic reaction. Just as perceptions about women were more than just a reflection of the actions of a few female revolutionaries and were symbolic of ideas about the way society should be ordered, so too antisemitism was more than merely a reaction to the political activities of Jews. Antisemitism, like contemporary anti-feminism, was a way of expressing an anti-revolutionary and anti-modern worldview and it encompassed a political statement about one's attitude not only to Jews but also to democracy, social reform, and suffrage reform, as well as to technical and artistic innovation.

Jews played prominent roles in the revolutions and were later the main victims of the counterrevolutions. But we must look past this apparent causal narrative to the underlying processes to understand how the Jewish leadership of the 1919 revolutions was connected to both existing antisemitic attitudes and the anti-Jewish violence of the counterrevolution. There had been similar manifestations of popular antisemitism in Munich and Budapest in the decades before World War I, even though the objective reality of Jewish economic and cultural participation in the two cities was very different, as was the proportion of Jews in the population: Jews constituted less than 2 percent in Munich, while they made up 23 percent in Budapest. A comparative examination of the two cities not only helps us to grapple with the issues of antisemitism and anti-feminism, it gives us a picture of how the collective understanding of the revolutions developed within these two settings in the wake of events. In this way, we can understand how three weeks of revolutionary rule in Munich and four months of revolutionary rule in Budapest could be popularly perceived as "reigns of terror," understood as similar to the much more consequential Russian Revolution, and blamed for the disruption of traditional gender norms through modernization, and specifically for the role of Jews in both this modernization process and the revolutionary events themselves.

Budapest and Hungary: Urbanization and Urban Alienation

At the end of the nineteenth century Budapest was the site of the Hungarian Millennium Exhibition, which celebrated the presumed arrival of the Hungarians in the Carpathian Basin under their leader Árpád around 896 CE.[5] This event was reported around the world as a "Great Exposition" devoted to a celebration of Hungarian history and achievement.[6] In preparation, several major public-works projects were undertaken in Budapest, including the construction of a massive new national parliament building on the Pest side of the Danube and an equally massive "heroes' square" at the end of the elegant Andrássy út (avenue), under which was located the first underground subway line on the European continent, built and opened for the millennium celebration

---

[5] Excellent histories that cover Budapest becoming the Hungarian capital and the exhibition are Alice Freifeld, *Nationalism and the Crowd in Liberal Hungary, 1848–1914* (Washington, DC: Woodrow Wilson Center Press and Johns Hopkins University Press, 2000) and Robert Nemes, *The Once and Future Budapest* (DeKalb, IL: Northern Illinois University Press, 2005).

[6] For example, in the *Washington Post*, "Hungary's Millennium: Buda-Pest to Celebrate Her Thousandth Anniversary. Emperor and Sultan Aid. All Hungary's Heterogenous Life and Heroic History Will Be Represented in a Great Exposition and Reproduced in Elaborate Fetes," October 6, 1895.

in 1896.[7] Other national landmarks, including two new bridges over the Danube, the National Opera House, the National Museum, the Academy of Sciences in Pest, and the new palace on the hill in Buda, were also products of this late nineteenth-century period of confident expansion and celebratory display in the Hungarian capital.

Even as Budapest was presenting itself to the rest of the world as the face of Hungarian creativity and achievement, many nineteenth-century social and cultural critics, as well as most vocal Hungarian nationalists, increasingly criticized the capital city as an alien place, disconnected from the remainder of the Hungarian nation. They considered Budapest a foreign behemoth grafted onto traditional, agrarian Hungary, resounding with German and other languages, linked to the international world of trade and commerce, and with a large and visible Jewish minority. Even progressive critics, like the circle of intellectuals around the social scientist, historian, and progressive politician Oszkár Jászi at the journal *Huszadik Század* (Twentieth Century), viewed the massive public-works campaign as a fancy cover-up for the deep political and social problems of the capital and the country. They pointed out that the new parliament building on the banks of the Danube, the largest parliament building in Europe, was built to house a parliament elected by the narrowest electoral franchise in Europe: only 6 percent of the kingdom's population. Similarly, Hungary's national minorities – Croats, Romanians, Serbs, and Slovaks – decried the mythic view of Magyar rule presented in these public-works projects, such as the massive statues of Magyar ancestors in Heroes' Square. The narrative of the "land-taking" by equestrian riders from the steppes, which was central to the myth of the millennium celebration, ignored the ethnic complexity of the nation, the other people who had lived in the land, and the often violent nature of Magyar ascendency.

The 1867 Settlement (*Ausgleich*) with Austria had made the Kingdom of Hungary an effectively autonomous state ruled by the Habsburg family and sharing only military and certain financial institutions with the rest of the Habsburg Monarchy.[8] Nevertheless, Hungarian nationalists' aspirations for independence remained a powerful and often disruptive force in late nineteenth-century Hungarian politics, despite the rapid growth and prosperity Hungary enjoyed under the so-called Dual Monarchy. During this period Hungary's industrial and agrarian production increased relative to the rest of Europe and

---

[7] London's first steam-powered underground railway opened in 1863, but the line in Budapest (today's M1) was the first on the continent and the first electric-powered line. The subway line was included in the UNESCO World Heritage List as "Andrássy Avenue and the Millennium Underground" (extension to "Budapest, the Banks of the Danube and the Buda Castle Quarter") in June 2002 (https://whc.unesco.org/en/news/156).

[8] The shared finances were essentially to fund the military, as in most aspects even the finances of the two entities were autonomous.

Austria, growth which stimulated rapid urbanization in Budapest, by far the largest city in Hungary.

The population of Budapest kept pace with the rapidly expanding urban centers elsewhere in Europe. Between 1869 and 1910 the population of Budapest increased from 270,000 to 880,000, or 1.1 million if the suburbs were included.[9] Though still less than half the size of the metropolises of Vienna and Berlin, Budapest, Hamburg, and Warsaw were the only other really large Central European cities, far larger than Munich, Frankfurt, Dresden, Amsterdam, Prague, or Rome.[10] In 1873, the two cities of Buda (called Ofen in German) and Pest, as well as Óbuda (Ancient Buda), were administratively and legally merged into a single, large municipality. Of the two larger parts, Buda and Pest, Pest was the more recent, more dynamic and modern. Buda, though also expanding, grew more slowly, keeping its image as more traditional, more Habsburg, and more German-speaking. Yet while the population of the capital grew dramatically, the Kingdom of Hungary as a whole remained predominantly agrarian, dependent on the export of unprocessed agricultural goods, such as grains and cattle, and finished agricultural products, such as flour and wine.[11] As a result, for many rural Hungarians the rapid expansion of the capital's population and the simultaneous industrial transformation of its economy seemed to make this dynamic city a foreign and even dangerous place.

Hungarian nationalists' mounting antipathy to Budapest was clearly rooted in their perception that the city's "cosmopolitan" population was, in effect, a colonial occupation. At the end of the nineteenth century, the city was home to an ethnically and religiously diverse population: speakers of German, Slovak, Romanian, and Serbo-Croatian, and Jews, Protestants, Catholics, and Orthodox Christians, as well as smaller groups. And, despite the Magyar-centric dreams and delusions of Hungarian nationalists, the Kingdom of Hungary itself was very ethnically diverse. Hungarian speakers were the largest single ethnic group, but they constituted only a small majority of the total population as measured by language statistics.[12] Ethnic diversity was, however, manifested

[9] "Urbanization and Civilization: Vienna and Budapest in the Nineteenth Century," in Péter Hanák, *The Garden and the Workshop: Essays on the Cultural History of Vienna and Budapest* (Princeton, NJ: Princeton University Press, 1998), 12.

[10] Populations of various continental European cities in 1910: Berlin, 2 million; Vienna, 2 million; Hamburg, 931,000; Warsaw, 872,000; Amsterdam, 574,000; Munich, 596,000; Dresden, 548,000; Rome 542,000; Frankfurt, 415,000; Prague, 224,000. Figures from B. R. Mitchell, ed., *International Historical Statistics: Europe, 1750–2005*, 6th edition (New York: Palgrave Macmillan, 2007), 75–7.

[11] Péter Gunst, "Agricultural Exports in Hungary (1850–1914)," *Acta Historica Academiae Scientiarum Hungaricae* 35, no. 1/4 (1989): 61–90.

[12] Hungarian speakers (the census category) made up 51.4 percent of the population of the Kingdom of Hungary (not including autonomous Croatia) in the census of 1900, this went up to 54.5 percent in the last pre–World War I census of 1910. This included the vast majority of people who designated their religion as "Jewish" in the same census.

differently in the capital than elsewhere. In the provinces of the Kingdom of Hungary, ethnic Magyars were often outnumbered by Romanian, Slovak, or other ethnic peasant populations whom they believed they had the right to rule, regardless of relative numbers.

The situation was different in nineteenth-century Budapest: non-Magyars included not only, as in the countryside, many disenfranchised workers and former peasants but also politically and financially powerful groups. These "non-Hungarians" included many groups that had assimilated to the dominant Hungarian national culture over the course of the previous century and whose numbers created the small Hungarian-speaking majority in the census. Many Hungarian-speaking Jews and Germans, and some Greek merchants, as well as some Slovak and Serb workers, had even "magyarized" their names in the last decades of the century. As this process of assimilation proceeded in the nineteenth century, Budapest's minority populations changed the statistical portrait of the city that was registered by census takers. While the nationalists in government were thrilled by the growing number of Hungarian speakers shown in every census, some worried that the modernizing capital, while nominally Hungarian-speaking, was becoming less and less Hungarian culturally and ethnically.[13]

For Hungarian-nationalist critics of this urban transformation, the population that symbolized all that was wrong with Budapest was the city's large Jewish population. According to the 1910 census, though they made up less than 5 percent of the total national population, Jews accounted for 12.4 percent of all urban dwellers in Hungary and 23 percent of the population of Budapest.[14] At the turn of the century, when more than 60 percent of Hungary's population still worked on the land, to Magyar nationalists the Jewish population of Budapest seemed to embody both modernization and urbanization. They believed that Jews, whom they associated with all the ills afflicting modern urban society, were disproportionately represented in the capital relative to the rest of the state. Karl Lueger, the early twentieth-century antisemitic mayor of Vienna, famously promoted this emerging antisemitic tide when he coined the name "Judapest" for the Hungarian capital, thus rallying his antisemitic followers to his anti-Hungarian stance.[15]

---

[13] In the famously multinational empire, after 1867 the census of Cisleithania (the "Austrian half") asked for "language of use" and the Hungarian census for "mother tongue," though both categories were open to subjective decisions and demonstrated dramatic changes over the final decades of the monarchy.

[14] Paul Lendvai, *The Hungarians: A Thousand Years of Victory in Defeat*, translated by Ann Major (Princeton, NJ: Princeton University Press, 2003), 328; George Barany, "'Magyar Jew' or 'Jewish Magyar'? To the Question of Jewish Assimilation in Hungary," *Canadian-American Slavic Studies* 8 (1974): 1–44.

[15] Lueger was quite proud of this coinage, saying that he had "thought of something so clever at the time" about "the connection between the two evils of the empire," the Jews and the Hungarians. Lendvai, 329.

Literacy rates were higher among Jews than among the general population: 90.2 percent as opposed to 71.9 percent in 1910. Thus, Jews also constituted a high proportion of urban and middle-class professionals. For example, 12.5 percent of Hungary's industrialists, 33.6 percent of engineers, 45.2 percent of lawyers, 48.9 percent of doctors, 42.4 percent of journalists, and 26.6 percent of writers and artists were of Jewish origin.[16] Not surprisingly, considering their professional distribution, Jews also made up a large portion of students at universities and medical and law schools. In 1913/14, Jews made up 46.7 percent of medical students; in 1903/4, 27.5 percent of law students and 33 percent of students at technical colleges.[17] Many contemporary observers described this remarkably successful integration of Jews into Hungarian economic and cultural life in the nineteenth and early twentieth century, sometimes explaining it as a result of a mutually beneficial "pact" of sorts that had developed between the often Jewish capitalist elite and the large rural landowners who dominated Hungary's politics in the nineteenth century. In return for social status and the ruling Liberals' philo-Semitic encouragement of assimilation, Jews became both staunch Magyar patriots and loyal Liberal voters. This was especially important in Budapest because of the limited franchise. Because the right to vote was based on the level of taxes paid, Jewish success in education and well-paid liberal professions, as well as the wealth of some Jewish merchants and industrialists, meant that Jews (or people of Jewish origin) made up almost half of enfranchised voters in the capital.

The spectacular success of Hungarian Jewish assimilation in the late nineteenth century contrasts starkly with the twentieth-century history of their persecution and murder. Scholars and memoirists have therefore devoted much attention to discovering the seeds of later catastrophes in the fin-de-siècle golden age of apparently successful assimilation. Certainly, Jewish cultural integration and financial success found not only admirers such as the Liberal Party politicians Count Gyula Andrássy (prime minister 1867–71; foreign minister 1871–9) and long-time prime minister Kálmán Tisza (prime minister 1875–90) but also many detractors. Antisemitism and anti-Jewish agitation began to pick up and become more politically noticeable towards the end of the nineteenth century. Did these doubts and condemnation from Hungarian nationalists and Jews, who

---

[16] Rolf Fischer, *Entwicklungsstufen des Antisemitismus in Ungarn, 1867–1939: Die Zerstörung der magyarisch-jüdischen Symbiose* (Munich: Oldenbourg, 1988), 36–7. For a wonderful study on the history of these professions and the fate of their Jewish members, see Mária M. Kovács, *Liberal Professions and Illiberal Politics: Hungary from the Habsburgs to the Holocaust* (New York and Washington: Columbia University Press and Woodrow Wilson Center Press, 1994).

[17] In 1910, 18.5 percent of Hungarian Jews had completed at least four years of higher education, compared to 3.3 percent of Catholics, 3.2 percent of Reformed Hungarians, and 4.4 percent of Lutherans (Germans). For their relative percentages at further institutions of higher learning, see Fischer, *Entwicklungsstufen des Antisemitismus in Ungarn*, 37.

were themselves sometimes critical of the process, signal that the process of Jewish assimilation in Hungary was superficial, lacked intensity, or had gone awry? Or were they responses to its successes?

The pace and breadth of Jewish assimilation in Budapest was only one of many nineteenth-century processes that seems to have fed the growth of antisemitism as a cultural trend and a political platform throughout Central Europe. Detractors of Jewish assimilation could always raise the bar of intensity for would-be assimilated Hungarians. Once their Jewish conationals had adopted the Hungarian language and Hungarian names and social habits, these nationalist critics could always assert the need for the achievement of intangible (and for Jews unattainable) measures of full integration, such as the development of a "Magyar soul." A similar argument can be made about the course of Jewish assimilation and rising antisemitism in the German Empire.

Nonetheless, political expressions of antisemitism in Hungary never achieved the level of popular political support demonstrated in contemporary Austria or Germany, perhaps in part because of Hungary's more limited suffrage. In Budapest, where the assimilating Jewish population made up almost a quarter of the total population, and almost half of the voters, overtly antisemitic politics found little traction. Lueger, for example, was elected mayor of Vienna many times on a popular antisemitic platform, while at the same time Ferenc Heltai, a man of Jewish heritage, was elected chief burgomaster of Budapest in 1913.[18] Interestingly, the virulent antisemitism so characteristic of Viennese politics in this period was directed against a Jewish minority that made up only 8–9 percent of the city's population, though some of its members had attained great influence, particularly in the financial and cultural spheres. And because of the introduction of universal manhood suffrage in Austria in 1907, Jews made up a much lower percentage of voters than in Hungary, where the franchise was restricted to the highest taxpayers.

In addition to the ethnic and religious differences in Budapest there were also the vast class disparities common to rapidly industrializing cities. While class differences sometimes coincided with ethnic fault lines, this was not always the case. Despite recent historiography's tendency to focus primarily on the conflicts between nationalities in the last decades of the multinational Habsburg Monarchy, Hungarian society and politics in the nineteenth century were also distinguished by deep divisions between rich and poor and between rural and urban. Many contemporary observers remarked on the rigid social stratification in Hungary at the turn of the century. According to 1910 government statistics, just over 5,000 of the largest landowners – members of a small stratum of the wealthiest families, many of them the same Hungarian families who dominated

---

[18] Heltai was the nephew of Theodore Herzl, the founder of the Zionist movement, also from Budapest.

the country's politics – owned almost a third of all cultivated land in Hungary. By contrast, two-thirds of the nation's seven million poor peasants and agricultural workers (about 40 percent of the population), many of them ethnic minorities, owned a half hectare or less on average.[19] Though Hungarian peasants had been legally freed in 1849 there had been no land reform following emancipation. The political effects of this economic stratification were dramatic because of the nation's electoral laws. Suffrage, and therefore political influence, was available only to a limited stratum, around 5 percent, of tax-paying citizens.

Class differences that made manifest the deep inequalities in wealth and political power were reinforced by prejudices that reflected the Hungarian elite's contempt for their social inferiors. Ottokár Prohászka, the prominent and anti-semitic Catholic bishop of the diocese of Székesfehérvár, observed these preju-dices clearly, remarking in 1899 that "in Hungary ... the gentleman sees the peasant not as a person, but in line with the old caste conception as half a head of cattle."[20] Prohászka's comment, ironic when one considers his own extreme racism, demonstrates vividly the way class provided (like race and gender) legible and indelible categories with which the elite viewed their own society.

In the fast-growing capital, Budapest, an expanding government bureau-cracy and the new urban financial and professional classes embodied a new "middle class," whose increasing political and economic prominence mitigated and transformed the social relationships and attitudes that defined class rela-tions in the more traditional countryside, where a chasm often separated the landowning nobles or gentry and the poor peasants, who in many regions even spoke a different language than their lords. Even in the capital, however, social and cultural life remained stratified, with the nobility and gentry separated socially from other classes and organized in their own clubs and social circles, into which professionals and civil servants had little entry in the pre–World War I era. Even within these elevated social strata both the nobility and civil servants maintained intricate interior hierarchies that included a dozen levels of titles and unique forms of address that connoted subtle differences in social standing.[21] While facing challenges in the late nineteenth century, this social system persisted to the time of the 1919 revolutions (and beyond).

[19] Miklós Molnár, *A Concise History of Hungary*, translated by Anna Magyar (Cambridge: Cambridge University Press, 2001), 218–19.

[20] Prohászka quoted in Lendvai, 325. Székesfehérvár is a diocese in the Esztergom–Budapest ecclesiastical province. Prohászka was a prominent figure in early twentieth-century Hungary who wrote widely on antisemitic topics as in "Die Judenfrage in Ungarn" [The Jewish question in Hungary], (Hamburg: Deutschvölkische Schutz- und Trutzbund Hamburg, 1920) and *Heft 21 der Hammer-Schläge* (1920). For more on Catholic antisemitic intellectuals in Hungary, see Paul Hanebrink, *In Defense of Christian Hungary: Religion, Nationalism and Antisemitism in Inter-war Hungary, 1890–1944* (Ithaca, NY: Cornell University Press, 2006).

[21] The Hungarian language also has multiple grammatical levels of address, indicating both hierarchy and familiarity.

At the other end of the social spectrum, Budapest was also home to Hungary's other new, urban socioeconomic class: industrial workers. In 1919 the revolutionary government legitimized itself as the representatives of exactly this urban proletariat, but nationalist counterrevolutionaries denied that the industrial workers of Hungary had supported the revolution, which they portrayed not as a true class uprising but as a foreign or Jewish takeover that had manipulated the native workers. As we will see, the truth about the political loyalties and revolutionary politics of the Hungarian workers probably lay somewhere between these two views, with them being neither dupes of foreign machinations nor a vanguard of organized labor. At the turn of the century Hungary had a few centers of industry outside of Budapest, particularly in mining areas, but largely the country's growing numbers of industrial workers, as well as their political organizations, were concentrated in the capital city. In 1890, when the population of Budapest was about a half million, it was already home to 80,000 industrial workers. These numbers continued to increase as the city's population grew in the decades before World War I.[22]

Hungarian workers were able to forge an independent political movement over the last decades of the nineteenth century. The workers' political mobilizations began in the 1860s under the influence of the German socialist movement, with urban workers forming a German *Arbeiterverein* in 1867.[23] The first congress of the Social Democratic Workers' Party of Hungary was held in 1890, though the extremely limited Hungarian suffrage meant the group was not able to successfully contest elections. Rather, they could only push for suffrage reforms and labor organization rights. The next decades were marked by sporadic labor unrest in the capital, with illegal strikes organized by the party and affiliated trade unions. It is telling of Hungary's enduring rural character, though, that much of the era's most serious labor disruption, such as the bloody unrest in Békés County in 1891 and 1892, occurred among agricultural workers in the countryside rather than urban industrial workers, and, as the political scientist Andrew Janos has pointed out, it was ironically the rural "breadbasket" regions, not the capital, that sent the first socialist representatives to the Hungarian parliament.[24]

For the duration of the monarchy, Hungary's limited franchise made it impossible for the socialists to achieve the sort of parliamentary representation that the German Social Democratic Party (Sozialdemokratische Partei Deutschlands; SPD) had. Owing to the universal manhood suffrage granted

---

[22] Tibor Frank, "Hungary and the Dual Monarchy," in Peter F. Sugar, Péter Hanák, and Tibor Frank, eds., *A History of Hungary* (Bloomington: Indiana University Press, 1990), 260; also Molnár, *Concise History of Hungary*, 219.

[23] Andrew C. Janos, *The Politics of Backwardness in Hungary, 1825–1945* (Princeton: Princeton University Press, 1982), 161.

[24] Ibid., 160.

at the founding of the German Empire in 1871, Social Democrats were elected to the parliament as nonparty individual candidates even during the period of the Anti-Socialist Laws (1878–90).[25] However, in the Hungarian parliamentary elections of 1901, not a single one of the Hungarian Social Democrats' fifty-eight candidates for parliament was elected despite the party's 72,790 members and the 130,000 affiliated trade union members.[26] Although the Hungarian Social Democrats had proved unable to establish an effective presence in parliament, they proved more effective in mobilizing workers to represent themselves physically on the streets in strikes and demonstrations, including some involving as many as 200,000 participants, as in May 1912 when protesters demanding suffrage reform were involved in bloody clashes with the military outside the parliament building.[27] These demonstrations of workers' political strength were staged in Budapest's streets and factories, and in front of its government buildings. The mass organizations of Hungary's Social Democrats and the visible presence of workers in strikes or political demonstrations meant that, even without electoral reform on the German model, the masses had clearly entered the field of Hungarian politics, and this was evident both to observers on the street and to the politicians in parliament looking out their windows. But such visible manifestations of working-class political organizations and demands made the workers' movement a useful symbolic enemy for the conservative political elite in their effort to limit the franchise.

When analyzing the social composition of pre–World War I Budapest, we should add to industrial laborers a relatively large servant population. John Lukacs contends that "as late as 1870 every fifth person in Buda and Pest was a servant – a portion twice as large as that in Vienna, and three times larger than in Berlin."[28] For many families, keeping a servant was a sign of their bourgeois identity, even if they were themselves quite poor. As a group, servants had even less political representation than workers in Hungary, since they lacked not only the franchise but also political organizations to represent their interests. Some of these servants were young women from urban working-class families, who may therefore have heard of, and identified with, socialist ideas from their family and neighborhood. But many others came from rural backgrounds: small towns and villages outside the capital. Most of them lacked personal ties to the urban residents when they arrived. Because of the mixed socioeconomic composition

---

[25] This was true for elections to the imperial parliament (Reichstag), but the elections to the parliament (*Landtag)* of the individual German states (including the largest state, Prussia) were often determined by three-tier suffrage based on taxes paid, giving more representation to the wealthiest individuals.
[26] Janos, 160.   [27] Ibid.
[28] John Lukacs, *Budapest 1900: A Historical Portrait of a City and Its Culture* (New York: Grove Weidenfeld, 1988), 74–5.

of most of Budapest's neighborhoods at the turn of the century, even if, after their arrival, these poor migrants lived with the wealthy families they served, they were not separated physically from the urban poor, who sometimes lived in the basement and attic apartments of the same buildings. Rural migrant servants were likely to have met, socialized with, and most likely married other working-class urban residents.

Despite the growing numbers of laborers and servants in Budapest's population, and the growing numbers of famous noble families who built new urban palaces in the central Pest districts, most contemporaries and historians have emphasized the "bourgeois" character of Budapest around the turn of the last century. John Lukacs argues that "the working classes were the largest portion of the people of Budapest; but by 1900 the *tone* of Budapest was that of a bourgeois city. Perhaps in all of Eastern Europe it was the *only* bourgeois city."[29] There were signs of a flourishing bourgeois civic culture even though the franchise remained limited and middle-class political organizations were generally weak. Nearly every contemporary commentator sang the praises of the city's cafes, restaurants, clubs, and organizational life, as well as its relatively free and varied press, with more than twenty daily newspapers representing a variety of political perspectives. The sparkling surface of Budapest's literary and artistic world blinded many to the problems below the surface.

Across Europe the electoral franchise was expanded in the late nineteenth century. German Chancellor Otto von Bismarck famously gambled on the conservatism of Germany's rural masses, and, as a result, the German Empire was founded with universal manhood suffrage in 1871; by 1912, even after weathering a decade of illegality under the Anti-Socialist Laws, the SPD was the largest party in the German imperial parliament. In neighboring Vienna, capital of the other half of the Habsburg Monarchy, the franchise was slowly expanded by reforms in 1873 and 1897, which granted suffrage to most men over twenty-four regardless of income, but retained the tiered curial system that favored the wealthy. The Austrian Social Democrats were able to win seats in parliament and from there to also push for universal manhood suffrage, which was finally introduced in 1907 following both Social Democratic parliamentary pressure and a general strike. They immediately became the largest party in the parliament, with 23 percent of the vote in the first democratic elections.[30]

[29] Ibid., 75. As evidence of the predominance of bourgeois social norms even among the workers, Lukacs shows a photograph (opposite page 99) of skilled workers at a factory bench wearing derby hats rather than the floppy workers' caps common elsewhere in Europe.

[30] Pieter Judson, *The Habsburg Empire: A New History* (Cambridge, MA: Belknap Press of Harvard University Press, 2016), 375; and more detail in John Boyer, "Power, Partisanship, and the Grid of Democratic Politics: 1907 as the Pivot Point of Modern Austrian History," *Austrian History Yearbook* 44 (2013): 148–74.

In Hungary, however, the fears of the Magyar nobles and elites in parliament of potential social and ethnic upheaval conspired to keep the franchise narrow. Turn-of-the-century debates over the expansion of suffrage in Hungary were indicative of many of the most serious problems the country suffered. Deep national and social conflicts were intertwined and resulted in parliamentary paralysis and the perpetuation of rule by what many proponents of suffrage expansion and democratization called the "old regime" or "semifeudal" leadership. This was demonstrated vividly in the 1906 suffrage crisis that arose during the decennial renegotiation of the 1867 Settlement Agreement. The Hungarian parliament was dissolved after the nationalist opposition defeated the ruling Liberal Party but couldn't form a government acceptable to their king, Francis Joseph. It seemed that there could be a more general nationalist revolt against the terms of the compromise and royal authority, especially regarding the use of German as the language of command in the joint military.[31] In response, Emperor Francis Joseph used the threat of universal manhood suffrage to prevent the aristocratic Hungarian parliament from rebelling against the crown. The political ploy worked, and opposition forces agreed to let the comprise survive intact. Hungarian nationalists worried that political parties representing ethnic minority groups, such as the Romanians, Slovaks, Serbs, and others, would have significant representation in a parliament elected with democratic suffrage and so backed down on their attempts to assert Hungarian national interests vis-à-vis Austria out of fear of the possible nationalist claims of these groups.

By the beginning of the twentieth century, a group of radical Hungarian social critics were already portraying their state as an ossified, elite-dominated political structure that was precariously hanging onto power in a country teeming with potential national and social strife. For many observers, the revolutionary events of 1918 and 1919 merely proved that the prewar situation had been untenable. In the 1920s, Oszkár Jászi, historian and former member of Mihály Károlyi's post–World War I democratic government (the one replaced by the March soviet revolution), offered an immensely influential interpretation of the end of the Habsburg Monarchy and the revolutions in Hungary. Jászi acknowledged both the uncontrollable "centrifugal forces" of nationalism that were pulling apart the monarchy and the thwarted desires for social change and greater equality that had not been met by timely reforms.[32] The progressive, although not revolutionary, novelist Dezső Kosztolányi's 1926 novel *Anna Édes* put a human face on this theory. Set in the months after the fall of the Hungarian Soviet, the murder of her masters by the servant Anna served as

---

[31] Judson, 367.

[32] Oscar [Oszkár] Jászi, *The Dissolution of the Habsburg Monarchy*, (Chicago: University of Chicago Press, 1929) and *Revolution and Counter-Revolution in Hungary* (New York: Howard Fertig, 1969).

a metaphor for the revolutions themselves. In Kosztolányi's famous novel this pointless act of violence, which only worsened Anna's situation, erupted (like the revolution itself) after her employers prevented her from improving her life through marriage and treated her generally unjustly and inhumanly.[33]

In the era of the 1919 revolution and the counterrevolutionary antisemitic hysteria that followed, many Jewish politicians and observers attempted to make sense for themselves of the events that the Hungarian masses now blamed on the Jews. In the wake of the failed revolutionary experiment, many right-wing political actors asserted that the old-regime Kingdom of Hungary had been politically and militarily viable before its artificial dismemberment at the hands of radicals, socialists, the minority nationalities, and the Entente powers in 1918. For Jászi, who was himself Jewish, it was important to demonstrate that "the dissolution of the Habsburg Monarchy was not a mechanical, but an organic process."[34] He refuted the Hungarian version of the "stab in the back" legend that was retailed in many European settings, most notably Germany, over the following decades. Instead, Jászi argued that the fault for the dissolution of both the monarchy and historic Hungary lay with the stubborn, self-absorbed ruling nobility and its refusal to address the twin issues of democratic and national reforms. In fact, Jászi argued, a direct line could be drawn from the dysfunction of pre–World War I Hungary, and its many unresolved issues with subordinated nationalities, to the appearance of a rabid postwar version of antisemitism. Fear of the Jews, according to him, replaced fear of the nationalities as a "bulwark for the maintenance of feudal privileges." In the smaller, ethnically homogenous "rump" Hungary that the Entente created after the Central Powers' defeat, "the pretext of the nationality danger ceased, but the system of class domination continued," as Jászi put it. "The theory of the 'Nationality bugbear' was transformed into that of the 'Jewish bugbear'!"[35] This contemporary explanation for the turn from assimilationist prewar Hungary to the antisemitism of the interwar period is an important rebuttal to the counterrevolutionary narrative, which blamed the activities of revolutionary Jews for the anti-Jewish politics and violence.

As we have seen, antisemitism had first become a force in Hungarian intellectual life even during the era of the "Nationality bugbear," and its appearance and rapid growth had a variety of social, economic, and psychological causes. But, for the generation of successful, assimilated Jews like Jászi, recalling these antecedents served to explain more "organically" and scientifically the tragic antisemitic atmosphere that afflicted postrevolutionary Hungary. He rejected the alternative, "mechanical" view, promoted by the

---

[33] Dezső Kosztolányi, *Anna Édes*, translated by George Szirtes (New York: New Directions, 1993).
[34] See Jászi, *Dissolution*, chapter 2.   [35] Ibid., 326.

triumphant conservatives, that claimed that antisemitism was spurred only in 1919 by the actions of "Jewish" revolutionaries (in other words, antisemitism was caused by the revolutionary politics of the Jews themselves somehow). Certainly, Jászi and his prewar collaborators at the influential journal *Huszadik Század* (Twentieth Century) had argued before the war for the Hungarian government to adopt a platform of democratization and nationalities reforms. Now, in the wake of the national disaster of the war and the destructive cycle of revolution and counterrevolution, they believed their warnings had been unheeded like Cassandra's.

Bavaria: Particularism and Modernity

At the beginning of the twentieth century, Bavaria, like Hungary, could look back on more than 800 years of statehood. Also like Hungary, during the nineteenth century a predominantly agrarian Bavaria had been transformed by the rapid growth of its urban centers, especially its capital, Munich. Munich, like Budapest, became the site of a flourishing literary and artistic modernism and the home of a growing population of workers and other urban poor. After German unification under Prussian leadership in 1871, Bavaria, like Hungary, was also defined by its position within a larger empire. Similar to Hungary, in the decades before World War I Bavarian political life was dominated by struggles over suffrage, social reform, and nationalism.

Munich's urban development in the nineteenth century, including the tension between the city and the countryside, was in many ways similar to that of Budapest. Like Budapest, Munich went from a modestly sized provincial capital at the beginning of the century to a large urban center by the end, with all of the benefits and problems that came with such rapid growth. By 1880 the relatively small royal-residence city of Munich had grown to an urban center of 230,000. Thirty years later, in 1910, the city was more than two and half times the size, with a population of almost 600,000, making it the third largest city in the German Empire, after Berlin and Hamburg, and slightly ahead of Leipzig.[36] As in Budapest and other rapidly expanding Central European cities, the tremendous population increase in Munich was mostly the result of migration. These migrants came from the surrounding Bavarian countryside and from "abroad," which often meant other German states. The primary stream came from linguistically and ethnically homogenous rural Bavaria and thus added a "peasant" but not a "foreign" flavor to the urban culture. The secondary stream came from other German states, such as Prussia, as well as from the

---

[36] Population statistics in Gerd Hohorst, Jürgen Kocka, and Gerhard Ritter, eds., *Sozialgeschichtliches Arbeitsbuch: Materialien zur Statistik des Kaiserreichs 1870–1914*, vol. 2. (Munich: C. H. Beck, 1975), 45–6; Volker Berghahn, *Imperial Germany, 1871–1914: Economy, Society, Culture and Politics* (Providence, RI: Berghahn Books, 1994), table 37, 312.

Polish territories and elsewhere in Central and Eastern Europe, adding new accents and sometimes languages to the urban soundscape. New arrivals made up a significant, and to observers remarkable, portion of the city's population. A 1910 travel guide to Munich gave an enthusiastic view of the city's diversity: "The Bavarian capital is cosmopolitan, crowded with adopted children: North Germans, who have settled by the Isar because here one draws his breath more easily than in the angular North ... Russians, who find it convenient to set another frontier between themselves and Siberia; painters, sculptors, musicians, men of learning and idlers."[37] Though turn-of-the-century Munich was less linguistically and ethnically diverse than Budapest (or Vienna or Berlin), residents comparing the city of 1910 with a few decades earlier were struck by the visible and audible increase in "foreigners."

Not all local observers were happy with this increasingly cosmopolitan Munich. As in Budapest, a portion of Munich's intellectuals fell under the spell of nationalism and its poisonous sibling, antisemitism. These modern "anti-modernists" often considered Jews responsible for the ills of urban society, both as industrial leaders and capitalists, and leaders of social democracy among the workers. Like many urban centers, Munich had seen its Jewish population grow at a rapid rate, more than doubling in the last quarter of the nineteenth century, from 3,451 in 1875 to 8,739 in 1900.[38] But although this increase seems dramatic, the population of Munich itself had more than doubled in the same period. So even with this increase, the Jewish population still made up less than 2 percent of Munich's 1900 population, and was significantly lower than the Jewish proportion of the population of Budapest, 23 percent, or Vienna, 9 percent.[39] It was probably not narrowly the growth of the Jewish population in Munich that incited the negative commentaries but the fact that many of the newcomers were Orthodox Jews who had arrived from Eastern Europe and who looked and sounded much more foreign than the native-born Jewish population and, for the nativist critics, were more visible and undesirable.

In his 1908 dissertation at Ludwig-Maximilian University in Munich, the statistician Jakob Segall pointed out what he considered the two key differences between the growth of Munich's Jewish and Christian populations. First, at least one third of the increase in the city's Christian population came through the physical incorporation of villages surrounding Munich into the municipality

[37] Henry Rawle Wadleigh, *Munich: History, Monuments, and Art* (London: T. Fisher Unwin, 1910), 13.

[38] David Clay Large, *Where Ghosts Walked: Munich's Road to the Third Reich* (New York: W. W. Norton, 1997), 12.

[39] Jewish population in Vienna: 1890, 8.7 percent of population; 1900, 8.8 percent; 1910, 8.6 percent – from Monika Richarz, "Demographic Developments," in Michael A. Meyer, ed., *German-Jewish History in Modern Times*, vol. 3: *Integration in Dispute, 1871–1918* (New York: Columbia University Press, 1997), 31, table 1.10.

during the last decades of the nineteenth century. These new city districts had almost no Jewish population.[40] Second, because the urbanized Jews of the German Empire, like middle-class urban populations in Europe in general, experienced a significant drop in birth rates in the late nineteenth century, the newly arrived Jewish immigrants, mostly from Eastern Europe, who had larger families, made up most of the increase in the Jewish population. This meant that though the relative portion of Jews in Munich's population remained almost unchanged in the last decades of the nineteenth century, their image was transformed. While many of the Christian "newcomers" in Munich in 1900 may well have been longtime residents of the surrounding villages, more and more of Munich's Jews seemed to be "foreigners," at least to the antisemites. In 1895, an observer wrote of the new immigrants, "Like the Chinese to California came the Jews to Munich: diligent, frugal, numerous, and thoroughly hated."[41] After the United States passed the Chinese Exclusion Act of 1882, Central European antisemites used this international precedent, and the comparison to the Chinese, to justify their numerous planned anti-Jewish immigration reforms.[42]

What drew these "thousands of Outlanders," as the 1910 guidebook called them, to Munich? According to many observers, Munich's charm lay largely in its feeling of comfort and friendliness – Munich's *Gemütlichkeit*. There is probably, from the nineteenth century onwards, no other adjective more frequently applied to Munich than *gemütlich*; an observation that is usually paired in later histories with a remark on the irony that it was this "comfortable" and friendly city, of all places, where Nazism got its start and that Hitler proclaimed the "capital of the movement." Behind the adjective *gemütlich* was a rejection of all the uncomfortable facts of urbanization and modern life. Like Budapest, Munich was considered a bourgeois city. Many Germans considered comfortable Munich a city of art and beer. It seemed to offer the pleasures of a large city without urban destitution and class conflict. An uncomplicated combination of low and high culture in Munich seemed unpretentious and inviting to many observers, particularly those worried by the conflicts of modern life elsewhere. Particularly with the hindsight offered by the terrible events of the later twentieth century, pre–World War I Munich seemed to glow with *Gemütlichkeit* and to have been a city without conflict. The liberal professor of economics and

---

[40] Jakob Segall, *Die Entwicklung der Juden in München von 1875 bis 1905: Eine Bevölkerungsstatistische Studie*, (dissertation, Ludwig-Maximilians-University, Munich, 1908), 3; for the populations of the new districts when they were added, see his note 8. The historian Mitchell Hart has written about Segall and his role as head of the Bureau for Jewish Statistics in Berlin in *Social Science and the Politics of Modern Jewish Identity* (Stanford, CA: Stanford University Press, 2000).

[41] Quoted in Large, *Where Ghosts Walked*, 12.

[42] For the pan-German politician Georg von Schönerer's use of the United States' act as a model for proposals to limit Jewish immigration to Habsburg Austria, see Carl Schorske, *Fin-de-Siècle Vienna: Politics and Culture* (New York: Vintage, 1981), 129.

prominent economic advisor to the early Weimar government Moritz Julius Bonn, in his post–World War II memoirs, describes Munich before World War I as "a city without class consciousness."[43] Like many depictions we see of Budapest at the turn of the century, Bonn's characterization of Munich made light of industrial development and emphasized the bourgeois look or feel of the working class, which he claimed "wasn't separated from other social strata either by its feeling or lifestyle . . . . The social life took place in the beer cellars. There people met without regard for rank or class; one seated oneself wherever there was room. In summer, one moved to the beer gardens, the small parks that surrounded the breweries."[44] Munich, though growing and industrializing, lacked large-scale factories or extractive industry and the local SPD was supported by employees of many small firms as well as civil servants under Georg von Vollmar's moderate leadership.[45]

In reality, Munich's bourgeoisie, like that of Budapest, ignored the housing and hygienic conditions in workers' districts, such as the Au in the southeast of the city, which were as cramped and unsanitary as those in most other urban centers. During the late nineteenth century the relatively hilly and scenic Westend area became, in the words of an urban historian, a district of "factory smells instead of bourgeois elegance."[46] In 1895, more than half of Munich's working-class families lived in squalid, one-room apartments, only half of which had a separate kitchen or chamber.[47] In fact, Munich was typical of European cities at the turn of the century in the contrasts, both architecturally and socially, between the worlds inhabited by the workers and the bourgeoisie, as is clear from contemporary writings by Oskar Maria Graf and Ödön von Horváth.[48]

A growing rift between city and countryside mirrored the social conflicts within the capital. Although Bavaria participated generally in the *Gründerboom*, (founder boom) of the early years of the German Empire, it

---

[43] M. J. [Moritz Julius] Bonn, *So Macht Man Geschichte? Bilanz eines Lebens* (Munich: Paul List Verlag, 1953), 142.

[44] Ibid., 143.

[45] Bonn's perspective is supported by the urban comparisons of Adam R. Seipp in *The Ordeal of Peace: Demobilization and the Urban Experience in Britain and Germany, 1917–1921* (Farnham: Ashgate Publishing, 2009), 40–1.

[46] Stephan Bleek, "Münchens Westend: Fabrikgestank statt Bürgereleganz," in Friedrich Prinz and Marita Krauss, eds., *München – Musenstadt mit Hinterhöfen: Die Prinzregentenzeit, 1886–1912* (Munich: C. H. Beck, 1988), 69–73.

[47] Table 65, "Size of Heatable Apartments by Selected Occupational Groups in Munich, 1895," in Berghahn, *Imperial Germany*, 325.

[48] Oskar Maria Graf, *Wir sind Gefangene: Ein Bekenntnis* (Munich: Deutscher Taschenbuch Verlag, 1981); Ödön von Horváth, *Der ewige Spießer. Erbaulicher Roman in drei Teilen* (Frankfurt a.M.: Suhrkamp Verlag, 1977). Graf was born in a small town in Bavaria outside Munich, the son of a baker. Horváth was born in Austria–Hungary, the son of a Hungarian officer in the Habsburg military. His family moved to Bavaria and Horváth studied in Munich, where he began his writing career.

continued to lag behind in industrialization and remained predominantly agricultural. Even at the end of the nineteenth century when, according to government statistics, the populations of Munich and Nuremberg had doubled and tripled respectively, there were still "less than a million 'workers' in all of Bavaria, of which no more than a third could be called 'industrial.'"[49] In this, too, Bavaria was similar to Hungary at the turn of the century.

Unlike Budapest, which had a central role in Hungary's industrial development, Munich was the capital and the political center of Bavaria, but it was not initially the center of the region's industry or its growing proletariat. In 1874, almost half of the members of the Bavarian SPD lived in Nuremberg rather than Munich, and it was the Nuremberg electoral district that sent the first Bavarian Social Democrat to the imperial parliament, the Reichstag, in 1881.[50] If Munich was not the undisputed center of the workers' movement, the workers' movement nonetheless came to play an increasingly important role in the city starting in the 1890s after the repeal of the Anti-Socialist Laws in the German Empire. Already in 1890, both of Munich's representatives elected to the Reichstag were Social Democrats.[51] In 1888, the daily newspaper the *Münchner Post* was established as the mouthpiece of the Bavarian Social Democrats in Munich, and its editor from 1890 was Vollmar – the Reichstag deputy from Munich and charismatic central figure of the Bavarian SPD. Under Vollmar, the Bavarian SPD took steps to broaden its appeal in rural areas and to agitate among the disaffected peasantry. Vollmar's attitudes and strategies regarding the "peasant question" and the Bavarian SPD's reformist platform were not well received by many in the national leadership of the SPD, but they did lead to electoral gains and a growing membership in the party.

Even as the SPD began to dominate Bavaria's cities at the turn of the twentieth century, the political force that most shaped pre–World War I Bavaria was not socialist but Catholic: the Bavarian branch of the German Center Party (*Deutsche Zentrumspartei* or just *Zentrum*).[52] While a popular

---

[49] *Statistisches Jahrbuch für den Freistaat Bayern* 1919 (Munich: 1919), 134–5, quoted in Alan F. Mitchell, *Revolution in Bavaria, 1918_1919: The Eisner Regime and the Soviet Republic* (Princeton, NJ: Princeton University Press, 1965), 10–11.

[50] Max Spindler, ed., *Bayerische Geschichte im 19. und 20. Jahrhundert, 1800–1970*, vol. 1: *Staat und Politik* (Munich: C. H. Beck, 1978), 308–9. This could be seen as a parallel to the irony noted by Andrew Janos that it was the rural districts of the Hungarian plains, with their peasant population, and not Budapest that elected the first socialists to the Hungarian parliament at the turn of the twentieth century. Janos, 161.

[51] Peter Jelavich, *Munich and Theatrical Modernism: Politics, Playwriting and Performance, 1890–1914* (Cambridge, MA: Harvard University Press, 1985), 14. Vollmar was elected in 1884 as Munich's first social democratic representative to the Reichstag.

[52] Like many new mass parties, the Center Party name and organization altered after its founding in the Rhineland in 1870, where its main purpose had been to defend the rights of Catholics and the Catholic Church in Protestant Prussia and against Bismarck's *Kulturkampf* struggle to weaken Catholic influence in the new empire after 1871. In the majority-Catholic Bavarian state, the party was not organized around minority rights, but rather focused on state rights and

Catholic party had been founded in Hungary in 1895 (*Néppárt*), the nation's limited franchise and the divisions between Catholics and Protestants prevented it from gaining great political influence until the interwar period.[53] In Bavaria, however, the struggle between the Bavarian state and the Catholic Church was the defining context of nineteenth-century-politics.[54] Political Catholicism in Bavaria played a contradictory role in the nineteenth century, and the Center Party's focus in majority-Catholic Bavaria was slightly different than that of the national German Center Party, with more emphasis on defending Bavarian particularism following the founding of the empire in 1871. Nonetheless, a struggle against the often-anticlerical liberalism of both the Reichstag and the Bavarian *Landtag* united Bavarian Catholic politicians to the national party and its goals.[55]

Catholic political organization in Bavaria had roots in a popular campaign of mass petitions in 1849 against a bill for Jewish emancipation that had passed the liberal parliament. James Harris has demonstrated that the Catholic Church used methods of mass mobilization to pursue a decidedly anti-emancipatory program to continue the oppression of the Jews. The Catholic campaign for suffrage reform, to enfranchise and politically emancipate its largely peasant base, was initiated in order to prevent the political emancipation of another group, the Jews.[56] The Bavarian Patriot Party, and later the Center Party, grew from this mid-century organization against Jewish emancipation. And that struggle, which had used antisemitism to mobilize the rural Catholic population against the liberal government in the capital, also colored Bavarian politics in the period leading up to the revolutions of 1918 and 1919 and the antisemitism that followed.

On the surface, nineteenth-century Bavaria seemed reliably stable; the Wittelsbach dynasty ruled it as a constitutional monarchy under the same constitution for a century before the revolutions in the fall of 1918. Yet, this surface stability proved to be quite fragile; the era of the constitutional

Bavarian particularism or regionalism. The Bavarian Center Party had originally been the Bavarian Patriots Party (*Bayerische Patriotenpartei*; formed in 1868), which joined the imperial German Center Party in 1887, changing its name to the Bavarian Center Party.

[53] For the development of Catholic politics in interwar Hungary, see Paul Hanebrink, *In Defense of Christian Hungary: Religion, Nationalism and Anti-Semitism in Inter-War Hungary, 1890–1944* (Ithaca, NY: Cornell University Press, 2006).

[54] Jelavich, 6–7 and 12–13.

[55] For more on the *Kulturkampf* and nationalist and liberal anticlericalism in the German Empire, see Helmut Walser Smith, *German Nationalism and Religious Conflict: Culture, Ideology, Politics, 1870–1914* (Princeton, NJ: Princeton University Press, 1995); and for another local case of Center Party development, David Blackbourn, *Class, Religion and Local Politics in Wilhemine Germany: The Centre Party in Würtemberg before 1914* (New Haven, CT: Yale University Press, 1980).

[56] James F. Harris, *The People Speak! Anti-Semitism and Emancipation in Nineteenth-Century Bavaria* (Ann Arbor: University of Michigan Press, 1994), 5.

monarchs was marred by electoral gerrymandering to favor the more urban, liberal constituencies and the rather frequent employment of ministerial rule to dismiss parliament when conflicts arose or challenges were raised to the dominant liberal governments. The techniques used in Bavaria were similar to those used by other Central European governments in the nineteenth century, most notably in Austria, in response to the rise of mass political parties such as the Christian Social Party of longtime Vienna mayor Karl Lueger and popular Czech nationalist parties in the Bohemian lands. In Bavaria, the mass political movement that caused the government to resort to ministerial rule was political Catholicism.

The most pressing local issue for Bavarian Catholics in the second half of the nineteenth century was that of German nationalism and the form that inevitable German unification would take. Even the original name of the Catholic party founded in 1868, the Bavarian Patriots Party, reflected the fact that, for Bavarian Catholics, protecting the rights of the church had become synonymous with preserving Bavarian independence from Protestant Prussia. In the nineteenth-century struggles over the question of national German unification, Bavaria was often on the side of Catholic Austria and a proponent of the so-called *großdeutsch*, or greater German solution, including Austria and possibly under the leadership of the Catholic Habsburgs. Catholic politicians feared Bavaria's being swallowed up in a majority-Protestant state under Prussian domination if Austria were excluded from a unified Germany. After the Prussian defeat of Austria and its allies, including Bavaria, in the Austro-Prussian War of 1866, the Bavarian government accepted the inevitability of its incorporation into the new German state under Prussian dominance. Inclusion in the new German Empire clearly meant a loss of sovereignty, even though the new *Reich* was a federation, with Bavaria allowed a number of political concessions to its independence.

The Bavarian Patriots Party, later renamed the Bavarian Center Party and united with the national Center Party in 1887, rallied support from the peasantry and even the middle classes against the government's program of secularization and economic liberalism. One year after its founding, and despite the restrictive franchise, the Patriots Party was able to win a majority of representatives in the parliament, the *Landtag*, and it held onto its majority for the almost the rest of the prewar period.[57] The Center Party exercised its influence through traditional means, such as the parish priests and their sermons, but also through novel political instruments such as the Christian trade unions and workers' associations, a direct response to the challenge of organizational efforts by the Social Democratic Party. Though no longer based on an explicitly antisemitic platform (as in the opposition to Jewish emancipation in 1849), the

---

[57] Jelavich, 6, 12–13; Mitchell, *Revolution in Bavaria*, 13–17, election results on 14 and 17.

Center Party's Catholic organization kept its membership exclusionary and its political worldview focused on religious affiliation.

After Bavaria's incorporation into the new German Empire – with its universal manhood suffrage – in 1871, the franchise for elections to the Bavarian state parliament remained much more limited than for national elections. A seemingly unlikely parliamentary alliance between the Bavarian Center Party and the Social Democrats led to franchise reform in 1906. Even after the reform, the king still could appoint and dismiss his ministers and there were still fewer enfranchised voters in Bavarian elections than in national elections for the Reichstag: of 133,000 voters in Munich for the Reichstag, only 89,000 were allowed to cast votes for the Bavarian *Landtag*.[58] This meant that, as in Hungary, franchise reform was at the forefront of all pre–World War I reform movements and political struggles in Bavaria. Both the Center Party and the Social Democratic workers' movement were profoundly affected by the inequities and peculiarities of Bavaria's parliamentary system. The disparity in the franchise at German national and Bavarian state level forced the development of strange, two-front strategies for the mass political parties in the pre–World War I decades. For the national elections, when they could count on their full electorate and where the Bavarian representatives would be joining large parliamentary contingents from their national party organizations in the Reichstag, the parties ran campaigns on different issues than for the local Bavarian elections, when they had to try to appeal to more nonparty members in order to get elected with the more limited suffrage. For example, the SPD in Bavaria presented a more peasant-friendly face to its electorate than the national party, and even entered into an election alliance with the Center Party at the Bavarian state level.

Conclusion

Although in 1919 many conservatives in Hungary and Bavaria nostalgically looked back on the prewar decades as a time of social harmony, in reality Munich and Budapest had both undergone a rapid and disruptive period of growth and industrialization in the second half of the nineteenth century. Jewish assimilation, in an era of rapidly growing Jewish populations in both cities, was linked by increasingly assertive antisemites to a range of social and cultural issues associated in popular opinion with modernization. At the same time, despite political restrictions, working-class parties grew to be a powerful force on the urban stage, though unlike Vienna and Berlin neither city experienced major labor unrest until the war. Even so, by the time World War I broke out in the summer of 1914, the fault lines for civil conflict were easily visible to critical observers.

[58] Spindler, *Bayerische Geschichte*, vol. 1, 320.

2   World War and World Revolution

In his diagnosis of the political and emotional state of the German nation in 1919, the Munich psychiatrist Emil Kraeplin noted that revolution often followed defeat in war. The "severe emotional shock disrupts calm objective reason, and the instinctual discharging of internal tensions replaces rational action."[1] Employing historical examples such as the Paris Commune and the Russian Revolution of 1905, Kraeplin and many other observers believed that the revolutionary upheavals in Austria, Hungary, and Germany in 1918 and 1919 should be understood in relationship to the shock of military defeat and therefore as part of a recognizable European experience of revolutionary activity.

Before the war, many observers had suggested the opposite, claiming that the patriotic fervor unleashed by the war would help to avert what they considered an impending social crisis and possible revolution and rallying behind German Kaiser Wilhelm's proclamation of a *Burgfrieden* or similar statements by other wartime leaders. By 1914, like other cities throughout Europe, Munich and Budapest seemed vulnerable to serious social and political conflict. The increasing power of mass parties and mounting calls for universal male suffrage left no room for the comfortable, *gemütlich* liberalism of the late nineteenth century. In societies anticipating calamity, many people believed that they had to take a side, either with the workers' movement for a more politically open and modern society, or against it, in alliance with religious authorities or imperial governments. In Bavaria as well as in Hungary, the national mobilizations that preceded World War I seemed at first to offer a release from the tensions of an impending clash between these two camps in society; perhaps the trajectory towards civil conflict would be avoided by the approach of international conflict.

It is one of the most vivid ironies of World War I that this last war fought by long-established European empires, a war initiated in defense of the honor of the house of Habsburg, led inexorably to the eclipse of the most important

---

[1] Quoted in Paul Lerner, *Hysterical Men: War, Psychiatry, and the Politics of Trauma in Germany, 1890–1930* (Ithaca, NY: Cornell University Press, 2003), 215.

European monarchies. The truth is that this imperial war began and ended with mass demonstrations across Europe – confirming for some that it was a people's war after all. But the masses' enthusiastic support of crown and king in 1914 can be interpreted as a nationalist rather than a monarchist or conservative sentiment. By 1918 circumstances had been altered by the terrible accumulations of death and injury and by the prospect of defeat. Among the Central Powers in particular, the interests of the crown and the people appeared to be irreparably divergent; it was a year of strikes, mutinies, and eventually revolution. That autumn, with military defeat on the immediate horizon, the once-broad support for the two monarchies collapsed and a revolutionary consensus formed. While each revolution took its own particular course, the phenomenon of overthrow and breakdown was a broad Central European one. In both Germany and Hungary, participants were aware of events unfolding elsewhere in the region and understood their own efforts to be part of the same historic struggle.

War and Revolution: Cause or Betrayal

Revolutions that began without bloodshed in the chaos of national military defeat in Munich and Budapest ended only months later in widespread violence and civil war. In both cases, an initial democratic revolution, like the establishment of the Provisional Government in Russia in 1917, was unable to withstand the pressure of attacks from the political Right and Left. Bereft of support by the spring of 1919, it might be accurate to argue that the Gustav Hoffmann and Mihály Károlyi regimes disintegrated rather than were overthrown. The trajectory of revolution in Central Europe followed the Russian model of the October Revolution, with proclamations of "all power to the councils," but unlike the Bolsheviks in Russia, these new Central European revolutionary governments were unable to stabilize the political situation or harness their early popular support to build institutions or structures.

Whereas in Russia the new communist government managed to survive a series of challenges that included civil war and foreign intervention, the Bavarian and Hungarian revolutions miscarried, becoming "failed revolutions," remembered and studied for different purposes than their successful Russian neighbor. Yet despite these large differences, I would argue that comparisons with the violent and uncertain situation in Russia can prove quite fruitful for understanding Central Europe in 1919 and the years that immediately followed. In Central Europe it was counterrevolution, not revolution, that became entrenched, but in similar circumstances to the creation of the new Soviet state. If the first years of the Soviet Union during the Russian Civil War are understood as "war communism," perhaps the establishment of the Horthy regime in Hungary should be understood as "war nationalism." In the end, chaos and counterrevolution overtook both Budapest and Munich, but this violence, which had been so universally predicted by those who feared revolution on the Russian model, arrived in the wake of the counterrevolutionary triumph, not as part of the revolutions themselves.

The early enthusiasm and societal unity proclaimed by governments and patriotic crowds at the beginning of the world war was a short-lived illusion; already in January 1915, the Hungarian novelist and journalist Gyula Krúdy was writing of "this war, which not so long ago still seemed a panorama of illusions, dreams, and fervent fantasies (seen from the distance through the astronomer's telescope, the poet's frenzy and the imaginings of young men)."[2] And the rumbling dissatisfaction of the poor over their treatment in the war may only have been a displaced frustration with the longue-durée structural inequities of Central European societies. But both the apparent national and imperial unity when the war was declared and the widespread disillusionment and anger of the population as the war's costs mounted were incredibly important reference points for contemporaries trying to understand the unprecedented events they were witnessing. To fully understand the relationship between the world war and the subsequent revolutions and counterrevolutions, therefore, we must place events within the context of popular interpretations that developed among various segments of the population. Both the idea that the war would solve all societal or political problems and later that the war was the source of all problems now seem unrealistic, but that did not make these potent, popular ideas any less powerful in shaping efforts to understand the events that followed. Similarly, powerful ideas and narrative scripts about revolution, derived from the French through the Russian revolutions, shaped the way that events unfolded even before the cessation of hostilities in November 1918.

War and Revolution in Hungary

For residents of Budapest, the world changed irrevocably on June 28, 1914 with the assassination of the Habsburg heir apparent to the throne, Archduke Francis Ferdinand, and his wife, Sophie Chotek, in Sarajevo. Yet, at the time, it was not immediately clear what this event would mean and how the citizens of the Habsburg Monarchy, or their allies, would react. Despite the stereotype, recognizable from postwar literature, of disloyal Hungarians cheering the assassination, the Hungarian population largely supported the declaration of war on July 28 and the outbreak of hostilities in Europe in early August, and various segments of society, such as minority religious communities and

---

[2] "Winter Campaign," in Gyula Krúdy, *Krúdy's Chronicles: Turn-of-the-Century Hungary in Gyula Krudy's Journalism*, edited and translated by John Bátki (Budapest: Central European University Press, 2000), 161.

women's organizations, outdid one another with patriotic expressions.[3] By mid-August, the Budapest socialist newspaper *Népszava*, as well as trade union papers, were unanimously declaring: "Class struggle has ceased in Hungary."[4]

After decades of bitter class and ethnic conflict, war appeared to be a panacea for all of Hungary's modern ills. In his report to the Hungarian parliament in November 1914, Prime Minister István Tisza expressed just this belief and hope.[5] "This struggle," he argued, "has put a stop to party strife; it has put a stop to the class struggle, relegated the nationality conflicts into the background, and given rise to the splendid manifestations of unity and mutual love both at home and in the battlefield."[6] But this apparent social unity, like the "emperor's new clothes" in the folk tale, was woven out of earnest proclamations by Tisza and other politicians, rather than from substantive changes to the nation's material or social conditions.

This mood of hopeful unity and war enthusiasm in the population during the fall of 1914 proved to be based on a series of false assumptions and nationalist enthusiasms. Like citizens and subjects elsewhere in Europe, the Hungarian public expected a short, decisive war. They hoped that the sacrifices they made now (especially those of the working and peasant classes) would be gratefully repaid by the nation's elite once the short conflict was over. As the war dragged on and ever greater sacrifices were required, the war effort became a divisive force rather than a unifying one. Different social and national groups became convinced that their privations were not matched by those of other groups, which they presumed had it easier.

In popular memory and in much historical scholarship, World War I is often viewed through the lens of the great trench battles fought in France and Belgium. The Eastern and Southern fronts where the Habsburg armies fought were not a part of this mythic struggle. Yet Hungary, allied with Germany as part of the Habsburg Monarchy, was one of the main belligerents in World War I. Austria–Hungary was second only to Germany in the number of soldiers mobilized relative to population.[7] The mobilization of over eight million soldiers by the monarchy during the war threw millions of citizens and their families into the crucible of world events. And the losses of the Austro-Hungarian Army in World

---

[3] A dramatic example of this stereotype is the Hungarian officers in Joseph Roth's 1932 novel of the end of the monarchy, *Radetzky March* (Woodstock, NY: Overlook Press, 1974).

[4] *A magyar munkásmosgalom történetének válogatott dokumentitmai*, 35–7, quoted in József Galántai, *Hungary in the First World War* (Budapest: Akadémiai Kiadó, 1989), 65.

[5] Prime minister 1903–5, 1913–17 (the son of Kálmán Tisza, Hungary's longest serving prime minister, from 1875–90).

[6] Tisza's speech in *A Magyar Országgyűlés nyomtatványai: Képviselőházi Napló*, November 28, 1914, quoted in Galántai, 70.

[7] The monarchy recruited 17 percent of the population into the armed forces, compared to 20 percent for the German Empire, see Galántai, 88.

War I were devastating: by one estimate there were 1.2 million dead, over 3.6 million wounded, and 2.2 million missing or held prisoner at the war's end – in other words, a casualty rate of almost 90 percent.[8] Of these, at least 3.8 million of those mobilized, 660,000 of the dead, and 740,000 of the wounded came from the Hungarian crown lands.[9] Finally, 730,000 Hungarians were taken prisoner, the majority of them by Russia.[10] As the scale of Hungary's losses makes clear, the country was not on the periphery of the World War I maelstrom but rather tragically in its full grasp.

A national sense of unusual and unrequited Hungarian sacrifice developed during the war years as a direct result of these immense losses. These remembered sacrifices fed the resentments of many Hungarians who believed their country had again been forced to bear unacceptable harm as a result of the 1919 revolution and counterrevolution. Linking these events together promoted a sense of Hungarian martyrdom, and the notion of a special national burden – the concept of a "Hungarian Calvary" – became widespread.[11] Initially prompted by belief in the inequity in the relative losses and sacrifices imposed on the peoples of the Habsburg Monarchy during the war, the idea of the "Hungarian Calvary" was later popularized as a metaphor for the effects of the 1919 revolution and the punitive peace treaty imposed by the victorious allies.

Postwar shortages and inflated prices for foodstuffs throughout the monarchy further compounded the suffering of Hungarian families that had been caused by mobilization and wartime casualties. Hungary, as the breadbasket of the monarchy, with less industry than Austria, had, in fact, suffered proportionally larger numbers of casualties than other regions of the monarchy. While workers in industrialized areas of Austria and the Bohemian lands were exempted from military service to support wartime industrial production, Hungarian peasants were conscripted and sent to the front in large numbers. And because the imperial government relied on wartime requisitioning of agricultural produce to manage shortages, Hungarian farmers were forced to sell to the government at controlled prices, levying, in effect, a tax on

---

[8] The figures for the casualties are from Martin Gilbert, *First World War* (London: Weidenfeld and Nicolson, 1994). Gilbert cites a slightly lower total for Austro-Hungarian men mobilized (7.8 million) – giving a 90 percent casualty rate.

[9] István Deák, "The Decline and Fall of the Habsburg Monarchy, 1914–18," in Iván Völgyes, ed., *Hungary in Revolution, 1918–1919: Nine Essays* (Lincoln: University of Nebraska Press, 1971), 18, gives a higher number of total men mobilized, 8.3 million, of whom 3.8 million (45 percent) were Hungarian citizens, more than Hungary's 41 percent of the population of the Dual Monarchy.

[10] Iris Rachamimov, *POWs and the Great War: Captivity on the Eastern Front* (Oxford: Berg, 2002), table 1.1, 39–40.

[11] For the parallel victim identity among Austrians, see Ke-Chin Hsia, "'War Victims': Concepts of Victimhood and the Austrian Identity after the Habsburgs," *Contemporary Austrian Studies* 27 (2018): 245–52.

agricultural producers. The result was that Hungarians bore a disproportionate economic burden in addition to disproportionate military service. The predictable result was that the government's manipulation of agricultural prices, intended to keep the price of rations low for the military and war-industry workers in urban areas, produced resentment among Hungarian farmers, who commonly assumed that they alone were being compelled to support the Habsburg war effort. They believed that their sacrifice was greater than that of the monarchy's other peoples. As Maureen Healy has wonderfully demonstrated, however, versions of this sense of grievance and injustice appeared elsewhere in the empire as the war continued. In the Austrian capital, for example, most Viennese, absorbed in their own experience of privation, viewed the Hungarians as privileged, with access to foodstuffs unavailable in Vienna.[12]

Letters from late 1917 – seized by Habsburg military censors – offer a perverse and apocalyptic version of Prime Minister Tisza's 1914 claim that the war would put a stop to class struggle. These angry and frustrated letters between soldiers and prisoners of war and their families show the spread of disillusionment and contrast with the patriotic narratives promoted by government censors. Poor peasants and workers had by this time been convinced that the rich were no longer united with them in suffering. Rather than an uplifting vision of national unity that would lead to victory, most predicted that the end of both the world war and the class war would likely arrive with their own annihilation. Many of the letter writers historian Péter Hanák has analyzed asserted that the war would lead inevitably to the destruction of the poor. Even writers who viewed the example of Russia's March revolution favorably often seemed to discard political optimism and embrace a defeatist outlook about the injustice of the world. In September 1917, for example, a Hungarian wife wrote to her soldier husband, "Why doesn't the earth simply open up and swallow the millions of poor, so that only the masters and bosses remain? I know that would soon put an end to the war."[13] Another woman wrote to her husband two months after the Bolshevik Revolution that November in Russia: "Our poor children suffer so, as soon as a child is born it should be immediately strangled, so that the emperor gets no soldiers."[14] In the most drastic expression of this view among the censored letters, of a redemptive self-annihilation of the poor, a woman whose husband was a Habsburg prisoner of war in Italy wrote, "if death does not free us from the world, we poor people will have to slaughter our children like pigs, so that we have something to eat and our children have peace, because they are whimpering from the time they wake in the morning

---

[12] Maureen Healy, *Vienna and the Fall of the Habsburg Monarchy: Total War and Everyday Life in World War I* (Cambridge: Cambridge University Press, 2004).

[13] "Vox Populi: Intercepted Letters in the First World War," in Hanák, *Garden and the Workshop*, 184.

[14] Ibid., 202.

and there is nothing to be done."[15] These too-common representations of societal or even familial self-destruction are a far cry from Tisza's 1914 proclamations of a national unity forged in opposition to foreign enemies.

In addition to threats of self-destruction, the letters also contain hints of a more hopeful vision of a better world. In the same letter that imagines a future in which the poor would "slaughter [their] children like pigs," the distraught soldier's wife describes how the anger of the poor might also be directed outwards, against the injustice of society: "We want to break down everything that stands in our way, if we are not better provided for, that is our ultimate goal."[16] One Hungarian wrote to his brother to predict a political change for the better: "because the belly will decide [the future], ours and other people's."[17] Hanák observes a clear "Social-Democratic vocabulary" in the censored letters of workers and the poor following the January strikes of 1918. In a letter written in late January, for example, a worker in the Budapest neighborhood Soroksár concluded that "war teaches the people how to arrange things better for the future."[18] This conception, that the war had "taught" the people to rebel against injustice and the old order, was widespread by the end of the war, among both those who welcomed and those who feared the revolutionary consequences of these "lessons."

During the final year of the war, when news of the revolutionary events in Russia had circulated widely among both soldiers and civilians, the battle, in effect, moved to the home front, making the streets of the capital, and even the countryside, sites of political struggle. A half million workers participated in general strikes in Budapest in January and July 1918. These strikes in Hungary's capital, which followed similar strikes in Germany, Bohemia, nearby Vienna, and elsewhere, brought masses of ordinary, disenfranchised workers onto the political stage for the first time. For many observers of these confrontations, the message was clear. In October 1918, a self-described "group of anxious patriots," including Count Mihály Károlyi and Oszkár Jászi, sent a "warning" to the Emperor Karl, who had come to the Habsburg throne in 1916 when his great-uncle Francis Joseph died, entitled "The Situation in Hungary."[19] They warned the young monarch that the precarious balance that had maintained prewar political inequality had been disrupted. With the example of the revolution in Russia and anger over war shortages, "this revolutionary atmosphere," they wrote, "will become yet more threatening because the demobilized veterans returning from the trenches will no longer be the blind, submissive, humble peasant mass of old."[20] These writers believed that the world had changed and so had Hungarian society: "The front has taught our people to think ... and they will no longer endure the

---

[15] Ibid., 186.   [16] Ibid.   [17] Ibid., 181.
[18] Ibid., 204. This was a working-class area. Soroksár's district, at the time Erzsébetfalva, was named Leninváros (Lenin city) during the Hungarian Soviet.
[19] Jászi, *Revolution and Counterrevolution*, 5–14.   [20] Ibid., 13.

domination of county pashas and city profiteers."[21] The authors argued that political change was necessary, that it in fact was already happening from below, without the leadership or guidance of the authorities. Conditions in the restive capital by late 1918 certainly appeared to confirm that their fears were justified.

Even before the exhausted belligerents signed the November 11 armistice in 1918, revolution had begun in Central Europe. The long-lived, once-powerful multinational Habsburg Monarchy quickly dissolved into a number of titularly "national" successor states, mostly themselves also actually multinational. Some, such as Czechoslovakia and Yugoslavia, were new states, declared in the waning days of the war. Others, such as Romania and Poland, were enlarged or revived versions of older states. As the rapid recalibration of the empire proceeded, Austria and Hungary were reinvented as diminished "rump" states, with their former royal and imperial capitals deprived of the vast territories they had long ruled over.

In his role as the final emperor of Austria, Karl had tried in vain to save the monarchy at the last minute by declaring it a federative state, with wide autonomy for the constitutive nationalities. Karl's efforts could not stop the rapid secession of most of the Habsburg lands and their declarations of independence, nor did they lessen the desire of the Entente Powers to see the Habsburg dynasty go. Almost immediately these new and enlarged states, conceived in most cases as ethnic homelands, began fighting on their respective borders to secure the territories each believed was integral to their new independent existence or to protect ethnic kinsmen now subject foreign domination, such as the Hungarians in Czechoslovakia, Romania, and Yugoslavia. With national boundaries and political institutions in flux, and the empire's constituent minorities struggling to assert themselves, democratic – or at least parliamentary – revolutions at the end of October 1918 dethroned the Habsburgs in the twin capitals of Vienna and Budapest.

The autumn revolution in Budapest was similar to the experiences of other cities in defeated Central Europe. The *Őszirózsa* (chrysanthemum or aster) revolution in the final days of October 1918 took its name from the flowers traditionally used to celebrate All Souls Day in Hungary. Soldiers and other demonstrators wore them in the protests that ignited the revolution in Budapest. These demonstrations persuaded Karl, as king of Hungary, to turn over power to a republican government on October 31. Károlyi formed the first democratic government, the National Council.[22] The October revolution was almost bloodless. The key exception was the murder of Tisza, the former prime minister. Tisza symbolized to many the intransigence of the old order. He had

---

[21] Ibid.

[22] Károlyi had been elected to the Hungarian parliament as a member of the opposition Party of Independence in 1910 but broke with the party in 1916 owing to his more radical opposition to the war. He demanded suffrage for veterans in 1915. His new party argued for peace with the Entente and broad suffrage reform, including women's suffrage, after 1916.

stood steadfastly against any political reforms during the war, even the proposal by Károlyi's party of a so-called hero's suffrage amendment that would have allowed veterans to vote without property or income restrictions. By October 1918, Tisza was widely blamed for the war as well as for all the inequities of the Hungarian political system. Almost more than the king, he had become the face of the old order to the angry masses. As such, he was hated by many and was the object of three earlier assassination attempts, one only two weeks earlier. Because he was a known target, the city swarmed with rumors of his death even before he was murdered. Tormay described hearing a crowd chanting "death to Tisza" along with "down with the King" on the day of his assassination, October 31, 1918.[23] But Tisza's assassination did not immediately unleash further violence, despite the fears of many observers.

The mass demonstrations of the October revolution in Budapest did not mean that the new government had the support of the whole population or the international community. Indeed, this government, composed of the former liberal opposition and various leftist politicians and formed under Károlyi, soon came under attack from both the Left and the Right and under international pressure from the victorious powers. Almost immediately there were calls from members of the organized Left to declare a soviet government on the Russian model, giving power to the workers' and soldiers' councils that had sprung up all over. In Budapest, although masses of citizens celebrated the declaration of the republic and the advent of democracy, many conservative Hungarians, like their contemporaries later in Weimar Germany, associated their country's new parliamentary government with the final defeat in the world war and with the punitive conditions that the Entente had imposed. For Hungarian nationalists, even the long-awaited independence from Austria was bittersweet because it was accompanied by military collapse and revolution. Moreover, conservatives opposed the National Council from the outset, asking "What is this obscure assembly after all? How dare it call itself the council of the nation? ... Eleven Jews and eight bad Hungarians! ... Good God, where is the King?"[24] Just as in the Russian Empire at the time of the February revolution, a popular revolution swept away an unpopular monarchy that had lost support even among many traditional allies. But also as in Russia, the government that was formed to replace the monarchy was in a difficult

---

[23] Tormay, *Outlaw's Diary*, vol. 1, 12. The identity of Tisza's assassins remains a mystery. A 1921 tribunal found the communist József Pogány (see more on his later roles in this and the following chapter) guilty *in absentia*, based on testimony by some of Tisza's relatives, but they later withdrew their witness statements and Pogány always maintained his innocence. On the assassination, see Ference Pölöskei, *A rejtélyes Tisza-gyilkosság* (Budapest: Helikon, 1988). There is an excellent biography of Pogány by Thomas Sakmyster, *A Communist Odyssey: The Life of József Pogány/John Pepper* (Budapest: Central European University Press, 2012); for the assassination of Tisza see page 18.

[24] Tormay, *Outlaw's Diary*, vol. 1, 6–7.

position: necessary, but unloved. The National Council under Károlyi was a compromise, not the answer to anyone's revolutionary dreams or plans.

In addition to the deep political divisions across the city, including vast differences even among their supporters, National Council leaders also found themselves confronted with the demands of the Entente and the humiliating territorial losses that had already been part of the armistice. Territories of the Hungarian crown that included Slovakia and Subcarpathia in the north and east, Transylvania in the southeast, and southern Hungary and the Kingdom of Croatia had been promised to and appropriated by Hungary's newly independent neighbors, such as Czechoslovakia and Yugoslavia, forged from the former empire, or to former enemies, such as Romania. Although some in Hungary hoped to negotiate for better territorial terms at the upcoming Paris Peace Conference, with the hope of reversing some of the fait accomplis on Hungary's new borders, the looming, and most likely disadvantageous, peace settlement hung over the Károlyi government.[25] The terms of the treaty, and the territorial losses finalized in the end, accelerated the crisis that led to the collapse of the October parliamentary government and to a second more radical revolution in March 1919. Economic collapse followed the military collapse, and the chaotic end of the war meant that tens of thousands of soldiers – many still carrying their army-issued weapons – quickly arrived in Budapest and other cities, unemployed and with what some referred to as "front syndrome," a sense that they could not easily be reintegrated into their previous civilian docility (as predicted by Jászi and his colleagues).[26] This proved a volatile mix for the new governments in Germany and in Austria as well, and in Hungary it may have been decisive in overthrowing the new government.

The arrival of hundreds of thousands of ethnic Hungarian refugees, fleeing from territories previously attached to prewar Hungary but now included within the boundaries of newly proclaimed successor states, further complicated the already deleterious effects of mass demobilization and defeat.[27] Refugee families, mostly from Transylvania, which was now part of an

---

[25] See Peter Pastor, *Hungary between Wilson and Lenin: The Hungarian Revolution of 1918–1919 and the Big Three* (Boulder, CO: East European Monographs, 1976).

[26] For an excellent treatment of questions raised by demobilization and the return of soldiers, see Maureen Healy, "Civilizing the Soldier in Postwar Austria," in Nancy Wingfield and Maria Bucur, eds., *Gender and War in Twentieth Century Eastern Europe* (Bloomington: Indiana University Press, 2006).

[27] For the refugee crisis and its political implications for Hungary, see István Mócsy, *The Effects of World War I. The Uprooted: Hungarian Refugees and their Impact on Hungarian Domestic Politics 1918–21* (Boulder, CO: Brooklyn College Press, 1983). Mócsy estimates that "426,000 Hungarians left the [ceded] territories" from the end of the war to 1924. "Of these, 197,035 came from Romania, 106,841 from Czechoslovakia, 44,903 from Yugoslavia, and 1,221 from the new Austrian province of Burgenland." These figures come from the National Refugee Office (OMH) and represent only the registered refugees, not the additional large numbers of those with means or connections in the city who did not seek out government assistance. Ibid., 10.

enlarged Romania, poured especially into Budapest, the center of the rail and transportation system, creating an acute housing crisis there. Without relatives to house them and unable to find or afford their own housing, the majority ended up in semipermanent refugee camps. These included converted schools and hospitals, and, quite dramatically, boxcars, where multiple families sheltered in the freight cars that had transported them as refugees from the ceded territories.[28] According to a contemporaneous report, the number of refugees living in freight cars in Budapest rail yards reached 16,500 in autumn 1920. Even as late as 1923, they numbered between three and four thousand.[29] As historian István Mócsy has shown, these refugee slums were breeding grounds of radical political organization on both the Left and the Right.[30]

Not only were large numbers of the refugees radicalized to socialist or right-wing politics, but their visible and destitute presence in the capital was a constant spark to others who claimed to act on their behalf. Indignation at the desperate poverty of the refugees from the lost territories led to some of the first manifestations of the social-reform photography movement in Hungary that was inspired by international examples like the Danish-American photographer and reformer Jacob Riis. The photographers Gyula Harsány and János Müllner published photos of Transylvanian refugees living in boxcars in the illustrated newspaper *Érdekes Újság* in 1919. A year later the journalist and social critic Kornél Tábori published a powerful photojournalistic album, *Egy halálra ítélt ország borzalmaiból: Razzia a budapesti nyomortanyákon* (On the horrors of a condemned nation: A raid in the slums of Budapest), which included many pictures illustrating the desperate living conditions of the refugees, particularly malnourished children.[31] These works by left-leaning progressive photographers were intended to spark social reforms by awakening sympathy with the poor through the connection of the photographic image.

Politicians and activists on the Right, such as the members of the *Ébredő Magyarok Egyesülete* (ÉME, Association of Awakening Hungarians) and the veterans' organization *Magyar Országos Véderő Egylet* (MOVE, Hungarian Association of National Defense), also called attention to the plight of destitute refugees living in camps in Budapest as a tactic to support their own calls for political action; in their case an antisemitic campaign for the deportation of thousands of so-called Galician Jews, or Jewish wartime refugees from other parts of the Habsburg Monarchy.[32] Protesters in Budapest wearing ÉME and

---

[28] Ibid., 92. [29] Ibid., 211, note 17 (numbers from the OMH report). [30] Ibid.

[31] Originally printed in Budapest in 1920; reproduced in Béla Albertini, *A Magyar szociofotó története a kezdetektől a második világháború végéig* (Budapest: Magyar Fotográfiai Múzeum, 1997), 35, 37.

[32] The ÉME was founded in November 1918 as a nationalist antisemitic organization under the leadership of Gyula Gömbös, the early Hungarian fascist leader, Tibor Eckhardt, a right-wing politician and leader of the National Party, and the two most infamous leaders of the White

MOVE insignias and carrying banners for these organizations demanded that the government house and care for the "Hungarian" refugees arriving from Transylvania and elsewhere in the ceded territories and not "foreigners," who were taking away needed resources. Of course, the "Galician Jews" described by the nationalist Right as "foreigners" had mostly come from Galicia and Bukovina, both provinces of the Austrian half of the Habsburg Monarchy before the war but not a part of the prewar Kingdom of Hungary. These anti-immigrant voices argued that the deportation of these "foreigners" would make room for "genuine" Hungarian refugees who sought housing and jobs.[33]

For the Károlyi government, the situation became even more precarious with the delivery on March 20, 1919 of the Entente's "Vix note." Named for the French colonel who delivered it, Fernand Vix, the note delineated Hungary's new borders and made clear the extent of territory that Hungary would be forced to cede to its neighbors in the coming Treaty of Trianon. This quashed the Károlyi government's hope that a democratic Hungary could negotiate a better settlement in Paris – a blow to the parliamentary camp and its promotion of a "Wilsonian" peace. Once the terms of the peace treaty and extent of territorial losses became known, public anger forced Károlyi's National Council to hand over power to a coalition of socialists and communists, which formed a new, united socialist party.[34] This merged socialist party, led by the communist Béla Kun, promised to fight against the terms of the "imperialist peace." Buoyed by the support of large numbers of demonstrators

---

Terror, Pál Prónay and Ivan Héjjas. Gömbös founded MOVE at the start of 1919 as a paramilitary group to defend Hungary's borders and fight the revolutionary government; the group formed the basis for what became the National Army under Horthy's command. Historian Béla Bodó has written specifically about Prónay and Héjjas, see *Pál Prónay: Paramilitary Violence and Anti-Semitism in Hungary, 1919–1921* (Pittsburgh, PA: Center for Russian and East European Studies, 2011) and "Iván Hejjás: The Life of a Counter-Revolutionary," *East Central Europe* 37/2–3 (2010): 247–79. He has also written about the social world of the men in these right-wing militias, "The White Terror in Hungary, 1919–1921: The Social Worlds of Paramilitary Groups," *Austrian History Yearbook* 42 (2011): 133–63.

[33] The wartime government of Hungary had also argued that refugees from Austria's eastern provinces were the responsibility of Austria rather than Hungary, as citizens of the other half of the Dual Monarchy, but the claim of "foreignness" by these virulently antisemitic groups was not about citizenship but about religious and national belonging. For the situation of Jewish refugees in World War I Hungary, see Rebekah Klein-Pejšová, "Between Refugees and the State: Hungarian Jewry and the Wartime Refugee Crisis in Austria–Hungary," in Peter Gatrell and Liubov Zhvanko, eds., *Europe on the Move: Refugees in the Era of the Great War* (Oxford: Oxford University Press, 2017), 156–76, and "The Budapest Jewish Community's Galician October," in Marsha L. Rozenblit and Jonathan Karp, eds., *World War I and the Jews: Conflict and Transformation in Europe, the Middle East, and America* (New York: Berghahn Books, 2017), 112–30.

[34] For Károlyi's version of the transfer of power, see Mihály Károlyi, *Fighting the World: The Struggle for Peace* (New York: Albert & Charles Boni, 1925) and *Memoirs of Michael Károlyi: Faith without Illusion* (New York: E. P. Dutton, 1957).

on the streets of the capital, Kun declared a *Tanácsköztársaság* (soviet republic) on March 21, 1919.

Anger at the territorial losses initially united a wide swath of popular support for this revolution, with a radical socialist government giving vent to frustrations framed in national and patriotic terms. At first, a desire to strike out against the Entente leaders in Paris and the dim prospect of retrieving the lost territories led many demobilized officers from the now-defunct Habsburg Army, as well as some Hungarian nationalists, to support Kun, though this obviously did not extend to the radical nationalists of the ÉME for whom Kun embodied the dual threat of "Judeo-Bolshevism." The Károlyi government had become increasingly unpopular during the general suffering of the first postwar winter. In part out of an excess of deference to electoral democracy, this provisional government had not acted on many pressing issues, such as land reform, deferring these decisions until there was a new constitution and an elected parliament. But these delays made it appear that the parliamentary government would not tackle the urgent problems the country faced. This apparent ineffectiveness was paired with the sense, since the Vix note, that the government was unable to defend Hungarian interests internationally. In this situation, with monarchy defeated and parliamentary government seemingly powerless, it seemed that a radical revolutionary regime might offer a last defense of national interests, and possibly even obtain the support of Soviet Russia for Hungarian territorial interests.

Initially, the newly formed Hungarian Red Army, led in part by patriotic Hungarian officers of the Habsburg Army hoping to regain lost territories, fought against the Romanians in the south to defend Hungary's borders and, if possible, retain Transylvania within them. Only after the first consequential military losses of the Red Army to the Romanians in late spring and early summer did the tables start to turn, as public support, especially among nationalists and former officers, declined. Military defeat again resulted in political instability, and the organizers of the counterrevolution gained popular support in rural areas and even in Budapest. By May 1919, the socialist revolution no longer seemed to offer the possibility of overturning the "dictates" of Paris. Soviet Russia was embroiled in its own bloody civil war and offered no support for the fledgling Hungarian Soviet; and, as with the provisional parliamentary government before it, the revolutionary government suffered from the curse of not only failing to meet its own world historical promises but of failing even to adequately provide basic services.

By summer 1919, Hungary had slipped into chaos, with remnants of the Red Army fighting Romanian forces, scattered revolts against the soviet government in the countryside and along the Danube, and a counterrevolutionary "National Army" organized in Szeged, in southern Hungary, under the command of Admiral Miklós Horthy, a hero of the Habsburg Navy in World War

I. As they gained strength, these Hungarian "White" forces perpetrated acts of counterrevolutionary justice, executing many purported revolutionaries – on the spot when they captured them or after summary courts-martial run by self-appointed White officer-judges. These forces also instigated widespread anti-Jewish violence and pogroms throughout the Hungarian countryside. Long before it took power, this nationalist movement revealed its antisemitic program.

Reports of the violence and anti-Jewish pogroms in Hungary were quickly conveyed to the delegates at the Paris Peace Conference and published in the international press. Fear about the violent retribution that the White forces might take against socialists and Jews in Hungary's capital led the Entente to forbid Horthy to enter with his forces until he had given assurances that his soldiers would not "punish" the city with violence. The Entente's well-intended intervention created additional incitements to violence. After Kun's soviet government fled on August 1, going into exile in Vienna, the Entente ordered that the city be first secured by the arrival of (much despised) Romanian troops on August 3 and 4. Only in November did the Entente finally allow Horthy to enter the capital with his National Army. This he did with great pomp on November 16, riding a white horse and wearing the ceremonial uniform of a Habsburg admiral. The sight of this "admiral on horseback" made a great impression on most observers as commanding and imposing, but the irony of an admiral at the head of a landlocked country did not escape either Horthy's critics or historians since.[35]

During the Romanian occupation, Budapest was subject to a series of short-lived, inept governments that were incapable of exercising real authority. After Kun and most of the leaders of the *Tanácsköztársaság* fled in August, moderate socialists attempted to stabilize political order through a coalition government. This effort was supported by Vilmos Böhm, the representative of the Hungarian soviet government in Vienna, who had been negotiating with Entente officials to this end since July 23, 1919.[36] The first fruit of his efforts was the creation on August 1 of a "trade union" government under Gyula Peidl, a long-time trade union leader and socialist.[37] The new government lasted only six days. In its

---

[35] Thomas Sakmyster's biography of Horthy is entitled *Hungary's Admiral on Horseback* (Boulder, CO: East European Monographs, 1994). The irony certainly did not escape Horthy's political opponents, either. József Pogány, the commissar for war of the Hungarian Soviet, described the official entry into Budapest as Horthy's "only glorious achievement, in that he finally made the old joke about a mounted navy into a reality," *Der Weiße Terror in Ungarn* (Vienna: Verlagsgenossenschaft Neue Welt, 1920), 15.

[36] Ferenc Pölöskei, *Hungary after Two Revolutions (1919–1922)* (Budapest: Akadémiai Kiadó, 1980), 9.

[37] Peidl (1873–1943) fled to Austria in August 1919 but returned to Hungary in 1921 and continued his political and trade union work. He was the leader of the Social Democratic representatives in the Hungarian parliament throughout much of the interwar period.

Figure 2.1 Miklós Horthy enters Budapest, November 16, 1919.
Source: Ullstein Bild via Getty Images.

brief existence, the Peidl government declared the Hungarian People's Republic, repealed unpopular communist policies, disbanded both the Red Guard and the revolutionary courts, and attempted to protect the key gains of the October revolution, including the establishment of a parliamentary democracy with universal suffrage, by winning the support of the Entente in the peace negotiations. This moderate, social-democratic program was put forward as a continuation of the bourgeois democracy of the Károlyi government. While pursuing these goals, Peidl's government abolished most of the institutions and programs Kun's soviet government had created.

On August 6, a group of counterrevolutionary officers – loyal to the Habsburgs and led by former Károlyi supporter István Friedrich – and a coalition of anti-revolutionary politicians drove out the Peidl government, demanding a return of the Habsburgs and King Karl. This government was reorganized several times in attempts to gain popular support and to satisfy the Entente, who considered the reinstatement of the Habsburg king to be out of the question. Friedrich himself was a quintessential figure of the turbulent postwar months, wearing a coat of many political colors. He first supported the Károlyists. He was rumored in various accounts to have ordered the assassination of Tisza, as well as to have offered his services to the soviet council republic of Kun. After the fall of the brief Kun government he redefined himself as a Habsburg loyalist but rejected the popular Habsburg Archduke Joseph August once he realized that the Entente would not allow a Habsburg as Hungarian head of state.[38]

After Admiral Horthy's military victory and his entrance into Budapest, a complicated negotiating process occurred between the leaders of the coalition of "Christian and National" parties to form a government acceptable both to the various counterrevolutionary groups, ranging from Habsburg loyalists to radical antisemites, and to the international powers assembled in Paris for the Peace Conference. Consultations between Horthy, the face of the counterrevolutionary National Army; Friedrich, who had overturned the Peidl government; prewar, "old regime" leaders from the Hungarian nobility such as counts Apponyi, Bethlen, and Andrássy; and even the Social Democratic leader Ernő Garami resulted in the formation of a "Christian and National" government under Károly Huszár, which took office on November 24, 1919. Elections to the new parliament, the National Assembly, were set for January 1920. This assembly once elected was dominated by the "Christian and National" bloc of parties. In its first year, the parliament appointed Admiral Horthy as regent and head of state of a new Kingdom of Hungary, a position he held throughout the interwar period, only leaving power in October 1944 when he was deposed by Nazi Germany after attempting to withdraw Hungary from World War II through a peace treaty with the Soviet Union. Since there was no ruling monarch, the position of "regent without a king" only extended Horthy's ironic position of the "admiral on horseback."

Germany and World War I

Though I have begun here by recounting events in Hungary, historians and contemporaries have rightly devoted more attention to Germany's decision to wage war in the summer of 1914 than to Hungary's, which was determined by the imperial government in Vienna.[39] There are many reasons for this focus among historians, and to understand the revolutionary situation in Bavaria at the end of the war, we will look briefly here at Germany in World War I as well.

---

[38] Archduke Joseph (1872–1962) was the grandson of the popular Habsburg Palatine Joseph, Viceroy of Hungary (1796–1847) and was a field marshal in the Habsburg Army. In October 1918 Emperor Karl attempted to appoint him as regent for Hungary, but Joseph asked to be released from an oath of loyalty to the emperor. In August 1919, the Friedrich government was initially established with Joseph as regent, but the Entente refused to allow a Habsburg head of state.

[39] I have chosen this order in part because it makes sense chronologically (the Hungarian events happened slightly earlier) and in part because the German events may be more familiar to the reader.

The debate over the causes of the war, and in particular German responsibility for its outbreak, has been raging among interpreters since 1914. Of particular interest to scholars is the German SPD's political about-face and decision to support the war-credits bill in the Reichstag in August 1914. This decision by the largest single party in the German parliament following the elections of 1912 (indeed the largest socialist organization in the world, with over a million members) provided a democratic sanction for the war.

After the delivery of the Austrian ultimatum and news of Austrian and Russian mobilizations, the Reichstag in Germany, like the parliament in Hungary, became the scene not of politics but of national theater. The SPD representative Eduard David, who was present for the vote on war credits, wrote in his diary afterwards, "The memory of the incredible enthusiasm of the other parties, of the government, and of the spectators, as we stood to be counted, will never leave me."[40] These fantasies of national unity, like those expressed contemporaneously by Tisza in Hungary, had a powerful effect on both contemporary politics and on later historical interpretation. It is only very recently that historians have begun to chip away at the "myth of August," the presence of a near-universal war enthusiasm.[41]

The replacement of politics with national melodrama was all the more striking in Germany since, unlike in Hungary, the Reichstag representatives who voted in favor of war had been elected by universal manhood suffrage and were, in their majority, members of the SPD, the left Liberals, and the Catholic Center Party. These were all mass parties with popular, reform-oriented platforms rather than supporters of traditional elites and the monarchy, as in Hungary. The political passions in August 1914 carried most German citizens along in a wave of patriotic enthusiasm, which left no place for measured discussion or rational argument, and the SPD was no exception to this general pattern. SPD leaders were not only afraid of a return to what they saw as Bismarckian political repression, they were afraid that by opposing the war they would become irrelevant to their base, the workers. Anti-Russian sentiment, or rather anti-tsarist sentiment, was widespread in a party whose members included many former subjects of the Russian Empire, such as the popular socialist orator Rosa Luxemburg.

The Bavarian Social Democrats in Munich followed a similar trajectory to that of the national SPD party during the July crisis. The author Oskar Maria Graf remembered how he sought in vain for his usual leftist friends in the cafes of Munich after war was declared: "Where had they all gone, those who had taught me that an anarchist must never serve the state in any situation, that he should especially avoid military or war service? They had run in droves to

---

[40] Quoted in Modris Eksteins, *Rites of Spring: The Great War and the Birth of the Modern Age* (New York: Houghton Mifflin, 1989), 91.
[41] See Jeffrey Verhey, *The Spirit of 1914: Militarism, Myth and Mobilization in Germany* (Cambridge: Cambridge University Press, 2000).

volunteer at the barracks!"[42] On August 1, the social democratic *Münchner Post* published an editorial proclaiming that "When it comes to the duty to protect our country from bloody tsarism, we will not allow ourselves to be considered second-class citizens."[43] Anti-Serbian sentiment and antagonism towards Serbia's protector, Russia, ran high in Munich after the assassination of Austrian Archduke Francis Ferdinand. The Munich police began to receive denunciations from the population about the many Russians and South Slavs resident in the city. The neighbors need not have worried about Munich's large population of Russian students, however, since most of them were staunchly opposed to the Russian tsar.[44] But rumors of foreign, especially Russian, spies flooded the city in the first days of August as war hysteria mounted.[45]

Though historians disagree about the exact mix of nationalist enthusiasm and territorial ambitions or general malaise and governmental impasse, there is general agreement that the decision to go to war was made in Berlin. What then was the reaction in Munich, where the decisions of the Berlin authorities were often met with misapprehension and distrust? By all accounts, news of the Russian mobilization and the following mobilization order for Bavarian troops were met with patriotic outbursts similar to those elsewhere in the German Empire. In his memoirs, the 1919 revolutionary leader Ernst Toller described returning to Munich from France, where he had been when war was declared. Along with other passengers arriving at the train station, he was handed postcards that featured a picture of the emperor and the statement, "right there in black and white" as Toller put it, "The emperor doesn't recognize any parties … nor the nation any races, everyone speaks one language and everyone defends one mother, Germany."[46] These patriotic sentiments were expressed by many in Munich who hoped that Bavarians would collectively demonstrate their loyalty and their credentials as "true Germans" when the fighting began. Later, after he had tried unsuccessfully to volunteer at the overfilled local army barracks, Toller walked through the city where he witnessed two women attacked by a crowd because someone had accused them of speaking French.[47] Similarly, nationalist enthusiasm at the beginning of the war led some hyper-patriots to demand that Munich's famous English Garden be renamed the "German Garden."[48]

---

[42] Graf, 143.

[43] *Münchner Post*, August 1, 1914; also quoted in Large, *Where Ghosts Walked*, 48.

[44] On anti-Russian sentiments in German universities, see Lisa Fetheringill Zwicker, "Antisemitism, the Limits of Antisemitic Rhetoric, and a Movement against Russian Students at German Universities, 1908–1914," *Leo Baeck Institute Year Book* 55/1 (2010): 193–203.

[45] Rumors in Ernst Toller, *Eine Jugend in Deutschland* (Hamburg: Rowohlt Taschenbuch Verlag, 1988), 39.

[46] Ibid.   [47] Ibid.

[48] That the municipal government refused this request, David Clay Large has aptly called "a rare act of sanity in this environment of patriotic breast-beating and intense xenophobia"; *Where Ghosts Walked*, 49.

Yet World War I, as we know, turned out to last far longer and to be far more destructive and costly than the quick triumph that Toller and Graf and their friends imagined when they volunteered. By the final year of the war, Germany, like its ally Austria–Hungary, was roiled by dissent and waves of strikes, which spread across Central and Eastern Europe as a result of the revolution in Russia and the worsening economic and military situation. The longest-lasting strikes were in Munich and Berlin. The Munich strikes came to an abrupt halt with the arrest of the popular Independent Social Democratic (*Unabhängige Sozialdemokratische Partei Deutschlands*, USPD) leader, Kurt Eisner, on January 31.[49] These upheavals were followed by relative quiet through the spring military offensives of 1918, when it seemed that Germany and its allies might be able to finally decide the war in their favor, but military defeats in the late summer and the prospect of a lost war set off a new wave of political upheavals across Germany in the fall of 1918.

On September 29, the German Empire experienced a "revolution from above," which led to the appointment of Prince Max von Baden as *Reichskanzler* (chancellor), and the emperor's acceptance of a new, British-style constitutional monarchy. In October, Baden ended the military rule of generals Paul von Hindenburg and Erich Ludendorff, who had effectively governed Germany during the last years of the war. Many German politicians hoped that these dramatic changes in the government would placate the Entente, which had previously demanded the end of the German Empire, and make peace possible. But subsequent events dashed their hopes.

The revolution from above could not keep pace with the proliferating demands from below. In the last days of the war, a wave of protest was ignited by mutinous sailors who refused orders for a final attack on the British Royal Navy, which they believed would be a "death mission." Surprised by the mutiny, the admiralty attempted to transfer mutinous elements of the fleet to Kiel, but the sailors went ashore and organized demonstrations and protests against the naval command. The riots and protests that followed in Kiel on November 4 quickly spread to other German cities. In all of these risings, the insurgents formed workers' and soldiers' councils (*Arbeiter- und Soldatenräte*). In many rural areas, especially in Bavaria, peasants' councils (*Bauernräte*) were formed in imitation of the urban and military models.

On November 7, 1918, King Ludwig III of the Bavarian Wittelsbach dynasty became the first German monarch forced to abdicate. Later the same day, Eisner declared the republic of *Freistaat Bayern*. On the following day a provisional

---

[49] The USPD was founded in April 1917 by left-wing members splitting off from what became known as the "majority SPD." The USPD was led nationally by Hugo Haase, who had been one of the few SPD members of the Reichstag to vote against the extension of further war credits in December 1916. The Bavarian SPD split as well, and Eisner was the leader of the Bavarian USPD.

government, with Eisner at the head, was established in Munich to govern Bavaria until elections to a parliament could be held.

The wave of royal abdications in Germany reached the imperial Hohenzollern dynasty in Berlin on November 9, when the imperial chancellor, Prince Max von Baden, announced the abdication of Emperor Wilhelm II and turned to the SPD leader Friedrich Ebert to form a new national government.[50] On the same day, the SPD leader and parliamentary representative Philipp Scheidemann proclaimed the German Republic from the Reichstag building. Scheidemann's announcement of the republic strengthened the movement to form workers' and soldiers' councils around the country. On November 10, the SPD and the USPD agreed on a provisional government, the Council of People's Deputies (*Rat der Volksbeauftragten* or RdV), under the leadership of Ebert and Scheidemann.

The USPD had split from the majority Social Democratic Party during the war, over the question of whether Social Democrats should continue to support a government bent on annexationist war aims. Now, after the precipitous fall of that annexationist, imperial government, the two socialist parties attempted a wary reunion to share power. The RdV government was officially responsible to the councils established on the local level, but tension between the councils and the RdV led to conflicts between the SPD and the USPD in the first months of the republic.

An agreement between Ebert and Ludendorff's successor, General Wilhelm Groener, for mutual assistance and military action against a Berlin mutiny was the pretext for the USPD to resign from the provisional government at the end of December 1918. The USPD and other groups to the left of the SPD protested against the "traitor" Ebert and his "counterrevolutionary" SPD-led provisional government. The USPD claimed that the SPD had put an end to the true revolution and was now joining forces with elements of the old order to keep the councils out of the new government. Agitation from the Left for further revolution reached its apex in January 1919 with the "Spartacus" uprising in Berlin, led by the Communist Party (formerly the *Spartakusbund*).[51] The SPD-led government employed full military force to crush the uprising, and right-wing soldiers assassinated the leaders of the movement, Karl Liebknecht and Rosa Luxemburg while they were held in police custody.

In Munich, the USPD prime minister, Eisner, managed, through appeals to Bavarian local patriotism and through great personal political skill, to avoid the violent winter upheavals that were occurring in the German capital. In Bavaria,

---

[50] Ebert had been elected leader of the SPD in 1913 following the death of August Bebel.

[51] The Spartacus League (*Spartakusbund*) was initially united with the USPD at the time of that party's creation, but its leaders Rosa Luxemburg, Karl Liebknecht, and Clara Zetkin declared it the German Communist Party (*Kommunistische Partei Deutschlands*, KPD) in December 1918 after the November revolutions and the conflicts with the SPD over council government.

the USPD remained in the provisional government along with the majority SPD, while the left-of-center coalition in Berlin splintered. Under Eisner's leadership, free elections were held in Bavaria for a new state parliament (*Landtag*) on January 12, 1919. The results of these elections, however, released some of the same radical protest from the Left that had torn Berlin apart earlier that month. Eisner's USPD received only 2.5 percent of the vote and only 3 out of 180 *Landtag* seats. The renamed Catholic party, the former Bavarian Center Party, now the Bavarian People's Party (*Bayerische Volkspartei*, BVP) and the SPD, on the other hand, received the most votes with 35 and 33 percent, respectively. Several other parties, including the liberal German Democratic Party and the farmer's party, the *Bauernbund*, also gained representation in the parliament.[52] Although Eisner himself was prepared to hand over power to this freely elected legislature, the majority of his party were unwilling to give up their leading role in the Bavarian revolution to what they viewed as a counterrevolutionary *Landtag*. They pressured Eisner to delay the transfer of power and threatened violence if he stepped down in favor of the new "reactionary" parliament.

In the end, however, the incitement to violence in Munich came from the Right and not the Left. On February 21, a young right-wing extremist and antisemite, Count Anton Arco, assassinated Eisner, who was on his way to the parliament to deliver his abdication speech. This speech would have handed over government to the majority Social Democrats under the leadership of Johannes Hoffmann and Erhard Auer. Arco shot Eisner three times from behind, and Eisner died on the spot; his bodyguards returned fire and wounded Arco, who was captured. The announcement of Eisner's assassination in the legislature led almost immediately to more violence and chaos among the delegates. Shots were fired during the parliamentary session and the majority socialist Auer, Eisner's main antagonist in the SPD, was seriously injured. Ironically, he and Arco were treated in the hospital by the same surgeon, who managed to save both their lives. Following their operations the men were placed in the same recovery room.

The assassination of Eisner before he had completed the transfer of power to the new government created a grave political crisis in Munich, similar to the effect in Budapest of the Vix note, which announced Hungary's territorial losses from the peace treaty. In the wake of both events it was not immediately clear where governmental power resided. In Bavaria, the newly elected *Landtag* and the workers' and soldiers' councils claimed legislative authority. The confusion was further complicated by the fact that Eisner had not legally

[52] The BVP had split from the national Center Party and renamed itself over the November revolutions. The BVP had a monarchist and Bavarian particularist program, in addition to continuing the Catholic clerical Center Party tradition. Election results in Mitchell, *Revolution in Bavaria*.

handed over executive power to a government chosen by the *Landtag* before his death. Equally paralyzing, neither the councils nor the *Landtag* were led by the sort of charismatic personality who might have taken over and reassured the now agitated population. Almost immediately there were calls from the Left to give "all power to the councils" and declare a *Räterepublik,* a republic of councils.

By mid-March, in the *Landtag,* an SPD-led government was finally formed, led by the moderate Social Democratic parliamentarian Johannes Hoffman. This government, however, found itself in a precarious legal and constitutional situation and was unable to combat the protests of both the Right and the Left. The deepening economic crisis across Germany deeply affected Bavaria, and the failure of the Eisner-initiated attempt to come to a separate peace agreement with the Entente for Bavaria led to a mounting government crisis in Munich.[53]

As in Hungary, the actual revolution in Bavaria was, in the end, bureaucratic rather than bloody. On the night of April 6, members of the SPD government held negotiations with a group of politicians and intellectuals who had been agitating for the declaration of a council or soviet republic, seizing power from the *Landtag* in the name of the workers', soldiers', and peasants' councils, as the Bolshevik Party had done in the October revolution in Russia. The SPD-led *Landtag* government then fled from Munich to Bamberg, refusing to recognize the new council authority. And from Bamberg, Johannes Hoffman and his *Landtag* colleagues continued to issue proclamations in the name of the government of Bavaria. In Munich, the Communist Party of Bavaria, under the leadership of Max Levien, decided not to join in the council government that was proclaimed on April 7. The communists announced that the time was not ripe for this second revolution. This led to the formation of what was often referred to by contemporaries as the "first *Räterepublik*" or the "*Literatenrat*" (council of writers), so named because of the communist absence and the many intellectuals, such as the pacifist and anarchist writers Gustav Landauer, Erich Mühsam, Ernst Toller, and Silvio Gesell, in the government. This first soviet government ruled in Munich for eight days before handing over power to a second, communist-controlled council government.

The transfer of power from the first to the second Bavarian soviet government of councils was instigated by an attempted counterrevolutionary attack on April 13/14 by a loosely organized coalition of right-wing military groups in alliance with the uprooted SPD-controlled *Landtag* government in Bamberg. Known as the Palm Sunday Putsch, this attack from the Right was the impetus

---

[53] Eisner had released documents from July and August 1914 from the Bavarian government representative in Berlin that demonstrated a reckless Prussian militarism. He hoped that the newly declared Bavarian Free-State would be able to conclude a separate treaty and not suffer from Prussia's war guilt, but there was no international interest in an independent Bavaria and France in particular felt all Germany to be equally at fault.

for the decision by the Communist Party's leaders, Max Levien and Eugen Leviné, to support the beleaguered council government. In fact, members of the Communist Party took almost all of the leading roles in the council government after April 15. Some of the most famous members of the first, "literary" *Räterepublik* government, such as Landauer and Mühsam, stepped down and had no official roles in the new government. Others, such as Toller, continued to have an active leadership role at the workers' and soldiers' council as well as in the Red Army. This "second *Räterepublik*" lasted only until the end of April.

On May 1, 1919, international workers day, the combined forces of the German Army, various voluntary milita organizations (the *Freikorps*), and their new recruits marched into revolutionary Munich to drive out the council government. The council's Red Guard, initially recruited to aid the workers' brigades as a class-conscious police force, also expanded massively through recruitment in the days leading up to this confrontation as Red Munich found itself surrounded. Initially, as the assembled White forces began to attack, the Red Army – organized earlier in April by the communist Rudolf Eglhofer – and the urban Red Guards fought back, particularly on the outskirts of town. A division of the Red Army under the command of Toller in Dachau, some eleven miles northwest of Munich, also came under attack and fought back, even as Toller himself tried desperately to negotiate a last-minute surrender and avoid bloodshed. As the White forces entered the city of Munich itself, there was street fighting throughout the day. By May 2–3, the city was almost entirely in the hands of the government and allied troops, but isolated fighting continued between these troops and members of the Red Guard or the Communist Party. The violent situation continued during the first week of May, with at least 600 people falling victim to gunfire or the summary justice meted out by the city's right-wing conquerors.

Assessing the Costs: Terror in Budapest and Munich

It is impossible to provide a reliable estimate for the number of victims during the revolutions and counterrevolutions of 1919. For both Budapest and Munich, we have conflicting, sometimes deeply conflicting, contemporary reports. This is, in part, the result of the confused political and administrative conditions that pertained at the time. It is also the result of the political loyalties and intentions of those who made the estimates. It is undeniable that judgments about which deaths should be included or excluded were framed by the politics of the moment. Similarly, modern analyses of this topic by scholars have sometimes been influenced by political considerations as well.

This question is of special relevance for two categories of victims, those who died "in fighting" or "with a weapon in the hand" and those executed after a judicial decision Some of these "judicial" verdicts were issued *ex post facto* by illegally formed courts-martial. In many cases in Hungary, for example, verdicts by "field courts-martial" were issued after the fact to justify earlier murders of "known communists" by the National Army under Horthy or less formally organized right-wing military forces. Even where death sentences were issued by courts after some form of traditional legal inquiry, there is disagreement about how to categorize these victims. Should those sentenced to death by soviet revolutionary courts in Hungary be considered victims of the Red Terror? Or, alternatively, should those executed by order of the postrevolutionary courts be assigned to the White Terror? Both sets of verdicts were passed by undeniably partisan courts, for "political crimes." For these cases, the adherents of each side refused to recognize the legitimacy of their enemy's courts and, as a result, viewed these court-ordered executions as "murder."

Because both contemporaries and scholars disagree about when the terror began and ended, the passage of time introduces another complication to efforts to assess the number of deaths during the period of "terror" in Hungary and Germany. It would be hard to say that the deaths of the individuals responsible for carrying out the so-called *Geiselmord* (murder of hostages), executed months after the end of the revolution and after a well-publicized trial in Weimar Germany, were victims of "terror." But clearly the court in this case adjudicated the case politically when it sentenced to death for murder these Red Army soldiers who had followed the orders of their superiors. Political violence and political justice intertwined in the successful counterrevolutions.

Terror in Munich

Because the counterrevolutionary events in Bavaria mostly preceded, and certainly ended before, the events in Hungary, we will first examine the question of Red and White Terror for Munich. In considering the two cases, it is perhaps also important to keep another difference in mind. Most of the violence in Bavaria occurred in Munich or its immediate surroundings, whereas in Hungary, the majority of deaths occurred outside the capital Budapest. In the case of Munich, we are looking almost entirely at violence in an urban setting, as troops surrounded and then invaded the capital to drive out the revolutionary government and forces. The lowest estimate for deaths in Munich during the revolutionary government's struggle with the counterrevolution, 557, was furnished by the victorious White military officials on June 10, 1919. They, in turn, relied on a report prepared by municipal police authorities and published in the *Münchener Neueste Nachrichten* (Munich Newest News) under the heading, "Official Report." In his 1922 book *Vier Jahre politischer Mord* (Four years of political murder), the liberal statistician Emil Gumbel criticized the estimates presented by the Bavarian military and judicial authorities. In a careful review of the sources, he argued that either the military figure was far too low, or it had assigned at least 161 political murders to the category of "fatal accidents."[54]

Nevertheless, many historians have relied on a version of the military estimates adjusted to reflect for Gumbel's cases and other verifiable political murders. In his 1965 book *Revolution in Bavaria,* for example, historian Alan Mitchell wrote that by May 3, 1919, the date on which the Whites triumphed, a total of 600 people had lost their lives from political violence in Munich. Similarly, the Bavarian historian Ludwig Morenz based his 1968 estimate of 625 deaths on the police report as well as other deaths from political violence recorded in the city chronicles.[55] Higher estimates include that of Wilhelm Hoegner, Social Democratic politician and minister president of post–World War II Bavaria, who gave the number of victims as 1,100 in his 1958 book *Die verratene Republik* (The republic betrayed).[56] Similarly, a 1939 history of the *Freikorps* claimed that 1,000–1,200 people had died in Munich; this estimate was referred to as "conservative" by Robert Waite in his 1952 history, *The Vanguard of Nazism.*[57] But, as Mitchell pointed out in 1965, the evidence for these higher numbers was based on contemporary reports in leftist newspapers such as *Rote Fahne* (Red Flag), *Vorwärts* (Forwards), and *Rote Hand* (Red Hand), without additional documentation of specific cases.

Gumbel provided the most careful accounting for the human costs of political violence across Bavaria during the revolutionary and counterrevolutionary periods. His first important discussion of political violence and political justice, "Zwei Jahre politischer Mord" (Two years of political murder), was published in 1920. In the introduction to the fourth and later editions of this work, entitled *Vier Jahre politischer Mord* (Four years of political murder), Gumbel stated that he had expected one of two results from his first documentation of over 300 unprosecuted political murders: the judicial authorities would believe him and prosecute the murderers or they would not believe him and would prosecute him for libel. In the end, neither of these possible outcomes occurred.[58] It was not until the new edition was published in 1922 that the justice ministries of three Weimar states (Prussia, Mecklenburg, and Bavaria) sent reports responding directly to Gumbel's findings to the federal government at the request of the

---

[54] Emil Gumbel, *Vier Jahre politischer Mord* (Heidelberg: Verlag Das Wunderhorn, 1980).

[55] Mitchell, 330–1; Ludwig Morenz, ed. *Revolution und Räteherrschaft in München: Aus der Stadtchronik 1918/1919.* (Munich: Albert Langen – Georg Mueller Verlag, 1968).

[56] Wilhelm Hoegner, *Die verratene Republik: Geschichte der deutschen Gegenrevolution* (Munich: Isar Verlag, 1958), 36. Hoegner wrote the book in exile in Switzerland in 1934, but claimed in the preface that in the intervening years "politics kept him too busy." He was Bavarian minister president from 1945–6 and subsequently justice minister; he helped to write the postwar Bavarian constitution.

[57] Robert G. L. Waite, *The Vanguard of Nazism: The Free Corps Movement in Post-War Germany, 1918–1923* (New York: Norton, 1970), 90.

[58] Gumbel, *Vier Jahre,* 6.

Social Democratic *Reichsjustizminister* (federal minister of justice), Gustav Radbruch.

The Bavarian report confirmed the facts of most of the cases identified by Gumbel in his publications. But the intent of the report's authors was undeniably political. They obscured available details that identified the guilty parties and denied the political nature of certain murders, redefining some murders as accidental rather than intentional. Gumbel poignantly described the report's obfuscation:

> If we hold the data in the ministry report to be true, then the normal Bavarian case looks something like the following: N. N. was taken from his apartment on the such and such day of May by soldiers whose identity it is impossible to establish, on orders from an officer whose identity it has been impossible to establish, on the basis of a denunciation from a civilian whose identity has not been established, and then killed in an undiscovered manner. This information was procured as a result of a prolonged investigation.[59]

In other words, the ministry admitted in 1922 that murders had been committed in putting down the revolutionary government in May 1919 but claimed the crimes were impossible to investigate or prosecute.

In reaction, Gumbel attempted to uncover the details of the crimes as well as the identities of both victims and perpetrators. He found the Bavarian report troubling because it seemed to treat these numerous deaths as part of a mass phenomenon, rather than as individual crimes. For example, the Bavarian judicial report classified twenty-two of the murders reported by Gumbel as "legal executions" even though the authors of the report admitted that the executing field courts-martial did not have legal status. Despite the authors' obvious efforts to suppress the number of deaths attributable to the Whites, the report acknowledged 193 cases that could only be classified as political murders and which had not been prosecuted.[60]

Because the Bavarian Justice Ministry report relied on Gumbel's research, there was little disagreement about the number of political deaths during the Red, or revolutionary, Terror. Gumbel claimed that twelve people were murdered under the revolutionary regimes of 1919. This included the ten victims of the so-called *Geiselmord*, plus two *Räteregierung* (soviet government) officials who appear to have been murdered by other revolutionaries. In the case of the two officials, the murders were never investigated by judicial authorities.[61] One of the victims, Max Weinberger, had been the Red city commander for Munich but was fired after it was reported that he had given false identity papers to members of the counterrevolutionary and antisemitic Thule Society. Following these reports, he disappeared. His body was found after White forces had taken

---

[59] Ibid., 127.   [60] Ibid., 130.
[61] See the full discussion of the Munich *Geiselmord* in Chapter 3.

the city.[62] These twelve murders represent the largely undisputed total of victims of the Red Terror in Bavaria.

The estimates for victims of White Terror has remained much more controversial because so many deaths that occurred during the armed struggle with Red forces and during the first stage of White ascendency fall into very subjective categories. The initial attribution of causes of death was typically made by the military forces who were responsible for these deaths in the first place. In the first days of May, the citizens of Munich were ordered by White military commanders to stay off the streets in order to avoid civilian casualties. Nevertheless, crowds of civilians swarmed the streets to greet the victorious troops as they entered the city on May 4. Despite the masses of civilian onlookers crowding the streets, elements of the White forces executed the locksmith Heinrich Schermer as a "spy" because he had watched the White forces with binoculars.[63] In another case Gumbel reported, twenty-three-year-old Maria Kling was arrested on May 1 along with her father as they served as medics for the Red forces. Neither was armed and both wore white armbands with a red cross. Although a White Army court-martial acquitted them, Maria was killed soon after. When her father arrived at the Stadelheim prison to pick her up, he was informed that his daughter had been shot "for target practice" by unknown soldiers. The Bavarian Justice Ministry report claimed that she was shot because she had given "signals to the Red Army." The fact she had previously been acquitted of these charges is not mentioned in the report.[64]

Citizens of Munich had also been ordered to turn in all weapons ("including antiques") at the time of the White takeover. But citizens desiring to follow these orders faced a dangerous dilemma since appearing on the street with a weapon, even if one intended to surrender it at a collection point, could be grounds for arrest or even execution (as "opposing government troops with a weapon in the hand"). Because many German soldiers had taken their regulation weapons home with them after demobilization in 1918, and the *Räteregierung* had distributed weapons to workers' organizations, working-class men were particularly vulnerable. If they took their weapons to the collection point, they could be arrested. However, if they left a weapon in their home and were denounced, they could face arrest or worse. For example, one worker, Josef Sedlmaier, was killed by the White forces simply for not being able to prove that he had no weapon. According to the officer who ordered his arrest, Sedlmaier was taken into custody on May 2 "because he couldn't prove to me that he had really turned in his weapon on April 27."

---

[62] More on the Thule Society and its role in both political intrigues and violence in Munich in Chapter 3.
[63] Gumbel, *Vier Jahre*, 129.   [64] Ibid., 127.

Taken to the courtyard of a leather factory where other "Spartacists" had already been shot, Sedlmaier and two neighbors were shot by White soldiers.[65]

On May 14, 1919, the White military authorities in Munich reported their version of fatal casualties during the "battle to retake Munich." Among "sparticist" losses, they counted "77 shot, approximately 433 battle wounded," additionally, "58 Russians who opposed government troops with armed force were shot." The Russians listed in this report were probably the fifty-three Russian prisoners of war (from the world war) who were captured by counterrevolutionary forces and executed by the order of an illegal court-martial outside of Munich on May 2. Only one of the fifty-three Russian prisoners could speak German, and he was asked if the group had fought for the revolutionary government. All of them had been unarmed when captured (they were on their way to Munich to try to get paid by the revolutionary authorities). They were collectively accused of opposing the government and executed on the spot. Most had not even been asked for their names by the "court" prior to execution.[66]

Though it would seem that the murder of unarmed prisoners of war would have been an embarrassment to the White military authorities, the presence of "Russian soldiers" among the enemy forces in the revolutionary city affirmed the perception of many conservatives that they were battling an international revolutionary force. Though the Russians were former POWs and not revolutionary reinforcements sent from the Soviet Union, their capture and their deaths enhanced the Bavarians' sense of participating in a world historical struggle.

On June 2, the official police report of losses in the "defeat of the Munich *Räterepublik*" was published in local newspapers, giving the widely accepted total of 557 deaths. This report claimed that thirty-eight federal government soldiers and *Freikorps*, along with ninety-three "members of the Red Army" had been killed in battle. A further forty-two Red Army members were "executed by orders of courts-martial." Of the 335 civilian dead, 7 had been killed "in battle," 144 "executed by court-martial," and 184 were "accidental deaths." A further forty-two victims listed in the report were described as unidentified, but this figure was reduced to twenty-three through the research of Gumbel and the use of fingerprints.[67]

As historian Heinrich Hillmayr pointed out in his 1978 study *Roter und Weißer Terror in Bayern* (Red and White Terror in Bavaria), from November 7,

---

[65]   Ibid., 35.

[66]   BHSA IV, Kriegsarchiv, Höhere Stäbe, Bund 1, Akt 3; 1 c, General Kommando Oven, May 14, 1919.

[67]   See the report of the Kriegsgeschichtliche Forschungsanstalt des Heeres, *Darstellungen aus den Nachkriegskämpfen deutscher Truppen und Freikorps*, vol. 4: *Die Niederwerfung der Räteherrschaft in Bayern 1919* (Berlin: F. S. Mittler, 1939); and the tables in Gumbel, *Vier Jahre*.

1918, the day of the Eisner-led revolution, through April 30, 1919, the final day
of revolutionary rule in Munich, there were a total of forty-six deaths. This
number includes Eisner himself as well as the *Geiselmord* hostages. Then,
according to military and police sources, between May 1, when federal government troops arrived, and May 14, 557 people lost their lives in Munich.[68]
Despite the persistent perception that the majority of the political violence and
deaths had happened during the revolution, the opposite was clearly the case.
The great majority of deaths occurred at the hands of White forces during and
after the collapse of the Red government in Munich.

Contemporaries often referred to revolutionary rule in Munich as "bloody,"
and it is certainly true that revolutionary rhetoric included a great deal of
violent language and ideas, but actual acts of violence and deaths were largely
products of the counterrevolutionary assault.[69] In other words, although the
counterrevolution portrayed itself as an intervention to stop bloodshed, it was
the intervention itself that caused most of the bloodshed.

Terror in Budapest

By all measures, the magnitude of events in Hungary was greater than in
Bavaria: the revolutionary government held power longer; the counterrevolutionary effort to overthrow the Kun government took months rather than days;
and, not surprisingly, both the level of political violence and the number of
victims were much higher. It is perhaps also not surprising that efforts to
estimate the exact numbers of victims have been more contentious in the
Hungarian than in the Bavarian case. This is not only because of the larger
numbers involved, but also because of this nation's more politicized historiography of the 1919 events – contemporaneously, during the post–World War II
state socialist regime, and since 1989. However, despite the contested nature of
these estimates, it is clear for Hungary, as for Germany, that deaths due to
counterrevolutionary violence were an order of magnitude greater than those of
the revolutionary era that preceded it.

While the precise number of deaths attributable to the Red and White Terror
in Hungary remains in dispute, we can establish fairly reliable estimates. The
most detailed examination of deaths under the revolutionary regime was
provided by the state prosecutor, Dr. Albert Váry, in his book, *A vörös uralom
áldozatai Magyarországon* (The victims of the Red regime in Hungary),
published in Hungary in 1922. This was the same year Gumbel published

---

[68] Heinrich Hillmayr, *Roter und Weißer Terror in Bayern nach 1918: Ursachen, Erscheinungsformen
und Folgen der Gewalttätigkeiten im Verlauf der revolutionären Ereignisse nach dem Ende des
Ersten Weltkrieges.* (Munich: Nusser Verlag, 1974), 150.

[69] A comparison could also be made here to the October Revolution in Russia versus the bloodshed
of the Russian Civil War.

Vier Jahre politischer Mord in Germany, and the two books provide an interesting comparison.

Gumbel published his books in the hopes of pressuring the Bavarian Justice Ministry to investigate and prosecute the vast number of cases of unresolved deaths, mostly committed during the counterrevolution. Váry, on the other hand, was writing from within the Hungarian justice system and was concerned almost entirely with deaths during the period of revolutionary rule. Yet, despite the differences in authorial intention, the two works have a number of similarities, both in their format and in their attention to the details of individual cases. The two authors, writing from what might appear to be opposing political positions, offer similar, largely non-polemical lists of incidents, including great detail about individual cases and the identities of the individual victims.

In *A vörös uralom áldozatai Magyarországon,* Váry presented, in table format, a list of all known deaths from the revolutionary period. His chart gave a total of 590 victims and provided some information about each case, in columns listing the identity of the victim, the identity of the killer, the place and date of death, and some of the circumstances of the death, where known.[70] Yet it is clear from Váry's own descriptions of the deaths that many cases can only be considered "victims of the Red regime" in a very broad sense. But, by classifying all 590 deaths that occurred during the period of the soviet government as victims of the Red Terror, Váry was able to make the revolutionary government guilty of every act of violence and lawlessness in Hungary in the spring and summer of 1919.

When historian Gábor Pajkossy reclassified these cases using the circumstances of death described by Váry and supplementary information from other sources (Table 2.1), he found that over a third of the deaths that Váry attributed to the Red Terror were in fact deaths that occurred in military action, many of these along Hungary's disputed borders.[71] A third of those killed in this armed fighting were identified by Váry himself as members of a revolutionary military force, such as the Red Army. Certainly, it is difficult to accept that Red Army soldiers who died defending the revolutionary government, either against foreign armies or counter-revolutionaries, were victims of "Red Terror." In other cases presented by Váry, it is unclear on which side battlefield casualties served or whether they were unfortunate bystanders killed in the violence. Once identified, these problems of categorization make clear that Váry's original estimate has to be adjusted before we can separate victims of political violence from casualties from the border fighting that followed the end of the war and the breakup of the Habsburg Monarchy.

---

[70] Albert Váry, *A vörös uralom áldozatai Magyarországon: Hivatalos jelentések és bírói ítéletek alapján írta és kiadja*, 3rd edition (Szeged: Szegedi Nyomda, 1993). This work was reprinted in post-socialist Hungary during the 1990s.
[71] Gábor Pajkossy, correspondence with István Deák, 2000.

Table 2.1 *Cause of death for 590 Váry victims of Red Terror*

Cause of death (for 590 victims)	Percentage*
Sentenced to death and executed by a revolutionary or summary court	11%
Sentenced to death and executed by commandos of the soviet government, or victims of the arbitrary actions of such commandos	44%
Killed in action (total)	35%
Killed in battle or in the line of fire (whether armed or unarmed)	24%
Members of a soviet institution (soldiers, guards) killed in action	11%
Soldiers killed as disciplinary action	3%
Cause of death remains unknown	8%

*Numbers are rounded up so the total is more than 100%.
Source: Percentages from Gábor Pajkossy, correspondence with István Deák, 2000.

Many of the victims listed in Váry's *A vörös uralom áldozatai Magyarországon* are not identified by age or profession and their murderers are identified in his examination as "Red soldiers" or occasionally as "Red soldiers or terrorists."[72] Even given these very consequential problems, it is possible to use Váry's data to produce an adjusted estimate that at least 325 people, or possibly more, were victims of the revolutionary regime in Hungary, or the Red Terror, broadly understood.

Like the Red Terror, the White Terror in Hungary has been the subject of polemical writing since 1919. Because of the large-scale influx of refugees and the disorderly situation on the various military fronts, many people simply vanished from the record. Other deaths attributed to the White Terror may have been victims of the Romanian Army in cases where the details of their deaths are not known. Not only do the estimates provided for the victims of each "terror" vary widely but the numbers have been drawn into an explanatory relationship with one another.

In his 1923 account, *Revolution and Counterrevolution in Hungary*, Oszkár Jászi, the bourgeois radical and member of the 1918 Károlyi government, calculated that "During the four months of the [proletarian] dictatorship its victims numbered at the most four hundred."[73] After remarking that "four hundred deaths is a terrible thing in the eyes of the moralist," he noted that the figure included deaths from the armed civil war and border conflicts that had taken place. Having recast the total number of deaths attributable to the revolutionary regime, he put these amended deaths in a comparative moral context with the comment, "It is also certain, though this does not absolve the Red Terror from its heavy responsibility, that the White counterrevolution

---

[72] See for example the twenty-one victims of the "battle for the Kecel township," Váry, 82.
[73] Jászi, *Revolution and Counterrevolution*, 120.

which followed it claimed at least ten times as many victims."[74] Jászi's effort to apportion responsibility for deaths during revolutionary and counterrevolutionary eras in Hungary produced results that were broadly similar to contemporary estimates for deaths in Munich and Bavaria during the revolution and counterrevolution there; deaths from counterrevolutionary violence were at least ten times the number for deaths during the revolutionary governments' rule.

Hungarian counterrevolutionaries found that a high estimate for the number of victims of Red Terror, such as the one Váry provided, proved useful in later justifying the levels of White violence. In the eyes of these triumphant conservatives, the deaths at the hands of the White forces were not the result of an antisemitic policy of the National Army or, later, the Horthy government. For them, the White Terror was unfortunate but predictable, given the extremes of the Red Terror. White "excesses" flowed naturally from the natural desire for revenge among the White soldiers. The Horthy-era historian Albert Kaas explained the White Terror as a sort of "people's justice" or a "thirst for vengeance, for retaliation" on the part of the counterrevolutionary militias, and thus "the statesmen with foresight and vision [i.e. Horthy] were quite unable to impose their own sane and rational judgment on these impetuous elements."[75] By putting the blame for the violence on the White troops rather than their leadership, Kaas not only exculpated the Horthy government from legal responsibility for the murders but he also shifted the blame to the revolutionaries themselves, who he claimed had created this natural and insatiable "thirst for vengeance" by their actions while in power.

At the low end of estimates for White Terror victims in Hungary is the one provided by Gusztáv Gratz, another member of the Horthy government. In his 1935 history of the "revolutionary era," Gratz estimated that only 202 people died as a result of actions by the Whites *after* the fall of the revolutionary government. He did not propose an estimate for the period of struggle between the two sides that preceded this date.[76] Additionally, according to Gratz, ninety-seven death sentences were imposed by the counterrevolutionary government, sixty-eight of which were carried out. Since these death sentences were for political crimes, it would seem, following Gratz, that there were 270 deaths that could be attributed to the White Terror.

By way of comparison, Jászi reckoned that 4,000 died from White violence in Hungary during this same period. Roughly at the same time, 1922, a report on anti-Jewish violence in Hungary published in Vienna with the title *Martyrium* claimed that the results of "present research show that more than

---

[74] Ibid.

[75] Albert Kaas and Fedor de Lazarovics, *Bolshevism in Hungary: The Béla Kun Period* (London: Grant Richards, 1931), 312.

[76] Gusztáv Gratz, *A forradalmak kora: Magyarorszag törtenete 1918–1920* (Budapest: Akadémiai Kiadó, 1992).

3,000 Jews were murdered in Transdanubia," the broad region of Hungary east of the Danube river.[77] To this figure we would presumably have to add some number of non-Jewish victims of the White Terror, not reported by *Martyrium*, to arrive at a total. Although this number is more than ten times that estimated by Gratz, it is not the highest. There is an estimate of 5,000 White Terror victims that has been repeated by various authors since 1919/20. Most famously, Vilmos Böhm, the former commander of the Hungarian Red Army, used this estimate in his memoir, *In the Crossfire of Two Revolutions*, which he published from exile in Germany in 1924. In fact, Böhm seems to suggest the total number of victims might be even higher, claiming that "hundreds of innocents were murdered" as well as that "more than 5000 revolutionaries were murdered."[78]

Böhm's high estimate might have originated with József Pogány, another member of the revolutionary government, who mentioned 5,000 deaths in his *Der Weiße Terror in Ungarn*, published in 1921 in Vienna. Pogány's book discussed many White atrocities; some evidence he borrowed from non-communist sources. But Böhm did not acknowledge Pogány as the source for his estimate, and this number has been dismissed by some critics as a propagandist creation. Some dismissed Pogány as a Red terrorist himself and therefore an unreliable source for any assessment of the period's body count. He was, in fact, tried *in absentia* by the Horthy regime in 1921 and found guilty of complicity in Tisza's murder, along with others. Despite the criticisms and dismissals, the estimate of 5,000 dead as a result of White violence has endured for generations in the histories published by the socialist party functionary Dezső Nemes in the 1950s and 60s.[79]

Even today it is still difficult to establish an acceptable estimate for the number of victims attributable the White Terror. In his 1997 book *A Magyar Golgota* historian Péter Gosztonyi, for example, offered the fairly low estimate of 500 or 600 deaths that resulted from the actions of the White forces.[80] But the consensus among historians favors a higher number. Pajkossy assembled a list of documented pogroms and other White murders all over Hungary. He initially

---

[77] Josef Halmi, "Akten über die Pogrome in Ungarn," in Jakob Krausz, ed., *Martyrium: Ein jüdisches Jahrbuch* (Vienna: 1922), 59.

[78] Vilmos Böhm, *Im Kreuzfeuer zweier Revolutionen* (Munich: Verlag für Kulturpolitik, 1924), 538.

[79] Dezső Nemes, *Az ellenforradalom hatalomrajutása és rémuralma Magyarországon, 1919–1921* (Budapest: Szikra, 1953); Dezső Nemes, *Az ellenforradalom története Magyarországon, 1919–1921* (Budapest: Akadémiai Kiadó, 1962).

[80] Péter Gosztonyi, *A Magyar Golgota: A politikai megtorlások vázlatos története Magyarországon, 1849–1963 és egyéb korrajzi történetek* (Budapest: Heltai Gáspár, 1997), 34. Gosztonyi bases this number on one estimate from László Fogarassy, a historian who in 1988 calculated 500 cases between August 1919 and November 1920 where death resulted from the action of White forces, and the estimate from the New York socialist publication, *Ember*, which in 1926 found in 140 police records or protocols for 626 deaths owing to the White forces.

documented around 360 murders by White troops and officers, based on a geographically narrow selection of cases that would definitely underestimate the total for the whole country.[81] He concluded that the number generally agreed upon by historians now is 1,500–2,000. On the eightieth anniversary of the end of the *tanácsköztársaság* (soviet republic) an article entitled "Számolni nehéz: A tanácsköztársaság áldozatai" (Counting is difficult: The victims of the Soviet Republic) in the popular Hungarian magazine *HVG* (*Heti Világgazdaság* or Weekly world economy) presented a similar consensus view of 1,500–2,000 victims of the White Terror.[82] In 2011, historian Béla Bodó concluded that the number of victims lies around 3,000, higher than the more conservative consensus but lower than the symbolic 5,000 of the socialists.[83]

Because of the politically weighted debates on the numbers of victims, historical research on the circumstances of the terror and the motivations of the men involved was quite sparse until recently. In particular, Bodó has investigated the social world and beliefs of the Hungarian paramilitary leaders Pál Prónay and Iván Hejjás, as well as their followers.[84] Participation in the various paramilitary groups around Hungary was a mass phenomenon. Bodó estimates that in 1920 as many as 10,000–12,000 men may have been involved.[85] That so many people took up arms and adopted political militarism as their vocation is a striking feature of postwar Hungarian society, and these men, with their uniforms, banners, and weapons would have been a visible feature of the social and cultural world, as is evidenced by the prominence of photographs and postcards of these groups in flea-market and antiquarian offerings in Budapest still.[86] (Figure 2.2) Though a small minority of the male population was directly involved, their visibility amplified the influence of their activities to family members, neighbors who may have taken a vicarious pride in their vocation, and to groups such as Jews, national minorities, and organized workers, who may have feared or dreaded their uniforms and symbols. Recent work on the Hungarian militias has provided

---

[81] Gábor Pajkossy correspondence with István Deák, 2000.

[82] Illényi Balázs, "Számolni nehéz: A tanácsköztársaság áldozatai," *HVG* (July 31, 1999): 86–9.

[83] See Bodó, "White Terror in Hungary," 133, n. 1, for his discussion of the numbers debate. For a full history of the Terror, see his book, *The White Terror: Antisemitic and Political Violence in Hungary, 1919–1921* (New York: Routledge, 2019).

[84] Bodó, *Pál Prónay* ; Bodó, "Iván Hejjás."

[85] Bodó, "White Terror in Hungary," 141. Along with Prónay and Gyula Ostenburg-Moravek, Héjjas was a leader of the White officer brigades most often held responsible for the terror and anti-Jewish violence. He was a member of the ÉME and a member of parliament. Many Hungarians considered him a hero, in part for his resistance to the transfer of Burgenland to Austria in 1921 and the attempted royal coups by the Habsburg King Charles.

[86] Whenever I am in Budapest looking at old photographs and postcards for sale, I am struck by the number of such mementos of young men of the ÉME or the MOVE. Though perhaps their sale is caused by families more recently finding such pictures uninteresting or embarrassing, the items may also be popular with the new Hungarian right-wing.

Figure 2.2 Commemorative photo postcard of a MOVE squad from
May 1921 "Patriotic Celebration."
Source: Postcard in possession of the author.

an opportunity for rich comparisons to the research on early Nazi supporters
and members of paramilitary groups in Weimar Germany and even elsewhere
in post–World War I Europe.[87]

An important reason for the different historical debates over the Red and
White Terrors of 1919 in Germany and Hungary was Cold War politics.
Although both countries had state socialist regimes in post–World War II,
divided Europe, Bavaria was not a part of the German Democratic Republic
and so belonged to the "West," while Hungary was in the Soviet-dominated
"East." Perhaps in large part because of this, the Bavarian revolution and the

---

[87] Gerwarth and Horne includes a broad comparison of paramilitary groups.

events in Munich in 1919 did not play a large role in the historical narrative of German revolution promoted by the East German regime, which instead paid greater attention to events such as the January 1919 Spartacus Uprising in Berlin. And, to be clear, in the post–World War II era, German communists had many more heroes and important events to look back on for historical legitimation than did their colleagues in Hungary. The failed Bavarian revolution, brief and without real charismatic communist leadership, could be easily brushed aside.

This was not the case in postwar state socialist Hungary, where 1919 provided an important proof of a national communist prehistory. However, as we will see in Chapter 6, because many of the 1919 revolutionary leaders fell out with Stalin, they themselves were not the main focus of research for historical legitimation; rather the national history of revolutionary struggle was portrayed, especially the suffering of the country in the White Terror and under the counterrevolutionary regime. For this reason, the violence of the White Terror received much more academic attention in Hungary over the postwar decades than the Red Terror, until the post-socialist 1990s. This has had a number of effects. First, suspicion about the manipulation of the events of 1919 for propaganda by the postwar regime led to cynicism about history and a sense among many Hungarians that truths about the revolution remained hidden. In its worst version, this has brought the resurgence of antisemitic tropes about so-called Judeo-Bolshevism.[88] Second, the relative inattention to the Red Terror by historians for many decades had the ironic effect of leaving the original claims of the 1919 counterrevolutionaries unexamined. For example, Albert Váry's 1922 book on victims of the Red Terror described above was republished in Hungary in 1993, and Gusztáv Gratz's 1935 history of the 1919 revolution was reprinted in 1992. It would seem that the post-socialist republication of the works of Váry and Gratz was meant to serve as an "antidote" to the many volumes published in the preceding decades of socialism about the horrors of Horthy-Hungary.

As we have seen, the establishment of the facts of the revolutions and counterrevolutions has been quite contentious and complicated by politics. This has been even truer for the allocation of guilt for the crimes committed. In the following chapters we will look at the way that the definition of crimes and the attribution of responsibility was handled by the courts after the fall of the revolutionary governments, and how these questions of revolutionary guilt shaped the politics and culture of interwar Central Europe more broadly.

---

[88] A full discussion of the effects of this myth in 1919–21 is in Chapter 5; also Ablovatski, 137–54; and Hanebrink, *Specter Haunting Europe*.

3 Rumor and Terror
Revolutionary Script and Political Violence

Men make their own history, but they do not make it as they please; they do not make it under self-selected circumstances, but under circumstances existing already, given and transmitted from the past. The tradition of all dead generations weighs like a nightmare on the brains of the living. And just as they seem to be occupied with revolutionizing themselves and things, creating something that did not exist before, precisely in such epochs of revolutionary crisis they anxiously conjure up the spirits of the past to their service, borrowing from them names, battle slogans, and costumes in order to present this new scene in world history in time-honored disguise and borrowed language. Thus Luther put on the mask of the Apostle Paul, the Revolution of 1789-1814 draped itself alternately in the guise of the Roman Republic and the Roman Empire, and the Revolution of 1848 knew nothing better to do than to parody, now 1789, now the revolutionary tradition of 1793–95.

From the declaration of the council republics in March 1919 until the revolutions' respective defeats in May and August, Munich and Budapest appeared in leading roles on the stage of the ongoing drama of world revolution. The script for this revolutionary drama was well known to all the participants, both revolutionaries and counterrevolutionaries. Media reports from these two cities as well as from Berlin and Moscow, fortified by well-known accounts of the French Revolution and Paris Commune, formed the building blocks of a narrative for understanding local events. By 1919 it was a well-rehearsed and broadly disseminated story that carried in its wake a developed set of expectations that made plausible the circulating rumors and threats that so often provoked violence. This chapter analyzes rumor and terror, both shaped by these revolutionary scripts, and the political violence that erupted after the creation of council governments. These new governments, namesakes of the revolutionary government in Russia, deployed a revolutionary vocabulary that seemed to make concrete all the ideas of radical political discourse. Rhetoric about class warfare appeared to transform into reality with the appearance of armed workers brigades patrolling the streets. This embodiment of previously theoretical concepts was empowering to those playing the roles of revolutionary heroes and terrifying to those who suddenly found themselves cast as enemies in a dramatic new reality. As we explore events in Budapest and

Munich, we will see how expectations of violence, shaped by revolutionary scripts, influenced the ways in which residents of the two cities understood political events and provoked new rounds of violence.

The declarations of soviet-style revolutionary governments in Munich and Budapest broke through the political paralysis that followed the assassination of Bavaria's USPD Minister President Kurt Eisner on February 21, 1919 and Hungary's receipt of the terms of the Paris Peace Conference with the Vix note of March 19, 1919. Not only politicians but also residents of Munich and Budapest were acutely aware of the revolutions and civil war in Russia and, as a result, there were many who anticipated the declaration of revolutionary soviet or council governments, some impatiently but most with dread. It seemed that history was being written on a large scale since the world war, with the ongoing civil war in Russia and signs of revolution all over Central Europe. With the creation of the revolutionary governments, most people understood local events to be part of a larger, international armed struggle. Local events were perceived in an international and world historical context.

During the 1919 revolutions, individuals' previously held ideas about revolution, especially the Russian Revolution, facilitated the circulation of rumors in Munich and Budapest and colored the reactions of the public. Although neither Munich nor Budapest had a real revolutionary heritage, city dwellers on the Left and the Right interpreted "revolution," when it occurred, through the lens of a well-known script. Key roles, in support and opposition, were widely anticipated, as were plot lines; only local casting and staging remained unresolved. Many contemporaries judged local events against world historical archetypes like the French and Russian revolutions or the Paris Commune, calling the local communist leaders of their era "Robespierre," "Lenin," or "Raoul Rigault" depending on their political point of view. The narrative framework suggested how they should act, react, and understand the actions of others.

In 1919, certain catchphrases from the revolutionary vocabulary, including Red and White Terror, Spartacist, Jacobin, White Guardist, and hostage, had functions that proved to be more prescriptive than descriptive. These terms, in common usage at the time, may be considered misnomers from a historical perspective. For example, in Bavaria, were troops under the command of Berlin's Social Democrat-led government really "White forces"?[1] In retrospect, we can see that contemporaries applied labels like this to create and shape popular perceptions and mobilize political support. Rather than merely note or even "correct" these mistakes or misinterpretations by contemporary

---

[1] The troops used white armbands to distinguish themselves from the Red military formations, which wore red armbands. Since many of the soldiers on both sides still wore their war-issue "field gray" uniforms, the armbands were necessary to identify the side for which each soldier fought. I also use the designation "White forces" as a shorthand for "government troops and Freikorps" in analyzing the fighting between "Red" and "White" in Munich.

participants, this chapter examines the profound influence the often-hyperbolic revolutionary language had on unfolding events. When the revolutionaries called the troops fighting under the SPD-led Berlin German republic "White forces," it associated them with the crimes of the Russian White forces in the ongoing civil war and made it easier to believe rumors of their mistreatment of prisoners and civilians. The relationship between what was said to have happened and concrete evidence was woven with threads of fantasy and terror. Across postwar Central Europe thousands of people were victims of real political violence, but in the press and in imaginations of the time thousands of additional alleged victims washed up in the rivers, were left mangled on the street corners, or were slaughtered by firing squads. Both the real corpses, as well as the rumored or imagined corpses, were terrifying to the people who lived through the times and they served to justify more violence on both sides.

Examining the origin and transmission of rumors is especially important and revealing for the study of revolution and counterrevolution. In times of political or military crisis, the usual flow of information in a city is disrupted. Physical barriers to information arise when newspapers disappear, post and telegraph service becomes irregular, and halted public transportation prevents the usual interchange between residents in different areas of the city. Similarly, military and civilian authorities all-too predictably attempted to censor any remaining publications, while at the same time they printed propaganda and posted informational announcements encouraging citizens to embrace the government's policies and objectives. As with the shortage and rationing of material goods, the shortage and rationing (or control) of information leads inexorably to a black market of sorts, where the demand for information is met in the form of rumors. Like many black-market goods, rumors are of uncertain origin, unreliable in quality, and sometimes costly for contemporaries, in the sense that they may lead to further tragic violence.

Well before the Central European revolutions in the spring of 1919, World War I had already established the conditions for an active market in rumors. In the days leading up to war, rumors circulated in Munich that Serbs had poisoned the Isar River, and the writer Ernst Toller witnessed a crowd of ruffians attack as a spy a man unfortunate enough to take off his hat and reveal the French milliner's name inside.[2] The wartime regime of censorship and propaganda in Germany and Austria–Hungary only worsened the situation and made each country's population cynical and skeptical, as well as oddly susceptible to believing even outlandish rumors. It was as if the increasing hunger for reliable information provoked by censorship and the disruptions of traditional news media made these populations willing to swallow almost any information, especially when hoped-for or feared versions of stories came from unofficial or conspiratorial sources. As popular confidence in government dissolved over the course of the war, certain types of

---

[2] Toller, *Eine Jugend in Deutschland*, 39.

unverifiable rumor gained strength; the idea that "of course you haven't heard anything, *they* don't want us to know" or "my informant knows the *real* situation, which of course no one is telling us" gained credibility when the government really did restrict information, made painfully obvious by wartime newspapers that were covered with the black boxes of the censors. These conspiratorial claims to secret (and true) information must have been incredibly tempting in a wartime diet that was dominated by self-serving government propaganda.

During the war, rumors with unverified information could save lives and determine political events. The relationship between rumor and the black market was real and vital for women trying to feed families during the war.[3] Without confidential sources and information about the availability of food-stuffs, urban families could go hungry. In Munich and Budapest, rumors arguably helped to propel the revolutions of November 1918 when masses of protesters overthrew their monarchs, inspired as much by tales of governmental incompetence and indifference as by a positive revolutionary platform or an organized revolutionary cadre. The government-instituted shortage of informa-tion during the world war had trained citizens to look to other sources for information, and these informal sources such as neighbors, fellow line-standers, and even strangers were accorded similar levels of trust to more official outlets such as newspapers, government proclamations, and the police.

Distrust of official information and the hunger for news from what was perceived to be more trustworthy sources created the market for rumors, but the actual content of the rumors was shaped by a matrix of expectations and practices. Why did people believe and spread certain rumors and not others? In order to survive and gain traction, a rumor must fit into the expectations of its audience. Believable rumors offered new information that fit well with what the listener already knew or believed. These tales could be rooted in universally known facts, such as food scarcity, but were supplemented and expanded by unverifiable information that gave the suspicions substance: who was hoarding food, who was responsible for the scarcity. Maureen Healy has shown how existing ethnic prejudices and distrust shaped the stories the Viennese told about hoarding and food prices during World War I.[4] To be credible, these supplements to known facts needed to resonate with the listener's existing store of beliefs and stereotypes.

During the 1919 revolutions, rumors spread in Munich and Budapest based on previously held ideas about revolution –from knowledge of the French Revolution and the Paris Commune and, of course, news from the ongoing revolutionary struggle in Russia, as well as events in other Central European cities. These rumors often served to confirm contemporary assumptions about how these societies were organized. Rumors that confirmed racial and gender stereotypes often found immediate traction as they simultaneously reinforced

---

[3] See Healy, *Vienna and the Fall of the Habsburg Monarchy.*   [4] Ibid., esp. chapter 1.

those stereotypes and recirculated them in new guises.[5] Listeners who already held antisemitic opinions, for example, found rumors linking Jews to revolutionary atrocities or to economic crimes believable because they fit centuries-old stereotypes and prejudices that were rooted in assumptions about racial difference. Understanding this flow of rumor and popular information helps us to unpack the relationship between antisemitism, antifeminism, and counter-revolutionary violence. It was not only that Jews were blamed after the fact for the actions of the revolutionary governments but that popular antisemitism coded political enemies as biologically different and made it possible for people to believe all kinds of claims about the revolutions.

Rumor and Terror in Munich

The bloodshed in Munich took place during the fighting to overthrow the soviet government in the first days of May 1919, with a few isolated incidents in the next weeks; over 600 people lost their lives in total. Two notorious crimes that were caused by rumor and terror, the *Geiselmord* and the Karolinenplatz murders, bookended this violent period. Of the two, it was the so-called *Geiselmord* on April 30 that for many residents of Munich best symbolized and encapsulated the disaster of the soviet experiment. This "murder of hostages" refers to a Red firing squad's execution of ten people in the Luitpold Gymnasium in the center of the city, by the English Garden. At the time, the school was serving as the barracks and headquarters of the Red Army. When news of the executions and rumors about the desecration of the corpses reached the besieging government forces and *Freikorps* this information and misinformation inspired them to brutal acts of revenge. These included the torture and murder of twenty young Catholic journeymen who had been denounced as Spartacists on May 6, an event known as the Karolinenplatz murders. In both of these mass killings, one perpetrated by the Left and one by the Right, the guilty soldiers, militiamen, and vigilantes were motivated to brutal violence by their exposure to rumors of terrible crimes and cruel actions that had very little basis in fact. The two incidents horrified Munich's residents and yet somehow did not completely surprise them, given popular expectations about the nature of the revolutionary struggle. News of both atrocities circulated across Central Europe, gaining enormous symbolic importance for contemporaries in the interwar period. The

---

[5] Two books offer compelling comparative perspective on anti-Jewish violence: Irina Marin's *Peasant Violence and Antisemitism in Early Twentieth-Century Eastern Europe* (Cham: Palgrave Macmillan, 2018) is an intriguing study of the pivotal role of antisemitic rumors about Jews and "foreigners" in the 1907 uprising in rural Romania. Daniel L. Unowsky, *The Plunder: The 1898 Anti-Jewish Riots in Habsburg Galicia* (Stanford, CA: Stanford University Press, 2018), argues that "exclusionary violence" against Jews was a product of modernization rather than a sign of backwardness.

political impact of each event, in the end, seemed to fit an existing script: Red Terror and a responding White Terror.

The first act of this cycle of terror, the killings at the Luitpold Gymansium, occurred in an atmosphere already thick with rumor and primed with the expectation of violence. The terrorizing of bourgeois hostages was an expected part of the drama of revolution. In his April 27, 1919 "Message of Greetings to the Bavarian Soviet Republic," Lenin had asked his German comrades, among other questions, "have you taken hostages from the ranks of the bourgeoisie?" He advised the leadership that "The most urgent and most extensive implementation of these and similar measures ... should strengthen your position."[6] Revolutionaries understood the taking of bourgeois hostages, like taking over the banks and arming the workers (two of Lenin's other suggestions), to be a tool of the revolutionary trade. While in the Munich case the executed prisoners had not been seized as hostages but rather they had been arrested for counterrevolutionary crimes, both the Right and the Left immediately used the term *Geiselmord* to describe the killings. This crime illustrates the powerful effects of revolutionary language and rumor, especially when word-of-mouth diffusion was magnified by transmission through media – posters, printed proclamations, and later also photographs and news reports. Fighting between the Red Army and White forces had already begun around Munich on April 29 and, by the morning of the April 30, the whole city was already roiled by rumors of White atrocities, especially among the nervous recruits in the Red Army barracks in the Luitpold Gymnasium on Müllerstrasse.

A flyer from the Communist Party (*Spartakusbund*), widely distributed in Munich on April 30, claimed that "White guardists" were shooting even those Red troops who attempted to surrender and that many noncombatants had been executed as well. The flyer repeated a rumor that, in nearby Starnberg, White forces had attacked and killed a group of Red medics and ambulance workers, clearly wearing medical armbands, who were tending to the wounded.[7] In his 1938 *Revolutionstagebuch* (Diary of the revolution), the conservative literary scholar Josef Hofmiller reproduced the text of the flyer, with his reactions to its various claims in brackets. Reporting on the story of the medics' execution, he wrote simply, "That is so nonsensical that I don't believe it." Hofmiller also suggested that for his neighbors and acquaintances in the Munich middle classes, at least, the revolutionary call to arms had the opposite effect of reassuring them of their impending release from what he said people were calling "this red puppet

[6] Lenin, *Collected Works*, 325–6.
[7] For the story of the ambulance workers in memoirs of the revolution, see Erich Wollenberg, *Als Rotarmist vor München* (Hamburg, Internationale Sozialistische Publikationen, 1972), 152–3, as well as 90, for a discussion of the "bounty" offered for Spartacists; Graf, 497; and Ernst Niekisch, *Gewagtes Leben: Begegnungen und Begebnisse* (Köln and Berlin: Kiepenheuer & Witsch, 1958), 77. Gumbel cites a September article in *Kampf* that reports that the victims were "20 unarmed red soldiers who were surprised in Starnberg ... three medics, working on transporting the wounded in Possenhofen, and a 68-year-old man"; Gumbel, *Vier Jahre*, 28.

show [*Kasperltheater*]." He here implied both the relief of the Munich bourgeoisie at the arrival of government forces to free them but also their strong contempt, rather than fear, of the revolutionary government.[8]

From April 29 to May 1, Red authorities responded to news of the fighting, as well as the rising tide of rumors, by printing and distributing throughout the city posters calling for volunteers to help defend revolutionary Munich in a "battle to the death." These same posters warned the public to expect additional White atrocities if the battle were lost and "the Prussians," as they called the federal German troops, took the capital. The flyer from April 30 claimed, "The capitalists will never forgive you for what they experienced in these weeks . . . . They will never forgive you for their fear as they saw you march by armed. "[9] The violent revenge of the Whites was not only predicted but was used to encourage resistance, if more out of fear than ideological commitment. Propaganda from the revolutionary government almost universally referred to the White forces encircling Munich as "Prussians" and "capitalist mercenaries" to inspire fear and resistance among Munich's residents. The famous novelist Thomas Mann, himself a Prussian living in Munich, called this equation of Whites and Prussians "demagogic" in his diary entry for April 30, 1919.[10]

On the morning of April 30, Fritz Seidel, the commander in charge at the Luitpold Gymnasium, received an order, apparently stamped with the signature of the Red Army Commander, Rudolf Eglhofer, to execute the group of prisoners, described as "White guardists," imprisoned in the barracks. At ten in the morning, guards led two prisoners into the courtyard, and they were executed by a firing squad. These first two victims were members of General Burghardt von Oven's federal German army; forty-one year old Lance Corporal Fritz Linnenbrügger and nineteen-year old cavalryman Walter Hindorf of the Eighth Prussian Hussar Regiment were natives of Berlin.[11] They had been captured two days earlier and interrogated. Put under great pressure, both had reportedly confessed that a bounty had been placed on the heads of revolutionaries and that their regiment had been involved in the assassination of the popular revolutionary leaders Rosa Luxemburg and Karl Liebknecht following their arrests in

---

[8] Josef Hofmiller, *Revolutionstagebuch 1918/19: Aus den Tagen der Münchener Revolution* (Leipzig: Karl Rauch Verlag, 1938), 209–10. This diary, which largely held Jews responsible for the revolutions, was published by Hofmiller's widow after his death. She dedicated the 1938 publication to "the young greater Germany" (*Dem jungen Großdeutschland*) and to her two sons in the Nazi Wehrmacht.

[9] Ibid., 208.

[10] Mann, 217. Whether calculated or not, the expression found traction in the public; see for example Victor Klemperer's diary entry for May 3, 1919; Klemperer, *Leben sammeln, nicht fragen wozu und warum: Tagebücher 1918–1924*, edited by Walter Nowojski (Berlin: Aufbau Verlag, 1996), 107.

[11] Oven himself was a Prussian as well. The Red Army and even local counterrevolutionaries resented that a Prussian had been given control of the government forces fighting to defend the Hoffmann-led Bavarian government. Anti-Prussian sentiment was even used to recruit Bavarian men into the *Freikorps* (along the lines of "don't let the Prussians defend you, defend yourselves").

Berlin during the January 1919 Spartacus Uprising. On the night of April 29, their captors set the stage for the executions by using the presses of the liberal *Münchener Neuesten Nachrichten* to print posters containing these incendiary allegations and then posting them throughout the city.[12]

By all accounts these posters, along with the incendiary rumors of White atrocities in the hinterlands of Munich that circulated through the besieged city, transformed the treatment of civilian prisoners being held at the Luitpold Gymnasium. According to later testimony by surviving prisoners, until April 29 their situation had been quite tolerable. Up to that point they had played cards with their guards and even been permitted to receive outside visitors. According to the other local Bavarian prisoners, the guards treated only the two Prussian soldiers badly. Witnesses testified that the mood changed between five and six in the morning of April 30, when a Red Guardist stormed into the prisoners' room and read aloud the poster announcing White atrocities on the outskirts of Munich. This set the tone for a terrifying day for the prisoners as well as for many of their guards. In their testimony during the trials held in September 1919, both firing squad members and surviving prisoners cited this poster with its announcement that the captured Prussians had confessed that there was a bounty for revolutionaries. They attested that the false information on this poster was used in the barracks to gin up support for the executions of White prisoners. One of the surviving prisoners from the gymnasium, a legal counsel for the city of Munich, Adolf Konrad, testified that he believed "those who, against their better judgment, drew up the announcement on that poster are responsible for the *Geiselmord*."[13] Nonparticipants, unattached to either Red or White organizations, also made this connection at the time of the killings. In his diary, Mann, for example, recognized the cycle of violence spurred by the posters' provocative language and the publication of unconfirmed reports of illegal executions and the murder of prisoners by White forces. He believed that the murder of prisoners by the Reds originated with the allegations of White Terror in Starnberg spread through the city on the posters.[14] The language used in the poster – "White Guardists," "bounty," "shooting of prisoners" – helped incite the Red soldiers at the barracks to a new round of violence, violence they saw as necessary.

On the morning of the Luitpold Gymnasium murders, civilian prisoners were taken from their rooms, supposedly to peel potatoes, but were left standing near the school's courtyard. From there, they witnessed the mid-morning execution

---

[12] The poster is reproduced in Karl-Ludwig Ay, *Appelle einer Revolution. Das Ende der Monarchie. Das revolutionare Interregnum. Die Ratezeit. Dokumente aus Bayern zum Jahr 1918/1919. Zusammenstellung und historische Einfuhrung* (Munich: Süddeutscher Verlag, 1968); the poster is described by contemporaries as in Hofmiller's memoir, 207–9, and Hillmayr, 106.

[13] Staatsarchiv München (StAM) Polizeidirektion(Pol. Dir.) 677, Geiselmord Protokoll.

[14] Mann, May 1, 1919, 218.

of the two Prussian soldiers.[15] At noon, Commander Seidel received a second order signed by Eglhofer, to shoot the remaining prisoners, starting with arrestees who were members of the *völkisch*-nationalist Thule Society and a group of aristocrats. The former had been accused of plotting a coup against the revolutionary government and had reportedly possessed stolen or forged stamps of the revolutionary leadership's seals and signatures. Over the course of the afternoon, eight prisoners, including the Thule Society members, were brought into the courtyard. They were shot in pairs by an ad hoc firing squad whose members had been recruited from among the crowd of Red soldiers then at the school awaiting their pay and drinking free beer in the cafeteria.[16]

News that prisoners, or rather "hostages" as they were called, had been executed at the Luitpold Gymnasium spread rapidly. Wild, often conflicting, stories circulated through the city. Accounts of the events vary wildly: the number of the dead, the identities of the victims, and the condition of the corpses. With each retelling it seems that shocking or titillating information, whether correct or incorrect, was amplified. The rumors people heard about the killings sometimes doubled or tripled the number of female victims, or the number of professors or members of the princely family of Thurn and Taxis among the victims. In actuality there was only one victim from of each of these categories among the dead. As stories with false or inaccurate information were repeated, they added to the imagined body count as Munich residents attempted to confirm the identities of the dead. Piecing together information from various friends who called or visited on May 1, Mann came up with a working list of nine victims; this included "Privy Council Döderlein ... Lindpaintner ..., Count Arco, a Countess Arco, Prince and Princess of Thurn and Taxis." The friend who confirmed this list claimed "the others were unidentifiably mutilated."[17] Hofmiller's mother reported a similar list of victims when she visited him on May 4, "Countess Arco along with her son, Eisner's assassin, the Princess of Thurn and Taxis, and Count Bothmer."[18] These rumored lists of victims are quite revelatory for how rumors spread and were evaluated in Munich in these days when, as Hofmiller pointed out, they were totally without information, there having been no newspapers since April 13. All of the incorrect names on the lists reported by Hofmiller and Mann were people who seemed to fit the narrative of Red Terror, which was what made these lists believable as people passed the information on. Most of the phantom

---

[15] The description of the morning's events comes from the testimony of a fellow prisoner, Dr. Konrad. His article in the *Münchener Neuste Nachrichten* is reprinted Josef Karl, *Die Schreckensherrschaft in München und Spartakus in bayerischen Oberland:Tagebuchblätter und Ereignisse aus der Zeit der "bayr. Räterepublik" und der Münchner Kommune im Frühjahr 1919 nach amtlichen Quellen* (Munich: Hochschulverlag, 1919), 86.

[16] StAM Pol. Dir. 677, testimony at Geiselmord trial – defendant Johann Hannes, Geiselmord Protokoll.

[17] Mann, see entry for May 1–4, 1919.   [18] Hofmiller, 215.

victims were nobles, which fit with the idea of class warfare; some of them were even well-known as enemies of the revolution, like Eisner's assassin Count Arco and his mother or Count Felix von Bothmer, a Bavarian member of the German military high command during World War I and an associate of Prince Rupprecht of Bavaria (Wittelsbach). That the list of female victims expanded in the popular imagination also fit with preexisting fears and stereotypes of Red savagery against defenseless victims, presumably apolitical noblewomen. Like the friends and relatives who passed on the rumors to them, these conservative diarists were enraged when they heard about the reported victims, especially the women among them. But most of the victims in the lists, whose deaths they rued in their diaries, were later revealed as victims only of the imagined terror of the grapevine and not of the actual *Geiselmord*.

By the evening of the executions at the barracks, the revolutionary soviet government had already condemned the murders. As the Red government stumbled towards collapse, Toller and the leadership of the workers' and soldiers' council published statements expressing their "deepest disgust" at what they called the "bestial shooting of hostages."[19] These words sounded hollow to the Munich bourgeoisie. Hofmiller found the regret suspicious, writing that "Hostages are taken in order to be killed in an emergency." He then argued that the council should have understood, as he did, the lessons of history and known how the revolutionary narrative would play out. As he put it, "If the workers' council only took the hostages to scare the bourgeoisie, they should have known that in every revolution hostages are shot at the last minute, and it was therefore a crime not to release them earlier. Or they were taken prisoner in order to shoot in case of emergency, in which case, why the 'deepest disgust' afterwards?" Hofmiller believed not only that he knew "that in every revolution hostages are shot" but also that the revolutionaries themselves must have known this. Therefore, from his perspective, the council government was guilty, even before the murders happened, of not preventing what they had to know was inevitable "in every revolution."[20]

After the revolution's defeat on May Day, the city's new military authorities, the Bavarian Army under the command of General Arnold Ritter von Möhl, issued proclamations that informed the population about the *Geiselmord*, but these were initially incomplete. Reports in the first newspapers, distributed on May 4, contained entirely fabricated details, including two particularly inflammatory falsehoods. They declared that the murders had actually been planned as a signal for a revolutionary, conspiratorial uprising in the working-class population, in other words that the hostages had been killed as part of the planned defense of the revolutionary government. They also gave new,

---

[19] Mann, 218; Hofmiller, 211.   [20] Hofmiller, 211.

incorrect details about the actual executions, claiming that "Russians had been made to drink until they were complete animals and then were let loose on the unlucky hostages."[21] Like the false reports of the identities of victims, this piece of information seemed to fit with what the citizens of Munich believed they knew about revolutionary violence. They already associated this behavior with Russians from the Russian Revolution, and it was a common German stereotype that Russians were drunk and primitive. If the *Geiselmord* was "bestial," as everyone agreed, then it was easy to imagine Russian "animals" committing the crime.

Eventually both newspaper articles and military reports corrected the most extravagant claims of the rumors about the *Geiselmord*. But they retained the provocative tone as well as the militant language of the conservative versions of revolutionary script, justifying and valorizing White military action. Just as Munich's Red government poster denouncing White atrocities had radicalized Red soldiers, inciting them to acts of terror and violence, the story of the *Geiselmord* in all its variations incited White troops to acts of retributive and punitive violence. These included the murder in the Stadelheim prison of around thirty prisoners, including Gustav Landauer, an intellectual leader of the first soviet government, who was beaten to death by White soldiers yelling antisemitic taunts. Revolutionary leaders such as Eglhofer and other, less prominent suspects were shot after their arrest or "while trying to escape."[22] At the same time illegal courts-martial ordered other executions that were little more than vigilante justice. The men responsible for these unauthorized executions and killings were never prosecuted.

The single most deadly act of political revenge the Whites committed was the murder of fifty-three unarmed Russian prisoners of war on May 2 outside Munich in Gräfelfing. Captured late in the war, before the March 1918 Treaty of Brest-Litovsk, they were still wearing their Russian army uniforms when a firing squad executed them. Although this killing involved five times as many prisoners as the earlier *Geiselmord*, this massacre did not attract much public attention at the time. Gumbel's accounts in 1920 and 1922 included the most detailed retelling of this event.[23] The false rumors, which were printed on May 4, that claimed that Russian soldiers were the "animals" who shot the *Geiselmord* hostages were likely to have already been circulating two days earlier when the Russian POWs were killed. This could have encouraged their killing as a justified "revenge" and certainly poisoned any sympathy for them as victims in the general population. For most Bavarians, the Russian prisoners were already doubly marked as enemies: first of all as enemy POWs captured in

---

[21] Ibid., 217.

[22] I discuss the widespread phenomenon of "shot while trying to escape" in Chapter 2.

[23] Gumbel's work is discussed in detail in Chapter 2.

the world war, and second as probable revolutionaries after the Russian Revolution, at a moment when "Russian" seemed to equal "Bolshevik" for most Central Europeans. For all of these reasons, these murders do not seem to have been taken up at the time as a cause for indignation at the White Terror. In fact, quite the opposite seems to have been true. Hofmiller reported overhearing a young woman "agitating" in line during the two-hour wait to buy meat. The woman was bemoaning the White violence and complained that "The Russians killed the hostages, but of course the workers are the ones who get shot."[24] Far from showing sympathy towards the dead Russian POWs, this woman seemed to hold "the Russians" responsible for the White forces' violence against the Munich working class.

The majority of Munich's population considered the most notorious act of counterrevolutionary terror to be the murder of twenty-one prisoners in the barracks at the Prince Georg Palace at Karolinenplatz on May 6, 1919. On that evening, right after the military curfew, soldiers at the City Command received a denunciation from a civilian in the bohemian and working-class neighborhood Schwabing in northern Munich, an area that had loyally supported the revolutionary government. White officers were informed that a group of Spartacists, possibly armed with a machine gun, was meeting at 71 Augustenstraße, in the basement of the dormitory of St. Joseph's Church. When White Army soldiers burst into the basement, they discovered a group of twenty-four young men.[25] They met no resistance and discovered no weapons. The soldiers herded their captives out of the basement with bayonets and through the streets to the military police headquarters at the Prince Georg Palace. Along the way, a large crowd of onlookers gathered to yell and spit at the band of alleged Spartacists.[26]

Once they arrived at the palace, the prisoners protested their arrest and tried to present their papers and offer explanations for their assembly to the City Command officials there. Nevertheless, without a formal hearing or trial, overexcited soldiers almost immediately shot seven of the prisoners in the building's courtyard. The others were taken into the basement where they were tortured and otherwise abused. The soldiers, many of them now drunk, stepped on the prisoners, beat them with rifles, and in some cases stabbed them with bayonets. When all of the prisoners appeared to be dead, the soldiers robbed the corpses of shoes, watches, and other valuables.

Three men survived this savage treatment, though severely wounded, by pretending to be dead.[27] One of them later reported in court that two soldiers had "performed a real Indian dance next to the corpses."[28] According to depositions taken from witnesses by White military authorities, the corpses

---

[24] Hofmiller, 218.   [25] Karl, 151.   [26] *Leipziger Neueste Nachrichten*, May 8, 1919, 1.
[27] Karl, 153.
[28] Report in *Der Bayrischer Kurier*, October 23, 1919, at the time of the trials, quoted in Gumbel, *Vier Jahre*, 41–2.

"looked horrible. One's nose had been trampled into his face and another was missing half of the back of his head."[29] A colonel who finally entered the basement shortly after the killings, despite warnings that the enlisted men were "wild," testified that although he had seen a lot of carnage in the recent world war, the sight in the basement was "the most impressive" he had seen.[30]

Many people in Munich at first understood this violence as part of the "necessary excesses" that some leaders of White forces had predicted, given what they thought to be provocations and excesses by the Red forces. Major Schulze of the *Freikorps Lützow* summarized this point of view two days earlier in a speech to his troops on May 4: "Those who don't understand that we have to resort to quite drastic measures, and those crippled by their conscience, they should just stay away. It's better that a few innocents die than that even a single guilty person get away."[31] On the day of Schulze's speech, the *Freikorps* shot twelve prisoners they took at the Hofbräuhaus in the district Perlach without any formal arrests or trials. The impunity suggested by Schulze's speech seems to have been widespread, not only in the often far-right *Freikorps* but also among the regular German federal army troops (the "Prussians," as they were popularly known). In fact, one of the soldiers involved in the brutal killings in the basement at Karolinenplatz unapologetically informed his superiors, after the majority of the prisoners had been beaten to death, that his unit had shot twenty-one Spartacists.

But unlike some other victims of White Terror, the men killed in the basement at Karolinenplatz had not been Red Guardists or even sympathizers with the revolution. They were members of a Catholic journeymen's society; their killings were not just "excesses" but mistakes. They were nineteen to twenty-six years old and the "sons of good families" as one survivor put it.[32] Anger at the murder and torture of the young men swirled through Munich in the next few days, with much resentment focused on the role of "Prussian troops" in the event and in the city more generally. Blaming the "foreigners" in the federal army fit with Bavarian stereotypes of Prussian brutality and into particularist narratives of Bavarian victimization at the hands of Prussia. But although some troops from Berlin and elsewhere in Germany were involved in the atrocity, there were Bavarian soldiers and local *Freikorps* in the Karolinenplatz basement as well.

The mass murders carried out by White forces altered the political opinion of many of Munich's burghers, who had previously cheered their actions uncritically. On May 5, the day before the Karolinenplatz murders, for example,

---

[29] Ibid., 41.   [30] StAM, Staatsanwalt München I, 2766/II, quoted by Hillmayr, 147.

[31] Dominick Venner, *Ein deutscher Heldenkampf. Die Geschichte der Freikorps 1918–1923*, 99, quoted in Ralf Höller, *Der Anfang der ein Ende War: Die Revolution in Bayern 1918/19* (Berlin: Aufbau, 1999).

[32] Ibid.

Mann noted in his diary "one breathes much easier under the military dictatorship than under the rule of crooks," meaning the revolutionary government.[33] Even on the morning of May 7, Mann remarked with pleasure on the presence of so many armed soldiers on the streets. He listened with satisfaction to the military band at the Feldherrnhalle, noting, "[martial] music means order."[34] Then later that afternoon he read about the murders of the Catholic journeymen and, as a result, felt the need to take a stance against the violence in the city. That evening Mann worked on an open letter for the newspapers calling for a "politics of reconciliation" that was signed by his brother Heinrich Mann and other writers living in Munich at the time of the revolution, such as the poet Rainer Maria Rilke.[35] Like many residents of the city, Rilke felt himself to be a victim of the counterrevolution after soldiers searching for the communist leader Eugen Leviné or other revolutionaries ransacked his apartment, and he left Munich soon after.

Perhaps because the Karolinenplatz murders couldn't be explained as harsh but necessary justice against revolutionaries, they stiffened the backs of people like Mann in demanding accountability from the various armed forces. Partly in reaction to the public outrage over the deaths of the Catholic journeymen, the Bavarian military commander General Arnold von Möhl issued an order on May 8 that took away the impunity described only four days earlier in Major Schulze's speech to his *Freikorps* troops. Möhl ordered that no executions be carried out without a trial and that even executions ordered by a court-martial required a ministerial signature from the government in exile in Bamberg before being implemented.[36] The brutal murders of the journeymen in Karolinenplatz and the public outrage that followed effectively ended military control over Munich and put an end to most of the random violence of the White Terror.

The murder of the twenty-one young Catholic journeymen was a turning point in the violent struggle between revolution and counterrevolution in Munich and led to a rapid de-escalation of violence in the city. But long after the suppression of physical violence, events like the Karolinenplatz murders committed by the Whites and the so-called murder of hostages by the Reds had important symbolic roles in contemporaries' understanding of this period's violence in general. One enduring assumption was the presumed causal link between the two crimes. Many later emphasized that the *Geiselmord* had led inexorably to the second, larger atrocity. Posters published by White military authorities to announce the murder of the journeymen at Karolinenplatz, began with the comment: "The rage over the *Geiselmord*, and over the tenacious and insidious resistance of the Spartacists, has led to an abhorrent crime."[37] While

---

[33] Mann, 227.   [34] Ibid., 228.
[35] Ibid., 230; see also Stadtarchiv München/ Oberbayern (StadtAMü), *Stadtkronik*, May 7, 1919.
[36] StadtAMü, *Stadtkronik*, May 8, 1919.   [37] Karl, 150.

admitting their forces had committed these murders, triumphant White authorities assigned ultimate responsibility to the defeated revolutionaries (for their earlier crime). Once the two events were linked in this self-serving manner, the resulting narrative left a legacy in which all of the violence of the period came to be associated with the revolution, rather than with its conservative opponents.

After the revolution's defeat, the German reading public had an insatiable interest in the *Geiselmord*, and a veritable library of publications was produced over the interwar period and later to meet this demand.[38] The press worked to uncover details and titillate their readers with information about the last days of the victims, heroic details of their deaths, coroner's reports, and the supposedly psychopathic character of the revolutionaries who ordered and conducted the murders. The *Münchener Neue Illustrierte*, for example, published a special "Geisel edition" after the first set of trials of the accused perpetrators in September 1919. The issue included photos of the basement at the school where the prisoners were held, the courtyard where the executions took place, the bullet-marked wall, and the dust heap where the bodies were left, with captions claiming that the photos were taken "directly after the acts."[39]

As intended, the photos and text from these publications inspired fear of communist excesses among readers. The publication also had unambiguous antisemitic content, although none of the men later convicted for the murders were Jews. The preexisting association of Jews with Russia and revolution meant that listeners to unofficial information networks readily believed rumors about the revolutionary leadership, who were portrayed as universally Jewish. To this day, Max Levien, leader of the Munich Communists is often referred to as a Jew. In fact, he was a Russian of non-Jewish Huguenot descent. A vocabulary of preexisting stereotypes, particularly the idea of "Judeo-Bolshevism," played an important role in the transmission of rumors describing the origins and key events of the Munich revolutions. This cognitive elision lent credence to many rumors – if one part of the equation could be proven or believed (Jewish, Russian, or Bolshevik/socialist identity), then the other part of the equation (cruel, greedy, violent) must be true.[40] In the wake of the revolution's defeat, these executions came to be seen as examples of a presumed "Jewish-Bolshevik" depravity, a depravity anticipated by the antisemitism already long-established in conservative circles on the right. Much

---

[38] See for example, *Der Münchener Geiselmord: Wer traegt die Schuld?* (Berlin: Der Firn, 1919); *Der Münchener Bluttat* (Berlin: Wilhelm-Wagner, 1919).

[39] *Münchener Neue Illustrierte*, "Special-Geisel-Nummer," September 29, 1919, reproduced in Rudolf Herz and Dirk Halfbrodt, *Revolution und Fotographie: München 1918/19* (Berlin: Verlag Dirk Nishen and Münchner Stadtmuseum, 1988).

[40] The Judeo-Bolshevik myth is discussed in full detail in Chapter 5.

reporting on the *Geiselmord* emphasized "depraved" aspects of the story, even when they contradicted known facts.

An anonymous exposé, *Der Münchener Geiselmord: Wer traegt die Schuld?* (The Munich *Geiselmord*: Who is responsible?), published in late 1919 by a social democratic publisher in Berlin informed its readers that "these barbaric brutalities, these unbelievable tortures and then finally the horrible deaths of these defenseless prisoners is not hard to understand when one understands the spirit that prevailed among the Red troops in the Luitpold Gymnasium."[41] That spirit was described as a "dirty bordello atmosphere." So that this "bordello atmosphere" would not be confused with the usual interest of simple soldiers in occasional visits to prostitutes, the author emphasized that the moral corruption came from the leadership. "Even in the 'higher' command posts," argued the book, "raping another comrade's lover wouldn't even affect the friendship." Sexual depravity was paired with alcohol and gluttony, "alcohol flowed in streams" in the gymnasium, and on the night before the murders there was a "champagne party." The author suggested that the Jewish Red leaders made a habit of visiting and viewing their prisoners as the culmination of various orgiastic events.[42]

The murder of the one female *Geiselmord* victim, Countess Hella von Westarp, was held up as an example of particular barbarity, both by diarists at the time of the event and in the retellings of the following years.[43] Many publications implied that either the countess or, after her murder, her corpse had been sexually violated.[44] As the coroner's report showed, this was not the case; Westarp's body had been left in a heap with the others after her death from a shot in the throat. But the rumor that she and other victims' corpses had been robbed and desecrated persisted, despite official reports to the contrary.[45]

By May 2, the coroner's report had already explained that all the unusual wounds found on the victims were the result of shots having been fired at close range. But this did little to dampen the rumors at the time and stories continued to surface even years later about abuses suffered by the prisoners before and after their deaths. Newspapers published some of the photos of the corpses taken by the court medical institute for the criminal investigation, and these enflamed public opinion. The photos showed the victims on autopsy tables, both clothed and undressed to better highlight their wounds for the public.[46]

---

[41] *Der Münchener Geiselmord*, 12; also Herz and Halfbrodt, 187.   [42] Ibid.

[43] Hofmiller, for example, found her death deplorable because, according to him, unlike the other Thule Society members she had only been formally involved with the society (as their secretary) for a few days before her arrest, 225.

[44] "Ein dünsterer Jahrtag," *Münchner Zeitung*, April 30, 1920, evening edition.

[45] See for example the May 6 press report from Oberkommando Möhl, BHSA IV, Kriegsarchiv, Höhere Stäbe, Bund 3/4.

[46] Herz and Halfbrodt, 186–7.

Westarp's body was the image most reprinted in the city's illustrated papers, although her wounds were not the most gruesome.

The image of this naked, murdered woman confirmed the worst of what conservatives had feared and expected from the communists all along. The photograph of Westarp's body resonated so deeply because it was already familiar. The vulnerable, often naked, female victim of revolutionary violence was a visual representation that people had seen many times before in political propaganda. Residents of Munich had seen just such an image hanging all over the city as recently as the January 1919 elections for the Bavarian *Landtag*. A poster for the anti-communist voting bloc, designed and printed well before either of the Munich soviet governments had been declared in April, showed a naked woman prostrate before a landscape of gravestones with the caption, "a bloody sea, an army of graves – that is bolshevism."[47] In May 1919, with the violence of the *Geiselmord* now universally recognized and the photograph of the murdered Hella von Westarp prominent on the pages of popular newspapers, the poster's prophecy seemed fulfilled.

Historical scripts, such as the common narratives attached to the murders of hostages during the Paris Commune in 1871 (an event still in recent historical memory for many in 1919), made wild rumors about hostage taking and the murder of hostages in Munich believable. Because the rumors endured far beyond the end of the revolutionary regime, sometimes reappearing in historical scholarship, iconic images and symbolic vocabulary had a significant effect on popular views of the events of 1919. Labels like Bolshevik, once attached to an event, often made a connection between local events and the world historical drama of revolution. This was also true of the word *Geiselmord* itself once it was fully identified with the narrative of Red violence and Jewish culpability. The identification stuck, even though none of the ten people murdered on April 30 had been taken as a hostage. Two were the captured Prussian soldiers and the rest, with one exception, were members of the *völkisch* Germanic Thule Society, arrested for forgery and possessing illegal weapons. The final victim was Professor Ernst Berger, an artist and instructor at a Munich gymnasium. Berger was arrested after a patrol of Red Guardists saw him tearing down a poster from the revolutionary government, and his inclusion in the executions seems to have been a fatal misunderstanding. Dr. Konrad, a prisoner who survived the executions, testified at the *Geiselmord* trial that Berger had demanded to be included on the list with the Thule members, perhaps under the false impression that this group of nobles would be treated better. In any case, though his arrest and murder were tragic and criminal, he was certainly not taken prisoner as a "bourgeois hostage."

[47] Reprinted in ibid., 28.

The revolutionary government had, in fact, left Munich's middle classes largely unharmed and, with the exception of automobiles, no property was confiscated. To use the vocabulary of the counterrevolution, there was no "red justice" in Munich. However, the specter of hostage taking had spread terror among the middle classes long before the event. One of the most broadly circulated rumors at the time and long afterward was that Eglhofer had ordered all of Munich's burghers who were held as hostages to be shot during the battle with the White forces.[48] Application of the words "murder of hostages" to the events at the Luitpold Gymnasium united its victims with the general population, reminding the burghers of their long-held fears as well as the actual dangers they had faced.

The majority of the *Geiselmord* victims, members of the antisemitic Thule Society, had a complicated symbolic role as victims of Red Terror. They were first portrayed as victims of class warfare but, years later in altered political circumstances, they were reinvented as early martyred heroes of National Socialism, with which they shared their "Germanic" swastika symbol and antisemitic ideology. In initial reports of the murders, however, the Thule members were portrayed as innocent "hostages" and their society referred to as a "study group for old Germandom." The police report on the identities of these victims, written in the immediate aftermath of the event, stated that in several cases the deceased "was an antisemite," or that the "ground for [the prisoner's original] arrest was membership in the so-called Thule Society."[49]

Though all the victims were portrayed as innocents, as apolitical hostages, in the case of Countess Westarp, most published examinations of the *Geiselmord* used her gender and her class to emphasize the horror of the murders. From this perspective, Red forces had brutally murdered an innocent woman. In the police file produced during the inquiry into her murder, authorities indicated her prior political activity and active membership in the Thule Society, as well as her employment as its secretary. Her landlord testified to the police that she was a known "antisemite who had made derisive remarks about Jews." Despite evidence of her active political participation during the counterrevolution, the police report concluded that "it is unlikely that she had participated in any of the counterrevolutionary activities, [since] she was too naïve."[50] Westarp was more understandable as a victim embodying the horrors of the Red Terror when viewed as a representative of her gender, age, and class – a young noblewoman. This portrayal of her as a defenseless female victim proved more compelling and enduring than the actual political realities of her life as a right-wing activist and conspirator.

---

[48] See Mann; Hofmiller ; and Ernst Müller-Meiningen, *Aus Bayerns schwersten Tagen: Erinnerungen und Betrachtungen aus der Revolutionszeit* (Berlin: Walter de Gruyter, 1924).

[49] StAM Pol. Dir. 10014, "Berger, Ernst," Betreff: Geiselmord im Luitpoldgymnasium.

[50] Ibid.

In 1919, all of the Thule victims of the Red firing squad were portrayed in Munich newspaper reports as martyrs of class warfare, "bourgeois hostages," not prisoners arrested as antisemitic or counterrevolutionary militants. As a group of mostly titled nobles, their deaths seemed to symbolize iconoclastic revolutionary violence, like the persecution and guillotining of nobles in the French Revolution. In addition to the Countess Westarp, the victims of the *Geiselmord* comprised a prince of Thurn and Taxis, a baron, and another noble.

However, after the Nazi takeover in 1933, the symbolic significance of the Thule Society victims grew. They were perceived not as innocent victims of class warfare but specifically as martyrs to a German antisemitic ideology who died for their beliefs. A 1933 book on the antisemitic Germanic orders was dedicated to the Thule members "martyred" in 1919: "Now [after Hitler's seizure of power] . . . it no longer needs to be concealed that those seven Thule members did not die as hostages . . . rather they were murdered because they were antisemites. They died for the swastika, were sacrificed to Juda."[51] Indeed, throughout the 1930s, there were annual memorial events in Munich dedicated to the victims of the *Geiselmord* held by local Nazi groups. These public stagings of this controversial event served the double purpose of recalling and memorializing the Nazi avant-garde and reminding the city's bourgeoisie of the terrors of Bolshevism, a set of associations that tended to obfuscate any bourgeois fears about the terrors of Nazism.

In 1919, nothing was spared by the reinstated Bavarian government in the investigation and prosecution of the *Geiselmord*. Justice Minister Ernst Müller-Meiningen allocated 30,000 Marks for a special investigation into the *Geiselmord* in September, before the trials, so that, in his words, the public would not forget these "Bolshevik crimes." The trials were held in September and October; the two Red commanders at the Luitpold Gymnasium, Johann Schicklhofer and Fritz Seidel, were sentenced to death, as were four Red Guardists who participated in the executions. The final results of the three trials were a total of eight court-ordered executions. Ten other men received sentences of fifteen years' imprisonment, and one a sentence of seven years. Another Red commander, Willi Haußmann, had committed suicide immediately following the shootings on the evening of April 30, and Eglhofer was murdered in police custody before the trials. By the end of this messy process, a total of ten of the men responsible for the *Geiselmord* had paid for their actions with their own lives.[52]

Contemporary methods of identification and policing then in common use played powerful roles in these events. Some of the arrests and prosecutions

---

[51] Rudolf von Sebottendorf, *Bevor Hitler kam: Urkundliches aus der Frühzeit der nationalsozialistischen Bewegung* (Munich: Deukula Verlag Graffinger, 1933), dedication.

[52] StAM Pol. Dir. 677, "Geiselmord Prozeß: Protokoll."

depended heavily on biographical information, in the absence of fingerprints or other forensic tools. One example of this is the way Fritz Seidel's name was used to pull others into the investigation. The family name Seidel (or Seidl) is common in Bavaria. In addition to the Red military commander Fritz Seidel, one of the Red Guardists sentenced by the court for his role in the executions was Josef Seidel. A Karl Seidl was also arrested and interrogated when authorities discovered that he had been at the Luitpold Gymnasium at the time of the *Geiselmord*.[53] Both of these men were originally arrested as the police searched for Fritz Seidel, not on the basis of direct denunciations of them as individuals. However, the questioning that cleared up the mistaken identity (that they were not Fritz Seidel) led to the discovery that each had been at the Luitpold Gymnasium and may have also been involved in the executions.

The White soldiers who were responsible for guarding Eglhofer at the former royal residence planned his murder on May 3. Their planning is what distinguishes this event from the wild and unplanned murders on May 6 of the Catholic journeymen. Several witnesses, including an ambulance worker and the palace superintendent, testified that they heard officers assigned to guard Eglhofer swear that he would not leave the palace alive. The murder was a calculated decision by these soldiers to "sentence" Eglhofer themselves rather than give him over to civil or judicial authorities. It was not a case of "unfortunate excess" due to "excited emotions," as other murders by White troops – such as those of the Russian POWs, the Catholic journeymen, or the prisoners from the Perlach Hofbrauhaus – were often described in military briefings.[54] The typed report retained in Eglhofer's police file states that he "was killed" on May 3, but these words are crossed out and replaced with the handwritten statement, "shot while trying to escape."[55] We can safely presume that Eglhofer's death was planned in response to the rumors and reports that associated him with the *Geiselmord*. It was, therefore, a premeditated act by soldiers who did not trust the recently created judicial authorities to sentence with sufficient harshness what these White soldiers saw as Red political criminals.

The soldiers may have assessed correctly what Eglhofer's likely fate would have been before a court. Even in the later *Geiselmord* trials, Eglhofer's role in the murders could not be definitively proven. Immediately after the ten executions carried out by Red soldiers were made public in Munich on April 30, Eglhofer joined other communist leaders in the proclamation denouncing them. It was also true that several forged stamps with Eglhofer's signature were known to exist; in fact, one had been found in the Thule Society headquarters

---

[53] StAM Pol. Dir. 10151, "Fritz Seidel."

[54] See for example the report "Ehrfahrungen bei der Operation gegen München," May 21, 1919; BHSA IV, Kriegsarchiv, Höhere Stäbe Bund 3/2.

[55] StAM Pol. Dir. 10040, 23, "Rädelsfuehrer zur Zeit der Räteregierung in München."

at the Four Seasons Hotel. This forged stamp had ironically been part of the grounds for the arrest of the Thule members. Both Eglhofer and his posthumous supporters argued that the written orders had been a forgery. But from testimony at the trials, we know that many people saw and read the slip of paper with the order to shoot the hostages and all of them believed it to be authentic at the time, including the two Red Guardists who carried the note from police headquarters over to the Luitpold Gymnasim and several soldiers who were recruited for the firing squads but demanded proof of the order before agreeing to serve.[56] The paper itself was lost or destroyed when the Red forces abandoned the school the next day, and so at the *Geiselmord* trials the authenticity of Eglhofer's signature could not be proven. What was clear, however, was that many people read the paper that morning, and all believed it to be a direct order from Eglhofer, the commander of all Red forces. Eglhofer's authority was understood to be behind the order, but the court may not have been able to establish his guilt.

Descriptions of property loss give another example of the power of revolutionary vocabulary to shape perceptions of the Munich events. During the weeks of revolutionary government, many Munich burghers waited in fear of what they were sure would be the inevitable Marxist attack on their property, through confiscation or expropriation, as their diaries and memoirs attest. Yet in 1919, the actual loss of property in Munich was limited to the damage caused by the fighting in the first week of May. It was the White troops who brought heavy artillery to bear on the city, including the use of incendiary ammunition. Following the White victory, many Munich residents, as well as politicians and commentators, applied the costs for nearly all the damages experienced by the city to the account of the revolution. This calculation, once in place, seemed to demonstrate the destructive costs of the soviet experiment. For postrevolutionary Munich, the destruction of private property was viewed as a confirmation of Red Terror. The government commission created by the *Landtag* to assess damages and hear appeals for restitution was named, as a result, the "Committee for the Restitution of Revolutionary Losses."

Photographic postcards disseminated in the wake of the White victory confirm the success of this effort to attach the material and human costs of this conflict to the Red government and its defenders. The archives in Munich contain thousands of postcards and photos of ransacked offices, damaged buildings, and the bodies of victims of the violence. By 1919 the advance of photographic technology enabled the use of powerful visual images that could make the connection between destruction and revolution. Many surviving examples of these postcards from Munich retain the written comments of

---

[56] Karl Seidl (one of those arrested because of his name) argued in his defense that he had demanded to see the orders to shoot prisoners.

Figure 3.1 Freikorps Görlitz on Goethestrasse, Munich, May 1919.
Source: Photo by Heinrich Hoffmann via Universal History Archive/Getty
Images. Bayerische Staatsbibliothek, Bildarchiv.

residents confirming the horrors of the revolution. Most had been sent by
residents to friends and relatives as proof of Munich's suffering.[57]

Because of the seemingly authentic, documentary character of the photographs, these postcards seemed to offer objective evidence about the consequences of revolution. Yet the photographs themselves were often fakes or
were published with misleading captions. Many photos claiming to show the
"capture of Munich" that were published in books or printed as postcards were
actually staged after the fighting was over, with government soldiers standing
in for "Reds."[58] Photographs and physical descriptions of participants in the
revolutions, often manipulated for antisemitic effect, served as references to
a stock of stereotypes, especially those of "Judeo-Bolshevism" and "Red
Terror," with which the viewer was already familiar.

Many photos and postcards showed the physical destruction that occurred at
the hands of White forces as they advanced on the city but were given captions
that claimed that the damage had been caused by the revolutionary government

[57] Several photos that are included in the catalog to an exhibit at the Munich city museum vividly
demonstrate the way photography was politically manipulated in the production of images of
revolution. Photos of the damage done to buildings in Munich in the fighting were labeled and
cropped for the greatest effect; Herz and Halfbrodt, 194.
[58] Ibid.

Figure 3.2 Damage to Mathäser Brewery caused by incendiary artillery,
May 1919.
Source: Ullstein Bild via Getty Images.

or the Red Army. Among the most widely circulated were postcards showing
serious damage to the Mathäser Brewery, which caught fire as a result of artillery
fire from government forces, not the Red Army (Figure 3.2). Another postcard
seemed to show the mangled corpses of animals killed by "revolutionary barbarism" but in reality displayed the contents of a taxidermist's office hit by a shell.[59]

Despite the fact that the Mathäser Brewery, the city's largest brewery, suffered
massive damage, the city's Brewers Union was among the many groups that wrote
to General Möhl, as commander of the White forces, expressing their thanks "to all
of those who participated in this redemptive liberation."[60] "In the last hour," they
continued, using a metaphor wonderfully suited to their profession, "before the
Bavarian capital was forced to drain the bitter cup of the Bolshevik reign of terror,
the Bavarian and federal forces freed our beloved Munich from the blind rage of
terror and saved Bavaria from the flood of Bolshevism."[61] The letter, written on
May 23, attempted to persuade Möhl to keep troops in the city to prevent any
revival of revolutionary activities. They claimed that the city was not yet quiet and
that troops should remain to secure law and order.

[59] Ibid., 194.   [60] BHSA IV, Kriegsarchiv, Höhere Stäbe, Bund 3/2.   [61] Ibid.

The Munich brewers were not alone in their lingering fears of a Spartacist revival. Many middle-class residents feared the revolution could be renewed if not kept in check by the continued presence of the armed counterrevolutionary forces. Yet by mid-May, according to the military's own records, almost all of the shooting and disturbances in Munich were being caused by the government's own "nervous soldiers." An army report on May 25 complained about troop behavior, stating that "the citizens of Munich are still being disturbed by reports of shots fired in the night, but explanations for the shooting are not reported." Soldiers and guards were, therefore, asked to "account for every bullet fired and to give a report of any shootings."[62] Rather than being grounds for ending the military occupation, the fact that the White forces were still shooting inside the city at the end of May kept the citizens of Munich "nervous," and encouraged them to ask the military to stay longer.

The cycle of fear was fueled not only by the continued sound of gunfire from occupying troops in the streets of Munich but also by a steady stream of vicious rumors and denunciations. To return to the metaphor of the black market, if rumors are goods, then we need to know who produced them and who profited from their circulation. As historians, we encounter rumors in a variety of sources: police and military reports, diaries, memoirs, and court documents, among others. Unlike some other historical records, rumors can seldom be traced back to a specific author or source. It is easiest to detect authorship in rumors that seem to serve a narrow personal objective or to reflect an identifiable grievance. Contemporaries were justly suspicious of such cases of personal and malicious attacks. In some cases, the author of a rumor was identified as the result of a police investigation or legal action. In Munich there were many cases of anonymous denunciations or intentional misrepresentations given to the authorities that were later investigated by the police or courts. One woman in Schwabing, for example, posted a declaration to her neighbors "to protect myself from further slander and wild rumors," offering proof from the authorities that they had searched her apartment and found nothing incriminating and threatening one neighbor with a lawsuit if he "doesn't stop spreading outrageous gossip" about her and her daughter's morality and political affiliations.[63] This atmosphere, in which individuals felt themselves under suspicion by their neighbors and compelled to offer public proclamations of their political (and moral) reliability, was one consequence of the politicization of private life and private interactions due to the 1919 revolutions.

Rumors attacking or slandering a large group are harder to track down. In the case of the rumors in Munich that blamed violence, property destruction, and

---

[62] BHSA IV, Kriegsarchiv, Höhere Stäbe, Bund 3/4, "Korpsbefehl," May 25, 1919, Generalkommando Oven.

[63] StAM, Akten der Staatsanwaltschaft, Fasz. 153, 2106/1 – "Leviné" (Ebert), 230.

shortages on the "Judeo-Bolshevik" government, the city's Jewish community sought to defend itself and refute the malicious content but with limited success. Who was behind these persistent rumors, and why couldn't they be proven incorrect? Many of them were disseminated in the antisemitic press and even the conservative press, and they were repeated years after the events, throughout the Weimar period (and even later), becoming a part of the collective European understanding of post–World War I events.

The proliferation and dissemination of rumors in revolutionary and counter-revolutionary Munich raised the level of terror and contributed to the rising levels of violence in the city, stoking antisemitism in particular. Wartime experiences made the city's residents distrustful of official information. As a result, even after the defeat of the revolution, efforts by the Jewish community or others to "set the record straight" lent further credence to rumors of Judeo-Bolshevik and other conspiracies. Similarly, the rumors about 1919 Munich both built on and reproduced the earlier scripts and stereotypes they were created out of. Their longevity and repetition added to their strength, reinforcing the same revolutionary archetypes.

At the end of April, as government troops and volunteer White militias surrounded the revolutionary city, residents were already psychologically prepared for what they assumed would be inevitable bloodshed and destruction. When the attack by White forces began, news and rumors based on both real and reported crimes were grafted on to preexisting scripts to justify acts of revenge and even criminal behavior. It was rumors of White atrocities that led the soldiers in the Luitpold Gymnasium to shoot ten of their prisoners (the *Geiselmord*). News of these murders and rumors about the desecration of corpses by Red forces then led to acts of revenge by White forces, a brutal reckoning that resulted in over 600 victims.

Oskar Maria Graf described a visit to the Ostfriedhof cemetery in Munich after the first days of fighting in May, where "the masses of working women, the bent men, girls and crying schoolchildren" searched in the piles of dead for their loved ones.[64] As Graf and the others filed past the "mangled" corpses, "the crying and moaning increased." Finally, he wrote, he couldn't stand the smell of blood and corpses and "the terrible expressions of those still searching" any longer and stepped out for fresh air. But once he was outside of the cramped cemetery, he realized that his discomfort continued. The recent violence had changed the whole city of Munich. "After I came out of the cemetery it seemed like the whole city stank of corpses."[65] For a few weeks in the spring of 1919, world revolution played out on a local stage, and Munich paid a high price in loss of life during the staging. Magnified through rampant rumors and inflammatory media reports, the narrative and language of revolutionary stereotypes

---

[64] Graf, 505–6.   [65] Ibid., 506.

created a framework in which people made decisions about who to blame and how to punish them. In Munich, the images and archetypes of a revolutionary narrative, and the expectations it aroused, had the effect of exacerbating the violence.

Rumor and Terror in Budapest

As we turn to analyze the role of revolutionary scripts in rumor and terror in Budapest, we observe how differences in historical circumstances meant that different revolutionary narratives framed the experience of Red and White Terror in Hungary. Although the Hungarian and Bavarian soviet republics were declared very close in time, at the end of March and early April respectively, the two consecutive revolutionary governments in Munich only lasted about three weeks, while the soviet in Budapest held out for 133 days. In Munich, there were certainly revolutionary changes of system, but the whole period was so brief and tumultuous that the new revolutionary institutions did not have much time to develop or exercise their functions. The entire soviet period in Bavaria was more transitional in nature than was the revolutionary experience in Hungary. In terms of the scope of the terrors, there was a parallel difference of scale in that the period of violent counterrevolution, which was confined to the first weeks of May in Munich, was drawn out for many months in Budapest and its surroundings. This meant there was more time for a real socialist revolution to be experienced in the day-to-day life of Budapest and its citizens, including more time for revolutionary justice and administration to function, constituting the Red Terror in the eyes of its critics. The feeling of being isolated and cut off from the world that diarists in Munich complained of in April lasted until August for Budapest residents. Rumors and news from battles between revolutionary and White forces in the Hungarian countryside shaped the experience and understandings of people living in the city during these long four months.[66] Though Budapest was, for the most part, spared a violent direct confrontation between Left and Right as happened when German federal troops invaded Munich on May 1, Budapest residents nevertheless suffered terror.

In Budapest, the revolutionary judicial tribunals represented the most public institution of the Hungarian soviet government during its four months of rule. They embodied the revolutionaries' claims of class justice and represented the Red Terror in the capital city. For the revolutionary regime's opponents, all of those subjected to the Red justice of the tribunals were victims of Red Terror,

---

[66] In this sense the case of Hungary is more akin to the French Revolution, where revolutionary and counterrevolutionary violence in the countryside and in Paris reinforced and spurred each other, whereas Munich may have been more similar to the Paris Commune (as contemporaries often claimed).

and the counterrevolutionary state prosecutor, Albert Váry, included all those sentenced to death in his count of 590 victims of the Red Terror.[67] The death sentences passed by these courts, which account for approximately 11 percent of the Red Terror victims cited by Váry in his 1922 book, fall into two general categories. In the first category are the political victims of a purposeful terror or class warfare, convicted for acts opposing the soviet government. In the second group are people tried and sentenced (in some cases to death) for nonpolitical crimes, some of which were related to the revolutionary situation, such as looting. We could argue that the Red courts had two functions, one revolutionary, in actually radically transforming society, and one governmental, in maintaining and protecting order. But since even in the second capacity, the order being protected was that of the new revolutionary regime, this distinction in function was only minimally recognized by counterrevolutionaries, if at all. On the other hand, both leftist Hungarians and international observers tended to call attention to the fact that despite the well-publicized political cases, most of the work of the courts was "normal" judicial business, a sign of an efficacious socialist order. In Munich, we saw how the revolutionary scripts around "hostages" shaped the *Geiselmord* and the Karolinenplatz murders. In Budapest, the familiar narrative of the Revolutionary Tribunal established in 1793 in France framed the experience of Red Terror and motivated the acts of White Terror.

The tribunals certainly provided terrifying examples of brutal revolutionary justice. These included victims who were sentenced to death by revolutionary courts for nonviolent political crimes. The bank official Géza Herczeg, for example, was arrested on June 22 in the Bazilika church.[68] He had been distributing antisemitic pamphlets "in the interest of a restoration of legal conditions," according to Váry. Unfortunately for Herczeg, Márk Féder, who had been assigned by the new authorities to watch for any anti-proletarian propaganda being disseminated at the church, was "kneeling piously among the believers." After receiving a copy of the brochure, Féder arrested Herczeg. The following day the counterrevolutionary banker was sentenced to death by a revolutionary tribunal and then executed three days later.[69] Herczeg was clearly a victim of Red Terror; his arrest and execution for the distribution of propaganda was intended to terrify the regime's opponents and make affiliation with the counterrevolution itself a criminal activity. For the regime's opponents, his death was a symbol. Cecile Tormay wrote in her *Outlaw's Diary* about Herczeg's death: "So a Hungarian has died because he distributed bills inciting his compatriots to rebel against the Jewish terror."[70]

It is probably not surprising that after the counterrevolutionary victory, the courts established by the triumphant White forces pursued a mirror course of

---

[67] Váry.   [68] Ibid., 11.   [69] Ibid., 11.   [70] Tormay, *An Outlaw's Diary*, vol. 2, 167 and 171.

political justice, seeking out and brutally punishing captured revolutionary officials. As Váry reported, the four judges who issued the death sentence for Herczeg were later sent to be tried by the Budapest criminal court established by the victorious Whites in June 1920. One of the four revolutionary jurists, Lajos Schreier, escaped capture. One of the three brought before the White court was sentenced to death and executed. The other two received sentences of life imprisonment and fifteen years' imprisonment.[71]

Not all the cases tried in the tribunals fit clearly into the characterization of Red Terror. In other cases, the courts of the Hungarian soviet government worked to create order rather suppress their opponents through terror. In these more common cases, the courts fulfilled the function of preserving law and order and represented the face of official governmental authority. On May 3, 1919, the "terrorist," meaning a member of one of the Red revolutionary armed groups, Géza Nemes, was sentenced to death as punishment for plundering by the same Budapest revolutionary tribunal that later sentenced the banker Herczeg. Even though he was a member of one of the soviet governments' own militias, Nemes was publicly executed in Parliament Square on the same day as his conviction.[72] Nemes and three associates had reportedly gone with a group of Red "terrorists" (Váry's term) to Budafok at the end of April, and had remained behind in order to rob and steal. The revolutionary court sentenced them as plunderers. In this case, the Red judges who sentenced Nemes to death received relatively light sentences of two and three years in prison from the counterrevolutionary tribunal that tried them later.[73] This lighter sentencing demonstrates that although all actions of the revolutionary courts were judged as "criminal" by the successor counterrevolutionary courts, these same authorities nonetheless recognized the imperative of keeping order and enforcing military discipline within the ranks of even Red forces and institutions and therefore gave more lenient sentences in these cases.

Several contemporary observers provide evidence that the newly installed revolutionary courts attempted to maintain law and order. On May 6, three days after Nemes was executed by firing squad on Parliament Square for plundering, the Prussian Consul General in Budapest filed a report to Berlin acknowledging the efforts of the revolutionary government to keep order and prevent general lawlessness, especially in the capital: "The council government has in fact taken specific measures in the last few days which demonstrate that they are serious about using all their energy to protect the population from the rioting mob and from Red Guard deserters from the front who are surely just waiting

---

[71] Váry, 11.   [72] Ibid.

[73] In the case of the revolutionary judge Izidor Rózsa, however, his sentencing three days later to life imprisonment for his guilt in the Herczeg case essentially nullified the light sentence of two years handed down in the Nemes case.

for the opportunity to plunder at will."[74] He continued, arguing that thanks to these "energetic measures" of the revolutionary government, public order, certainly in Budapest had not been "seriously disturbed." The consul apparently felt the need to contradict the wild stories circulating abroad about the situation in revolutionary Hungary. "All the rumors spread abroad about the plundering and murders that supposedly have taken place do not represent the facts here," he averred.[75] Some journalists and representatives of foreign governments echoed this impression of "surprising" calm in the Hungarian capital. A September 1919 issue of the American weekly *Literary Digest* included an article entitled, "A Non-Terrifying View of the Bolsheviki in Budapest," published somewhat belatedly after the regime's collapse in August.[76] Of course, for every one such "non-terrifying view," there were many more "terrifying" reports published in the international press.

Despite the horror stories of "Red Budapest" that circulated across Europe, the situation in the capital remained, as the Prussian consul reported, relatively calm throughout both the revolution and the counterrevolution. Budapest in 1919 was the populous capital of a small nation of roughly 7.9 million. The city's population of over a million residents had been swollen by refugees from wartime violence and then later from the territories transferred to neighboring states by the peace agreements. The fact that only 34 of the 590 victims of Red Terror identified by Váry, including the two cases described above, were killed in Budapest suggests the city's minor role in the political violence of the *tanácsköztársaság* (soviet republic). This was true for violence during the counterrevolutionary period as well.

Thus, the role of Budapest in the traumatic events of 1919 was, strangely, both central and peripheral. Political events in Budapest drove both the October and the March revolutions, but the battle for control of the country was largely fought elsewhere. As a result, the majority of those who lost their lives in the conflict lost them outside the capital. As we have seen, there was not the sort of direct confrontation between Red and White forces in Budapest as happened in Munich on May 1, 1919. But in other ways, Budapest was central to popular perceptions of the revolutionary events held by Hungarians. It was the political and intellectual center of Hungary. As such it hosted the national press as well as most international observers. It was where information about the violence everywhere in the country was digested and then disseminated. Pamphlets and reports on revolutionary Hungary were much more likely to be produced in the city and to bear titles such as "In Red Budapest" than to be written about the

---

[74] Bundesarchiv (BA), Berlin, Germany, Microfilm 53411, Bd. 6, Presse u. Propaganda Angelegenheiten, "Informatorische Aufzeichnung Nr. 23, General Konsulat Budapest, May 6, 1919."
[75] Ibid.
[76] "A Non-terrifying View of the Bolsheviki in Budapest," *Literary Digest*, September 27, 1919.

places where most of Váry's list of victims actually lost their lives.[77] Therefore, the citizens of Budapest may have suffered from a surplus of alarmist and propagandistic information that increased their feelings of terror under both the revolutionary and the counterrevolutionary regimes, even though the city's residents were seldom directly threatened by the violence.

Because the cycles of political violence in Budapest were unpredictable and episodic, residents never knew when the dreaded confrontations between Red and White, or between the "classes," would take place. News of every execution or murder was, therefore, understood as the potential opening of an era of cataclysmic violence. Intensifying cycles of Red and White violence and retribution were routinely inflated as they were disseminated by rumor, keeping alive the sense of terror in Budapest. While the frightened population's worst fears were never realized, Budapest did experience some casualties from political conflict, as during the attempted coup on June 24.

The majority of deaths that occurred in the capital during the revolution happened in the attempted overthrow of the revolutionary government on June 24, 1919. Fourteen people died in Budapest on that day alone, and the deaths of three others can be tied to either arrests that followed or to the atmosphere of fear and retribution that still pervaded the city on June 25.[78] The execution of Herczeg described above, for example, was actually ordered by the revolutionary court on June 24 in the midst of the attempted overthrow, although he was arrested earlier. Similarly, the murder of financial administrator Géza Taubinger on June 25 was related to the counterrevolutionary rising, though he was not directly involved in the attempted coup. He was shot by two Red soldiers for having "bourgeois jowls," according to Váry, an unusual example of class violence for the capital city, and an event most likely sparked by the atmosphere of fear and rumor during the fighting that day. Even cases of apparently random or spontaneous violence were often driven by a crisis like the June counterrevolution.

Before the June 24 revolt, the revolutionary government had faced increasing dissatisfaction among both workers and peasants. It also faced uprisings in the Hungarian countryside, especially along the Danube river, where conflict began on June 18. The suppression of these anti-soviet revolts was responsible for a large percentage of the political victims outside the capital identified in Váry's lists of victims of the Red Terror. The uprising in Budapest began while

[77] The title is from Eugen Szatmari, *Im Roten Budapest* (Berlin: Kulturliga, 1919).

[78] In total, thirty of the thirty-four deaths in Budapest during the revolutionary period took place in only three incidents. In addition to the seventeen deaths on June 24/25, there were two other periods that involved significant fatalities. Nine deaths occurred between April 19 and 23. Then on May 2 and 3, after the announcement of hostilities with the Romanian Army, four more people died in violence in Budapest. It is interesting to note here that even the judicial executions discussed above, of Herczeg and Nemes, fit into these totals, since Nemes was executed on May 3 and Herczeg on June 25.

the National Congress of Soviets was convened. On June 24, cadets of the Ludovika military academy took over the telephone exchange. In coordinated attacks, shots were fired by some disaffected military units quartered in the city and from a gunship on the Danube that targeted the Soviet Congress. Despite the participation of trained military units, revolutionary authorities succeeded in putting down the revolt by early in the morning of June 25.

As a response to what had been a well-planned and coordinated attack, the Central Executive Committee passed a resolution on June 25 calling for "exemplary punishment and increased powers for the security organs."[79] However, as historian Tibor Hajdu has noted, "the resolution passed showed determination but not even the sentences of the court of summary jurisdiction were carried out."[80] Even in this moment of class conflict in the capital, revolutionary justice was seldom lethal.

In the wake of the June 24 uprising and with increasing counterrevolutionary activity in the countryside, many Budapest residents anticipated what they assumed would be an inevitable violent confrontation between the *tanácsköztársaság* government and the White forces assembling under Miklós Horthy and the so-called Szeged government. For the citizens of Budapest, both news of the Romanian occupation of Hungarian territory up to the Tisza river and the successes of Horthy's forces in recruiting seemed to suggest that their city would soon be a battlefield. News of the White Terror, and the anti-Jewish violence of the White battalions in areas under their control, arrived in the capital and increased the level of anxiety for many Budapest citizens. The White Terror was directed in particular against Jews, and the specter of pogrom hung over Budapest's large Jewish population.[81]

The pattern described here for the revolutionary violence – mostly occurring outside the capital but terrifying to Budapest residents nonetheless – also held true for the counterrevolution as well. Nonetheless, reports submitted by refugees to the Pest Jewish community, the American Jewish relief agency, the Joint Distribution Committee (JDC), the British Labour commission, and Jewish organizations in Vienna give evidence of an atmosphere of threat and harassment faced by Jews in the capital city. People were stopped on the street and asked to identify themselves by religion. Julius Goldman, the European Director General of the JDC, sent a confidential report on the White Terror and pogroms in Hungary back to JDC Chairman Felix Warburg after a visit to Budapest in April 1920. Describing the situation in autumn 1919, after the departure of the Romanian troops, Goldman summarized, "Anti-Semitism became rabid, pogroms of the most mediaeval character were inaugurated – Jews throughout the country were killed by the hundreds and the remaining

---

[79] Tibor Hajdu, *The Hungarian Soviet Republic* (Budapest: Akadémiai Kiadó, 1979), 149.
[80] Ibid.   [81] The anti-Jewish violence is discussed more fully in Chapter 5.

ones fled from the country towns to Budapest in the hope that they would be safer there than in the country."[82] This influx of rural Jews to Budapest intensified the feeling of terror, both because of the horrors they were fleeing and reporting and because of fears that the refugee influx might increase antisemitism in the capital itself. Goldman wrote that in April 1920 even in Budapest, "No Jew, however prominent he might be, ventured even at the time I was in Budapest on the streets after dark and I was warned not to go out in the evening unless by automobile."[83] Goldman seems to have worried that the stories of Jewish persecution from Hungary might seem overstated, and says that, originally, "I was inclined to look upon the statements made to me as exaggerations." But his own experience of the fear of violence and supposed political retribution that hung over the Jews of Budapest left him reassuring Warburg that "All of this was vouched for to me by the most distinguished Jews of Budapest and I can speak from my own experience that the terror was so great, as to prevent any Jew, except with bated breath, to speak of the existing conditions." Vouching for the reports of the Pest Jewish community, he says, "Nothing I have heard can be looked upon as exaggerations and as being described in darker colors than actual conditions warrant."[84] In addition to the constant threat of harassment on the street reported by Goldman, once brought in for questioning by police or militia members, Jews were attacked with the antisemitic libel of revolutionary responsibility, versions of the myth of "Judeo-Bolshevism."

In late 1919 and in 1920, after the flight of the *tanácsköztársaság* government, Budapest was full of tangible reminders of the threat of anti-Jewish violence. In February 1920, an antisemitic and nationalist crowd destroyed the offices of the socialist newspaper *Népszava*. White militia members lynched the paper's Jewish editor, Béla Somogyi, and the reporter Béla Bacsó, whose bodies were thrown into the Danube. Between the corpses in the river and the destroyed newspaper office (Figure 3.3), this notorious attack confirmed the sense of Jews being helpless before these uncontrolled antisemitic forces. From the banners and insignia of the ÉME and MOVE to the sensationalist publications on all the newsstands, Jews in the capital moved in a space full of visual danger signals. Alongside the sharply censored daily papers, appeared cheap, five-korona flyers with titles like "The Terror," purporting to reveal the crimes of the revolutionary government.[85] All of this combined to make Budapest feel

---

[82] Letter, Julius Goldman to Felix Warburg, April 13, 1920, JDC-NY Collection 1919–1921, file # 148 [Hungary, General, 1919–1920], p. 144.

[83] Ibid.   [84] Ibid.

[85] One example, written by the leftist writer Vilmos Tarján, and with a foreword by another leftist, László Fényes, was nonetheless illustrated on the cover with a graphically antisemitic drawing of the "Red terrorist" Otto Korvin. Vilmos Tarján, *A Terror* (Budapest, 1919).

Figure 3.3 Destruction of the *Népszava* offices, February 1920.
Source: Bettmann via Getty Images.

very unsafe, despite the relatively low numbers of victims of the White Terror in the capital city.

By all accounts, counterrevolutionary violence was worst in the Hungarian countryside. Because of the Entente-ordered Romanian occupation of Budapest in August 1919, Horthy's National Army was only allowed by the Entente to enter Budapest in late November 1919. As a result, the city was saved from the feared armed confrontation between the forces of Left and Right in the streets. Budapest was not subjected to weeks of sporadic artillery and rifle fire as in Munich in the first weeks of May. Nor was it the scene of street fighting or wild shootings by soldiers as had happened in Munich. Nevertheless, the citizens of Budapest did not entirely escape from the horrors of civil violence. Hundreds of residents were arrested. Many were mistreated by the police in police stations and prisons, and many were deported to the large prison camps established elsewhere in the country, such as the one at Hajmáskér. Some of those incarcerated never returned, while others sustained serious physical and psychological injuries. Gangs of youths from right-wing organizations such as the ÉME and MOVE harassed people, especially Jews, on the streets and in cafes. The police themselves detained and questioned many with known leftist sympathies. To many residents it seemed that there was no protection from these vigilante gangs. Goldman, for example, was told that though the Hungarian government "while in the main imbued with the same spirit of anti-semitism prevailing in the military circles, does not look with favor upon the acts of barbarism perpetrated by officers and soldiers – nevertheless it is powerless to prevent such occurrences."[86] This interpretation of the relationship between government authority and right-wing violence, offered by the Budapest Jewish community to the JDC in 1920, is one that has largely been confirmed by historians evaluating in particular the responsibility of Regent Miklós Horthy himself for the paramilitary violence.[87] Horthy and his political allies did share many of the antisemitic prejudices of the militiamen, and especially the idea of Jewish responsibility for the revolutions. It also seems that the militia violence was outside of the command or control of the official government, at least in the year or so following the counterrevolution.

An atmosphere of intolerance for any criticism of the new counterrevolutionary government meant that many victims of abuse or illegal imprisonment by government officials or paramilitary groups feared to bring their complaints to the authorities. Press censorship was severe; already in August and September 1919 the Romanian military authorities prohibited the publication of even the major bourgeois liberal papers.[88] On September 10, 1919, the Friedrich government passed a decree that extended the wartime control over the press, ordering "the delivery and destruction of publications endangering public order and security."[89] When the Romanian occupation army withdrew from Budapest on November 1, martial law was implemented, a curfew was established, and telephone service was discontinued. The chief of police issued a decree that was published on posters all over the city. It announced: "it is a capital crime to violate the law by trying to restore the past bloody reign of terror by spoken or written word."[90] Under these conditions, it was difficult to collect information about atrocities the White forces had committed as under the new decree reporting White violence might come dangerously close to voicing support for their opponents, the revolutionary government, which was a capital crime. And the order also made it almost impossible for the press to inform the public about such reports as did exist. It is telling that so many of the

---

[86] Goldman to Warburg, April 13, 1920, JDC-NY Collection 1919–1921, file # 148 [Hungary, General, 1919–1920], p. 144.

[87] This is the conclusion of both Sakmyster in his biography of Horthy, *Hungary's Admiral on Horseback* and Bodó, for example, "White Terror in Hungary."

[88] Pölöskei, 52.   [89] Ibid.   [90] *Pesti Hírlap,* November 15, 1919, quoted in ibid., 40.

transcripts of reports of anti-Jewish violence towards the Pest Jewish community were published abroad, in Vienna or in Britain. The lack of reliable information fed an atmosphere of fear and terror in the capital.

During the Romanian occupation in August and September, as the counter-revolution raged in the Hungarian countryside, the complaints office of the Pest Jewish community recorded testimony about the White Terror from witnesses under oath. Jewish community officials then filed the reports with government agencies. Those testifying took great pains to differentiate between the actions of local authorities, who often attempted to maintain order, and the White "officer brigades," the militias loosely organized under the control of Pál Prónay and Iván Hejjás, who acted lawlessly.[91] The focus of these reports was on the anti-Jewish violence, and they made clear the nonpolitical and non-leftist credentials of the majority of the victims of White Terror. The careful differentiation between types of victims and types of perpetrators seems to acknowledge that revolutionaries, some Jewish, had perhaps rightfully suffered or been victims of political revenge. But the Jewish witnesses also established that the much wider experience of antisemitic violence in Budapest and in the countryside had not, in most cases, resulted from the Jewish victims having any direct participation in the revolutionary government and that the violence had been perpetrated by antisemitic paramilitary groups acting outside of, but tolerated by, government authorities.

Many testimonies by Hungarian Jews to the Pest Jewish community about violence they had witnessed were assembled by Josef Halmi for the 1922 book *Martyrium: Ein jüdisches Jahrbuch* (Martyrium: A Jewish yearbook) published in Vienna by Jakob Krausz. The book presented documentation of postwar anti-Jewish violence in Poland and Hungary as the latest example of the historical suffering of Jews in the diaspora. The very first report in the collection, given on September 10 by the merchant Salomon Weingarten in Budapest, is paradigmatic of many of the reports and their efforts to both document anti-Jewish attacks and defend the victims against the slander of Judeo-Bolshevism and accusations of political crimes. Weingarten reported that his brother-in-law Simon Fischl was dragged out of the synagogue in Gyönk in Tolna county when an armed soldier entered the building during Sabbath prayer services. Fischl was then held prisoner in the community meeting house, where he was apparently shot and killed several hours later. Weingarten reported, "my brother-in-law played no role during the entire Commune, and he himself only suffered under communism. He was accused of agitating the peasants against conscription [into the counterrevolutionary

---

[91] Though it seems oxymoronic, the term "officer brigades" was often used for these groups since they were not military units with soldiers serving under officers but rather militias made up mostly of former officers of the Habsburg Army as well as others who had been promoted or promoted themselves into various officer ranks.

National Army]." Weingarten protested that this accusation could "only be the result of some sort of intrigue," as Fischl "himself was among the first to answer the call for conscripts."[92] This report establishes a pattern: after describing the extrajudicial killing of his brother-in-law, the witness immediately answered what must have been the obvious questions for the time – had the brother actually played a role in the revolution? Was he in some way guilty to have been a target of the counterrevolutionaries? The depositions that follow Weingarten's in *Martyrium* take similar pains to separate Jewish victims from accusations of revolutionary activities.

Just as Weingarten's testimony outlined a discursive explanatory pattern of defending Jewish victims from accusations of revolutionary crimes, even in its brevity it followed another pattern in witness accounts. First, the violence in these narratives often appears suddenly, most often with the arrival of a White officers' detachment. When paramilitary brigades or sometimes groups of National Army soldiers arrived in a town, they ordered a mass meeting and then led groups of local people as they sought out and lynched local Jews. In the testimonies, the "officers" are often unknown, or only the infamous Prónay and Hejjás were named. But the witnesses often named neighbors and townspeople who joined the antisemitic mobs. Officers and local activists then removed Jews from the local counterrevolutionary citizens' militias and other civic institutions. Jews were often dragged from their homes and businesses and most were robbed and abused. Many were murdered. The murders often followed a "people's verdict," that is, public accusations of political activity either in support of the revolutionary government or against the counterrevolution (as with the claim of hindering conscription raised against Fischl). Many Jews reported instances where members of the local population or the local police authorities tried to step in to stop attacks. In one case, the city commander from the National Army, Captain Kelényi, tried to prevent bloodshed: when news arrived that the first thirty-five officers would be joined by fifty more, Kelényi cabled to the military base requesting that the officers not be allowed to come to Dunaföldvár, "because they would only make trouble here."[93] An elderly doctor, Samuel Markus in the town of Polgárdi (near Lake Balaton), described a pogrom on December 4–5, 1919, with plundering and violent attacks on Jews. He reported that during the attacks the notary of the Jewish community telephoned the gendarmes for assistance. The commander, who Markus said "I know to be a well-meaning person," informed them that "he couldn't do anything, because of orders from higher up not to intervene against the White Guard."[94] The testimonies presented the Hungarian Jews as not only unjustly persecuted on the basis of the antisemitic myth of Judeo-

[92] Krausz, *Martyrium*, 59.   [93] Ibid., 60.   [94] Ibid., 61.

Bolshevism but also unprotected by their own government and without the sympathy of the non-Jewish population.

Vienna hosted thousands of Jewish as well as non-Jewish Hungarian refugees after the fall of the communist regime.[95] Several investigative reports were published based on the testimony of these refugees, such as one submitted by an American member of the victorious Entente's military mission in Vienna.[96] "Report of the British Joint Labour Delegation to Hungary," published in May 1920, described many cases of intimidation, physical abuse, and judicial murder that were reported to a delegation sent by the British Labour Party and Trade Union Congress to Hungary to investigate the "allegations of persecutions of the working classes in Hungary."[97]

The British Labour Party had sent its own delegation to Hungary because they were dissatisfied with the British government's White Paper issued in February 1920, in which Admiral Ernest Troubridge had reported that "life is as secure here [in Hungary] as in England," calling the Horthy regime, "a Christian government in a Christian country." The Labour delegates noted, "this conveys a false impression unless it is fully understood that in Hungary the word Christian has a definite political significance."[98] In fact, the adjective "Christian" served as a political and racial descriptor, understood by its proponents as a defense against the "Judeo-Bolshevik" threat.

The Labour delegation, which included a member of parliament, Colonel J. C. Wedgwood, conducted interviews with witnesses in both Vienna and Budapest. Because of time constraints and the irregularity of the rail service, the delegates did not travel to all the sites of reported incidents of mass violence. They did send two members to Szolnok and Abony to gather information and interview victims and government officials. Their report is one of the few detailed contemporary sources about named individual victims of the White Terror. Because it was published abroad, it also avoided the intense press censorship in Hungary that prevented open discussion of the White Terror. Like the work of Gumbel in Germany, the report was based on the testimony of witnesses and was intended to spur governmental action to uncover the truth of the allegations and put an end to the widespread miscarriage of justice.

---

[95] Böhm claimed that 10,000 people had fled the country, but many refugees returned. Several reports on the White Terror in Hungary were prepared based on information the refugees provided. These included the Jewish Martyrium collection described above as well as Josef Pogány's 1920 *Der Weiße Terror in Ungarn*. In this book, Pogány, a former member of the soviet governing council and a Red Army commander, assembled evidence of violence from a variety of witnesses and published reports (mostly noncommunist).

[96] Nathaniel Katzburg reprints parts of this report in *Hungary and the Jews: Policy and Legislation, 1920–1943* (Ramat-Gan: Bar-Ilan University Press, 1981), 39–40.

[97] British Joint Labour Delegation to Hungary, *The White Terror in Hungary: Report of the British Joint Labour Delegation to Hungary* (London: Trade Union Congress & The Labour Party, May 1920).

[98] Ibid., 24.

The report seems to have had some political effect. The threat of a boycott of Hungary and Hungarian goods by international transport workers who were outraged by the Labour report caused politicians in the Horthy government to take public steps to curb the right-wing violence. The German ambassador to Hungary reported that the threat of boycott "finally woke the government and the National Assembly from their earlier apathy and forced them in the final hour to use the full weight of their authority to reestablish order in the country."[99] This assessment may exaggerate its influence, but clearly the convincing nature of the Labour report influenced both international opinion and the actions of the Horthy government.

Two of the dozen individual cases discussed in the report involve women. Reactions to these two cases offer an especially interesting perspective on the international perception of violence in Hungary as well as on the important role that female victims played in the propaganda of both the Left and the Right. We have seen how conservative groups symbolically used the image of the only female victim of the Munich revolution, Countess Westarp, to mobilize public anger against the depravity of "Jewish Bolshevism." At the same time these political groups obscured or misrepresented her actual political activities as a member of the antisemitic and counterrevolutionary Thule Society. In the British Labour delegation's report, these two aspects in the cases of the female victims are described similarly. The treatment of these women was held up as proof of the barbarous nature of the White forces, and the possible political activities or convictions of the women were swept aside in favor of their symbolic role as the ultimate victims.

One of the women who testified to the British Labour delegation was a young Jewish woman born in Putnok. Municipal authorities had arrested her in Budapest in October 1919 and taken her to the Mozsár utca police prison, where she was repeatedly questioned "about being a Communist," and then released.[100] She was subsequently rearrested and released twice; at one point she was beaten at police headquarters for refusing to admit that she was a communist. After Horthy's entrance into Budapest, she was recognized on the street by an officer and taken again to a police station, where she was locked up and threatened if she refused to sign an admission of being a "Socialist agitator."[101]

One of the police officers even refused to give her food unless she agreed to have sexual relations with him. After this denial of food, "he visited her cell at night and violated her. Two days later he violated her again."[102] After a guard left her cell door open, the girl was able to flee to Vienna, where she was

---

[99] BA, Berlin, Germany, Microfilm 53411, Bd. 12, Deutsches Generalkonsulat für Ungarn, 94–8, letter from June 9,1920.

[100] British Joint Labour Delegation, 16.   [101] Ibid.   [102] Ibid., 16–17.

interviewed by the British delegates, who reported also, "She is enceinte through [pregnant by] the officer who violated her."[103] At a time when pregnancy out of wedlock was a matter of great social stigma, this case seems to have been included in the report in order to shock its readers with the moral consequences of the violence in Hungary. The physical brutality described by the male witnesses included in the report is of such an unbelievable level of gruesomeness (including a castration and disembowelment from kicking and stomping) that it seems the case of this young woman, the final one described in the report, is included to trump the "merely" physical cruelty of the other cases with this example of moral cruelty.

The other female victim named in the Labour report was Mrs. Sándor Hamburger, "her husband's brother a known Communist and an ex-Commissary," as the report admits. She was picked up by the military in Budapest after her husband had fled to Vienna with his brother. She and her neighbor Béla Neumann were taken to the Kelenföld barracks and subjected to bloody and humiliating torture by officers, apparently including the infamous Lieutenant Héjjas.[104] They were held there for five weeks. During this time, Hamburger's friend and neighbor Neumann had all his teeth brutally pulled out by guards and was castrated for refusing to rape her after being ordered to do so by the prison officers.

Hamburger's story seems to have made a particularly strong impression on the Labour representatives. They interviewed her twice and her case was discussed at far greater length in their report than the others. Having described the sexual torture of Hamburger and her friend, the authors protest, "Mrs. H. is a quiet, unassuming and a highly respected woman, and we were informed by all who knew her that she possessed a moral character beyond reproach. No charge was ever made against her; there has been no semblance of a trial."[105] The British Labour delegation reported that they had pursued the Hamburger case with the Hungarian government but that their attempts to "get [a response] in writing" had failed.

The only official information was provided by the state prosecutor, Váry.[106] Váry admitted to the British Labour delegation that "a body had been washed up by the Danube that was supposed to be Neumann's, and that ... he had granted facilities to the relatives for identification."[107] The official story Váry and the Hungarian government presented followed a pattern, which reappeared later as the new governments in Munich and Budapest brought prisoners associated with

---

[103] Ibid.
[104] The torture of Hamburger and Neumann was reported not only in the British Labour report but also was mentioned by other witnesses in the protocols of the Pest Jewish community and a report of the JDC on the White Terror in Hungary. As I discuss in Chapter 6, this case was also the subject of an illustration in a book by the socialist artist Mihály Biró.
[105] British Joint Labour Delegation.   [106] Váry.   [107] Ibid., 10.

the two revolutionary governments to trial. Female political prisoners were presented as morally dangerous and incontrollable. "The Hungarian government admits," according to the report, "that Mrs. Hamburger was badly beaten, but alleges that she was placed in a cell in which there was one man, and that they were found misconducting themselves. She was removed to another cell in which there was another man, and again found misconducting herself and was consequently beaten disciplinarily."[108] In other words, although it would seem that the physical violence against Mrs. Hamburger violated the social and gender norms of civilization, the behavior was explained by attacks on the victim. In Váry's portrayal, it was not the prison guards who violated civilized rules by their abuse of a woman, but rather Hamburger herself had violated the gender and sexual norms by her "misconduct," which deprived her of the usual protections afforded to women (and other prisoners) in government custody. To counter these claims, the Labour report established a counter-memory of events, which relied on and reinforced gender distinctions and expected gender protections. As the authors stressed, Mrs. Hamburg was far from being the sexually depraved and dangerous prisoner described by the government; in fact, she was a paragon of bourgeois female virtue, married with two children. After quoting from the government's cruel justifications for her brutal treatment, the Labour report's authors reemphasized their portrait of Hamburger as a moral woman, claiming that, even disregarding "the inherent improbabilities of the semi-official Government defense," it should be noted that "Mrs. Hamburger appears to be a respectable woman of good education."[109] Hamburger's portrayal as an "respectable" female victim in the report echoes the images of Countess Westarp as a victim of the Red Terror in publications in Munich. In both cases, attacks on female bodies offered proof of the danger and immorality of the other side. The depictions resonated, not only with well-known narratives about political violence but also with underlying beliefs about gender and morality. Similar images of violated women were used to spark resolve in defending the political cause of either Left or Right.

Conclusion

The effect of the violence in both Munich and Budapest was to turn the cities upside down but not only in terms of gender roles. All that had represented the city and civilization seemed to be swept away in the atmosphere of terror. The organizations upon whose functioning the citizens of the city depended suddenly appeared as a danger; the police arrested and abused without charges, neighbors denounced each other, and the rule of law was applied arbitrarily if at all.

---

[108] British Joint Labour Delegation.   [109] Ibid., 11.

While the Red and White Terror in Hungary were very different from Bavaria's experience, we have seen that Budapest, like Munich, experienced extrajudicial arrests, imprisonments, and executions that spread an atmosphere of fear. This opinion was not limited to members of the Budapest Jewish community. The German embassy in Budapest reported an atmosphere of lawlessness in the city under White control in the summer of 1920, which it blamed on the activities of the "radical-antisemitic Awakening Hungary organization" and "military detachments."[110] The violence and harassment by radical groups like these was compounded by the impunity with which they seemed to operate, making both victims and potential victims feel terrorized.

In addition to the feelings of terror, there were many real victims of the White Terror in Budapest, most prominent among them the Jewish editors of the social democratic *Népszava* newspaper, whose bodies were washed up from the Danube. But the atmosphere of lawlessness and the lack of information multiplied these deaths into the sort of terror that was transmitted to Goldman by the leaders of the Jewish community. The inability to walk safely on the street, the rumors of corpses in the Danube, all of this made Budapest, too, a city that, as Graf described Munich, "stank of corpses." The attempt to create order out of lawlessness through the trials of revolutionaries is the subject of the following chapter.

---

[110] BA, Berlin, Germany, Microfilm 53411, 12, 94–8.

4   Revolution on Trial

In the months following the defeat of the revolutionary governments in Munich and Budapest, the legal and administrative situation in the two cities was tumultuous. Hundreds of people were victims of unofficial "people's justice" in the reaction that followed the 1919 revolutions. Volunteer militias, such as the *Freikorps* and MOVE, and civilians employed violence to punish or settle accounts with those they blamed for causing the revolutions. But the period of "fair game" was relatively short in the capital cities, only one week in Munich and just over two weeks in Budapest.[1] Through decrees on May 8 and August 19, respectively, the Bavarian and Hungarian counterrevolutionary authorities reasserted the government's monopoly on the use of force by regulating the imposition of the death penalty by summary courts-martial. In each case, judicial authorities regained sole responsibility for ascertaining guilt and determining punishment for revolutionaries.

This chapter examines how the police and the courts became the main audience for competing revolutionary narratives of guilt and victimization. People wanted to punish others and rehabilitate themselves. The courts functioned both as a sounding board for narratives through which one found resonance and affected verdicts and sentencing and as a transmitter of new narratives to the public, as court verdicts seemed to be the official or "true" story of the revolutions ("a convicted criminal" is different from "an accused or acquitted" person). The transnational comparison of Budapest and Munich shows that the narrative developed in each was quite different and led to differential severity of verdicts and sentencing, with the courts in Hungary being much more punitive. This situation in turn further radicalized Hungarians on the Left and the Right in the interwar period, with "judicial terror" added to the fraught narrative of revolution and counterrevolution. In Bavaria, though memoirs such as Ernst Toller's sought to rally supporters with examples of

---

[1] The German term *Freiwild* (fair game) was often used by both perpetrators and victims to talk about the extralegal violence. As discussed in the previous chapter, violence continued in the Hungarian countryside for months, but in Budapest it was brought mostly under control by the time of Horthy's entry to the city, with the notable exceptions I analyze in this and the previous chapter.

legal mistreatment, the revolution did not play as central a role in the symbolic world of Weimar German politics and was overshadowed by much more limited events such as the January 1919 Spartacus uprising and the martyrdom during that revolt of the communist leaders Karl Liebknecht and Rosa Luxemburg.

While the decrees in May and August ended the extrajudicial situation of battlefield justice, the military authorities in charge (the Bavarian Army command in Munich and the Romanian and later National Army command in Budapest) enforced this incompletely and the protection from vigilante justice was not always apparent to the civilian populations of the two cities. Though the work of determining guilt had been turned over to the courts officially, several circumstances contributed to an atmosphere where arbitrary justice continued at the hands of nongovernmental groups. The triumphant White governments that came to power in both cities needed time to organize new police and judicial institutions that could assume effective control. During this transition, a number of organizations and individuals continued to patrol the streets, checking documents, searching homes, and even making arrests. In addition to the official police force and the government military authorities, there were also numerous voluntary militias, such as the *Freikorps* and Munich's Civil Guard in Bavaria, and ÉME and MOVE in Hungary, all of whom continued to patrol streets, encourage denunciations, and search for fugitives. Representatives of these groups, often wearing armbands and badges with official-looking insignias, acted well beyond their official authorizations, most of which were limited to the right to patrol with or without arms outside of the military curfews in place in the cities.

Many witnesses to the counterrevolution described the intimidating and often self-enriching activities of these unofficial, self-proclaimed "forces of order." The experience of the women's rights and peace activist Constanze Hallgarten in Bavaria is illustrative. According to her friend Thomas Mann, as Hallgarten prepared to go to Zurich for the founding meeting of the Women's International League for Peace and Freedom in May 1919, "six men with machine guns visited her and questioned her about her political views, but decided she wasn't worth the trouble."[2] Though Hallgarten reported her interrogation to Mann with bravado, having your home entered and searched by armed men was a terrifying experience, especially with all the news and rumors of fatal "mistakes," like those leading to the Karolinenplatz murders. Those killings occurred on the same day as the search of Hallgarten's apartment, proof of the concrete danger many Munich residents faced. The evidence suggests that some vigilantes were merely seeking a bribe; others were using the power

---

[2] Mann, 229, entry for May 7, 1919. Mann quotes the phrase used by the armed men and related to him by Hallgarten, "aber es sei 'nicht gut Kirschenessen' mit ihr gewesen."

granted by their new armbands and weapons to bully immigrants, ethnic minorities, or people they associated with any form of leftist or progressive politics. Victims, especially those who had not actually participated in the revolutionary governments, found the experience understandably unnerving and were left with a sense of being at the mercy of political highwaymen.

In addition to the presence of nongovernmental militias and vigilante groups, denunciations were another factor that contributed to the continuation of the extrajudicial atmosphere even after the revolutionaries had been turned over to the courts. After the revolutions collapsed, letters from the citizens of Budapest and Munich flooded into the new governmental authorities and the informal militias, denouncing men and women they believed had participated in or actively supported the revolutionary governments. In most cases, they demanded the arrest of suspected communists and Spartacists, often with only suspicions or overheard phrases to back up their claims. This outpouring of denunciations contributed to a continued sense of emergency and danger while leading to the arrests of thousands of citizens in both cities. Tragically, they also led to some of the murders of the counterrevolution, such as those of the Catholic journeymen in Munich. This denunciatory atmosphere put the power of arrest into anyone's hands, and put many people at the mercy not only of the various armed groups or civic patrols but also of any angry or misinformed neighbor, acquaintance, or colleague who chose to exercise this power.[3]

Because a great number of police and military authorities – official and unofficial – were arresting and detaining people, the Hungarian and Bavarian governments' police and justice officials found it extremely difficult to interrogate prisoners in a timely manner, or sometimes even to locate those who had been detained. The result was a nearly insurmountable backlog in resolving criminal cases associated with the revolutionary period and releasing those who had been mistakenly detained. In Munich and Budapest, many hundreds of prisoners were kept in overcrowded and poorly equipped prisons and camps for weeks without the opportunity to hear the charges against them, defend themselves, or speak to their families or a legal counsel. As jails overflowed, the newly installed Hungarian authorities were forced to transfer prisoners from

---

[3] Jan Gross calls this the "privatization of the public domain" in his article on the Soviet occupation of eastern Poland after the Hitler–Stalin Pact, "A Note on the Nature of Soviet Totalitarianism," *Soviet Studies* 34/3 (July 1982): 367–76. Gross argued this formed an important characteristic of totalitarianism, but this function of denunciation applies much more broadly to circumstances in which denunciations have or appear to have the ear of the authorities. See Peter Holquist, "'Information is the Alpha and Omega of Our Work': Bolshevik Surveillance in its Pan-European Perspective," *Journal of Modern History* 69/3 (1997): 415–50; Maureen Healy's work on World War I Vienna, especially, "Denunziation und Patriotismus: Briefe an die Wiener Polizei im Ersten Weltkrieg," *Sozialwissenschaftliche Informationen (Sowi)* 27/2 (1998): 106–12; and Nancy Wingfield on the role of denunciations in the policing of prostitution, *The World of Prostitution in Late Imperial Austria* (Oxford: Oxford University Press, 2017).

Budapest to a series of internment camps in Hajmáskér, Zalaegerszeg, Esztergom, Csót, and Inota. Similarly, Bavarian officials moved several thousand prisoners to prisons outside Munich, such as the fortress in Ingolstadt.

It is against this background of mass arrests and imprisonments and the harsh application of justice that the trials of those who were neither fortunate enough to be released nor unfortunate enough to be among those summarily executed must be examined. Surviving records of the counterrevolutionary courts provide us the best point of access to assess the objectives and actions of the triumphant postrevolutionary governments. They also provide illustrative comparisons between the situation in Hungary, ruled by a self-proclaimed "Christian and national" White government, and in Bavaria, where the postrevolutionary courts were operating under the Weimar German constitution and the Bavarian state government was, in fact, led by the SPD initially.

In this context, of course, the explanations given in court by defendants and their attorneys had acquittal as their first goal. They introduced numerous possible mitigating circumstances that might result in acquittal or reduce the punishment imposed on the defendants. Because a charge of treason, for example, could result in the death penalty or a long prison term, defendants and their attorneys did all they could to escape these consequences. In many cases, attorneys attempted to explain their clients' actions in ways that fit with the still materializing "official version" of the events surrounding the revolutionary period. Through their verdicts, the courts in turn attempted to further crystallize this official story by assessing ultimate guilt for the upheavals and reestablishing the moral authority of the new conservative regimes, as well as by serving the pedagogical purpose of warning against further left-wing radicalism.

The postrevolutionary trials constituted a turning point in the process of dealing with the societal trauma of the revolution and the armed conflicts. The trials made the still volatile narratives about the revolutions legible, with the force of law: witnesses testifying under oath and evidence submitted to the court. What previously had been in the realm of the individual – rumors or conversations overheard, denunciations made or received, observations and fears – were put into the public record, elaborated with other documentation, and often challenged by the opposing side in the courtroom. If the denunciations, arrests into protective custody, and, above all, the "wild" extrajudicial executions of the terror were all part of a process of revenge taking, I would argue that following this period the dialogue (unequal, unfair, and stilted though it was) that occurred in the courts and courts-martial between defendants and judges marked the beginning of a long process of coming to terms or making amends.

The first stage of the process of adjudication of revolutionary guilt led, over the months in which the courts dealt with these cases, not only to the determination of individual guilt and responsibility of thousands of defendants but also, perhaps inexorably, to the creation of a sort of official narrative of events. In the process of trying the accused, the language used to describe revolutionary activities and the values against which revolutionary actors were judged became more uniform. This led ultimately to the development of agreed upon narratives and scripts that would broadly influence politics in both Hungary and Germany in the interwar decades.

The narratives created by the trials helped standardize the distinct and scattered experiences of individuals into collective revolutionary scripts that motivated people to action, for or against the revolution. These scripts clarified the confusion of the revolutionary period and became a framework for under- standing recent events. The narratives generated in court were not universally dominant, in fact they produced a wide range of counternarratives, but the process of consolidation, from rumor and personal experience to shared col- lective memory, was similar for the interwar Left and Right; I analyze this process in Chapter 6. As the stories moved from anecdote to historical evi- dence, they gave meaning to their tellers and listeners. As the courts, and the governments they served, settled on an official view of the immediate past, defendants and their lawyers were forced to fit their explanations and justifica- tions for past actions to this new reality. As a result, some sought to twist government rhetoric to defend their anti-government activities. A successful defendant was sometimes able to translate his or her revolutionary actions into the explanatory language of the postrevolutionary era, such as the Munich baker's assistant described below. In the case of a Budapest schoolteacher, we see that her attorney's attempt to wield the language of the counterrevolution appears not to have swayed the courts. A survey of counterrevolutionary court verdicts allows us to see both an evolving official view of revolutionary events and the efficacy of defense strategies, some of which found resonance with official ears.

Following the defeat of the revolutions, thousands of revolutionaries were tried in Munich and Budapest. Accusations included a wide variety of crimes based on the defendants' activities during revolutionary rule, ranging from serious crimes that qualified for the death penalty, such as high treason, unlawful imprisonment, hostage taking, and murder, to noncapital crimes such as blasphemy, incitement to class hatred, extortion and blackmail, rob- bery, distribution of illegal printed materials, fraud, and misappropriation of public funds. In addition to the leaders of the revolutionary governments, hundreds of ordinary men who had served in the Red armies and Red guards were put on trial, as well as a small number of women who had been members of revolutionary institutions and a larger number of women charged broadly with supporting the revolution through public statements or even in private conversations. In both countries, the period of revolutionary upheavals that followed the end of World War I was viewed as a continuation of the legal state of war and martial law, so many of these trials took place before special summary courts set up specifically for trying the revolutions or even "drumhead" courts-martial based on wartime legal conditions.

In Bavaria and Hungary, the new governments took similar legal measures following the defeat of the revolutionary governments, extending the state of emergency from the war, creating legal institutions to expedite the handling of court cases stemming from the revolution, and making provisions for the detention of citizens without trial in political cases. Yet we will see that although the police and the courts in both Munich and Budapest were mobilized for political justice, the legal verdicts issued in the two cities deviated notably from one another. The fact that leaders of the victorious forces in the two cities came to accept distinct, and divergent, explanations for the origins and trajectories of revolutionary events in 1919 was the major reason for the contrast in trial outcomes.

The primary difference in the ways the two cities assessed blame was that in Hungary, from Horthy's victory speech at the National Museum onwards, the city of Budapest itself was held responsible for the excesses of the revolutions (including the first parliamentary government of 1918), as well as for the lost war and the terrible economic situation that followed. Counterrevolutionary forces had gathered their troops and solidified their victories in the Hungarian countryside, and they also drew on the long anti-Budapest tradition of Hungarian nationalism and antisemitism. In Munich, the language and sentencing suggest that the judges and authorities understood the deprivations of the war and the economic distress caused by inflation as mitigating the guilt of the urban working classes for the revolutions. Anti-urban rhetoric, though it made periodic appearances, was not dominant and the capital was not contrasted with "the nation." It was almost the opposite in Hungary, where the forces supporting Horthy saw the Jewish population and workers of Budapest as responsible for the military defeat, the breakup of the monarchy, and the revolutions that followed. While Bavarian antisemites held the Jews of Munich responsible for the city's suffering, antisemites in Hungary viewed the capital city itself as Jewish and foreign and, therefore, applied collective punishments to compensate for the suffering of the entire country.

The documentary record for the administration of postrevolutionary justice in the case of the Munich revolution is both simpler and more complete than in Budapest. By February 1920 (nine months after the defeat of the *Räterepublik*), more than 5,000 trials had been held in Bavaria. As will be analyzed below, the first cases were brought before courts-martial. Later cases came before a newly created civilian court, the *Volksgericht*. The files of the state prosecutor from 1919 and the following years are complete and available. The case record contains not only the verdict from the trial itself (this was often brief and cursory) but also, in many cases, the supporting documentation provided by the defense, including letters from family members, statements of defendants and witnesses, and other evidence. The richness of these records allows us to recover a full and fairly clear picture of postrevolutionary judicial proceedings in Munich.

The judicial record for Budapest is less complete than the record for Munich and more complicated for several reasons. First, and most importantly, the Romanian invasion and the quick procession of short-term governments that came to power in Budapest following Béla Kun's resignation in August prolonged the period of "summary court-martial" and extraordinary justice. In Hungary as a whole, the period of White Terror and summary justice began in many regions already in early summer, while the Red regime still held power in the capital. We have seen that, in Munich, public outrage after the murder of the Catholic journeymen on May 6, 1919 (a mere week after the defeat of the revolution) resulted in civilian authorities almost immediately putting an end to vigilante justice. From this point, efforts to resolve accusations of revolutionary criminal activity were conducted by the police and the courts. In Hungary, civil officials tolerated extrajudicial procedures much longer, even passing new emergency laws in 1920 that placed civilians accused of crimes in the revolutionary period under the judicial authority of the military. Thus, thousands of people who were accused of revolutionary activity were not tried before a court but were deposed by what was called euphemistically "people's justice," the supposedly uncontrollable, but understandable, rage of the common people against the revolutionaries. In most cases, however, it was the arrival of the White officers' brigades in an area that stirred up if not instigated this rage. In this environment, with little formal supervision by courts and civilian officials, thousands of innocent people were, in effect, casualties of proto-judicial whims and vigilante attacks. Most of these innocent victims were Jews. Despite this wild, so-called people's justice, which often had the character of a pogrom in Hungary, revolutionary officials and minor participants also found their way before formal courts in far greater numbers than in Bavaria. The total number of cases tried in Hungary was high; according to an attorney in the postrevolutionary justice ministry, "when the old order was restored it was found necessary, as a result of the denunciations received, to institute proceedings in no less than 15,000 criminal cases,"[4] or three times the number tried in Bavaria.

Another important structural factor influenced both the practice of justice and the character of archival records in Hungary. The special courts set up to deal with political crimes in 1919 were "councils of five" established within preexisting courts rather than new, separate institutions created to deal with

---

[4] Oscar Szollosy [Oszkár Szőllősy], "The Criminals of the Dictatorship of the Proletariat," as appendix in Tormay, *An Outlaw's Diary,* vol. 2, 223.

purported crimes during the era of the Red government, like the Munich court-martial or the *Volksgericht*. This meant that while decisions in court cases having to do with the Bavarian revolution are concentrated in the records of these two judicial institutions, the records of trials for similar crimes in Hungary are dispersed in multiple judicial jurisdictions as well as within the archives of both regular and summary trials. This diffusion of archival materials from the trials tracked the dispersion of both revolutionary and counter-revolutionary violence across Hungary following (and in some areas even preceding) the collapse of the Kun government. In Bavaria, violence was largely contained within Munich and the resulting judicial records were also clustered within the capital and a few of its suburbs.[5]

The massive political upheavals that have continued to affect both nations since the 1920s have also influenced the location and organization of archival material related to the trials in Munich and Budapest in 1919. During the post–World War II state socialist regime in Hungary, many court files were moved from the National Archives (*Országos Levéltár*) to the archives of the Institute for Political History (*Politikatörténeti Intézet Levéltára*). In this archive, files from the trials are not kept together as court records but are located in the personal files of individual Communist Party members from all decades. Therefore, in Hungary the cases for which records are available are not necessarily representative of the full array of cases tried before the courts of the postrevolutionary judiciary. Among the cases preserved in the Institute for Political History archives, in particular, trials of self-proclaimed socialists are likely to be overrepresented relative to the other groups brought before the courts in 1919. Only those defendants from 1919 who later were members of the post–World War II governing socialist party would have a personal file or would have donated their personal papers to the archive.[6] Although the trials of the leaders of the Budapest revolution have been the object of much historical inquiry, information about the trials of second-tier participants in the revolutionary events, seen by many as "followers," has been more haphazardly excavated and examined because of this organization of archival materials.[7]

---

[5] Some of the other available trial records from 1919 cases in Hungary are appeals located in the Military Archives (*Hadtörténelmi Levéltár*) and the Budapest City Archives (*Budapest Főváros Levéltára*); some appeals proceedings for cases tried in both Budapest and elsewhere are in the justice ministry files of the National Archives; as described above, some files were moved to the Institute for Political History.

[6] From 1948 to 1956 this party was the Hungarian Working People's Party (*Magyar Dolgozók Pártja*, MDP) and after 1956 the Hungarian Socialist Workers' Party (*Magyar Szocialista Munkáspárt*).

[7] For thorough coverage of the trials of the revolutionary leadership, see Erika Rév, *A Népbiztosok Pere* (Budapest: Kossuth Kiadó, 1969). For a partisan contemporary analysis, see "Gesetzliche Morde," in Pogány, 65–84.

A thorough discussion of the activities of the courts in Munich, based on surviving trial records, defense statements, and the reports in the contemporary press, is a sensible starting place for our comparison of how justice was practiced in both cities. By comparing the trials of revolutionary leaders with those of minor figures swept up in the counterrevolutionary reaction, we can see how the courts distributed responsibility for the revolutions and how the motivations and actions of participants were assessed. The courts served several functions in the postrevolutionary period; they apportioned guilt and punishment as well as offering a public forum for discussion of the revolutions and their meanings. They also served a self-conscious pedagogical function, attempting to dissuade citizens from committing similar political crimes and to inoculate the public against leftist seductions. By comparing the sorts of excuses and explanations offered by defendants with the sentences they received, we can tease out the coalescing official view of the 1919 upheavals.

These same records allow us to examine the ways that defendants attempted to shape their motivations and experiences to take advantage of the emerging official narrative that was becoming manifest in the judicial process. In Munich, an explanatory narrative developed that allowed judges and prosecutors to grant significant leniency to minor figures from the revolution who were caught up in the legal system. By claiming naivety or denying that their actions had a political character, revolutionaries who were not clearly active in the leadership were often able to partially or fully acquit themselves. This narrative from the Munich trials is foundationally different from the quickly evolved narrative developed by the Horthy government in Hungary. Transcripts from the trials in Budapest and across Hungary reveal near total rejection of claims of mitigating circumstances that were brought forward by defendants and their attorneys as prosecutors uniformly demanded harsh sentences, demands that were seconded by the Hungarian press.

Munich Trials

A glance at Table 4.1 shows the leap in judicial activity in Bavaria in the wake of the 1919 revolutions in Munich. Even though the revolutionary upheavals in the spring forced a period of interruption in the activities of the courts, the increase in convictions at the level of the Bavarian state courts (the courts-martial and *Volksgericht*) demonstrates the large number of cases tried in connection with the revolutions. These numbers are for all of Bavaria, but in Munich alone over 5,000 separate legal cases connected with the revolutions were brought by the prosecuting attorney's office.[8]

---

[8] Gumbel, *Vier Jahre*.

Table 4.1 *Bavarian justice statistics, 1918–19*
Source: BHStA, MInn, 71655, film 11, "Justizstatistik, 1910–1919."

Convictions by courts	1918	1919	% change
District courts	184,019	210,020	14.1
Bavarian state courts	**8,005**	**11,299**	**41.2**
Trials by jury	134	210	56.7
Total convictions	192,158	221,259	15.1

Until July 31, 1919, revolutionary cases were tried in Munich before a special court-martial established for that purpose. After that date, trials and appeals were held before a new institution of the Bavarian state court, the *Volksgericht* or people's court. The *Volksgericht* was a creation of the first democratic regime under Kurt Eisner in the fall of 1918. It was established initially to fulfill a democratic and socialist ideal of judgment by one's peers. Each court had a panel of two professional and three lay judges. A supermajority of four votes (thereby including at least one professional judge) was needed for a conviction. The courts also provided for the expedited treatment of the mass of criminal cases brought in the wake of the German military defeat and the revolution of autumn 1918. The courts were understood to be "summary" courts with expedited procedures and no right of appeal. They were established to deal with certain serious criminal violations, but in January 1919 their competence was extended to several political infractions. In September 1919, with the new constitution, the Bavarian *Landtag* reaffirmed the *Volksgericht* and its competence was extended to include the charge of high treason. All trials arising from the revolution that were not tried before courts-martial were tried before the *Volksgericht*.[9]

The *Landtag* also legally extended the "state of war" to the end of 1919, well past the November 1918 armistice and the signing of the peace treaty that ended the war on June 28. This extension of the state of war permitted the authorities to place citizens in protective custody. Afterwards, a continued state of emergency remained in effect in Bavaria until September 1922, and after the failed *Hitlerputsch* in 1923 it was reinstated. During the actual wartime of 1914–18, the government made more sparing use of emergency laws than after the 1919 revolutions. As shown in Table 4.2, almost twice as many people were held without trial in Bavaria in 1919 than in the previous year, even though the strikes of January 1918 had led to the arrest of many strike leaders and participants. Most strikingly, we notice

---

[9] BHSA I, MInn 66252, 3.9.1919, in Thomas Lange, *Bayern im Ausnahmezustand, 1919–1923: Zur politischen Funktion des bayerischen Ausnahmerechts in den ersten Jahren der Weimarer Republik* (dissertation, Ludwig Maximilians University, Munich, 1989), 56.

Table 4.2 *Bavarian justice statistics, prisoners*

Prisoners held	1918	1919	% change
Imprisoned awaiting trial	5,685	10,828	90.5
Sentenced prisoners	8,093	6,368	−21.3
Total	19,526	25,545	30.8

Note: The annual total includes prisoners of other penal institutions.
Source: BHStA, MInn, 71655, film 11, "Justizstatistik, 1910–1919."

the huge disparity demonstrated by the 90 percent increase in the number of untried prisoners and the parallel decrease in the number of convicted prisoners serving sentences. These two vivid anomalies demonstrate the harsh reality described by many contemporary observers: thousands of prisoners held indefinitely – often as a result of denunciations or the slimmest evidence – without the opportunity to hear the charges against them or to defend themselves in court.

While the postrevolutionary arrests mounted, the number of sentenced prisoners actually declined, as Table 4.2 shows. This resulted from several factors, including the inability of the courts to process all the cases associated with the revolution and the release of some prisoners during the brief period of revolutionary rule. The tendency towards leniency with minor figures in the revolution that was repeatedly demonstrated by the Bavarian courts also played a role in the relatively low number of sentenced prisoners serving time in Bavarian prisons in 1919.

In Bavaria, many revolutionary leaders and functionaries were tried for their participation in what the counterrevolutionary government viewed as the worst crimes of the revolutionary government, such as the *Geiselmord*. Many others were tried for what they believed had been their professional responsibilities at the time of the revolutionary government. For example, the execution of arrest orders on behalf of the revolutionary government was viewed by the counterrevolutionary authorities as unlawful imprisonment and kidnapping. Similarly, house search and confiscation orders issued by revolutionary functionaries were tried as the crimes of unlawful search and seizure or burglary. In all these cases, claims that the defendant was following orders or acting within the guidelines set by the government then in power were dismissed by judicial and police authorities as possible grounds for acquittal, as the revolutionary government itself was not recognized as a legal authority.

Defendants' claims that any refusal to follow orders would have resulted in penalties were seldom viewed as exculpatory, though in a tiny minority of cases these claims were seen as a mitigating circumstance for the soldiers of the Red

Army. More typically, soldiers were held fully accountable for the violence they perpetrated. The judges of the *Volksgericht* who decided the *Geiselmord* trial in September 1919, for example, specifically noted that no soldiers were forced to participate and that all members of the squad had responded to a call for volunteers. The soldiers on the firing squad that executed the Thule Society members and the two White Army prisoners were convicted of murder. Even the soldier who was accused of delivering the written order for the execution from Fritz Seidel to Willi Haußmann in the courtyard was found guilty of accessory to murder, "because he was aware of the criminal contents of the order which he delivered."[10] In all of these cases, the counterrevolutionary authorities refused to recognize the revolutionary laws, judicial institutions, or judges established by the brief soviet government. Instead, they held that the legal code of the prerevolutionary (and even prewar) system was valid throughout 1919, despite the revolution and multiple regime changes.

Once in the settings of the court-martial or the *Volksgericht*, both prosecution and defense focused on identifying or disputing the criminal activity of the accused. Perhaps because of the superheated political environment that followed the collapse of the revolutionary government, defendants seldom challenged the authority of the court to adjudicate such cases. Yet the legal authority of the special courts, and even of the government that created them, was not at all clear. In particular, the ubiquitous charge of "high treason" or "abetting in high treason" was a problem when applied to actions against a government that itself had come to power through the overthrow of the monarchy and claimed popular rather than historical or constitutional legitimacy.

Despite the abdication of the Wittelsbach dynasty in November 1918, a new democratic constitution for Bavaria, the *Bamberger Verfassung*, was not ratified until August 14, 1919, after the trials of most of the revolutionaries. The ratification of this constitution solidified the achievements of the democratic November 1918 revolution and finally ended any official legislative or administrative role for the ad hoc councils. Despite the widespread popularity of monarchists and the anti-republican stance of many Catholic politicians, only three *Landtag* representatives of the USPD opposed the ratification. This near-unanimous vote for ratification offered strong retroactive support to the Hoffmann government and to the actions it had taken in the name of the Bavarian state since Eisner's assassination in February 1919. But regarding the legal status of the postrevolutionary courts, the fact of this late (post-*Räterepublik*) ratification of a democratic constitution, combined with the uncertain legal status of the councils up to that point, created a legally complicated situation.

---

[10] StAM Pol. Dir. 677, "Geiselmord Prozeß."

Not surprisingly, it was the leaders of the defeated revolutionary governments rather than the more insignificant Red soldiers who challenged the
authority of these courts. One of the few defendants to challenge the legal
basis of the charges against him was Dr. Eugen Leviné, leader of the second,
communist-led revolutionary government in Munich. Leviné was actively
pursued by the new conservative government because they associated him
with some of the most brutal actions of the revolutionary period. Posters
offering a reward were circulated across the city and region, alleging crimes
of high treason and murder. His presumed authorship of the order to kill the
"hostages" in the Luitpold Gymnasium was used to justify the murder charge.

Leviné was finally arrested on May 13 in his hiding place in the apartment of
a friend, the artist Botho Schmidt, in the working-class neighborhood of
Haidhausen. A reward of 10,000 Marks had been offered for his arrest, and
information about his whereabouts had poured in from Schmidt's neighbors
and others eager to denounce the former leader. In the end, many of these tips
proved to have no merit. Some of them denounced unrelated people, such as the
barber at the Park Hotel, who was anonymously denounced to authorities on
May 13, perhaps by a business competitor using the manhunt to settle personal
grievances. The barber was denounced as a "dangerous communist," and of his
purchase of the hotel barbershop business two weeks earlier the letter claimed
"it is said that the money came from Leviné-Niessen."[11] In the end, it was
Dr. Mattissen, a *Freikorps* member who had functioned as a mole within the
Communist Party during the revolutionary period, who revealed Leviné's
hiding place and received the reward. Mattissen discovered the hiding place
by offering his own identity papers to members of the Communist Party to
facilitate Leviné's escape and was rewarded with the fugitive's whereabouts.
He then passed this location to the police. He claimed the reward money offered
by the authorities but requested anonymity.[12] Leviné's trial before the court-
martial began on June 2; his lawyers had been allowed only two and a half days
to inspect his files.[13]

Leviné's trial was the first for a leader of the Bavarian revolution. Eisner, the
leader of the November revolution of 1918, had been murdered on February 21,
1919. Gustav Landauer, the anarchist philosopher and member of the first
"literary" soviet government, had been murdered in police custody, as had
the Red Army commander Rudolf Eglhofer. Both Ernst Toller, writer and the

[11] StAM Pol. Dir. 10110, "Levine-Niessen, Eugen," 70,143.
[12] StAM Pol. Dir. 10110, "Levine-Niessen, Eugen," letter from Otto Herb, Kriminalwachmeister.
Herb said that Mattissen applied for the reward money but did not want his name made public.
That he had been a spy in the party comes from Rosa Leviné, who identifies him as "the doctor
of theology Mattissen." Rosa Leviné, *Aus der Münchener Rätezeit* (Berlin: Vereinigung
Internationaler Verlags-Anstalten, 1925), 63.
[13] Höller, 263.

commander of Red forces in Dachau, and Max Levien, the head of the Munich Communist Party, had evaded capture and remained in hiding at the time of Leviné's trial.

Public interest in Leviné's trial was therefore high across Central Europe and, as a result, the courtroom proceedings were fully reported in the print media across Germany and in many foreign newspapers. Perhaps because his trial represented the first example of the judicial effort to assess guilt for the 1919 revolutions, Leviné came to be seen as a symbol of the revolution by its supporters and its opponents. His Russian and Jewish origins made him exactly the sort of foreign, Jewish Bolshevik that the revolution's opponents had vilified and campaigned against during the violent political struggle that brought an end to the revolutionary government. For the supporters of the revolution, Leviné's credentials of having participated in the 1905 Russian Revolution and his experience of subsequent imprisonment by the tsarist government, as well as his close ties to Rosa Luxemburg, Karl Liebknecht, and the Berlin Spartacists, gave him a revolutionary pedigree that had helped raise the revolution in Munich to the world stage.

Because of the high emotions surrounding Leviné's trial, the prosecuting attorney's office asked the Munich police to use "all available measures" to get the prisoner securely from his holding cell in the Stadelheim prison to the district court building at Mariahilfplatz.[14] They were worried that supporters could be planning Leviné's escape. At the same time, they also feared that he might be lynched by the crowd. Low-profile prisoners, they confided, could be conducted to their trials "in the usual manner."[15]

Once in the courtroom, Leviné seemed to have an electrifying effect on both his supporters and his opponents. In his testimony before the court, Leviné argued that although he didn't recognize the authority of the court or the legitimacy of the charges against him, he would proceed with his defense in order to set the record straight about his actions and the key events of the revolutionary period. He went on to state that if his goal was merely to achieve a milder sentence, he would have turned over the defense entirely to his attorneys, "who are surely politically and socially closer to you."[16] Instead, he went on, he felt the need to address "the most dreadful rumors that are being circulated in the press and the general public about the Räterepublik, about me personally, and about events in general. I cannot let these rumors go unanswered."[17] Leviné worried that "the Munich working class knew me

---

[14] Letter from Staatsanwalt bei dem standgerichtlichen Gerichte für München, May 18, 1919, in StAM Pol. Dir. 10110, "Leviné-Niessen, Eugen," 81.

[15] Ibid.

[16] Leviné's defense speech was reprinted abundantly at the time, in the press and in brochures. My translation here is from the reproduction in his wife's 1925 memoir; Leviné, 67–8.

[17] Ibid., 68.

only briefly, and some of them might now begin to doubt whether they gave their trust to someone who was worthy of it."[18] Seizing upon the didactic potential of his own trial, Leviné testified that it was his duty, as a member of the Communist Party, to explain to the working class the reasons for his actions and the actions of his party.[19]

Leviné's dramatic speech in his own defense was quoted widely and was even reproduced in full in many German periodicals of the time. During the interwar years, this speech became one of the most symbolically potent legacies of the martyrdom of the German Left. In addition to a highly emotional profession of his belief in the communist and revolutionary causes, Leviné challenged directly the legitimacy of the charges levied against him and other leaders of the revolutionary government, as well as the legality of the courts and prosecutorial officials of the new regime. It raised the important question: did the court have a legal right to try these revolutionaries for treason?

After all, until the ratification of the new Bavarian constitution in August 1919, months after the fall of the *Räterepublik*, the legal role of the councils, in whose name that government was declared, was not clear. The initial decision to call for a republic of councils at the beginning of April was made by the Congress of Bavarian Workers', Soldiers' and Peasants' Councils at a moment when the newly elected *Landtag* was paralyzed by the violence associated with Eisner's assassination. A representative of the Hoffmann SPD government participated in this decision and signed the declaration of a republic of councils on April 6.[20] In his speech, Leviné argued, "there is only [the accusation of] high treason because the *Räterepublik* was defeated." He noted further that even the liberal *Münchener Neuste Nachrichten* had written in a lead article, "only failed high treason is actually high treason, every successful high treason is not." "High treason," Leviné concluded in his defense testimony, "results from political considerations and not judicial."[21]

Leviné's challenge to the now-dominant republican parties was difficult to answer since they, too, were theoretically guilty of an earlier treason against the monarchy in the wake of military defeat in 1918. Predictably, the court-martial ignored this question of legitimacy in its verdict. Instead, the court offered an almost organic definition of "high treason." Acknowledging that Leviné had actually argued against the proclamation of the first ("literary") council

[18] Ibid.

[19] Leviné had been released by Russian authorities in 1908 for medical reasons and allowed to go to Germany. He became a German citizen and joined the SPD; he volunteered for the German army in 1914 and had a medical discharge in 1916. After the SPD split in 1917, Leviné was a member of the USPD and then the newly formed KPD and edited the *Rote Fahne*. He went to Bavaria in 1918 to work for the KPD in Munich.

[20] Minister Schneppenhorst of the Hoffmann government was present at the deliberations on April 6 and signed the declaration of a republic of councils, as is clear from the archival record.

[21] StAM, Staatsanwalt München I, Film 310, File 2106/1–2, "Leviné-Niessen, Eugen."

government on April 6 and 7, the court claimed that because of his later, "fanatical" defense of the second revolutionary government, "his conduct justifies the verdict of high treason." "Leviné," wrote the court, "was a foreign interloper in Bavaria, and didn't care in the least about its constitutional conditions. He followed his goals without any consideration of the good of the whole population, even though he knew that the country desperately needed domestic peace."[22] The language of the verdict, which sentenced Leviné to death, put his treason against "the Bavarian people" ahead of any consideration of the government against which the treason legally should have been committed. Its description of him as a "foreign interloper" also excluded Leviné, a naturalized German citizen and veteran of the German Army in World War I, from the political nation. His execution was carried out the following day after a governmental review that was perfunctory at best.

Leviné's challenge to the legitimacy of the judicial authorities who tried him and his questioning of the legality of the charge of "high treason" were renewed even more eloquently two weeks later at the trial of Ernst Toller. Toller had been leader of the first "literary" revolutionary republic of councils from April 7–14, and he also served as commander of the Red Army in Dachau during the fighting that defeated the revolution. The prominent socialist lawyer and politician Hugo Haase argued on Toller's behalf during his trial. "The [royal] criminal code existed in order to protect the constitutional system at the time of its creation ... against violent attacks. It would be absurd to assume," claimed Haase, "that it also existed to offer protection to a new 'constitution,' created through violence. Just as the laws on *lèse majesté* are no longer valid, neither are those on high treason."[23] In his memoir, published in 1933, Toller reiterated Haase's points about the charge of high treason for which he was ultimately sentenced to five years imprisonment by the Munich court-martial. He playfully described the irony of the charges against him:

The judges call what I have done high treason; they point to the royal code of law, by which they now judge. They are certainly cleverer than the old working woman; they ignore her healthy, common-sense understanding that the paragraph on high treason in that book was supposed to protect the monarchy and the monarchy was dethroned long ago.[24]

---

[22] Verdict from Leviné, 66.

[23] See Haase's speech reprinted in Ernst Toller, *Justiz-Erlebnisse* (Berlin: E. Laubsche Verlagsbuchhandlung, 1927), 9–11. Haase was an important SPD representative in East Prussia and as a lawyer successfully defended many socialists. Along with Ebert and Scheidemann, he was one of the SPD party leaders and head of its Reichstag faction. He was one of the cofounders of the USPD in the spilt in 1917 and as a USPD representative was a member of the post–World War I RdV, but resigned over the handling of the Berlin winter uprisings. He died in November 1919 from wounds received in an assassination attempt a month earlier.

[24] Toller, *Eine Jugend in Deutschland*, 132.

"In regard to the charge that I overthrew the constitution," Toller continued, "it's the same thing; the old constitution was overthrown by the very ministers who are now putting me on trial, and there wasn't a new one yet."[25]

During the trial, Haase had pointed out the inapplicability of the royal treason law to the actions of the 1919 revolutionaries. He argued that it was "nonsense" for a government founded through revolution to try others for revolutionary treason. He also noted that the royal law that the prosecutors were attempting to apply was particularly unsuited to the defense of a democratic regime, especially because it allowed death sentences for treason and political crimes. "None of the parliaments existing today, if they tried to protect their new constitutions against treasonous activities, would set the sort of sentence contained in the old [imperial] criminal code."[26] That punishment, he argued, "could only be understood as part of the monarchist conception of the state," implying that by using not only the criminal code but also its harsh sentencing, the democratic regimes were representing a monarchist and anachronistic worldview.[27] With his arguments at Toller's trial, Haase provided additional legal and philosophical depth to the challenge Leviné had mounted in his own defense.

Toller's trial is of particular interest in comparison with that of Leviné. Both men were well-known as leaders of the revolution and both had been the object of well-publicized manhunts and calls to bring them to justice. And we have seen that Toller, like Leviné, questioned the legitimacy of the courts and new political authorities to try him for treason. In both cases, the court ignored this legal argument, finding both Leviné and Toller guilty of treason. However, the similarities end there – Leviné was sentenced to death and executed two days later, while Toller received five years imprisonment, the minimum sentence for the crime of high treason. It is impossible to know for certain the extent to which the evidence and defense arguments affected the judges' decisions. However, the marked difference in the sentences of Leviné and Toller, tried less than two weeks apart by the same court-martial for the same crimes, offers us an opportunity to examine the understanding of responsibility, morality, and justice that had developed among the ascendant new political leadership in Munich in the early days and weeks following the defeat of the revolution.

The brevity of Toller's sentence in comparison to that of Leviné can be explained by two main factors, public opinion and individual moral consideration. The trial and execution of Leviné earlier in the month of June had caused a wave of local and international criticism of "White Terror" and "exceptional" justice in Bavaria. During the forty-eight hours while Leviné's death sentence was out for ministerial review, the government in Bamberg was flooded with telegrams from prominent figures and organizations across Germany and

[25] Ibid.   [26] Toller, *Justiz*, 11.   [27] Ibid., 11.

Europe calling for amnesty or a stay of execution. In a telegram sent from Berlin, for example, a group of self-described "members of all political parties" warned that the court-martial in Munich, the trials generally, and Leviné's execution in particular, "in the current heated political atmosphere," would, "arouse the passions of the people once again." They called on the courts "not to distance themselves from the principles of justice and humanity."[28] The signatories included such prominent Weimar era figures as Albert Einstein, Maximilian Harden, and Karl Kautsky.[29]

This telegram in support of Leviné is noteworthy, not only for the famous signatories but because of the language it used to plea for leniency in the punishment of this well-known revolutionary. With an argument similar to that used by many of those calling for the swift execution of the revolutionary "Munich criminals," the writers pleaded for leniency by claiming it would facilitate a restoration of civil order. According to these prominent figures, the courts should follow the "principles of justice and humanity," but they should also be careful not to "arouse the passions of the people."[30] In other words, leniency was proposed as a way to prevent further revolutionary upheavals.

Johannes Hoffmann, the head of the SPD-led government in Bavaria, did not attend the ministerial meeting during which Leviné's execution was sanctioned. This allowed critics on both sides to attack what they saw as a sign of Hoffmann's moral weakness. The Right claimed that Hoffmann had shown his true colors by refusing to deal harshly with the revolutionary leader. Critics on the Left, on the other hand, even many members of Hoffmann's own majority Social Democrats, profoundly disapproved of the death penalty for political crimes (treason) and were troubled that the SPD had not taken a stance against the execution. Those further on the Left, such as the USPD and Communists argued that, for sanctioning the murder of workers or their leaders, Hoffmann's hands were now "bloody" like those of Gustav Noske in Berlin, who had put down the Spartakus Uprising with deadly force.[31]

The execution provoked a scandal within the Bavarian Social Democratic Party. On June 14, nine days after Leviné's execution, the SPD-run *Münchener Post* found it necessary to publish an explanatory editorial titled, "Social Democratic Ministers against Leviné's Execution." It stipulated, "false reports that the Bavarian Ministerial Cabinet had unanimously approved Leviné's death sentence have led to serious attacks on the Social Democratic members

---

[28] Telegram in StAM, Staatsanwalt München I, Film 310, File 2106/1–2, "Leviné-Niessen, Eugen."

[29] Ibid.; other signatories were: Karl A. Aner, Graf von Arco, Pfarrer August Bleier, Ernst Cassirer, Pastor Hans Francke, Hellmut von Gerlach, Adolf Grabowsky, Max Hodann, Walther Koch, Georg Friedrich Nicolai, Elisabeth Rotten, Hugo Simon, and Helene Stoecker.

[30] Ibid.

[31] See for example, *Bayerischer Weckruf* 10, July 7, 1919, "Die Entscheidung der Regierung im Falle Leviné!"

of the cabinet and confusion in the party." The editorial claimed that Hoffmann had not attended the meeting that sanctioned the death sentence and that the four SPD members present had not signed the approval. The editors hoped that "the establishment of these facts, however late, should produce the necessary clarity and pull the rug out from under the wild attacks on the party." In this case, however, it seems that the rumors can actually be substantiated using the archival record. The reality was that while Hoffmann was indeed absent from the critical cabinet meeting, the signatures of three other majority SPD cabinet members (Martin Segitz, Ernst Schneppenhorst, and Fritz Endres) were indeed on the approval sent to the prosecuting attorney's office, contrary to these declarations in the *Münchener Post*.[32]

The outcry over Leviné's execution and the negative reports of summary executions and miscarriages of justice in the press may have influenced the sentence given to Toller. The moral and ethical opinions of the individual judges also guided the court towards Toller's relatively mild sentence. Unlike Leviné, a Russian-born communist and professional revolutionary, Toller was a relatively well-known German writer at the time of the trial and had many advocates. Several of them appealed to the judges to recognize that Toller had acted with moral conviction. From Vienna, a telegram with well-known signatories, including Sigmund Freud, Hugo Hoffmannsthal, Robert Musil, Jakob Wassermann, and Franz Werfel, pleaded for mercy.[33] Toller's Viennese supporters presented moral aspects of his behavior that warranted the leniency of the court-martial. They emphasized in particular Toller's "idealism."

The authors of the Vienna telegram reminded the judges that during the war Toller had been "one of the champions of understanding amongst the nations" and that "during the [November 1918] revolution he had fought alongside Eisner, and after the latter's death had continued on the course of true humanitarianism."[34] They also mentioned Toller's attempt to prevent the taking of hostages. More telling, they reminded the court that Toller left his position with the Red Army in Dachau in an effort to prevent the executions in the Luitpold Gymnasium. It concluded, "Enough victims have been lost, we appeal to the Munich government to spare his life as he spared the lives of

---

[32] The ministers who signed the approval of the death penalty were: Segitz (SPD), Müller-Meiningen (Dem.), Speck (BVP), Freyberg (BVP), Frauendorfer (no party), Endres (SPD), Hamm (Dem.), Schneppenhorst (SPD), and Ackermann. StAM Staatsanwalt München I, Film 310, file 2016/2 "Leviné."

[33] BHSA, Bamberger Akten, MA 99926, telegram dated June 12, 1919. The signatories were: Hermann Bahr, Direktor Alfred Bernau, Franz Blei, Dr. R. K. Coudenhove, Karl Etlinger, Prof. Sigmund Freud, Egon Friedell, Direktor Emil Geyer, Rudolf Goldscheid, Prof. Josef Halban, Direktor Albert Heine, Hugo Hoffmannstal, Marta Karlweiss, Selma Kurz, Hr Lederer, Alexander Moissi, Robert Musil, Josef Popper-Lynkeus, Ida Roland, Rudolf Schildkraut, Otto Soyka, Jakob Wassermann, Franz Werfel, and Grete Wiesenthal.

[34] Ibid.

others."[35] Though we cannot know the effect of the telegram in achieving its goal, Toller's life was in fact spared by the court.

These calls for compassion and reconciliation by prominent figures enraged many on the political Right, however. On June 12, the same day that the Viennese petitioners sent their appeal for leniency, the conservative *München-Augsburger Abendzeitung* published an angry letter that demanded that Toller be forced to pay a heavy price for his actions during the revolutionary period. The letter was a response to an "Open Letter" to the government that the paper had published two days earlier, which made a plea for leniency for Toller. The author of the response, which was entitled "A Politics of Reconciliation?," identified himself only as a student and a volunteer with the Bavarian Schützenkorps, one of the local *Freikorps*. He wrote that he was frustrated with the appeals for leniency for the revolutionaries. He complained that at Leviné's trial, "this man, on whose shoulders the guilt for the spilt blood in Munich mostly lies, was suddenly stamped an 'idealist.'"[36] "Now that Toller has been arrested," he continued, "we read again the pleas for clemency and leniency."[37] In response he argued, "We [militia] volunteers are the last to clamor for the death penalty; all we want is to get the chance to finally return to our studies." He and his fellow *Freikorps* members were hindered in this goal by the shortsighted leniency of the courts, he argued: "If we always let the rabble-rousers free, there will never be peace and we have to deal with the fact that some sunny day the 'idealist' Toller from Samotschin or his Bavarian followers might decide to throw us out of the university again."[38] To dispel the image that he and his allies were "blood-thirsty," he offered the unlikely hope, "If there was some way to make Toller, Sauber, Levien, and whatever they are all called, permanently harmless without shedding blood, we would be satisfied with that."[39] But the tone of his letter implied that, of course, no such other solution existed.

This self-identified student and *Freikorps* volunteer framed his argument in terms that dominated the postrevolutionary discussion in Munich. His central objective, he asserted, was to reestablish the social order, in his case specifically "returning to our studies." He argued that the death penalty for Toller and the others would actually aid in the restoration of law and order, rather than merely satisfy a desire for revenge or bloodlust. He also directly confronted the question of political "idealism," the argument Toller's defenders had used to plead for leniency. Here the "student" argued idealism and political engagement, such as Toller's, presented an ongoing danger to public order. For the anonymous writer, the revolution had not developed independently in Munich

---

[35] Ibid.
[36] "Versöhnungspolitik?," *München-Augsburger Abendzeitung* 225, June 12, 1919; StAM Pol. Dir. 10110, "Leviné-Niessen, Eugen." 135.
[37] Ibid.   [38] Ibid.   [39] Ibid.

but had been imposed on the city by foreign "idealists," like the outsider Toller from Samotschin. The letter-writer linked Toller to the east with this identification and perhaps to the *Ostjuden*, or East European Jewish immigrants. The tag of "from Samotschin" may have been an attempt to identify Toller as foreign, or even Polish, but the town was located in the Prussian region of Posen, and Toller had been born a citizen of the German Empire in 1893.

In the letter, the anonymous student writer further maintained that he and the other militia "volunteers" were ready to work, unlike the "so-called workers" of the Red Army and Red Guard. These self-defined proletarians, he claimed, had left behind a mess in the barracks. He and his friends, not those now calling for amnesties and class reconciliation, represented the city's future. According to his version of events, the "rift between the bourgeoisie and the workers in Munich was only created by these foreign screamers," and for this rift to ever be breached, it must be through the "work" of those like him, meaning the patrolling and policing work of the volunteer militias, and not through various government amnesties.[40]

In the wake of conservative victories in Munich and Budapest, the question of "idealism" and the role it played in the revolutions of 1919 became a topic of great debate in Central Europe, far beyond the cases of individuals like Toller. Was the alleged idealism of revolutionary participants something that warranted leniency? For some of those favoring leniency, the revolutionaries had erred politically but had been motivated by a desire to help their fellow citizens make the best out of the terrible situation at the end of the war. But, as both Leviné's judges and the student/soldier saw it, this ethereal idealism had disconnected the Left from "real people" and facilitated the era's worst crimes. In Toller's case, claims for leniency based on his alleged "idealism" found greater purchase than had occurred in Leviné's case, perhaps because his profession as a writer was not directly political.

The controversial notion of the revolutionary leadership's "idealism" (whether judged good or bad) had its flipside in the widely circulated opinion that the working class who had supported the revolution had been naive and therefore easily misled by the revolutionaries. This asserted dichotomy of idealist or fanatical leaders and naive or misled followers became a powerful and enduring explanatory model for the post–World War I revolutions. It solved several conceptual problems for the postrevolutionary political establishment. By laying all of the guilt for violence and property destruction on relatively few leaders, it seemed to prepare the ground for reconciliation with the majority of the working class. It effectively depoliticized the revolutions; they became the escapades of a few criminals rather than focused demand for wholesale change by organized workers. It also held the potential to offer forgiveness to those

[40] Ibid.

workers who denied the political nature of their actions while at the same time driving a wedge between the working class and its radical leadership.

This double-sided explanatory coin of idealist leaders and naive followers that was minted in Munich was already in general circulation in June when the court-martial heard the first criminal cases, playing a decisive role in guiding judgments and sentencing. Predictably, in trials of the "rank and file" of the revolution, the majority of defendants attempted to deny participation in the actions that had led to their arrests or to minimize individual responsibility. A significant number claimed that the accusations against them were based on unreliable denunciations. This was certainly plausible.[41] The authorities in postrevolutionary Munich were awash in denunciations from the general public. Both military and civilian authorities repeatedly reminded police and soldiers that, as Commissioner Hermann Ewinger wrote in an order to all magistrates and gendarmes, "Denunciations should be treated with skepticism." While reports from dependable sources could be helpful in initiating an investigation, "Anonymous charges are always an act of cowardly revenge. It is hereby expressly forbidden to make arrests on the basis of anonymous denunciations."[42] But the fact that orders like these were so often repeated suggests that the problem of denunciation was ongoing and difficult to control.

In many of the court cases, however, the revolutionary acts of the defendants were undeniable. There were either too many witnesses or their names were found in the rolls of the Red Army or on the payrolls of other revolutionary organizations. The artist Botho Schmidt, for example, had not played a significant role in the revolutionary government or in resistance to the White military forces. He had allowed Leviné to escape arrest by hiding in his apartment. As a result, the prosecuting attorney held Schmidt for questioning after Leviné's discovery and arrest. In a letter signed by several character witnesses, Schmidt's lawyer argued that his client was very poor and had not participated in revolutionary political events. Schmidt, he claimed, had only allowed Leviné to stay with him "out of purely personal motives that had nothing to do with politics. Everyone who knows Schmidt knows that he would help anyone in need, merely because they were in need or presented themselves as in need ... even at times beyond his own strength and without worrying about anything."[43] In all such cases, the defendants, their lawyers, and their families (and often their employers) wrote to the prosecuting attorneys or the

---

[41] See note 3 in this chapter as well as Sheila Fitzpatrick and Robert Gellately, eds., "Practices of Denunciation in Modern European History, 1789–1989," special issue, *Journal of Modern History* 68/4 (December 1996), especially the editors' introduction, and the articles by the two editors.

[42] BHSA IV, Kriegsarchiv, Höhere Stäbe Bund I/4, 37: May 12, 1919, order from Staatskommissar Ewinger to all magistrate's offices and gendarmes.

[43] StAM, Staatsanwalt München I, Film 310, File 2106/1, "Leviné-Niessen, Eugen," 57–9.

military governor seeking to explain their actions. These letters and pleas most often focused on the defendant's youth, their weakness, and their political naivety, or conversely on the external pressures which had forced them to act as they did.

These explanations were often successful. The twenty-year-old factory worker Josef Lämmle from Immenstadt was arrested in Munich on May 2, 1919, the day after the fall of revolutionary Munich, in his room at the Hotel Schweitzerhof.[44] His name appeared on the roster of the Red Army, and on this basis, he was interned without interrogation for a week. On May 9, he was finally questioned and allowed to make a statement in his defense. He claimed that he had been stuck in Munich at the end of the war after being decommissioned from his wartime service in a German infantry regiment. He only joined the Red Army out of material necessity. He was trapped in Munich because he could not find work and was unable to return home to his parents in Immenstadt because the rail lines were blocked, and he needed a source of income. In his testimony he claimed that he had never been issued a weapon by the Red Army. He also claimed that he had never taken part in any of the battles with White forces in Munich or its surroundings and never served in police functions on the city streets. According to him, he had quit the army by April 28, three days before government troops entered Munich.[45]

Following his interrogation, Lämmle continued in protective custody awaiting his court-martial. Four weeks later (after a total of five weeks in custody), his father wrote an urgent request to the military commander for Munich, General Möhl. In his letter, the father restated his son's claims that he had only joined the Red Army out of economic necessity after being released from his demobilized German regiment and that he had not participated in any armed resistance to government forces. This anxious father emphasized that his son had not understood the consequences of joining such a political army due to his youth and naivety. Finally, the father appealed to the patriotism and sympathy of the military command. He told them that the news of Josef's arrest was an exceptionally hard blow to him since he had only recently learned of the hero's death (*Heldentod*) of his first son, Eduard, who had been missing in action from World War I.

Josef Lämmle's case was heard the following day by the court-martial and he was acquitted of the crime of abetting high treason. In his explanation of the verdict the chairman of the court-martial, Judge Reidel, noted Lämmle's military service during the war and his desperate material circumstances, as well as his youth and inexperience. He also highlighted the fact that Lämmle had not actually taken up arms against the government. While his father's reference to the family's patriotic sacrifices may well have helped in getting

---

[44] StAM, Staatsanwaltschaft München I, Film 310, File 2098.   [45] Ibid.

this case heard more quickly, it was not specifically cited by the court as a reason for the young man's acquittal.

It is not surprising that most other defendants tried to depoliticize their activities in the Red Army or Red Guard, as had Lämmle. Many claimed to have had no strong political ties to the Left. These defendants asserted that they were led to recruitment centers by friends, brothers, or coworkers and joined revolutionary military units without any ideological commitment. One of the most astounding explanations encountered in the records of the public prosecutor's office was provided by the thirty-one-year-old pastry chef Max Kainz. According to his testimony to the military police, he had worked for the gingerbread manufacturer Johann Platzröder. When on April 24 the revolutionary council government announced that automobiles and motorcycles would be confiscated, Kainz joined the Red Guard in an effort to protect the bakery's continued access to a motorcycle used for deliveries. Because of engine trouble, however, Kainz was unable to use the motorcycle on behalf of his employer or to transport the Red Guard.

Satisfied with this explanation, the police released Kainz without charges but did ask him to testify about events he had witnessed as a Red Guard stationed at the Luitpold Gymasium on the day of the *Geiselmord*. This proved to be a dead end for the prosecutor. Although Kainz had bragged to his friends that he had been present for the killings, he proved unable to remember the names of anyone who participated in the executions or to supply any other useful information.[46]

A sampling of cases tried before the Munich court-martial demonstrates that length of service in the Red Army or Red Guard often proved to be the most influential evidence in determining verdicts. A defendant's actual military service, including even limited action such as receiving a weapon or being sent to a position to confront government troops, was viewed by the court as proof of criminal activity.[47] Yet, in Bavaria, as in Hungary, the enlisted ranks and even officer corps of the Red forces were in constant flux during the brief revolutionary period. Large numbers of decommissioned soldiers from the demobilized German and Habsburg imperial armies, as well as workers laid off from war production, provided a massive body of potential recruits for both the Red and White forces in both countries.

The dire economic situation of recruits in both White and Red forces made them politically and militarily unreliable. This was also true of recruits into the right-wing *Freikorps* that aided German federal troops in retaking Munich from the soviet government. An officer of the second battalion of the *Freikorps Oberland* (one of the most notoriously right-wing of the voluntary militias) made this point clearly on June 2, after the Red Guard had been

---

[46] StAM Pol. Dir. 10151 (Fritz Seidel), 11.   [47] StAM, Staatsanwaltschaft München I.

defeated for over a month and all its leaders killed or arrested. He claimed that "if a Red Army were to come into being today and promise higher wages," than the *Freikorps*, he assumed about thirty percent of his troops would change sides "without giving it a thought."[48] Thus, although both sides painted the conflict in terms of a grand conflict of ideologies and both sides attempted to draw recruits by persuading them of the moral superiority of their cause there was tacit recognition that economic necessity was the most powerful motivator for most enlistments on both sides.

The relatively lenient verdicts of the courts-martial in Munich demonstrate their recognition of the economic motives of Red soldiers. Thus nineteen-year-old Karl Lichtenstern was acquitted of accessory to high treason although he joined the Red Guard (and the Communist Party!) in Munich on April 28, by which late date even the moderate leaders of the revolutionary government, such as Toller, were trying to negotiate the handing over of power to the government forces. In his defense, Lichtenstern claimed that he had been receiving unemployment payments, but because these were not enough to survive he joined the Red Guard. In court documents, he claimed to have no knowledge of the program of the Communist Party and to have acted solely out of economic necessity.[49] Given the intensity and visibility of the revolutionary government's recruitment propaganda, which called upon loyalists to fight to the end in a "life and death struggle" to save the revolution from the gathering White forces, such ideological innocence seems perhaps unconvincing, yet it found an ear in the Munich trials.

When compared to contemporary descriptions of the mood in Munich in the last days of April and the city's saturation with desperate propaganda posters demonizing the enemy, Lichtenstern's claim of political ignorance seems incongruous. The professor of philology and famous diarist Victor Klemperer wrote on April 28, the day Lichtenstern enlisted, that "certainty about the impending fall of the current [soviet] regime was widespread" in Munich.[50] In other words, by Klemperer's description, a recruit like Lichtenstern would have to have known he was signing up for a desperate last-ditch attempt to save the revolutionary government. But by the time Lichtenstern's trial began on June 26, 1919, almost at the end of the court-martial, there seemed to be a general tendency towards greater leniency. The fact that he was acquitted made clear the powerful resonance of his claims that his participation was based on apolitical economic necessity, rather than on any ideological commitment, with the judges of the court-martial.

---

[48] BHSA IV, Kriegsarchiv, Gruppenkommando 4, Bund 4/2.
[49] StAM, Staatsanwalt München I, Film 311, file 2107.
[50] Klemperer, entry for April 28, 1919, 104.

It might seem that the relative leniency of the court-martial in Munich in reaction to these claims of economic motivation might be explained by the constitution of the government that defeated the "commune" and reestablished order in the capital. The postrevolutionary Bavarian government was the Social Democratic– led parliamentary government under Johannes Hoffman that had been installed by the *Landtag*, democratically elected in January 1919. Because the Social Democrats in their Bamberg exile faced the difficult task of defeating and routing out the Communist leaders of the *Räterepublik* without alienating their working-class support base, they sought compromise. Leniency with those who had only been "followers" in the revolution or who had joined because of economic pressure or muddled political understanding were intended as signals that demonstrated the good will of the Bamberg government towards Munich's workers.

Yet this SPD attempt to mollify the Munich working class alone cannot explain lenient sentencing by the Bavarian courts. The SPD-led *Landtag* government did not directly control the verdicts and sentencing of the court-martial or later the actions of the *Volksgericht*. Neither the military nor the civil judges who served on the court-martial were appointees of the new parliamentary government. They were, instead, judges inherited from the pre-1918 system. These judges tended to be much more conservative, right-leaning, and less sympathetic to workers than the Social Democratic-led government in whose name they issued their verdicts. This was not only the case in Bavaria, but throughout Weimar Germany.

After taking power in 1918, the German Social Democratic government decided to proclaim the "independence of the judiciary" rather than fight against an institution that the party had criticized as an agent of "class justice" during the imperial government. Judges from the imperial government were offered the chance to retire with full compensation if they felt they could not serve the new republican government in good conscience. Only approximately 0.15 percent of judiciary employees took advantage of this option, as opposed to almost 10 percent of other government functionaries.[51] Erich Kuttner, an SPD delegate in the Prussian *Landtag* and editor of *Vorwärts*, described the situation in 1921: "The great majority of judges stayed in the service of the republic, although they are inwardly hostile to it."[52] The situation of the Weimar judiciary, staffed with imperial-era judges, can therefore not be a plausible explanation for the relative leniency shown by the courts in Munich in dealing with the 1919 revolutionaries. The willingness of even these conservative judges to accept a variety of mitigating circumstances in

---

[51] Statistics from Erich Kuttner's 1921 brochure, "Warum versagt die Justiz?," quoted in Heinrich Hannover and Elisabeth Hannover-Drück, *Politische Justiz, 1918–1933* (Frankfurt a.M.: Fischer, 1966), 22. Kuttner was murdered in 1942 in the Mauthausen concentration camp.
[52] Ibid.

considering cases was not caused by any SPD-government partisanship towards the working class but rather resulted from two intertwined factors.

The first had its roots in German legal tradition and the weight historically granted to considerations of the *Gesinnung* – the motivations and character of the accused. The legal foundation for the determination of *Gesinnung* rested on the 1871 imperial law code, StGB §20, which allowed for two different sorts of imprisonment (in a penitentiary versus in a fortress) depending on the "motivation" of the convicted individual in carrying out the crime. As Pamela Swett has shown, "Even though *Gesinnung* appears only in this one instance in the 1871 StGB, its significance was far greater."[53] She quotes a participant at the 1903 German Legal Scholars Conference: "this principle [*Gesinnung*] works like a central nerve throughout all main sections of the criminal law system and into its most outlying periphery."[54] The research of Swett and others has demonstrated that this legal concept of *Gesinnung* had a prejudicial effect in cases against political criminals on the Left in the Weimar years as the conservative judiciary as well as the police came to view the actions of communists as inherently criminal. This led, eventually, to a change in the earlier understanding of an "honorable" *Gesinnung*, actions that originated from "strongly-held political or religious convictions." If communist beliefs were themselves criminal, then someone who acted from strong communist "political conviction" could not be honorable in his or her intention. Instead, crimes committed by communists and other leftists were simple criminal activities undertaken for "dishonorable motives." This was a slippery interpretive slope that led in the Nazi-era to the creation of a legal code based on politically legislated morality. In the post-1934 National Socialist *Volksgericht*, *Gesinnung* alone, in the absence of any proven criminal activity, became grounds for conviction.[55]

In the context of such longer-term developments in interwar German legal thought and practice, the decisions of the court-martial and the Bavarian *Volksgericht* offer an interesting case study of the way the perceived character and motivation of the accused affected sentencing for obviously political crimes. This strong inclination to bend sentencing to fit the presumed motivations of defendants operated as a kind of ideological prophylaxis in the postrevolutionary courts, preventing the courts in Bavaria from becoming narrowly vehicles for retribution. While the evidence suggests relative leniency in the sentencing of the 1919 revolutionaries in Munich given the superheated

---

[53] Pamela E. Swett, "Political Violence, *Gesinnung*, and the Courts in Late Weimar Berlin," in Mark Roseman, Frank Biess, and Hanna Schissler, eds., *Conflict, Catastrophe and Continuity: Essays on Modern German History* (New York: Berghahn Books, 2007), 67.

[54] Kahl from the 26th Deutsche Juristen Tag, 1903, in Hans Lipmann, *Gesinnung und Strafrecht* (dissertation, University of Bonn, 1930),15, quoted in ibid.

[55] William Sweet, "The Volksgerichtshof," *Journal of Modern History* 46/2 (June 1974): 314–29.

rhetoric of the moment, these sentences must sensibly be compared with the frank sympathy and extreme leniency demonstrated in later right-wing political violence, especially in Adolf Hitler's famous trial in 1923 in Bavaria.

A comparison between the judicial actions in the 1919 trials of Bavarian revolutionaries and those experienced by the participants in the failed March 1920 Kapp Putsch shows how the application of *Gesinnung* by judges worked to the disadvantage of those identified with the Left.[56] The courts sentenced fifty-two leaders of the 1919 Munich *Räteregierung* to a total of more than 135 years' imprisonment. By way of comparison, only one of the almost 800 officers who participated in the 1920 Kapp Putsch was tried and sentenced for his part in the treasonous activities. That one officer, Traugott von Jagow, a former Berlin police chief who served as interior minister in the failed Kapp government, was pardoned after serving only three years of his five-year minimum sentence for the crime of abetting in high treason. At his trial, not only his own defense attorney but even the state prosecutor, Ludwig Ebermayer, emphasized that Jagow had "undoubtedly noble motives" and had acted "under the banner of selfless love for the fatherland."[57] So, while we must sensibly concede the courts' efforts to consider the role of ideology and idealism in the sentencing of the 1919 revolutionaries, the related application of this legal principle in cases where the political ideals of the defendant were more understandable and sympathetic to the conservative worldview of most of the Weimar era judges generally led to even milder sentences or, more often, acquittal or lack of criminal prosecution.

Leaders of the Munich *Räteregierung* were seldom seen as having acted out of "noble motives," even in cases where their "idealism" was acknowledged by the court. For the courts and prosecutors who were in place after the fall of the revolutionary government, communist "idealism" was understood to be a predictor of criminal acts. In fact, the judges who heard the case against Leviné expressly denied leniency based on idealism in their verdict. They

---

[56] From March 13–16, 1920, a right-wing putsch government was established in Berlin, and the SPD-led government fled to Stuttgart. The putsch began after an order to disband the *Freikorps* in line with the Treaty of Versailles. The army remained "neutral" and neither defended the government nor aided the putschists. The trade unions and leftist parties called a general strike to fight the putsch. This certainly played a role in the defeat of the putsch effort, but the radicalized workers who established "Red Armies" in the industrial Ruhr region were themselves violently put down by government forces. Many scholars have shown that the reprisals against these workers (who believed that they were defending the republic) were much more severe than those against the officers who had aided Wolfgang Kapp and Walther von Lüttwitz in their putsch. For more on this event and the way that the "apolitical" stance of the *Reichswehr* had tremendous political consequences for the Weimar Republic, see F. L. Carsten, *The Reichswehr and Politics: 1918–1933* (Oxford: Clarendon, 1966), 80–103.

[57] Karl Brammer, *Verfassungsgrundlagen und Hochverrat* (Berlin: Verlag für Politik und Wirtschaft, 1922), 121, quoted in Ingo Müller, *Hitler's Justice: The Courts of the Third Reich*, translated by Deborah Lucas Schneider (Cambridge, MA: Harvard University Press, 1991), 13. See also Gumbel, *Vier Jahre*, 95, 99 (table).

maintained that "because of his [Leviné's] high intelligence he could fully foresee the consequences [of his actions]. When someone meddles with the fate of a whole people like this, it is clear that his actions stem from dishonorable *Gesinnung*."[58] For this reason, the court refused to recognize any mitigating circumstances and sentenced Leviné with the full severity of the law, imposing the death penalty. In the case of the noncommunist Toller, the court accepted his "idealism," using it to justify a lighter sentence.

Similarly, judges weighed other factors that were extraneous to the facts of the case before sentencing defendants. Here again right-wing defendants were more likely to benefit from this mitigation than were revolutionary defendants. They included social factors, such as being well educated, coming from a "good" family, or having served in the army during the recently ended war. Right-wing defendants seeking judicial leniency were often able to cash in this social capital because they came from the same sort of social and educational background as the judges themselves. As the remarks about Leviné's intelligence suggest, similar qualities could be held against leftist defendants. If revolutionaries came from bourgeois or even aristocratic families, prosecutors presented their leftist politics as particularly perverse and treasonous, as was the case for Gabriele Kätzler, an admiral's daughter who was tried for supporting the revolution in Munich, whose trial I discuss in detail in Chapter 5. In Kätzler's case, judges viewed her support of revolutionary politics as a betrayal of her class and her father's service to the German emperor. Socialist politics appeared particularly unnatural and dangerous when expounded by members of the more privileged classes. And if the defendants were also educated and intelligent, their legal responsibility was judged greater, since, as the judges' reasoning went in the Leviné verdict, they should have been able to foresee the consequences of their revolutionary actions. Strongly held political conviction was, in the case of perceived traitors to their middle- or upper-class backgrounds, not a sign of honorable *Gesinnung*, but rather a perversion of honor, demonstrating criminal intentions.

Because the Bavarian revolutions arose in the turmoil at the end of World War I, and because soldiers and sailors played prominent roles in revolutionary activity all over Germany, it is not surprising that many of those tried in Munich were veterans of that war. It should also not surprise us that the meaning of this soldier identity was contested and subject to a variety of interpretations in postrevolutionary society and specifically in the courts. Whereas military service (particularly of long duration or with recognition for bravery) had long seemed to represent traditional qualities such as loyalty, bravery, and allegiance to crown and nation, recent events had turned some of the traditional views of soldiers on their heads. Were servicemen (enlisted men, as opposed to

---

[58] Leviné, 66.

officers or career military) now understood as particularly susceptible to revolutionary politics and activity (like the navel mutineers in Kiel), or could their veterans' status still signal traditional conservative qualities? Lawyers and families certainly argued for a traditional understanding of the soldier defendants, contrasting an honorable military identity with any suspected revolutionary activity. And they were often successful. As we will see, service in World War I was sometimes cited as a sign of character and a mitigating circumstance in the verdicts and sentencing of revolutionary fellow travelers, such as low-ranking members of the Red Army and Red Guard.

In the case of the revolution's leaders, however, courts and prosecutors used their military service during World War I as evidence of particularly "dishonorable motivation"; swearing an oath to defend the fatherland and then making revolution was evidence of deviousness or even psychopathic behavior. For example, in his memoirs, Toller used the case of a Red officer named Müller to demonstrate the courts' hypocritical understanding of "leadership." According to Toller, Müller was sentenced to one year and nine months in prison for "abetting high treason," although the court could not prove that he had given any orders to the revolutionary troops to fight. By way of explanation, the court said that he was someone who "should have used his influence over his troops to prevent them from fighting the government forces."[59]

Other circumstances, such as drunkenness, loyalty to a leader, standing up for a comrade, or following orders, appear in the sentencing notes as mitigating factors for minor figures but were conversely damning when describing a revolutionary leader. Drunkenness could help excuse the poorly thought-out actions of a young soldier, but the use of alcohol represented a sign of degeneracy in communist leaders. As in the case of the *Geiselmord*, anti-revolutionary literature often described the atmosphere in revolutionary meetings and barracks as awash in alcohol. Similarly, lower level (and often young) recruits to the revolutionary forces could defend themselves with claims that they signed up with brothers, friends, or comrades from their wartime military units or that they merely followed orders. But since the courts did not recognize any of the organizations as legitimate military units, the same claims of loyalty or duty were not considered exculpatory for Red organizers, who were viewed as criminals not soldiers.

In Munich, following the defeat of the revolutionary government in 1919, the courts slowly created a dominant narrative to explain recent political history that served as backdrop to the trials of Leviné and other leaders. In practical terms, mass responsibility for the revolution was reduced through the

---

[59] Toller, *Justiz-Erlebnisse*, 51–3. This is one of the examples Toller provided to demonstrate how loosely the court sometimes applied its definition of "leadership"; the name and sentence do not exactly match a case file from the Munich court-martial, though the officer he refers to could have appealed or been tried or sentenced later.

demonization of the leaders, most of whom were also characterized as foreign exotics. This willful misunderstanding of the revolution effectively denied the agency of the urban masses, placing the majority of revolutionary participants outside the frame of legal consequences. This same narrative that effectively depoliticized the actions of the mass of supporters of the revolution emphasized, reciprocally, the sinister and selfish influence of the ringleaders, who cynically manipulated the dire economic situation of the time to their own benefit. In this way Munich (and also, though to a lesser extent, its working-class population) came to be viewed as a victim of the revolution and not its perpetrator.

Trials in Budapest

In Hungary, the counterrevolution was prolonged relative to Munich and the cycle of reprisals and counterrevolutionary accounting extended over a wider geographic orbit. It was, therefore, the so-called National Army under Admiral Horthy's loose command, rather than the official judiciary or even special summary courts set up for revolutionary crimes, which became the site of what historian Ferenc Pölöskei referred to as "the main form of mass reprisal."[60] In Hungary, the violence associated with the revolutionary *tanácsköztársaság* government and its defeat was not narrowly focused in the capital Budapest. As discussed earlier, much of both the Red and White terrors took place in the Hungarian countryside, in particular in Transdanubia. The revolutionary leadership, as well as the majority of their supporters, however, had been based in Budapest.

What seemed an inevitable violent confrontation between Horthy's National Army and former revolutionaries in the capital was probably avoided by the Entente-supported Romanian occupation. In the wake of the collapse of the Kun government, White authorities in other parts of Hungary permitted a violent account-taking that included pogroms and brutal executions. When Horthy and his troops finally entered Budapest on November 16, 1919, ceremonially "retaking" the city, they had been put under immense international pressure to avoid similar bloodlettings in the capital.

The temporary "government of concentration" formed under Károly Huszár on November 24, after Horthy's entry into Budapest, immediately set about establishing the legal and judiciary regulations for the postrevolutionary period. A special decree was issued on December 23, 1919 that established a system of summary justice.[61] The Ministry of Justice based the decree on the

---

[60] Pölöskei, *Hungary after Two Revolutions*, 46.
[61] Andor Csizmadia, *A magyar állam-és az egyházak jogi kapcsolatainak kialakulása és gyakorlata a Horthy-korszakban* (Budapest, Akadémiai Kiadó, 1966), 144.

force of the 1912 Habsburg Law LXIII on wartime emergency, creating a legal link to the prewar and prerevolutionary Habsburg royal legal code and also equating the post-armistice period of revolution with the wartime emergency that had preceded it. The decree was intended to establish both institutions and procedures for punishing the participants in the revolutionary government and its military. Procedurally, the decree set aside the right to a trial by jury that was guaranteed by the nation's 1878 legal code. Section 18 of the emergency decree "temporarily suspend[ed] the jury in all courts of law and relegate[d] the trial to the sphere of authority of the courts of law."[62] Institutionally, the decree called for the creation of councils of five within every court district to try the "organs, authorities and commissariats of the Soviet republic" for "crimes committed to establish, maintain or restore the Soviet Republic."[63] These summary courts could sanction capital punishment following the procedures of an earlier decree on the imposition of the death penalty. This procedure allowed judicial review of death sentences by the Hungarian Supreme Court within twenty-four hours, and the Supreme Court did not have to explain its decision to grant or deny reprieve.[64]

These judicial institutions and procedures, resting on the 1912 State of Wartime Emergency Law, were extended again in early 1920 and remained in place even after the ratification of the peace treaty in July of that year. But even this summary justice, which included the death penalty, was seen by right-wing groups in Hungary, such as MOVE, as too slow and too lenient.[65] This critique from the right that the civilian courts were too "soft" meant that more and more cases came to be considered under military jurisdiction, both because police and prosecutors may have shared these sentiments and as a measure to keep the peace and prevent right-wing vigilante violence and lynchings, like the murder of the *Népszava* editor Béla Somogyi and journalist Béla Bacsó.[66] In thousands of other cases of political arrests, people were simply interned by armed forces and held without trial under the provisions of Law III of 1921, which allowed indefinite protective custody. Because the same decree allowed for the unlimited internment of people suspected of "communist crimes," some felt there was no need to go through the effort of holding trials and sentencing political prisoners – they could simply be imprisoned without trial, without the effort and expense of a court trial or the risk of acquittal or mild sentences. Given the relatively light sentences issued by the courts in Munich, even by a conservative judiciary, the Hungarian Right may have been correct to assume that court trials could lead to leniency.

---

[62] Pölöskei, *Hungary after Two Revolutions*, 46 n. 115.   [63] Ibid., 47.
[64] The Friedrich government's August 1919 decree, ibid., 48.
[65] Magyar Országos Véderő Egylet (more on the group in Chapter 3).
[66] These murders are discussed in more detail in Chapters 3 and 5.

Thus, in Budapest the extraordinary judicial situation of the immediate postrevolutionary period was extended in 1920 through laws and decrees that placed civilians under the jurisdiction of military courts and broadened the grounds for internment. But since all these actions were based on the royal law of 1912 concerning states of wartime emergency, the signing of the final peace treaty that ended Hungary's wartime status removed the legal basis for the decrees. The ratification of the Treaty of Trianon officially ended the war and meant that the emergency powers associated with the resurrection of the 1912 law had to be superseded by new legislation, Law III of 1921, the "Law for the Maintenance of Order," which was ratified on March 16. This law set out the criminal procedures that could be applied to political crimes and was in force throughout the interwar period in Hungary. Both before and after this law, however, revolutionaries were often charged with other "nonpolitical" crimes, including charges relating to murder, bribery, kidnapping, and so on. These charges would not have fallen under the provisions for political crimes but under standard criminal procedures.

The postrevolutionary trials in Hungary occurred in an atmosphere of severely limited civil rights. The early counterrevolutionary governments, from István Friedrich through Károly Huszár and even the parliament under István Bethlen through the 1920s, retained many features of the emergency decrees issued during World War I in addition to the restrictions on the right to jury trial and other judicial rights. Press freedom was limited, and the Press Law of 1914 passed by István Tisza's wartime government remained in force until the late 1930s.[67] This law imposed preventative censorship and proclaimed collective responsibility for published works so that the editor and publisher of a paper or journal would bear legal repercussions for the articles they printed, in addition to the author. This created a strong disincentive to editors and publishers to work with authors whose politics might put the survival of their enterprise at risk. This combination of official censorship and self-censorship by fearful editors meant that citizens of Budapest received only very limited information through the media about postrevolutionary arrests, incarcerations, and trials. Even newspapers that provided a steady diet of sensational stories of the crimes by the Red regime that seemed to justify the unacknowledged but well-known excesses of the Whites often appeared with censors' blackouts.[68]

As we have seen, censorship in Hungary both contributed to an atmosphere of fear and rumor for citizens of Budapest at the time and left an imbalanced legacy for historians. The reports in Budapest's censored newspapers were a stark contrast to the active and politically diverse press in Munich, where leftist

[67] Pölöskei, *Hungary after Two Revolutions*, 54.
[68] For complaints about newspapers, see BA, Berlin, Germany, Microfilm 53411, Bd. 6, Presse u. Propaganda Angelegenheiten, "Informatorische Aufzeichnung Nr. 23, General Konsulat Budapest, May 6, 1919"; also the British Joint Labor Delegation to Hungary, 20.

newspapers such as *Rote Fahne, Vorwärts*, and *Rote Hand* published articles on Leviné's execution and martyrdom while at the same time offering their readers a critical interpretation of the postrevolutionary trials. The censorship in Hungary extended beyond the periodical press to other media as well.

While former Bavarian revolutionary leaders Erich Mühsam and Ernst Toller were able to publish books critical of postrevolutionary justice and the White Terror that could be bought in Munich's bookstores, Hungarian revolutionaries could only criticize from exile, and the sale of their works was banned in Hungary. In September 1919, the Hungarian Ministry of the Interior ordered socialist and other leftist books "confiscated and destroyed"; these included not only works by leaders of the *tanácsköztársaság*, such as Vilmos Böhm, Béla Kun, and György Lukács, and the editor of the socialist newspaper *Népszava,* Béla Somogyi, but also works by Marx, Engels, and Lenin. The ban even extended to works by members of the 1918 Mihály Károlyi government, such as Oszkár Jászi.[69]

One obvious manifestation of the greater severity of judicial decisions in Hungary was the large number of death sentences imposed for crimes associated with the revolution or the council government.[70] The Hungarian judiciary imposed ninety-seven death sentences for crimes associated with the revolution, and, in the end, sixty-eight people were executed.[71] Sixteen other prisoners who had been condemned to death were traded to Soviet Russia along with other political prisoners in return for Hungarian POWs. Thirteen others who had been condemned to death were pardoned.[72] The contrast with Bavaria is stark. In Munich, Leviné was the only person sentenced to death by court-martial. Another seven were sentenced to death in the autumn by the *Volksgericht* for their role in the *Geiselmord*, which meant that the postrevolutionary judiciary in Bavaria only sentenced a total of eight people to death for crimes to do with the revolutionary regime in Munich.

It would be easy to assume that the difference came from the fact that postrevolutionary Munich was controlled by a SPD-led government, while Hungary was led by Horthy's right-wing "Christian and National" government. However, as we saw above, by upholding the principle of the independence of the judiciary, the SPD-led Weimar government had effectively saddled itself with the old, imperial and often anti-republican judges, who were not inclined to sympathy with radical leftist politics.[73] So the judges in both places came

---

[69] Pölöskei, *Hungary after Two Revolutions*, 55.
[70] The exiled Hungarian revolutionary Pogány called his chapter on the trials "Gesetzliche Morde" (statutory murders).
[71] Gratz, *A forradalmak kora.*   [72] Gosztonyi, 37.
[73] Hungary had a similar continuity in judicial personnel, so in both places the judiciary was largely staffed by prewar judges. These judges, while most likely unsympathetic to revolutionary politics, also had strong institutional loyalties. They upheld the independence and integrity of the courts, which may have limited the use of the courts as active tools of political counterrevolution in both Bavaria and Hungary.

from the old, conservative judiciaries of the monarchies. Instead, the difference in severity of punishment originated in two key differences between the states during the revolutionary and immediate postrevolutionary periods. The first and most important was that the general level of violence and lawlessness in Hungary over the period of the revolution and counterrevolution was undeniably higher than in Bavaria. The scope of both revolutionary Red violence and counterrevolutionary White violence was vastly greater in Hungary. The process of "re-taking" control, first of the Hungarian countryside and later, ceremonially, of the capital, took months, rather than days or weeks as in Munich. During this longer period of effective civil war, many more people were victims of counterrevolutionary terror and summary or vigilante justice than in Bavaria. The prolonged period of violence and the greater loss of life meant that expectations of judicial retribution might have been higher among both the judges and the public in Budapest.

The second key difference had to do with the question of "idealism" or considerations of character. This proved to be much more influential in sentencing in Munich in than in Budapest. As we have seen, judges in Bavaria showed a far greater degree of tolerance for the naive "idealism" and economic motivations of workers who supported the revolution than their Hungarian counterparts. One of the profound differences between the two cities during the period of the trials was the contrast in understanding and sympathy for the claim of "idealism" in Hungary, both in the courts and more widely in the press and public sphere.

The "hard line" taken in Hungary was made clear by Horthy in a speech given on November 16, 1919, after his ceremonial entry into Budapest. After a ceremonial welcome from the city's mayor and receiving the key to the city, Horthy gave a speech that was shocking to many listeners in its lack of conciliatory tone and content. Horthy emphasized instead that the city of Budapest was "guilty" and "sinful." He claimed the capital had "denied her thousand-year history" and "dragged her crown and her national colors in the mud and covered herself instead in red rags."[74] Later, in a ceremony in front of the parliament building, Horthy called for the elimination of "poisonous elements" from the nation. Despite this extreme and uncompromising formulation of Hungary's future, he was then heralded as a national hero by officials of the Catholic and Protestant churches as well as by the National Association of Hungarian Women.[75] Film footage of Horthy's arrival and the ceremonies that day show the stark contrast between Horthy's words, which posited the capital Budapest as the enemy of the National Army, and the reality of the hearty welcome given to his troops all along their parade route and the massive

---

[74] *Pester Lloyd*, November 17, 1919. Horthy's speech was printed in most daily papers.
[75] Ibid.

cheering crowds at all stages of the festivities.[76] In fact there was no battle to take "Red Budapest," no fighting in the city, and no armed resistance by revolutionaries, not to the Romanian troops who arrived in August, and certainly not to Horthy's National Army when they arrived in November. The antiurban rhetoric of the Hungarian Whites ignored the reality of Budapest's large middle-class population and its relief at the end of the revolutionary experiment.

The differences in counterrevolutionary rhetoric and policy in Munich and Budapest are even more noticeable when we turn from the opinions of political leaders like Horthy to the verdicts of judges as representations of the postrevolutionary assessment of guilt. In Munich, defendants were tried for concrete actions; they had joined a revolutionary organization or acted on the orders of the revolutionary government by bearing arms or requisitioning property. It is true that in the first days of May many people were denounced to the authorities simply as "known Spartacists," and, as Emil Gumbel's research demonstrated, most of the victims in those first days of White Terror were innocent bystanders who had been falsely denounced. As order was restored after May 7, however, even the military authorities in Bavaria took care to remind their troops, "political *Gesinnung* alone is not grounds for arrest."[77] In Munich, though the authorities were sent hundreds of denunciations in which informants claimed that a neighbor or acquaintance had been overheard offering their support for the soviet regime, these denunciations were only rarely part of court records. They appear in the judicial files when they were the original grounds for arrest or questioning and as supporting evidence of *Gesinnung*, not as the basis for criminal charges.[78] In general, Bavarian military authorities as well as the police and judiciary appear to have been disinclined to pay attention to vague denunciations. This reticence was owed to the German legal tradition in which statements of political support (even for the revolutionary regime) were protected as freedom of speech.

In Budapest, courts often did not differentiate between word and deed in considering revolutionary politics. The government decree issued on November 1, 1919 expressly stated, "it is a capital crime to violate the law by trying to restore the past bloody reign of terror by spoken or written word."[79] Across Hungary, therefore, many people found themselves before the

---

[76] Newsreel footage: "Corvin híradó" 1 – 1919 November, "Horthy Miklós bevonulása Budapestre," Magyar Hiradók Gyűjteménye, Magyar Nemzeti Digitális Archívum és Filmintézet; also available through Film Hiradók Online (filmhiradokonline.hu).

[77] BHSA IV, Kriegsarchiv, Höhere Stäbe Bund 3/4, Korpsbefehl May 7, 1919, Generalkommando Oven.

[78] See for example the denunciation included in StAM, Akten der Polizeidirektion München, "Kätzler, Gabriele" 10.087, letter from Stadtkommandantur, Fahndungs-Abteilung, 75, marked as unreliable.

[79] *Pesti Hírlap,* November 15, 1919, quoted in Pölöskei, *Hungary after Two Revolutions,* 40.

postrevolutionary courts for making disparaging statements about the government or the military, or for voicing support for the revolutionary regime, rather than for actions they had taken. The verdicts of judicial authorities routinely averred that such utterances amounted to "taking active part in a movement aimed at upsetting the legal Hungarian government."[80] Although the decree that served as the basis for these arrests and convictions was issued in November 1919, after the revolutionary period, it was applied retroactively to the whole period from the democratic, so-called *őszirózsa*, revolution at the war's end the previous November, through the second soviet revolution and almost four months of revolutionary rule. This meant that all sorts of "fellow travelers" who had merely given verbal support to the communist government while it was in power could be tried for criminal political activity.

The case of the Budapest restaurant manager Géza Zemniczky demonstrates that accusations of verbal support for the revolutionary government could lead to a severe sentence in postrevolutionary Hungary. Zemniczky, a twenty-eight-year-old Roman Catholic from Tiszaörs near Szolnok in eastern Hungary, was a legal resident of Budapest and was employed there during the revolutionary period in 1919. He was tried on October 22, 1920, for charges relating to political statements he had made during the time of the revolutionary government. The prosecuting attorney's indictment focused on two charges. The first was that Zemniczky had made statements glorifying the communist goals of destroying the middle class and attacking private property. The prosecutor focused on an incident in which Zemniczky was reported to have said, "The bourgeoisie must be wiped out; this is the only way that communism can survive!" The defendant's statement was apparently made in front of several witnesses at what was described as a "public gathering" at his residence at Csengery utca 52 in the Terézváros neighborhood near the Nyugati train station.[81] If proven to be true this statement amounted to the crime of offering support to the revolutionary government "by spoken or written word," defined in the November 1919 decree as a capital crime.

Zemniczky was also charged with a second crime. The prosecutor claimed that on an "as yet undetermined date" in July 1919, he and two armed Red soldiers, "who remained unknown," forced their way into the apartment of his neighbor Jenő Mezei and searched it for rationed food items. Mezei and his wife appear on the list of nine witnesses to be subpoenaed for the prosecution along with eight other neighbors. Another witness, Imre Csengős, a physician, lived around the corner from Zemniczky on Izabella utca. Though the charges in this case were brought by the state prosecutor's office, this amounted to

---

[80] Magyar Országos Levéltár (MOL) K616 Igazságügyminisztériumi Levélár, Koronaügyészség 1920 IVy, 3–114.

[81] MOL K616 1920 IVy, 3–114, "88460 szám. 1920.k.ü. A budapesti kir. ügyészségtől."

a local case of neighbors testifying against neighbors about events that happened within the confines of their residential building without outside witnesses or consequences. In the end, the Mezei couple did not testify at Zemniczky's trial, and we do not know if they dropped their claim about his participation in the search of their apartment, nor do we know what their motivations may have been in reporting their neighbor in the first place. Without the Mezei couple as witnesses, this charge, with no date or specific information, was eventually dropped by the court.

State prosecutors were more successful in their pursuit of Zemniczky on the charge of incitment to overthrow the political order. After hearing the testimony of three witnesses from his building and the neighbor Csengős, the court found Zemniczky guilty of three counts of inciting class warfare and abetting the overthrow of the government.[82] The charge of abetting the overthrow of the government demonstrates that the revolutionary government was not legally recognized by the court since Zemniczky's statements were made in support of the soviet government during the period it was in power. According to the witnesses, Zemniczky made public statements in support of communism and the revolutionary government on more than one occasion during the revolutionary period. In all of these cases, the defendant had been standing in the courtyard of his building, a place the court considered a public location, thus making Zemniczky's comments an "open proclamation" in the eyes of the court. According to his neighbors, these declarations had been expressed in front of fifteen to twenty people or, in prosecutorial terms, "a gathering of people."

Because the laws did not differentiate between words and deeds, the public nature of Zemniczky's statements justified his guilty verdicts.[83] After hearing the witness testimonies by neighbors, the court was still not able to establish the exact dates of the alleged communication. It was only determined that Zemniczky had made the declarations "during the time of the proletarian dictatorship, and therefore under the state of war." Despite not being able to establish the dates of any of the inflammatory statements, the court held that "in three separate instances" Zemniczky had made such statements such as "the bourgeoisie must be eradicated, they must be hanged, because this the only way for communists to survive, and only under them can the proletariat be happy and there will be more money." In the court's opinion Zemniczky had intended his words to incite his own proletarian class against the bourgeoisie and private property.[84] As a result, he was sentenced to four years imprisonment for three instances of incitement under the law of 1912 for the state of war.

[82] MOL K616, Igazságügyminisztériumi Levélár, Koronaügyészség 1920 IVy, 3–114, 280.
[83] MOL K616, Igazságügyminisztériumi Levélár, Koronaügyészség 1920 IVy, 3–114, 279.
[84] Ibid.

Zemniczky's sentence is remarkable when compared with the majority of sentences imposed in the postrevolutionary trials in Munich. There, sentences averaged less than two years of imprisonment, and these were mostly imposed in cases where there was significant external incriminating evidence such as a defendant's presence on Red Army payrolls or his capture while armed. Zemniczky was sentenced to four years in prison for verbal support of the revolutionary government (the actual government in place at the time he spoke to his neighbors in the courtyard of his residence). Prosecutors produced no other evidence of revolutionary actions or active support for the Kun government; he was convicted based only on the testimony of witnesses, all of whom lived in his building or very nearby and knew him personally. The surviving evidence of this case does not permit us to speculate about the relationships between the neighbors, their relative wealth or class status (except in the case of the doctor), or about any personal motivations in reporting Zemniczky to the authorities. A comparison with some of the large number of denunciations received by authorities in Munich suggests that often such unspecific charges made in denunciations by acquaintances originated in personal animosity rather than genuine political concerns. However, even without knowing the interpersonal details in this case, we see that the attitude of the Hungarian courts was to take such denunciations seriously and give them credence in their verdicts.

In another Hungarian case, Anna Rivészi (the widow of István Pogány) was tried in September 1919 in an "accelerated" trial before one of the postrevolutionary courts and her appeal was held in Budapest in 1920. Rivészi was accused of political crimes against the state for statements she made to other passengers in her train compartment as she traveled from Szekszárd to Sárbogárd in July 1919 during the period of revolutionary rule.[85] Rivészi was a forty-nine-year-old Roman Catholic widow with nine children. Her husband had been a railway signalman and, like many in his profession, he may have shared her working-class politics. There are several typos in the court documents, and on one occasion Rivészi was referred to as "Mrs. József Pogány," probably a slip because of the similarity to the revolutionary leader József Pogány's name and his infamy among the counterrevolutionaries, since he was held largely responsible for the Red Terror. Just as we saw in Bavaria with arrests of men named Seidel or Seidl, it may have been her (married) name Pogány that brought Rivészi to the attention of authorities or which strengthened their association of her with radical revolutionary politics.

The remarks that resulted in Rivészi's arrest were made while traveling by train on July 20, 1919. The compartment was full, and the passengers were talking about the momentous and chaotic political situation in the country,

[85] MOL K616, Igazságügyminisztériumi Levélár, Koronaügyészség 1920 IVy, 3–114, 42.

exchanging information and rumors about what was going on. The passengers discussed the failed counterrevolution on June 24 in Budapest and the role of the military cadets from the Ludovika Academy who had supported the counterrevolutionaries. Rivészi's fellow passengers reported that the subject of the counterrevolution and the cadets had "enraged" her. Witnesses claimed that Rivészi had said "every one of the rascals and traitors should be hanged" in reference to the cadets from the Ludovika Military Academy who had been arrested after their failed coup.[86] Even though her strong statement against the counterrevolutionaries was in support of the existing Red government in Budapest, the other passengers felt comfortable enough in their counterrevolutionary politics, and possibly secure enough in the imminent collapse of the revolution, to press Rivészi to explain why she was defending the soviet government in Budapest.

As a widowed mother of several children and a Catholic, she apparently appeared an unlikely revolutionary. Because she did not fit the stereotype of the "Jewish Bolshevik" or the young, liberated, and unconventional "revolutionary woman" that the other passengers associated with socialism, they attempted to show her that her political views were opposed to her personal interests. One of the passengers asked her, "what she would say as a mother if in the pursuit of free love they 'communized' your daughters?" According to the witnesses, "she retorted that if such times came, she wouldn't regret it."[87] Rivészi demonstrated a willingness to accept, at least rhetorically, the consequences associated with the success of the communist government, even the fantastical idea of the "communizing of women," a *reductio ad absurdum* often proposed by right-wingers as a predictable consequence of revolutionary terror. Her passionate leftist political convictions shocked her fellow passengers, and she was denounced soon after the collapse of the revolutionary government.

Following her trial in September 1919, Rivészi was sentenced to two and a half years in prison and the loss of her civil and political rights for five years. Her sentence was later reduced on appeal to three and a half months imprisonment.[88] According to the original verdict, not only did her statements "glorify criminal acts," they also demonstrated active support for the revolutionary movement. The verdict made clear that her guilt under the Law for the Maintenance of Order and the emergency ordinances of November 1919 stemmed from the public nature of her statements. The train compartment contained many people and was, therefore, "a gathering," a public, open space. This meant that Rivészi's statements fell under the provisions of the law against inciting against the government, even though she spoke in support of a government that faced armed attacks by those she had condemned. In her case, as elsewhere, the law was interpreted to mean that support for the existing

---

[86] Ibid.   [87] Ibid.   [88] Ibid.

soviet government was, in effect, treasonous. Because the counterrevolutionary judiciary did not recognize the legitimacy of the *tanácsköztársaság,* the courts could retroactively judge all actions, and even statements, in support of the only government existing at the time to be criminal acts.

Personal grievances or prejudices such as antisemitism often played a role in generating charges of verbal incitement to overthrow the political system in postrevolutionary Hungary. To be considered grounds for legal prosecution, it was not necessary that public remarks directly supported communism or the goals of the revolutionary government. One exemplary case was that of Salamon Scharf, the twenty-four-year-old son of a Jewish pub owner, who was tried on November 11, 1920. In this case, a statement made by Scharf to two White soldiers during an argument over their wine order led to a sentence of eight days in prison and a fine of 600 Korona.[89] On April 5, 1920, the soldiers entered the pub owned by Scharf's mother and got into a fight with Scharf, who served as bartender. When the soldiers insisted on paying for a less expensive wine than they had been served, Scharf threw their money to the ground in protest. In anger, the two soldiers accused Scharf of staying at home while they fought in the war to defend him, echoing a common Central European antisemitic slander of World War I.[90] They went on to assert that they still were fighting for the sake of the country. In reply, they claimed, Scharf proclaimed that he had "had enough of this sort of military, who are only fighting *turós gáluskaért*" (for cheese dumplings). This remark was taken by authorities to be an insult to the honor of the National Army and grounds for prosecution.

After hearing witnesses, the court determined that the argument had begun when Private Pál Pácza tried to pay for the drinks with postal money orders, a situation made worse by the soldiers' demand to be charged for an inferior quality wine. Scharf protested that they were "even paying with that shit [*szar*] money." As things heated up, the second soldier, Corporal Ferencz Zatrok, replied that "he'd pay with the money he had," telling Scharf, "I suffered through the war on your account" while Scharf "sat home masturbating."[91] It was in response to this insult that Scharf made his comment about soldiers fighting for cheese dumplings.

Various witnesses remembered the wording of Scharf's remark differently from the two soldiers, and both Scharf and other witnesses claimed he had

---

[89] MOL K616, Igazságügyminisztériumi Levélár, Koronaügyészség 1921 IVa, 48, 13. The fine would have been changed to thirty days imprisonment if Scharf had proved unable to pay.

[90] This claim was widespread enough in Germany that in October 1916 the military authorities commissioned a census of Jews in the German Army, though they did not release the results. Similar claims that Jews were not fulfilling their patriotic and military duties were made in both halves of the Habsburg Monarchy.

[91] MOL K616, Igazságügyminisztériumi Levélár, Koronaügyészség 1921 IVa, 48, 13.

meant his remarks to apply to Corporal Zatrok, and that he had not meant his remark to imply that the whole National Army was fighting only for cheese dumplings. Unlike the cases of Zemniczky and Rivészi, the defendant in this case was not sentenced to a long prison term. Scharf's previously clean criminal record and the agitation caused by Zatrok's comments were recognized as mitigating circumstances in his initial sentencing. Eight months later, an appeals court determined that the initial verdict had been incorrect in assuming that Scharf's insult to Zatrok applied to the Hungarian National Army or to the defense ministry.[92] Though Scharf was largely exonerated, his prosecution and his initial guilty verdict makes clear the potentially serious legal consequences for belittling the motivation of the Hungarian National Army in the counterrevolutionary mood of the months following the defeat of the revolutionary government.

In Budapest, as in Munich, the authorities installed in the wake of the conservative victories paid particular attention to educators who had openly supported the revolutions. In her memoirs, the conservative and antisemitic Hungarian Women's Association founder, Cecile Tormay, lamented that during the revolution, "A new teacher walks among the children, a devilish red shadow has mounted the teacher's desk." She decried what she claimed was the replacement of religious instruction with sexual education, claiming that "Jewish medical students and lady doctors give erotic lectures to little boys and girls." She concluded that, "after the robbing of the land the theft of souls has started."[93] Both Tormay's antisemitism and the fear she expressed about the influence of revolutionaries and progressives on children were widespread in the counterrevolutionary Christian National coalition that took power in Budapest after the departure of Romanian occupying forces. In this postrevolutionary hysteria, disciplinary measures were taken against more than 800 out of 5,600 teachers in the capital city.[94] Those identified as leftists or, worse, supporters of the defeated Kun government faced loss of employment and even in many cases criminal conviction and imprisonment.

The trial of one of these Budapest educators, Gizella Berzeviczy, highlights both the severity of postrevolutionary justice in Hungary and some of the shared Central European assumptions about what was commonly called the "Judeo-Bolshevik conspiracy." Berzeviczy had become director of her school under the communist regime. After the counterrevolutionary victory, she was denounced by several of the teachers at her school.[95] She was tried in 1920 on three serious charges, each carrying a potentially long sentence. The first two, inciting class hatred and blasphemy, were common for cases against educators

---

[92] Ibid.   [93] Tormay, vol. 2, 281.
[94] Gábor Pajkossy, correspondence with István Deák, 2000.
[95] Politikatörténeti Intézet Levéltár (PTIL), Budapest, Személyi gyütemények, visszaemlékések, 822. f. "Berzeviczy Gizella."

or others who had spoken in favor of the soviet regime while it was in power. The final charge, extortion, was one that was more common in cases against higher-ranking officials of the defeated regime. This charge implied financial and moral impropriety and was commonly applied with a little-disguised antisemitic tone.

In Berzeviczy's case, the extortion charge was dropped after her defense lawyer called the testimony of an accusing witness into question. In a denunciation typical of the heated antisemitic rhetoric of this period, the witness had called Berzeviczy a "Polish-Russian Jewish anarchist." This claim was made at a time when the Galician Jews of Budapest were facing expulsion due to the demands of Hungarian refugee groups and the right-wing ÉME.[96] The witness sought to identify Berzeviczy with the Galician Jews being expelled from the country and with the antisemitic campaign around those expulsions. The claim of hyphenated "Polish-Russian" origins would have linked Berzeviczy with both Galician (Polish) Jews and with Russian revolutionary politics. Berzeviczy's attorney challenged the validity of this denunciation by a man named Horger, but his challenge affirmed rather than denied the basic antisemitic assumptions underlying the claims. The lawyer merely tried to convince the court that these racist assumptions were being applied to the wrong individual. Rather than questioning the relevance of the defendant's racial or ethnic origins to the charge of extortion, the lawyer himself took on the context of antisemitism that informed the moment, proclaiming: "Mr. Horger calls Gizella Berzeviczy – a member of the old nobility, a close relative of the president of the Academy of Sciences – Jewish? Polish . . .? Is it possible?" He then argued that testimony that was so inaccurate about Berzeviczy's race and origins could not be trusted for any accurate information, asking the court, "Can it be permissible to take this and other similar testimony into consideration? Is it possible to convict her of extortion for base motives on the basis of such testimony?"[97] In other words, far from contesting the antisemitic assumptions of the denunciation, that a "Polish-Russian Jew" would be a revolutionary and an extortionist, Berzeviczy's defense gave further emphasis to the underlying racist and classist argument that Hungarian ethnicity and upper-class

---

[96] Hungary had far fewer Jewish refugees during World War I than Cisleithanian Austria. Galicia, where fighting on the eastern front caused a major refugee crisis, was part of the Austrian half of the monarchy, and the Hungarian government had pushed the predominantly Jewish Galician refugees on to Austria, the Bohemian Lands and elsewhere in Cisleithania. The Hungarian government treated them as foreigners within the monarchy. Despite this official policy, thousands of refugees nevertheless ended up in Budapest, as did other Jews without Hungarian citizenship. See discussion in Chapters 3 and 6; also Klein-Pejšová, "Budapest Jewish Community's Galician October" and "Between Refugees and the State."

[97] PTIL "Berzeviczy," 1–2. The defense speech of her lawyer, Dr. Béla Gonda, is also published in Viktor Hubert and Gusztáv Müller, *Perbeszedek gyüjteménye* [collected trial speeches] (Pécs: Dunántúl egyetemi nyomdája, 1928), 373.

origins would preclude the sort of "base" criminality coupled in the denunciation with Jewish and foreign heritage. In this point, her lawyer's argumentation along the governing "National and Christian" lines found resonance with the court and the contested item of testimony and the extortion charge were thrown out.[98] In other words, both the prosecution and the defense were able to use the contemporary understanding of Judeo-Bolshevism to argue the question of guilt for some of the revolutionary activities of this (non-Jewish) teacher.

In his response to the charges relating to her alleged misuse of her position as an educator, Berzeviczy's lawyer was less successful. He defended her against the charge of "incitement to class hatred" on the grounds that she had given the incriminating speeches, which compared the teachings of Karl Marx and Christ and praised the Hungarian revolution, only to closed meetings of the school's faculty. The audience for her words was therefore entirely bourgeois and could not be incited to hatred of their own class. He also argued that the "scientific" discussion of the teachings of Marx and Christ could not be construed as blasphemy in such an academic setting. The court disagreed and found her guilty of three counts of incitement to class hatred and blasphemy and sentenced her to eight years imprisonment.[99]

The court was particularly severe with Berzeviczy because of her visible and influential role as an educator. In looking at the treatment of educators generally by the courts it is important to consider the influence of gender on the decision to arrest and convict, since not only were women widely employed as teachers but even women not employed outside of the home were considered by conservatives to be "the teachers of the nation" in their role as mothers. Given society's prevailing stereotypes of women as politically naive, it would seem female defendants could easily claim to have been misled or to have misunderstood the political consequences of their activities. In fact, this lack of political experience was genuine since women had not had the vote in either Hungary or Germany before the outbreak of the revolutions. A defense based on claimed naivety had proved highly successful for the youngest male "Red Guardists" in their trials in Munich. But in both cities female participants in the revolutions were often seen as being particularly traitorous, rather than naive or misled victims of a manipulative Left.

Berzeviczy's case makes clear the foundationally different defense strategies that were employed in Budapest and Munich. Berzeviczy's lawyer, as was the case for most defense attorneys in Budapest, avoided the pleas of naivety and idealism that had proved so successful in the defense of accused revolutionaries in Munich. The lack of a full court record in Budapest, in particular equivalents to the public prosecutor's files for the Munich court-martial, prevents a direct

---

[98] Ibid.   [99] Ibid.

statistical comparison of the two cities. However, surviving trial evidence and records of appeals allow some sensible comparisons to be made. Gizella Berzeviczy's eight-year sentence was typical of the severity with which the courts in Hungary convicted and sentenced fellow travelers and minor participants in the revolutionary government. In stark contrast to Munich, where we were able to observe an attempt by judges to rationalize support of the revolution by members of the working classes, the new government in Hungary acted with great severity towards workers and workers' organizations. As late as February 1920, a request from the county government of Komárom to intern 3,000 miners for political crimes was approved in Budapest, despite the fact that the workers in a mine nationalized during the revolution had almost no choice about whether to support the revolution or join the Red Guard or not.[100]

Conclusion

We have seen that the counterrevolutions in Munich and Budapest were similar in some ways, especially in the phase that led up to and included the military confrontation, with similar armed groups forming, spurred on by anti-urban and antisemitic agitation. However, as the dust settled and order was restored, their unique political, ethnic, and economic characteristics led to a divergence in the relationship between the counterrevolutionary leadership and the two urban centers. In this chapter, we have had a chance to see how these differences were played out in the trials that determined guilt for the revolutions.

In Munich, the old elites were able to reestablish themselves in power and regain control from the military and right-wing activists who briefly followed the revolutionary groups into power. In Hungary, on the other hand, the length of the military conflict and the Entente-supported Romanian occupation of the capital city between August and November allowed the counterrevolutionary military forces to create a center of power and government outside of and independent from Budapest's traditional elites. These differences in power relations led to the creation of two similar, but varying, dominant narratives of the revolutionary period. While the narratives that evolved in Munich and Budapest to explain defeat in the world war and the outbreak of revolutions shared a powerful antisemitic inclination to blame Jews and foreigners, they differed in assessing the blame of the city itself. In Munich, the counterrevolutionary courts and press portrayed the city primarily as a victim of the machinations of revolutionary leaders who took advantage of the lost world war and the economic disaster. In Budapest, however, counterrevolutionary voices portrayed the city itself as the author of the betrayals that led the rest of the country into disaster, including military defeat, territorial losses, and economic

---

[100] Pölöskei, *Hungary after Two Revolutions*, 49.

collapse. They viewed Budapest as outside the Hungarian nation, the host of a population that was both Jewish and foreign, and guilty of bringing the disasters to the country. While indictments of guilt for the events of 1919 certainly evolved in both countries throughout the interwar period, close examination of the trials highlights some of the main themes of these evolving national narratives of revolution.

In one of these Central European additions to the European revolutionary narrative, the idea of the 1919 revolutions as evidence of a Judeo-Bolshevik conspiracy, we can recognize a shared transnational culture that transcends the facts of the individual local revolutions (or for that matter the local Jewish populations). Chapters 5 and 6 will examine this transnational culture of memory and meaning in more detail. The court cases examined in this chapter have highlighted some of the national differences within this Central European shared culture, and we notice striking contrasts between the two cases in the way that the judiciary assigned responsibility for participation in the 1919 revolutions and the way that guilt was determined, as well as the severity of the sentences imposed. The main reason for this dissimilarity was the contrasting narratives of the 1919 revolutions that developed in the two cities.

The primary difference in the ways they assessed blame was that in Hungary, Budapest itself was held responsible for the excesses of the revolutions (including the first parliamentary government of 1918) as well as for the lost war and the terrible economic situation. In Munich, war and inflation were seen as mitigating the guilt of the working classes for the revolutions. It was almost the opposite in Hungary, where Budapest itself, and especially its Jewish population and workers, were seen as responsible for the military defeat, the breakup of the monarchy, and the revolutions. While antisemites in Munich held the Jews responsible for Munich's suffering, antisemites in Hungary viewed the capital city itself as Jewish and foreign and held it responsible for the suffering of the entire country. It seems that not only were the sentences in Hungary more severe but the two excuses of political naivety and idealism, which successfully mitigated the punishments and even verdicts for many participants in the Munich revolutions, were not mobilized as often or as successfully in individual cases in Budapest. To follow the sort of biological metaphors favored at the time, if in Munich the revolutions were judged to be mass "fevers," in Budapest the diagnosis was of a "cancer."

5   Seeing Red

Dangerous Women and Jewish Bolshevism

In his 1926 novel *Anna Édes*, the Hungarian author Dezső Kosztolányi described Budapest in the late summer of 1919 as "like a plague of locusts had devastated the place. Consumed and exhausted, the town lay on the rubbish heap."[1] Since the end of the world war in October, the city had been through two revolutions, the influenza epidemic, occupation by the Romanians acting as agents of the Entente powers, the arrival of a flood of refugees, and political violence associated with the Red and White terrors. Mass deprivation compounded the physical and mental exhaustion Kosztolányi described. As Hungarians tried to make sense of their situation, they tended to view their experiences through the lens of ideology, framed through the existing vocabulary of gender and racial hierarchies. In Budapest in 1919, politics was everywhere and political slogans and calculations informed even the most ordinary personal interactions, from common forms of address and greeting exchanged with neighbors and workmates to interactions with strangers on public transit. Preconceived notions about women and Jews shaped the experience of revolutionary events, and the actions of women and Jews were seen not as individual acts but as representative of larger truths.

In the postrevolutionary chaos that summer, Hungary's political and social elites began to reassert themselves and their values in a still-complex, still-contested environment where vestiges of the revolutionary era survived. As Kosztolányi remembered, "Trams which had been painted under Communist rule were still to be seen in their revolutionary scarlet with revolutionary slogans daubed across them, dashing suicidally through town like refugees from a mental institution."[2] In *Anna Édes*, the upper-class couple the Vizys observe their city that fall, noting that

there were also encouraging signs of improvement. Middle-class passengers on the tram were no longer afraid to stand up to the bullying conductress who addressed them rudely. They took pleasure in reminding her that this was no longer a Bolshevist state. Men once again began to give up their seats to ladies. It was a new and glorious flowering of the age of chivalry.[3]

---

[1] Kosztolányi, 74.   [2] Ibid.   [3] Ibid.

Many residents of Budapest and Munich closely associated the end of revolutionary rule and the reestablishment of "normalcy" with the reassertion of
prerevolutionary gender, race, and class hierarchies, as do the characters in
Kosztolányi's novel.

If revolutionaries had threatened to overturn the old world order and right
traditional injustices, then the end of the revolutionary threat was easily and
visibly demonstrated by the reassertion of the sort of differences revolutionary
ideology had aimed to eliminate. The reassertion of class hierarchy was among
the most obvious social changes visible in postrevolutionary Budapest and
served as the primary subject of *Anna Édes*. But this jarring and contested
endeavor to resurrect the social hierarchy of the prewar past developed simultaneously with an ambitious reassertion of traditional hierarchies of gender and
race, as the quote from the novel illustrates in its equation of "chivalry" with the
new, postrevolutionary political situation. The reassertion of political and
social power by the old elites was demonstrated through the affirmation of
class (the conductress should use proper honorific forms of address) and gender
roles (chivalry of the upper classes). As the front line in the perceived struggle
of cultures in 1919 Hungary moved from the world of armies and politics to the
personal lives of Budapest residents, the reestablishment of traditional gender
roles was an important part of the postrevolutionary, "National and Christian"
consolidation of power.[4] Memories of 1919 and explanatory narratives about
the revolution helped serve this restoration of order. In the preceding chapters,
we examined the immediate responses of the population to the revolutionary
upheavals they had witnessed; in this chapter we will begin to examine the
stage when personal experiences and memories began to solidify into a larger,
social whole, and we see the fashioning of collective memory.[5]

The battles over the meaning of the recent past began in the immediate
aftermath of the struggles for military and political control of Budapest and
Munich. The postrevolutionary governments of both cities as well as the
educated elites attempted to understand and explain the recent experiences of
revolution and civil war for themselves, for the outside world, and for the
"masses." As we have seen already, the majority of these explanations tended to

---

[4] For additional scholarship examining gender in counterrevolutionary Hungary, see
Emily Gioielli, "Enemy at the Door: Revolutionary Struggle in the Hungarian Domestic
Sphere, 1918–1926," *Zeitschrift für Ostmitteleuropa Forschung* 60/4 (December 2011):
519–38, and "'Home is Home No Longer': Political Struggle in the Domestic Sphere in Post-
Armistice Hungary, 1919–1922," *Aspasia: The International Yearbook of Central, Eastern, and
Southeastern European Women's and Gender History* 11 (March 2017): 54–70. Ilse Josepha
Lazaroms looks at the intersection of gender and race in "Humanitarian Encounters: Charity and
Gender in Post–World War I Jewish Budapest," *Jewish History* 33 (2020): 115–32.
[5] I am using this in the sense of Maurice Halbwachs' theory that memory is formed and recalled in
social contexts. See especially Halbwachs, *On Collective Memory*, edited and translated by
Lewis A. Coser (Chicago: University of Chicago Press, 1992); Peter Burke, *Varieties of Cultural
History* (Ithaca: Cornell University Press, 1997), 43–59.

focus on what many authors asserted to be the "foreign" nature of the revolution and the foreign origins and cultures of the revolutionaries (Jews; Russians; in Bavaria, Prussians; and in Hungary, Germans). The reciprocal narrative, asserted alongside the branding of revolutionaries as foreign, was the exposition of the naivety and apolitical nature of the masses, specifically the working population, who, it was claimed, had been swept into revolutionary events through the connivance and manipulation of revolutionary leaders. In both Budapest and Munich, the narratives we have already seen develop through judicial authorities, the press, and key members of the new conservative governments used powerful racial and gendered symbols and content. This chapter examines these antisemitic and misogynist narratives about the 1919 revolutions in greater detail because of the important role they played in framing Central European political commentary and conflict into the World War II period.

The Central European revolutions of 1919 served as a crucible in which two long-standing and powerful associations, of Jews as cosmopolitan revolutionaries and of revolutionary politics with bloody violence, were forged into a powerful myth of Judeo-Bolshevism. Although the association of Jews with communism (even the Polish term *żydokomuna*) existed before 1919, the specific term "Judeo-Bolshevism" came into use after the Russian Revolution introduced "Bolshevism" as a key term in the European revolutionary and counterrevolutionary vocabulary, and the 1919 revolutions in Central Europe were pivotal in articulating and circulating the violent narrative of the Judeo-Bolshevik myth which served in the interwar years as legitimation for a perceived existential racial struggle.[6]

Similarly, press coverage of the trials of women who participated in the two revolutions and representations of women in revolutionary crowds placed gender at the center of the effort to make sense of the revolutionary past.[7] Though women were mainly charged with relatively minor crimes, in the "court of public opinion," represented by the press, they were held responsible far beyond their actual legal liability, along with the "irrational" women believed to be at the center of food and political riots. Opponents of the revolutions used sexual

---

[6] See Ablovatski; for a pan-European study, Hanebrink, *Specter Haunting Europe*.

[7] Kathleen Canning has demonstrated the centrality of gender order for perceptions of the revolutionary situation of post–World War I Germany: "Gender and the Imaginary of Revolution in Germany," in Klaus Weinhauer, Anthony McElligott, and Kirsten Heinsohn, eds., *In Search of Revolution: Germany and its European Context, 1916–1923* (Berlin: Transit Verlag, 2015), 103–26; "Gender Order/Disorder and New Political Subjects in the Weimar Republic," in Gabriele Metzler and Dirk Schumann, eds., *Geschlechterordnung und Politik in der Weimarer Republik* (Heidelberg: Friedrich-Ebert-Stiftung, 2016), 59–80; and "War, Citizenship and Rhetorics of Sexual Crisis: Reflections on States of Exception in Germany, 1914–1920," in Geoff Eley, Jennifer Jenkins and Tracie Matysik, eds., *German Modernities from Wilhelm to Weimar: A Contest of Futures* (London: Bloomsbury Academic Press, 2016), 235–57.

difference and other biological categories to explain political violence and exclude the revolutionaries from the political body of the nation, thus absolving the "nation" of blame. Perceptions of race and gender profoundly affected the way people remembered the revolutions and attempted to create a postrevolutionary social and political order, and the lens of memory highlights the close link between antisemitism and anti-feminism.

Gender on Trial

World War I represented a watershed in the historical experience of European women. Female integration into the industrial economy was both accelerated and given official endorsement as the massive mobilization of soldiers created great manpower shortages.[8] The war seemed to promote and legitimize female political integration as well, as many postwar European governments moved to meet the basic aims of the previously thwarted women's suffrage movement. Despite these advances, World War I and the interwar years comprised an era that was fraught with conflicts over women's roles, rights, and responsibilities.

Across Central Europe, contemporary observers believed that the participation of women in radical left-wing politics in general, and in the uprisings and revolutions of 1918 and 1919 in particular, offered proof of the dangerous and mutually ruinous relationship between women's political participation and revolutionary politics. In his melancholic novella *The Emperor's Tomb* about the end of the Habsburg Monarchy, Joseph Roth represents the clash of the old (good, trustworthy) prewar society and the new (broken, untrustworthy) postwar world by contrasting two strong female characters, the main character's widowed mother and the woman (the "female professor") who seduced his wife and defrauded his mother during his absence at the front in World War I. Franz Ferdinand Trotta returns from the war to find that his cold and bigoted but

---

[8] There is a rich historical literature on European women and gender in World War I. For a good overview, see Susan Grayzel and Tammy Proctor, eds., *Gender and the Great War* (New York: Oxford University Press, 2017) and Susan R. Grayzel, *Women and the First World War* (New York: Routledge, 2002). For classic studies, see Laura Lee Downs, *Manufacturing Inequality: Gender Division in the French and British Metalworking Industries, 1914–1939* (Ithaca, NY: Cornell University Press, 1995) and Susan Grayzel, *Women's Identities at War: Gender, Motherhood, and Politics in Britain and France during the First World War* (Chapel Hill: University of North Carolina Press, 1999); as well as Deborah Thom, *Nice Girls and Rude Girls: Women Workers in World War I* (London: I. B. Taurus, 1998). For Germany, Ute Daniel, *The War from Within: German Working-Class Women in the First World War*, translated by Margaret Ries (Oxford: Berg Publishers, 1997). For Vienna, Healy, *Vienna and the Fall of the Habsburg Empire*. More recently, for the Habsburg Monarchy, see Matteo Ermacora, "Women Behind the Lines: The Friuli Region as a Case Study of Total Mobilization, 1915–1917," in Christa Hämmerle, Oswald Überegger, and Birgitta Bader-Zaar, eds., *Gender and the First World War* (New York: Palgrave Macmillan; 2014), 16–35; and Rudolf Kučera, *Rationed Life: Science, Everyday Life, and Working-Class Politics in the Bohemian Lands, 1914–1918* (New York: Berghahn Books, 2016).

"respectable" mother is lost and disoriented by the changed world of postwar society and by her loss of both financial security and social standing. He also discovers that a shorthaired woman, Jolanth Szatmary (Roth employs a Hungarian name, symbolizing what he considered the central role of Hungarian nationalists in bringing down the comfortable world of the monarchy), has seduced his naive wife and lost her family's fortune by investing in a venture to sell modernist arts and crafts after the war.[9] Like the narrator of Kosztolányi's novel, *Anna Édes*, Roth's Trotta finds some comfort in the symbolic but empty reassertion of aristocrats like his mother: "I was home, in the midst of a Fatherland laid waste [but] I was falling asleep in a fortress. My old mother with her old black stick was keeping all confusion at bay."[10] Conservative women like the fictional mother here were portrayed as strong bastions upholding the prewar order, capable of protecting society through maintaining traditional order within their own homes. This identity as female bastions of the nation was not only imagined by men but also embraced by right-wing women in their political activities.

In the postwar era, conservative critics almost routinely asserted that women revolutionaries were unwomanly, positing radical politics as antithetical to the "natural" or traditional gender order. These female revolutionaries in effect embraced radical political commitments at the cost of filling traditional roles as wives and mothers. These critical voices often proclaimed a somewhat contradictory judgment even when they represented revolution and change fictionally, as in Roth's portrayals of women in his novella. On the one hand, revolutions had brought these "unwomanly" women to the fore, made women less feminine. Yet, on the other hand, the male revolutionary leaders were portrayed as effeminate or womanly, and revolutionary politics and social changes were viewed as emasculating, as in the way the "female professor" Szatmary appropriated both Trotta's wife and his fortune in Roth's novella.

The image of revolutionary crowds led by angry women (an image subversive to the more common, masculine image of uniformed soldiers) is, of course, an old one. Artists, propagandists, and right-wing critics since at least the era of the French Revolution had often emphasized the presence of women in defining events such as the march on Versailles in October 1789 or the defense of barricades in 1830 and 1848. For generations of Europeans, especially for the generation of witnesses to the 1919 revolutions, the image most strongly associated with the Paris Commune of 1871 was that of the female Communard.

---

[9] Joseph Roth, *The Emperor's Tomb*, translated by John Hoare (New York: Overlook Press, 2002), originally published as *Die Kapuzinergruft* (1938), chapters 23–end; Trotta's mother cannot remember the name Szatmary and refers to Jolanth by a whole list of other Hungarian names, see for example page 114: "'what's all this about some Professor Jolanth Kerzkemet?' 'Szatmary, Mamma,' I corrected. 'Szekely for all I care,' said my mother."

[10] Ibid., 99.

Historian Gay Gullickson has argued that the Paris Commune was "a defining moment for Western conceptualizations of gender, not least because it gave birth to the powerful, evil, and imaginary pétroleuses (female incendiaries) who were accused of setting fire to Paris during the semaine sanglante."[11] Contemporary authors often compared women in the 1919 Central European revolutions to these French historical precedents by referring to any female revolutionaries as "communardes," and political observers from both Left and Right attempted to use the complicated relationship between women and revolution to explain contemporary events.

In the expanding field of the cultural history of World War I, the role of gender in society was long expressed almost theatrically through the fighting front/home front dichotomy. There was the experience of war at the fighting front, a masculine world of soldiers, and in contrast there was the realm of the home front where women experienced the war through a variety of domestic hardships or through an expanded participation in the economy. Of course, there were many men who remained on the home front: older men, government officials, and skilled workers in the war industries among them. Moreover, a limited number of women experienced the fighting front as volunteers, mainly through the medical services, and some were even forced into this world as civilians caught in the direct line of battle. And, with few exceptions, these boundaries, as conceptualized by historians, continue to endure, despite our expanding understandings of the period's complexities.[12]

Contemporaries also emphasized the idea of an often-gendered division of the wartime experience. But what of the experience of revolution and civil war in Central Europe in 1918 and 1919? Was the dichotomy of war front/home front as clear in these hotly contested and often violent venues?[13] How were these events experienced and remembered by participants and witnesses? Can the same gender differences that were so widely associated with large military events and related home-front adjustments be applied to these consequential, but less studied, events? How did the presence of women in revolutionary movements and crowds affect the dominant archetypes of the war experience: the myths of soldiers' honor and bravery, the images of the enemy and of battle?

---

[11] Gay L. Gullickson, *Unruly Women of Paris: Images of the Commune* (Ithaca, NY: Cornell University Press, 1996), 3; Gullickson's book offers an excellent treatment of women in the Paris Commune of 1871, to which the Russian Revolution of 1917 and the Munich and Budapest revolutions of 1919 were often compared.

[12] See for example, Iris Rachamimov, "'Female Generals' and 'Siberian Angels': Aristocratic Nurses and the Austro-Hungarian POW Relief," in Wingfield and Bucur, eds., *Gender and War*, 23–46; and Melissa K. Stockdale, "My Death for the Motherland is Happiness": Women, Patriotism, and Soldiering in Russia's Great War, 1914–1917." *American Historical Review* 109/1 (February 2004): 78–116.

[13] See Healy, *Vienna and the Fall of the Habsburg Empire*; Gioielli, "Enemy at the Door" and "Home is Home No Longer."

Events in Munich and Budapest in 1919 afford us the opportunity to examine some of these questions.

Indeed, the ways in which the lives and activities of women revolutionaries were portrayed reveal essential elements of the counterrevolutionary moment. Representations of women in major newspapers, in denunciations sent to the authorities by other citizens, and in police reports and judicial verdicts, are all essential sources for this complex historical moment. In the postrevolutionary period, aside from the trials of the most famous (or infamous) revolutionary leaders, the contemporary press across Europe as well as in Munich and Budapest was most interested in, and gave most coverage to, the limited number of trials of women arrested for their participation in the revolutions. There was widespread and enduring interest, although the women who stood trial were all minor figures. Women had no leadership roles in the revolutionary governments or fighting forces in these cities. And, in the months following the collapse of the revolutionary governments in Munich and Budapest, they constituted only a very small portion of those arrested or tried for revolutionary crimes. The sensationalist attention of the press to cases with female defendants demonstrates contemporary assumptions about women's place in society and their role in the revolutions. An excellent example was the sensational trial of the widowed children's home director Gabriele Kätzler and Hilde Kramer, her eighteen-year-old former charge. Their trial was held in Munich on July 31, 1919, the last day of the legal authority of the court-martial, and their case is particularly well-documented with full trial records and a large police dossier.

Kätzler and her extended family lived in the small Bavarian town of Riederau. They came to the attention of the Munich police through an anonymous denunciation, signed only "from a reliable source," which claimed that the Kätzler family members were "well-known Spartacists." Additionally, this anonymous informant claimed to the police that one of the Kätzler daughters had had a romantic affair with the nephew of the famous Berlin revolutionary Karl Liebknecht. The second daughter had been active in the Spartacist movement in Munich.[14] During her trial, the prosecution accused Gabriele Kätzler herself of spreading propaganda throughout the revolutionary period and of traveling by train to the countryside to incite the rural population to support the soviet government. On May 2, 1919, the day after Munich was successfully captured by counterrevolutionary forces, Kätzler, her daughter Luise, and her foster daughter Hilde Kramer were taken into protective custody to await trial, like hundreds of other Munich citizens.[15] On June 16, 1919, the family's lawyer, Philipp Theilhaber, sent a letter to the Munich Polizeidirektion

---

[14] StAM, Akten der Polizeidirektion München, "Kätzler, Gabriele" 10.087, letter from Stadtkommandantur, Fahndungs-Abteilung, 75.

[15] StAM Pol. Dir. 10.087, 82.

inquiring about his clients' whereabouts, since he had no access to them and they were not listed on any of the inmate lists although they had still not been released from custody. Theilhaber was a prominent Munich lawyer who represented many 1919 revolutionaries and socialists throughout the Weimar era.[16] Luise Kätzler was finally released without charge, owing to Theilhaber's efforts. In the end, only her mother and Hilde Kramer stood trial before the court-martial at the end of July 1919. Both were accused of several crimes; the most serious was aiding and abetting high treason.

Examination of contemporary reporting on the Kätzler and other trials reveals that analyses of women's participation in the revolution focused on three areas: the accused women's supposed lack of morality, their social and ethnic origins, and their roles in society or professions. Readers were propelled towards the authors' prejudice by signals provided in their descriptions of the women's appearance or their presumed psychological characteristics.[17] Descriptions of both the appearance and the psychology of the women often employed the common terminology of Jewish stereotypes to help frame the reader's opinion. Descriptive cues, such as "bandy-legged," "hunched," or "hook-nosed," from popular antisemitic stereotypes were used to help readers fit events and personalities into the dominant cultural code of the time. This mix of cue-words and stereotypes evoked a variety of already existing prejudices. Such a symbolic vocabulary allowed writers such as Cecile Tormay to describe in her *Outlaw's Diary* such an illogical character as "a Russian Jew, with a limp and curly hair ... in the habit of gouging out a bourgeois' eye with a single turn of his Cossack knife," a figure that promiscuously blended Jewish fears of the Cossacks in Russia with the antisemitic author's fears of Jewish Bolshevism.[18]

Contemporary perceptions of female revolutionaries were inextricably bound together with the ideologies of nationalism and antisemitism. By the early twentieth century, the belief that women played a crucial role in the moral life of the nation was already a long-established trope of nationalist and conservative political discourse. Women were mothers and therefore served as the irreplaceable teachers of the nation's future citizens and leaders. Women were also seen from this perspective to embody, more abstractly, the virtue of the nation, its purity and its traditions.[19]

---

[16] Theilhaber's memoirs are housed at the Leo Baeck Institute in New York and are available on microfilm at the Jewish Museum in Berlin, MM 51.

[17] For an interesting comparison with trials of female collaborators in World War II, see Benjamin Frommer, "Denouncers and Fraternizers: Gender, Collaboration, and Retribution in Bohemia and Moravia During World War II and After," in Wingfield and Bucur, eds. *Gender and War*, 111–32.

[18] Tormay, *Outlaw's Diary*, vol. 2, 226.

[19] For a similar phenomenon elsewhere in post-Habsburg Central Europe, see Cynthia Paces, "Gender and the Battle for Prague's Old Town Square" in Elena Gapova, ed., *Gendernye istorii Vostochnoi Evropy* [Gendered (Hi)stories from Eastern Europe] (Minsk: European Humanities

The revolutionaries had also claimed to speak in the name of the nation (or rather the people), of course. But once they had been defeated and criminalized, it was important to conservatives and nationalists to demonstrate that the revolutionaries had not been "of the nation." According to the ascendant counterrevolutionaries, neither the Hungarian nor Bavarian revolution had sprung from local causes or been led by authentic members of the nation. In both Munich and Budapest this effort to exclude the revolutionaries from the nation, and the revolutions themselves from the nation's history, was most commonly expressed through the discourse of antisemitism, since antisemitic tropes assumed Jews were perpetually foreign and forever unintegrated culturally. Gender stereotypes as well as anti-feminist views helped to reinforce this surging antisemitic worldview or cultural code. Women, because of their importance to the discourse and imagery of the nation, were subject to this process of exclusion and discrediting. In this discourse, the gendered categories of social roles (mothers and teachers), morality, and origin all flowed together, supporting a general nationalist perspective. The gendered vocabulary of anti-semitic stereotypes allowed non-Jewish women to be made "Jewish" simply by being revolutionaries and Jewish women, whatever their politics, to be tarred as revolutionaries.

Rumors of licentious behavior by female members of revolutionary organizations during the soviet period became part and parcel of the myth of the revolution created after its repression and continued throughout the interwar years. In Munich and Budapest during the summer and fall of 1919, the personal lives of women were used as a means of incriminating them in denunciations to the police, press reportage, and testimony before the court. Men "coming and going at all hours," soldiers living in their homes, and their real or imagined romantic relationships were all offered in denunciations as evidence of their more general guilt for the national "shame," as the revolutions were seen. We have seen how allegations of sexual perversion were often paired with descriptions of revolutionary activities as a means for separating revolutionaries from the accepted body of society and recreating a stable social order.

For the women who appeared as defendants in the courts of Budapest and Munich, more attention was paid to information about their sexual morality than to the specific facts of the criminal accusations against them. For example, in the trial of Kätzler and Kramer, prosecutors presented the court with an array of evidence about their private and romantic lives based on a large number of

University Press, 2002), 124–31. See also the classic collection edited by Ida Blom, Karen Hagemann, and Catherine Hall, *Gendered Nations: Nationalisms and Gender Order in the Long Nineteenth Century* (London: Berg, 2000). More recently, Judith Szapor and Agatha Schwartz, "Gender and Nation," special issue, *Hungarian Studies Review* 41/1–2 (Spring–Fall 2014).

personal letters that had been confiscated from the Kätzler home. One newspaper correspondent described how Kramer's letters demonstrated a "lavish" use of exclamation marks, and several descriptions of her lovers such as "he's a dark, revolutionary type" were read into the court record. Kramer's claim in another letter, that "in Bavaria free-love is common," was read by the judge with the remark to the courtroom, "this must be why so many non-Bavarians have come here!"[20] The young Kramer seems to have stood by her political beliefs in court, only denying the specific charge that in her capacity as a secretary at the revolutionary city headquarters she personally signed arrest warrants or had access to public funds. She did not defend her morality against the charges made in court; in fact, according to the press, she seemed to enjoy shocking the public in her testimony. She felt no need to defend herself against the charges of the establishment because she did not believe the free movement of women, regardless of their marital status and whether in mixed company, to be wrong or something to be denied.

Kramer was unusual in her lack of concern for propriety; she was perhaps young enough and radical enough to flaunt traditional views of women even as she faced the hostility of the anti-revolutionary court. She, in effect, refused to let the moral condemnation of the conservatives define her. When charged by the authorities or denounced by their neighbors, most women, however, defended their honor as vehemently as they defended themselves against charges of treason or other political crimes. Many women made an effort to clear their names and good reputations, especially those who had been detained or arrested due to denunciations that focused on their personal or sexual lives.

Theilhaber, who served as Kätzler's attorney, demanded an official statement from the police verifying that they had found nothing incriminating during the search of the apartment of another of his clients. This woman then posted the official police statement in her building, along with a letter to the other inhabitants explaining that alleged "male company at all hours" was nothing other than her doctor and a male neighbor who had come to make sure she was surviving in such dangerous times. She also threatened to sue another neighbor for libel if he did not apologize for spreading rumors about her morality and behavior.[21] Such efforts by women to defend their honor, sexual morality, and behavior against anonymous attacks as well as formal charges worked to reinforce traditional morality and the often-oppressive restrictions on women's freedom of movement and association that had predated the revolutions.

The focus on women's sexual mores was often paired with a concern for racial and class origins and ethnic purity. Critics of the revolutions routinely

[20] "Die Sekretärin des Stadtkommandanten," *Münchner Neuste Nachrichten*, 303, August 1, 1919; StAM, Pol. Dir. 10.087.
[21] StAM, Akten der Staatsanwaltschaft, Fasz. 153, 2106/1 – "Leviné" (Ebert), 230.

equated Jewishness with revolutionary activity. One common antisemitic tactic used to attack gentile women on the left was to link them socially or romantically with Jews. Tormay wrote of a chance meeting during the revolutionary period with a young noblewoman of her acquaintance who had become a communist and was at the time accompanied by a man Tormay described in graphic antisemitic terms. The description demonstrated how an alert observer could even "see" certain stereotypical physical features that were not there by extrapolating from other physical cues. Tormay said of the companion, "His narrow shoulders bent forward and his back looked humped; he hadn't really got a hump, but his face gave one the impression of a hunchback as well. He was remarkably pale, and only his big, Jewish nose shone red in his face between his dark eyes."[22] Tormay showed her readers how from "only his big, Jewish nose" one could recognize the full racial stereotype (even the nonexistent humpback in this case). This physical profile then implied an entire political and moral worldview as well, representing a dangerous and corrupting influence on the young noblewoman.

After describing the girl's good family and her protected upbringing in the family castle, Tormay asked: "How could a girl like that fall into the company of the Communists?"[23] The answer, she asserted, was that the young woman "had learned Russian within the last few years and had translated several Communist works, and under the influence of two Jewish friends, one of them the son of a rich banker, had professed Syndicalist principles."[24] Tormay's lament for the young noblewoman infected by the "epidemic of Bolshevism" gives us an example of the other main stream of what I would term the "origins" argument. In this argument, responsibility for the revolutions lies mostly, but not only, with foreigners and Jews (these critics most often consider them one and the same) but also with the "fallen" nobility and the "misled" simple people.[25] The plot of Dezső Szabó's wildly popular, Hungarian best-selling novel of 1919, *Az elsodort falu* (The swept-away village) focuses similarly on the "infection" of a young nobleman in Budapest by cosmopolitan politics and attitudes and his eventual "rescue" through his return to the village of his birth and his marriage to a peasant girl.[26]

---

[22] Tormay, *Outlaw's Diary*, vol. 2, 236.   [23] Ibid., 237.   [24] Ibid., 236.

[25] This hatred of noblewomen who were believed to support socialism or befriend Jews is similar to attacks on white Southerners who were abolitionists or, later, who fought for civil rights. In 1959, the journalist William Peters remarked, "It would appear that this is the point where Southern male chivalry ends, for the fact that a renegade Southerner is of the gentler sex provides no assurance that her punishment will be correspondingly gentler," in *The Southern Temper* (New York: Doubleday, 1959), cited in G. McLeod Bryan *These Few Also Paid a Price: Southern Whites Who Fought for Civil Rights* (Macon, GA: Mercer University Press, 2001), 81–2.

[26] Dezső Szabó, *Az elsodort falu: Regény három kötetben* (Budapest: Genius Kiadás, 1919).

In the Munich revolution, Kätzler presented another example of this trope of fallen nobility. As many newspaper reports hastened to mention, her father was a titled admiral of the German Navy, Baron Max von der Goltz. In view of the tremendous importance of the navy to German nationalism in the early twentieth century, her father not only represented his aristocratic class but also German nationalism more generally. In the portrayals in the press, she was also characterized as a fallen daughter of the nation. During her trial, Kätzler explained that she had broken with her family at a very young age because of her leftist political beliefs. Her husband – who died in 1918 after a serious illness – had been a socialist and a language teacher, and together they had suffered great economic difficulties. After his death, she worked in a variety of children's homes.[27]

Kätzler's occupation as an educator of young children brings us to the third category (after morality and ethnic origin) of criticism leveled against women revolutionaries: their role in society. As mothers and teachers, women were seen as essential role models for children and were therefore seen as responsible for the inculcation of values and the transmission of national morals and traditions from generation to generation. In both Munich and Budapest, postrevolutionary authorities paid particular attention to punishing those educators who had openly supported the revolutions. The case of the Budapest educator Gizella Berzeviczy, described in the previous chapter, illustrates the harsh punishment that Hungarian courts imposed on teachers and other educators who had propagated leftist ideas among the youth during the revolutionary period. Berzeviczy's long sentence of eight years also showed that, despite stereotypes of politically naive women, Budapest judges dealt harshly with female revolutionary offenders. In fact, the feminized profession of teaching children made Berzeviczy's political stance seem even more treasonous, as it was counter to the nationalist view of women as mothers and teachers to the nation.

We have seen that the sentences given to revolutionary defendants were generally more lenient in Munich than in Budapest. This pattern was equally true among female defendants. In the end, Kätzler was acquitted and the case against her student and foster child, Kramer, was sent on to a civil court when the criminal case collapsed owing to lack of evidence after a key prosecution witness failed to appear. Despite the limited evidence the prosecution produced and the fact that both women escaped conviction for any crime, the bourgeois and right-wing press did not hesitate to condemn them. In the court of popular opinion, Kätzler's guilt was linked to her failures as a mother and as an educator of youth. Instead of inculcating national values and morality, Kätzler had, in the

---

[27] "Revolutionsdamen vor dem Standgericht," *Münchner Augsburger Abendblatt* 131, July 31, 1919; StAM Pol. Dir. 10.087.

view of these journalists and editors, abused her role and had led her daughters and young charges to embrace socialism. As reported in the newspapers, the fact that Kätzler had admitted in court that she had "raised and influenced her student Hilde Kramer in her own political beliefs" was conclusive evidence of criminal activity.[28] Shored up with long quotations extracted from Kramer's fearless evocation of radical political opinions during her trial, the papers emphasized that "this wild revolutionary thing" (Kramer) was the "product" of the Kätzler children's home. At the conclusion of their trials, the prosecuting attorney called for both women to be sentenced to one-and-a-half-years' imprisonment. While he acknowledged that Kramer had played a much greater role in the revolutionary unrest, he saw her youth and the "unhealthy influence" of Kätzler to be mitigating circumstances in her case.[29] For him, Kätzler, as an educator, should be held responsible for the actions and opinions of her former student.

Prosecutors also offered evidence about the political activities of Kätzler's two adult daughters, although no criminal charges were brought against them. Newspaper articles focused on this family network of female revolutionaries. Having one daughter in the USPD and the other daughter in the Communist Party further proved Kätzler's guilt, even though both political parties were legal, both daughters were adults, and neither lived in Munich at the time of the 1919 revolutions. Nevertheless, the political affiliations of the two young women were put on the record as evidence that their mother had been a bad role model as both mother and teacher. The prosecution's intent was to implicate Kätzler in the revolutionary excesses that had occurred, even though she did not directly participate in any significant way in the revolutionary government. To the bourgeois press and its readership, Kätzler, as a representative of all the women tainted by association with dangerous ideas, was on trial as a mother and educator rather than narrowly for the specific charges relating to inciting the peasants to revolt by traveling in the countryside by train. In fact, the press almost never mentioned the specific criminal charges against her. Instead, the press tried her for the crime of raising revolutionary daughters and found her guilty for her failures as a woman and mother.

Writers in the periodical press applied many descriptive stereotypes to revolutionary women. Among the most widely circulated described a woman with short hair in a "reformed" dress, meaning a modern, straight-cut dress that did not require a corset.[30] This image of female modernity was repeated often and was certainly one in which many of the female participants in the

---

[28] *Münchner Augsburger Abendblatt* 131, July 31, 1919; StAM Pol. Dir. 10.087.   [29] Ibid.

[30] See Rebecca Houze. *Textiles, Fashion, and Design Reform before the First World War: Principles of Dress*, (Burlington, VT: Ashgate, 2015); and Katherina Motyl, "Bodies that Shimmer: An Embodied History of Vienna's New Woman, 1893–1931," (dissertation, University of Chicago, 2017).

revolution had, in fact, taken a good deal of pride. In a letter Luise Kätzler wrote to Hilde Kramer from Berlin in the winter of 1918/19, she described a political rally she had attended and the excitement she felt at seeing an "army of women in modern dresses." Upon hearing that Hilde had cut her hair short, Luise (or Wiese as she was called) wrote, begging Hilde to send a picture of the new, revolutionary hairstyle (which she was sure was very becoming). Luise herself worried constantly in letters to Hilde and to her mother and sister about the damaging effects of the many food-shortages on her own appearance and reported that a great deal of her hair had fallen out.[31]

This same uniform of short hair and reformed dress that was an object of pride among many politically active women was also the focus for negative commentary among conservative observers, who likewise identified the style with a left-radical and feminist political worldview. A conservative Bavarian reporter wrote of the Kätzler–Kramer trial, "Despite her youth, Miss Kramer is a fanatical Communist; her behavior during the proceedings made a very poor impression . . . . In both her appearance and her manner [she is] extremely un-womanly and no political direction is radical enough for this young know-it-all."[32] The reporter for the liberal *Münchner Neuste Nachrichten* also focused on Kramer's appearance, noting first that "with her appearance [in the courtroom] it was clear that the nickname she'd had during the revolution, as the 'revolutionary girl with the Titus-Head' was in at least one sense no longer applicable, since she had let her hair grow out during her time in custody."[33]

The same newspaper report went on to sarcastically describe how "Even this wild young girl . . . couldn't completely deny the milder side of her femininity. Of her own accord, she went to the headquarters [*Kommandantur*], and offered to make curtains, which was apparently very much needed and which was greeted by a storm of protest from the *Kommandantur* officials of both sexes."[34] There may have been some truth in the story of the revolutionary leadership's derision towards Kramer for this suggestion of domestic improvement. The anarchist revolutionary Erich Mühsam ridiculed Kramer as a "silly young thing" in his 1931 memoirs, echoing the gender stereotypes from the conservative press and portraying Kramer's work for the revolutionary authorities as trivial.[35] As the Bavarian feminist Christiane Sterndorf-Hauck pointed out in her book on the role of women in the Bavarian revolutions of 1918 and

---

[31] StAM Pol. Dir. 10.087, police-typed copies of confiscated correspondence seized in the Kätzler home at the time of their arrest – undated and unnumbered letters.

[32] "Junges naseweises Ding," "Revolutionäre Frauen," *Bayerischer Kurier* 63, August 1, 1919; StAM Pol. Dir. 10.087.

[33] "Die Sekretärin des Stadtkommandanten," *Münchner Neuste Nachrichten* 303, August 1, 1919; StAM, Pol. Dir. 10.087.

[34] Ibid.

[35] Christiane Sternsdorf-Hauck, *Brotmarken und rote Fahnen: Frauen in der bayrischen Revolution und Räterepublik 1918/1919* (Frankfurt/Main: isp-Verlag, 1989).

1919, women's issues and the female political activists who supported them were routinely sidelined in favor of more "pressing" business in the debating sessions in the revolutionary councils.[36] The enthusiasm of young, radical women for the 1919 Central European revolutions was certainly not mirrored by concern for women's issues on the part of the male revolutionary leadership.

In Hungary as well, authors on the Right used the modern fashion of short hair and reformed dress as an effective stereotype to alert their readers to the political orientation of the activist women they described. In Tormay's description of her meeting with the young, "fallen" noblewoman described above, she used the woman's "Jewish" companion as an indication of her subservience to "foreign" ideology. She also used the visual cues of hair and dress to alert her readers to the woman's politics, commenting, "The fair face of the girl was familiar to me. She wore her hair after the Bolshevik fashion."[37] Oszkár Szőllősy, an attorney in the postrevolutionary Hungarian Ministry of Justice published articles for a popular audience on "the chief actors in the terror," with graphic descriptions of what he called their sadism. Szőllősy gave female criminals far greater coverage in his discussion of revolutionary excesses than was probably merited by their small numbers the postrevolutionary trials. He cleverly combined the commonly circulated use of the word "hysterical" to describe women's activities during the revolution with a description of the "Bolshevik hairstyle" discussed above: "Hysterical women, too, were given a plentiful scope of activity by Bolshevism, which induced women to wear short hair in order to be more like men, whereas the men wore long, flowing hair, after the Russian fashion."[38] From Szőllősy's perspective, the revolution had reversed the usual physical markers of gender while also overturning established social and economic hierarchies.

In a nationalist discourse that was guided in large measure by a strong sense of biological determinism, these references to physical appearance were very closely linked to the imputed psychological, moral, and intellectual health or rational capacities of the individual. The sensationalist nature of Szőllősy's presentation of women's participation in revolutionary violence was highlighted by his use of a photograph of a female physician, Johanna Peczkai, who he reported had "assisted with pleasure at executions." Peczkai was a minor figure in the revolutionary regime, and this photograph of her with a severe expression and wearing a masculine high-collared shirt with a necktie was used effectively to show his readers what a revolutionary woman looked like.[39] The photo

---

[36] Ibid.   [37] Tormay, *Outlaw's Diary*, vol. 2, 236.

[38] Oskar Szőllssy [sic], "Bolshevistische Verbrecher," in Karl Huszár, *Die Proletarierdiktatur in Ungarn: Wahrheitsgetreue Darstellung der bolschewistischen Schreckensherrschaft* (Regensburg: Verlag Jos. Koesel, 1920), 46.

[39] Oscar Szőllősy, "The Criminals of the Dictatorship of the Proletariat," in Tormay, *Outlaw's Diary*, vol. 2, appendix, 226; originally published in *The Anglo-Hungarian Review*, a journal published by the Oxford Hungarian League for Hungarian Self-Determination.

seemed to offer visual evidence of the revolutionary transformation of gender. Both antisemitic and gender stereotyping thus played important roles in the pathologizing of revolution, even as these stereotypes misappropriated what appeared superficially to be biological, scientific systems of classification to smear the reputation of revolutionaries.

Women, Gender, and Memory

The use of gender stereotypes to frame and give meaning to the postrevolutionary trials continued long after they had ended and the defendants had been sentenced or acquitted. Once established, stereotypes describing revolutionary women and the 1919 Central European revolutions played important roles in European anti-revolutionary writings for decades, conjuring fears of the profound and unnatural effects of revolutions. An ideology of gender struggle informed much conservative and right-wing writing in the interwar period, making the case for a manly defense against the emasculatory effects of revolution and the transformations of modern society and politics.

The interwar ideology of gender struggle has been particularly well-documented and researched for the German case. The work of Klaus Theweleit in the 1970s, which linked the soldiers of the "White Terror" in interwar Germany to the rise of fascism, has been particularly influential.[40] Theweleit pointed to a specific masculine psychology that feared women and crowds and was expressed through violence and a peculiar set of gendered literary tropes in the soldiers' memoirs. But these tropes were not limited to Germany and not to male writers either. Because of his insights from the psychoanalytic tradition and his focus on a single generation of German men, Theweleit produced what is at its core a psychological and even biological explanation for right-wing violence rooted in the masculine experience of a generation of men raised in Imperial Germany.

By examining similar stereotypes and themes in Tormay's memoirs, we can expand upon links derived from Theweleit's analysis.[41] The writings of a counterrevolutionary woman like Tormay are interesting because they offer their own conservative, often nationalist, argument for what she presumed was the centrality of women in society and national politics, a point of view which echoed many of the same stereotypes applied contemporaneously by men. Once Tormay's opinion is added to the mix, we see that gender stereotypes of the pure "white" woman versus the dangerous "red" woman were not narrowly the product of the male soldier's experience at the front nor of the masculine

---

[40] Klaus Theweleit, *Männerphantasien*, vol. 1: *Frauen, Fluten, Körper, Geschichte*, vol. 2: *Männerkörper – zur Psychoanalyse des weißen Terrors*, paperback edition with new epilogue by the author (Munich: Piper, 2000).

[41] Tormay, *Outlaw's Diary*.

culture of Imperial Germany but were much more generally the gender assumptions of both men and women on the political right all over interwar Central Europe. These were stereotypes and assumptions that were used by both sexes and across generations, not only by the men who had fought in the war and experienced the horrors of the trenches.

Because so many scholars have been driven by the desire to discover the roots of the Nazi dictatorship, interwar perceptions of dangerous challenges to received ideas of gender and the connections of these issues to the rise of right-wing extremism in Weimar Germany have received much more attention from scholars than have related phenomenon in interwar Hungary. The insights gained from the historiography of Weimar Germany can in fact help us to understand interwar Hungary, as long as we maintain a disciplined awareness of each nation's unique historical character. A Hungarian myth of "threefold suffering" developed in 1919 and, surprisingly, has endured to the present: the world war, the revolution, and the territorial losses of the Treaty of Trianon. This image of national suffering and martyrdom has often been portrayed through the use of gendered imagery and language, and the origins of this point of view can be already be found in contemporary perceptions of the roles of women at the time of the revolution and counterrevolution in 1919. How did the national idea of Hungary's special and unique suffering, relative to other European nations, affect the way that this society was imagined and portrayed, both in memories of the past and in plans for the future?[42] The social and psychological insights gained from research into the rise of Nazism in Germany help us understand Hungarian society in the years immediately after World War I.

In his 1977 book *Men's Fantasies*, Theweleit analyzed descriptions of women in the memoirs of hundreds of veterans, *Freikorps* soldiers, and future Nazi fighters, "soldier males" as he called them. He found that these men were generally afraid of women; they divided them into pure, good, and asexual "white" women: the nurse, the mother, the widow; and their opposites: the degenerate, polluting, and sexually dangerous "red" women. The revolutionary masses and these dangerous "red" women were portrayed via similar metaphors, as liquid dangers, dirty fluids, and powerful floods. In these portrayals Theweleit diagnosed a negation and denial by these "soldier males" of their own bodies, of the real fluids and needs of their own individual corporeality. He asserted that this repression found its release only in the White Terror, in the moment where soldiers and demobilized veterans suddenly operated as a crowd themselves. While fighting what they saw as the menacing Red crowd of the revolution, they themselves were able to surrender and become part of

---

[42] Of course, Hungary is not alone in having this myth of unique suffering. Poland in particular has a similar idea of national suffering.

a communal mass and act destructively, creating other common images of fluids and masses: the blood and broken bodies of their enemies.

Theweleit's work was pathbreaking when it appeared, highlighting and analyzing the most common symbols, myths, and narrative tropes found in the large body of *Freikorps* and soldiers' memoirs that were published in Germany during the Weimar Republic. His use of psychoanalytic method imposed an ahistorical focus on psychological causes, leading Theweleit to presume a "timeless quality" of "the problem of sexual antagonism," to use Joan Scott's description of this style of analysis.[43] Theweleit's goal had been to discover the reasons why the "soldier male" type developed and to uncover the psychological causes for dysfunctional socialization, which he asserted lay in the authoritarian family structure of the German *Kaiserreich*, offering a psychoanalytic version of the historical *Sonderweg* argument by identifying the psychological origins of fascist violence in Imperial German society.[44] Here, Scott's advice against similar ahistorical types of gender analysis are well warranted. In trying to examine the issue of gender in the 1919 revolutions and counterrevolutions, Theweleit's work proves less fruitful for historians. After all, many of the revolutionaries grew up in the same sorts of authoritarian bourgeois families and many of these committed revolutionaries had also served at the front. Yet, despite these similarities in familial background and experience, they developed very different behaviors and attitudes. Theweleit's work has the problem of pathologizing the cultural context that produced both the revolutionaries and their "White" opponents. We should also recognize the historical dependence of such psychological diagnoses, especially the notable difference in the perception of pathology between 1919 and post-1968 West Germany. Writing in the 1970s, after the upheavals in German universities led by the 1968 generation, Theweleit viewed the interwar "White" personality as psychologically damaged. Whereas, during the interwar period, professional psychiatrists and academics almost universally described the revolutionaries as "psychopathic."[45] That is, when the representatives of two different academic generations applied similar analytical methods and psychological vocabularies

---

[43] Joan Wallach Scott, *Gender and the Politics of History*, revised edition, (New York: Columbia University Press, 1999), especially 39–41.

[44] The *Sonderweg* (special path) argument was a long-standing view that Germany's late unification into the relatively authoritarian politics and culture of the *Kaiserreich* perverted or turned Germany's modernization onto a "special" path that led not to the parliamentary democracies of France and Britain but to Hitler and fascism. In *The Peculiarities of German History: Bourgeois Society and Politics in Nineteenth-Century Germany* (Oxford: Oxford University Press, 1984), David Blackbourn and Geoff Eley, successfully pointed out that not only was the argument flawed in its view of the German Empire, which was much more dynamic and liberal than the traditional portrayal but that the argument also depended on a romantic and unsubstantiated idea of the development of France and Britain. At the time of Theweleit's research, the *Sonderweg* concept of a direct line from empire to Nazism was widely accepted in Germany.

[45] The psychological diagnoses of the revolutionaries are discussed in Chapter 6.

to the same violent, troubled period they came to diametrically opposite conclusions.

By historicizing the White Terror and using a transnational comparative context, we can utilize some of Theweleit's insights to help us better understand interwar society in Central Europe while avoiding his essentializing tendencies. Compared to the situation for Weimar Germany, where a fascination with cultural questions has long been prominent, there has been less research on interwar Hungary and until recently most historical analysis focused on political history. Adding a gender analysis gives us a better sense of 1919 Hungary. The comparison with Hungary also serves as a check on some of the conclusions of authors whose focus has been limited to Weimar Germany. For example, Theweleit's research does not consider that the violent themes used by his *Freikorps* memoirists were widespread elsewhere in interwar European society, well beyond the geographical realm of the German proto-fascist militias. The images and tropes he uncovers in the writings of German "soldier males" were, as the Hungarian case illustrates, part of a broadly shared political vocabulary of the Central European right-of-center, as we demonstrate when we include of the writings of right-wing women in our analysis of interwar antisemitism and political violence.

Perhaps the best example of this phenomenon is Tormay's two-volume memoir, *An Outlaw's Diary*.[46] Born in 1876 into a wealthy and influential noble family of German heritage, Tormay was already a well-known Hungarian writer by the turn of the century. She was the author of a series of novels, with romantic nationalist themes, many of which had been translated and published successfully in western Europe, such as the novel *The Stone Crop*, which idealized the hard life of a family of Croatian peasants who remain steadfastly loyal to their Hungarian lords.[47] One of a very limited number of female authors in Hungary at the time, Tormay was well-respected, especially in conservative and nationalist literary circles, and served as the first editor of the literary journal, *Napkelet* [Orient], founded in 1923 as a nationalist counterpoint to the famous journal, *Nyugat* [West].[48] Even before the soviet revolution, Tormay helped to found and served as president of the counterrevolutionary National Association of Hungarian Women in January 1919. Already before the *tanácsköztársaság*

---

[46] Most recently, see Judith Szapor's discussion of Tormay in *Hungarian Women's Activism in the Wake of the First World War: From Rights to Revanche* (London: Bloomsbury, 2017); and on the reception of Tormay, see Anita Kurimay, "Interrogating the Historical Revisionism of the Hungarian Right: The Queer Case of Cécile Tormay," *East European Politics and Societies* 30/1 (February 2016): 10–33. For parallels in Germany, see Christiane Streubel, *Radikale Nationalistinnen: Agitation und Programmatik rechter Frauen in der Weimarer Republik* (Frankfurt: Campus Verlag, 2006).

[47] Tormay, *The Stonecrop, a Novel* (New York: R. M. McBride & Co., 1923).

[48] Albert Tezla, *Hungarian Authors: A Bibliographical Handbook* (Cambridge, MA: Belknap Press of Harvard University Press, 1970).

(soviet republic) was formed in March, Tormay and her associates viewed the autumn 1918 revolution as a Jewish and foreign assault on historic Hungary. After Béla Kun formed the radical government, their aggressive antisemitic politics intensified.

As the representative of the National Association of Hungarian Women, Tormay participated in ceremonies welcoming Horthy as "liberator" of Budapest in November 1919 and presented him with a banner from "the women of Hungary" at a ceremony in on the steps of the parliament. In his memoirs, Horthy described accepting this "splendidly embroidered banner . . . from the women."[49] This ceremony followed Horthy's famous speech condemning the capital city. Earlier in the day at Gellért Hill, Horthy had called Budapest "the sinful city" for having "dragged the Holy Crown and the national colors in the dust" and "clothed herself in red rags."[50] Now, before the parliament, he asked Hungarians to join him on a "holy cause" and called for the "nation's soul" to be purged of all "poisonous elements."[51] Hungary should follow the new "Christian and National" political course. In her memoirs of the revolutionary period, Tormay gave vivid literary imagery to this "Christian and National" program and its version of recent history.

An Outlaw's Diary first appeared in Hungary in December 1920 and was quickly translated into English and published in England as well. It featured a foreword by Alan Percy, Duke of Northumberland, a prominent English antisemite.[52] An American edition appeared the next year, and a French edition followed soon afterward.[53] All editions sold well and had multiple printings. Like the memoirs of former *Freikorps* soldiers examined by Theweleit, Tormay's book did not have the goal of self-explication (psychoanalytical or even political but focusing on the effects of the outside on the subjective) but rather served as an analysis or explication of contemporary events, self-consciously written with the authority of a witness.

Her work is a vivid example of the combination of nationalist politics with the moral dichotomy of women as either "angels or whores." Tormay viewed the women participating in the revolution (either in the rare cases where they took an active political role or as part of the masses in demonstrations) not only as politically dangerous but also as sexually dangerous and physically degenerate. Women on the Right were totally depoliticized, which in this work served to celebrate their flawless moral standing. Their supposed political naivety,

---

[49] Miklós Horthy, *Memoirs* (New York: Robert Speller, 1957), chapter 9.
[50] *Pester Lloyd*, November 17, 1919; see also Horthy, *Memoirs*.
[51] Sakmyster, *Hungary's Admiral on Horseback*, 42.
[52] He was the author of such works of the antisemitic canon as: *The First Bid for Jewish Power*, *History of World Revolution*, *The Downfall of Russia: Judaism and Bolshevism*, and *The Victories of Israel*, all of which are still reprinted and distributed by right-wing organizations.
[53] Cecile Tormay, *Le Livre Proscrit* (Paris: Libairie Plon, 1925); a second edition was published in 1933.

though making them morally irreproachable, made them weak and susceptible to the influences of others. In this sense, women were both the saviors of the nation and at the same time needed to be protected by it. In *Outlaw's Diary*, all of these ideas of gender roles and explanatory models are paired with an explicit antisemitic message. She paid close attention to the ethnic origins of all political actors. She used the method (also common in the Nazi papers of Weimar Germany) of hyphenating Jewish politicians' names with an "original" or invented and obviously Jewish name. For her, Jews had made the Hungarian revolutions and therefore their "Jewish" leaders had to be "unmasked" for her readers.

Tormay described how she and her fellow Red Cross volunteers were sent away from their location at the train station by socialist newcomers who arrived to take their place welcoming returning demobilized soldiers after the October democratic revolution. She contrasted the noble nature of her colleagues – Red Cross nurses as the epitome of the national feminine ideal, helping and ministering to the soldiers – with the physically and politically dangerous women who replaced them:

There was great activity at the station today. The old refreshment shed of the Red Cross has been transformed into a refreshment room for returning soldiers. We who had for many years worked there with the Red Cross offered our services in vain. White bread, which we had not seen for a long time, and sausages, were distributed to the soldiers by Jewesses who wore neither hat nor cap and looked unkempt and untidy. They had been sent by the Social Democratic party, and care for the soldiers was only a secondary part of their duty: they distributed handbills and talked propaganda to the returning men.[54]

Here the danger to the vulnerable young soldiers from these women, despite their unclean appearance, was not narrowly sexual; it was also their cynical use of scarce foods (decadence in the face of rationing) to further the subversive political agitation of the Left.[55]

Elsewhere in the *Outlaw's Diary*, Tormay decried the desecration of Hungarian culture, again using the idea of unclean (also Jewish) women and unclean food to dramatize her point:

A new kind of public invades the restaurants, the theatres, and the places of amusement: plays, written by [Jewish] writers, are played to full houses; people in gabardines occupy the stalls, while in the boxes Orthodox Jewish women in wigs chatter in Yiddish, and in the interval eat garlic-scented sausages in the beautiful, noble foyer of the Royal Opera, and throw greasy paper bags around.[56]

[54] Tormay, *Outlaw's Diary*, vol.1, 173.
[55] For arguments about how food became a moral symbol in World War I see Belinda J. Davis, *Home Fires Burning: Food, Politics, and Everyday Life in World War I Berlin* (Chapel Hill: University of North Carolina Press, 2000), on women and rationing and luxury foods in wartime Berlin, as well as Healy, *Vienna and the Fall of the Habsburg Empire*.
[56] Tormay, *Outlaw's Diary*, vol.1, 197.

Though Tormay also made accusations of sexual depravity and raved against the supposed orgies and "evenings of mixed company" that took place in the hotel occupied as the socialist headquarters, she more often focused on such images of filth and gluttony to represent the physical dangers of revolutionary women.

Tormay also vented her anger at another type of dangerous woman, the seductress or coquette. She condemned such women on two levels, as immoral and insincere and, perhaps more importantly, as distractions for men, who, she argued, needed their full energies for the national crisis. According to her, one such coquette was Countess Károlyi (Katalin Andrássy), the wife of the 1918 democratic revolution leader Mihály Károlyi. Like her husband, the countess was from one of Hungary's most important political families, the Andrássys. Thus, she could not be criticized as "foreign" or "coarse." Instead, Tormay presented her illustrious family heritage as a responsibility that this young woman had not taken seriously. Her insincerity compounded what Tormay described as the physical and mental degeneracy of her husband.[57]

Tormay described the couple as they drove by the crowds in Budapest in the former king's automobile. She compared Károlyi unfavorably with the conservative István Tisza, who had been assassinated in the fall of 1918. The late Tisza represented the ultimate ideal of Hungarian national manliness in many of Tormay's fantasies. Károlyi, in her description, however, was physically degenerate and weak. But as much as she scorned Károlyi, Tormay seemed more affronted by his attractive wife, who "was rouged in a doll-like fashion and her beautiful big eyes sparkled. Her voluptuous young mouth smiled in rapture, and she seemed to be drinking her success from the air greedily."[58] The perceived danger to the nation from such a vain and seductive woman caused Tormay to reflect, "the smile of those painted lips had left a trail of corruption over the suffering, harassed people . . .. The army goes to pieces; the throne has fallen . . .. The rabble robs and pilfers. A Serbian army has crossed the frontier. And the painted lips smile, smile."[59] Tormay considered the beauty of Károlyi's wife inauthentic and dangerous.

The antithesis of the dangerous revolutionary woman or the seductive coquette was the "white" angel of the nation. She was not only described by Tormay but was also subsumed into Tormay's self-image and self-description. Already a prominent figure before and during the war, she took an active role in trying to organize and shape a female counterrevolution against the Kun government. István Bethlen, the future prime minister under Admiral Horthy,

---

[57] Ibid., 71. Known as Katinka, the countess was the granddaughter of the powerful politician Gyula Andrássy (the elder), Hungarian prime minister 1867–71 and foreign minister 1871–79. Her father, Tivadar, and uncle, Gyula Andrássy (the younger), were also prominent politicians of the prewar period. On Katinka Andrássy, see Szapor, 36–9, 44–9, 53.

[58] Tormay, *Outlaw's Diary*, vol.1, 72. [59] Ibid.

had invited her to join in the conspiratorial planning meetings held in Budapest during the winter.[60] She was friendly with almost all the Hungarian political elite, especially those, such as the counterrevolutionary interwar minister of education, Count Kuno Klebelsberg, who were involved in literature and culture.

Yet, in *An Outlaw's Diary* she described all of her own political activity, as well as that of her organization, as nonpolitical, calling herself "a stranger in the world of politics."[61] In an address to a group of fellow female conspirators, she delineated the battlefronts for women during the revolution: "I address the women and tell them that our fortress is a triangle, the three advanced outworks being our country, our faith, and our family. These three outworks are threatened by Jewish socialist communism. Before the foe can storm the fort we must strengthen the souls of the defenders so that the offense collapses."[62] Women's role, according to this leading voice of the Right, was one of support, "strengthening the souls of the defenders," the men.

Tormay portrayed the particular danger revolution posed to women. She referred to the myth that under communism there would be "free love" or the "nationalization of women." According to Tormay,

Of all humanity, women will be the heaviest losers if the war is lost and the communists win, for women are to be common property once the home is broken up, and God and country have been denied . . .. We who fight on the soil of dismembered, trampled Hungary do not fight for ourselves alone, but for every Christian woman in the world.[63]

Hungary had long portrayed itself as the defender of Christian Europe during the Turkish wars, and here Tormay saw the battle over the future of Hungarian women as one fought symbolically on behalf of all European women.

Women, in Tormay's description, were both the nation's bulwark and its most endangered members. A poster printed and distributed by the propaganda department of the military command in Munich made a similar point in a poem addressed to "the women of Munich."[64] In this poster, the military command addressed women as both a potential defense and a potential threat in the looming political battle for Munich. The anonymous author first praised their valor through the hardship and privation of the war: "You were our example, helped us to continue in the worst danger; we could see in your eyes what duty and honor offered us." But the author implied that this sturdy example had faded, calling on women to "rejoin their efforts." Women, the author suggested, had wavered in their role as protectors and angels, and the results had been disastrous. "Women," the poster proclaimed, "turn away from delusional enterprises, and stop the Red Terror at the gates." What was needed now, was

---

[60] Ibid., 231.   [61] Ibid., 229.   [62] Ibid., 197–8.   [63] Ibid.
[64] BHSA, Höhere Stäbe, Bund 1/4, "An Münchens Frauen!" (undated handbill), 47.

for each woman to "press your hand on the bleeding heart" of the city; women were exhorted "don't allow fraternal blood to spill again." The women were warned to return to their wartime roles: "Be protective angels for your husbands and sons in the dark night," otherwise, the poem warned, "our homeland will be a grave for us all." In bold print spread across the bottom of the poster was the exclamation, "hunger is terrible, but communist rule of terror is worse!" According to this interpretation, women, as food rioters and instigators, were now partly guilty for the revolutionary upheavals. But if they would return to their traditional supportive roles, they would "give their men strength in the face of Satan's efforts."[65] Women here represented both a potential barricade against the danger of communism and a potential vulnerability that communists could exploit.

The myth of the "nationalization of women" under communism, though seldom precisely defined, was one of the most common horrors that was circulated to inspire fear of revolution. It seems that what was meant was both a breakdown of traditional marriage and its power and property dynamics and the introduction of "free love," or sex outside marriage. Since revolutionaries wanted to nationalize other economic "resources," the idea was that they would similarly "nationalize" (i.e. take for the state and away from private "ownership") women as well. This phrase was used as a rallying cry for counterrevolutionary troops. The anarchist writer Erich Mühsam, one of the leaders of the first government of councils in Munich, later reflected on the effects of this myth in an article entitled, "Republic of Councils and Sexual Revolution." He wrote that "The terrible murder of Gustav Landauer ... can only be put down to the fact that the soldiers on those black lists were convinced that Landauer and Mühsam had wanted to nationalize the women."[66] He recognized that the myth that communists would "nationalize the women" and break up the family was perceived as particularly threatening to the counterrevolutionaries and was a source of their rage and violence against the revolution.

Even if women were not "nationalized," it was widely assumed that the revolutionaries intended to shake up the long-established patterns of family and authority. Revolution, the Right claimed, threatened paternal authority over children as well as the authority of husbands over wives. These perceived threats were terrifying to conservatives. Writing from Budapest in 1919, an American reporter for the New York, socialist *Call* attempted to contradict rumors that the revolutionary government would destroy the family. The reporter, Grace Hunter, reassured her American audience that reality was quite the opposite, the regime promoted marriage. "Thanks to increased wages and sundry governmental provisions relative to housing," she wrote,

[65] Ibid.   [66] Sternsdorf-Hauck, 31.

"people in Budapest can now marry with impunity."[67] She quoted Dezső Somló, the people's commissar for housing, who claimed that

ten thousand couples have married in Budapest within the last two weeks and come to me for furniture and rooms. The business of my department was originally intended only as a clearing-house to bring empty rooms and homeless proletarians together, but now that the working man and woman get a living wage with a surplus, they seem to get married very fast.[68]

For Hunter, who was sympathetic to the Hungarian soviet regime, this information was proof of the improvements in the lives of proletarians, who now were free to pursue romantic happiness. Emancipation did not mean moral degeneration; it meant social regeneration. Furthering her argument that socialism promoted morality, she also described the decisive actions of the revolutionary government against prostitution and "houses of ill-repute." Hunter defended the regime against its critics; did this encouragement of marriage and attack on prostitution, she asked, "look like communism would abolish the home and encourage free love?"[69]

For many observers, however, it did look exactly as if the abolition of home and family was, if not communism's conscious goal, then at least its logical result. In 1920 the prime minister of the first postrevolutionary "Christian National" government, Károly Huszár, organized the publication of a German-language report, *Die Proletarierdiktatur in Ungarn: Wahrheitsgetreue Darstellung der bolschewistischen Schreckensherrschaft* (The dictatorship of the proletariat in Hungary: A faithful portrait of the Bolshevik reign of terror). Addressed to an international audience, the book sought to catalog the horrors of revolutionary rule and thus garner support for the counterrevolutionary regime. The majority of contributors to the volume held posts in Hungarian local and national government. The chapter by the counterrevolutionary mayor of Budapest, Tivadar Bódy, is quite interesting because its focus is not so much on revolutionary violence (of which as we have seen there was relatively little in the capital city) but on the pernicious effects of the revolution on the social fabric. In his chapter, the same wave of revolutionary marriages that Hunter had found inspiring and morally reassuring was portrayed as the disintegration of traditional family roles in society. Bódy complained that during the revolution the age of majority was lowered to eighteen and, as a result, "Many people who were not yet twenty-four married without the permission of parents, guardians or the juvenile authorities. It happened that many foolish, careless marriages were entered into."[70] In a report titled "A faithful portrait of the Bolshevik reign of terror," the concern that young people had entered "foolish,

---

[67] Article from the *Call* in *Literary Digest*, August 30, 1919, 102–3.   [68] Ibid.   [69] Ibid.

[70] Theodor Body, "Bolschewistische Willkürherrschaft in der Landeshauptstadt Budapest," in Karl Huszár, ed., *Die Proletarierdiktatur in Ungarn: Wahrheitsgetreue Darstellung der bolschewistischen Schreckensherrschaft* (Regensburg: Verlag Jos. Koesel, 1920), 135.

careless marriages" seems perhaps trivial, but conservatives took the challenge posed to the social order by lowering the majority and loosening marriage laws very seriously. The revolution threatened to emancipate women not only politically, but also socially.

The fear of women's emancipation was at the heart of a dilemma for an active, conservative woman such as Tormay. She was an unmarried, financially independent writer who was politically connected, a well-known literary figure, and a nationalist.[71] She was, by most definitions, politically and socially emancipated for her time and place. Yet her nationalist politics were anti-emancipatory. She took great pains to portray her own political activity, as well as the realm of women's political activity she advocated as appropriate, within the framework of traditional feminine roles. In December 1918, as she began to organize women, Tormay wrote about the role she imagined for women. Unlike the women of the Left, "Red" women who made real politics, giving speeches and distributing pamphlets, Tormay and her followers would strive for a behind-the-scenes political influence that left the traditional ideals in place. For them, this was not merely "traditional" or conservative in a universal sense; it was highly national in character. She believed that Hungarian ethnic traditions and Hungarian history at the border of "Christian" Europe against the Muslim Ottoman Turks had created a special strong and silent role for women.[72] The national character of Hungary's women, according to Tormay, particularly suited them to counterrevolutionary work. Comparing the present danger of Bolshevism with the Turkish invasions, Tormay wrote, "we all knew that the women would respond to our call and would sow the seed of the counter-revolution. Not at meetings, not in the market-place, but in their homes, in the souls of their men exhausted by the hardships of war."[73] Meetings and markets were the places where revolutionary women acted, counterrevolutionary women would work in the domestic and familial spheres. The active work of organizing the counterrevolution would require, in her words, "a man who was brave and strong, who knew how to organize and how to give orders, who could lay his hand on destiny at the brink of the abyss."[74]

For Tormay, as for many Hungarians, Miklós Horthy was just the man to steer the nation away from the abyss. "Hungary's admiral on horseback," as a 1994 biography of Horthy is titled, can appear today as an almost a comic figure: an admiral with no navy, a regent without a king.[75] In 1919, however, both Horthy's clout as one of the Habsburg Monarchy's few war heroes and the stirring image of him in his admiral's uniform mounted on a white horse

---

[71] Kurimay argues that Tormay's paradigmatic position on the Right has been impervious even to the scandal of her alleged homosexual affair with the wife of a high aristocrat. Horthy himself intervened in the court case on her behalf at the time, and she remains popular today including with the anti-gay Right despite her alleged homosexuality.

[72] Tormay, *Outlaw's Diary*, vol. 1, 182–3.   [73] Ibid.   [74] Ibid., 91–2.

[75] Sakmyster's excellent biography, *Hungary's Admiral on Horseback*.

Manno Miltiades plakátja, amelyet a magyar nemzeti hadseregnek
Budapestre való bevonulása után ragasztottak ki.

Figure 5.1 "Horthy!" 1919 poster by Manno Militiades.
Source: Photo12/Universal Images Group via Getty Images.

represented powerfully the reassuring bulwarks of traditional social order and masculine authority. This combination of symbols was powerfully broadcast in one of the most widely reproduced and distributed posters for Horthy in 1919–20, which showed only powerful hands firmly grasping the helm of a ship. The message was clear: Horthy would steer the nation to safety like a ship in a stormy sea.[76]

---

[76] The artist Manno Militiades (1880–1935) who designed this poster was also responsible for a large number of antisemitic posters in the counterrevolutionary era. Militiades' work employed the language of stereotyped bodies to send a powerful political message, with muscular male bodies representing the Hungarian nation and hook-nosed, hunchbacked, hairy "Jews" representing the communist revolution. One of these took Mihály Biró's famous large red worker with a hammer, gave him stereotypically antisemitic features, and showed him with the hammer over a destroyed map of the Kingdom of Hungary. Another showed an antisemi-tically caricatured people's commissar with his arms full of jewels and treasure (likely meant to

The writings of Tormay and other right-wing women in both interwar Hungary and Germany reproduced the gendered counterrevolutionary literary tropes of floods, liquids, and filth. They reinforced the dichotomy drawn by nationalists between the dangerous "Red" woman and the nursing, sacrificing "White" woman. In seeking the roots of German fascism, there has been much greater attention paid to the memoirs of the *Freikorps* soldiers and their use of this set of gendered ideals. As a result, a particularly masculine problem, the fear that the "soldier male" had of both women and his own body and suppressed desires, has been placed at the center of scholarly attention. After comparing these sources with Tormay and other authors who focused on the cultural power exercised by women, I would argue that the discoveries Theweleit made in his *Freikorps* research were not representative of a special "soldier male" psychology but rather were representative of the symbolic vocabulary of a wide section of interwar society in both Germany and Hungary. This symbolic vocabulary was part of a cultural code that was understandable to all generations. And, even though the content is misogynist, this vocabulary and this code were used and understood by women themselves. While this understanding may reduce the explanatory power of this symbolic language for determining the psychology of early fascist street fighters, the payoff is great in its potential to illuminate the mental outlook of the political Right in interwar Germany and Hungary.

1919 and the Myth of Judeo-Bolshevism

The prominence of Jews in the revolutionary leadership was a central concern of regional Jewish leaders as well as counterrevolutionaries and antisemites. Jewish community leaders were almost universally troubled that the revolutions were perceived as "Jewish" by the public and worked to uncouple the two halves of the fast-emerging construct of Judeo-Bolshevism. In the cases of Munich and Budapest specifically, there were attempts to refute the asserted allegation of Jewish responsibility for the revolutions, Judeo-Bolshevism, by various official and unofficial sources in the Jewish communities of both nations. But the rumors and allegations persisted throughout the interwar period (and even later). Even today this potent and defamatory slander endures in popular understandings of post–World War I events.

The popular presumption that Jews were the instigators of the Central European revolutions seems to have originated in the midst of the revolutions

---

be Kun because of the widespread rumors about his theft of jewels) running away from his victim, a one-legged war veteran in uniform lying on the pavement with his crutches (the strong male nation, maimed by the war).

themselves. Already in 1918, as the Habsburg and German empires collapsed, rumors and broadsheets in both Munich and Budapest associated government collapse, military defeat, and the autumn revolutions of 1918 with specific Jews and with a shadowy, general "Jewish conspiracy." We have seen how Jewish politicians, such as Oszkár Jászi in the Károlyi government in Hungary or Prime Minister Kurt Eisner of the first postwar Bavarian government, played leading roles in the 1918 revolutionary governments. Men of Jewish heritage played even more prominent roles in the later soviet revolutions in the spring; by the criteria used by most contemporaries and historians, the majority of the commissars in the Hungarian revolutionary government counted as Jewish.[77] But even from the moment of those first autumn revolutions, the participation of Jews was seen as a defining characteristic and was used to either justify or assign blame for the potent antisemitic reaction. Explanations for Jewish participation in revolutionary politics are entangled with the complex genealogies of Central European antisemitism.

As most observers writing on the topic have pointed out, most of the 1918 and 1919 revolutionaries counted by contemporaries or historians as Jews did not themselves consider this their identity, either in terms of religion or certainly "nationality." Ernst Toller and others have written about the role of antisemitism in their own intellectual development.[78] Others also openly discussed their Jewish descent and heritage. Efforts to "unmask" Jews among the revolutionary governments seems to still incite interest and debate, as recent academic inquiry into the "Jewishness" of the early Russian communist leadership demonstrates.[79] Although the magyarizing of last names was relatively common in dualist Hungary – not only for Hungarians with "Jewish" last names but also those with German or Slavic names – in the case of the 1919 revolutionaries, the practice among right-wing writers and newspapers of printing these people's "original" names alongside their legal names seemed to imply a dishonesty or masking.[80] The use of "Korvin/Klein" or "Lantos/

---

[77] By one count, thirty out of forty-eight commissars were "of Jewish origin"; William O. McCagg, Jr., "Jews in Revolutions: The Hungarian Experience," *Journal of Social History* 6/1 (Autumn 1972): 78–105. McCagg's numbers are based on the biographical entries in the 1929 *Magyar Zsidó Lexikon*, edited by Péter Ujvári. Other historians give the figure twenty of twenty-six commissars (using different criteria for both Jewishness and commissar), following the research of Shlomo Yitshaki, "Ha-yehudim be-mahapehot hungariya, 1918–1919," *Moreshet* 11 (1969): 113–34. The important point, I would argue, is one István Deák has often made, which is that Jewish identification in early twentieth-century Eastern Europe was very much "in the eye of the beholder." So, just as contemporaries estimated the "Jewishness" of the regimes by their own criteria, so too historians must choose the criteria for their own counts of Jewish revolutionaries.

[78] See Toller's memoir, *Eine Jugend in Deutschland*.

[79] The most interesting of these is Yuri Slezkine's *The Jewish Century* (Princeton, NJ: Princeton University Press, 2004).

[80] Victor Karády has shown that Jews predominated among magyarizers in the late dualist period, though other groups, especially Catholic Germans and Slovaks, were what he calls "strategic

Löwi" in counterrevolutionary texts allowed authors and propagandists to emphasize the Jewishness of revolutionary leaders while disguising their intentions as the provision of additional information to readers. This method of adding a hyphenated "original, Jewish" name (a hyphenated name that the person in question did not use) was quickly adopted by the antisemitic press in Germany and became the origin of many lawsuits against the Nazi *Völkischer Beobachter*, including one brought in the 1920s by Kurt Eisner's widow.

In interwar Hungary this same practice was rampant, especially in works about the 1919 revolution. Hyphenated "Jewish" names even appear in an official German-language edition of excerpts from the trials of selected revolutionaries printed by the counterrevolutionary Hungarian government in 1920.[81] In their efforts to identify Jews in the revolutionary leadership, White propagandists seldom proved scrupulous in researching the backgrounds of their targets. The head of Munich's Communist Party in 1919, Max Levien, for example, was persistently misidentified as Jewish. Eventually, the *Encyclopedia Judaica* added an entry explaining that Levien, though definitely Russian, was not Jewish. Nevertheless, he was often counted as a Jew (including in many historical accounts of 1919 and with incredible persistence in internet descriptions of the revolution).[82] The persistence of these sort of anxieties about correcting or discovering the Jewish identity of the 1919 revolutionaries shows the power of the myth of Judeo-Bolshevism in shaping even historical readings of the events.

From the first revolutions at the end of the war in autumn 1918, the Jewish communities of Budapest and Munich were concerned about the mounting perception that Jews had made the revolution. Officials of Jewish organizations attempted to diffuse intensifying antisemitism through making appeals to their fellow citizens in hopes of making clear the apolitical and nonrevolutionary stance of the Jewish community. In open letters to newspapers, leaders took pains to distance the Jewish community from the actions of actors who one such Jewish leader described as "such foreign … fantasists and dreamers, unfamiliar with the Bavarian character."[83] It is likely that such letters, because they repeated the antisemitic characterizations of Jewish revolutionaries as "foreign" and un-Bavarian, had the opposite effect. The Munich Jewish community wanted to differentiate between itself and "foreign" Jews in the

---

Magyarizers." See Karády, "Symbolic Nation-Building in a Multi-Ethnic Society: The Case of Surname Nationalization in Hungary," *Tel Aviver Jahrbuch für deutsche Geschichte* 30 (2002): 81–103.

[81] *Aktenstücke aus dem Archiv ungarischer Gerichtshöfe über die Prozesse einiger Kommunisten, 1919–1920* (Budapest: Königl. Ung. Staatsdrukerei, 1920).

[82] The similarity of the last names of Max Levien and Eugen Leviné (who was Jewish) has also led to some confusion.

[83] Sigmund Fraenkel, "Offener Brief an den Herrn Erich Mühsam, Dr. Wadler, Dr. Otto Neurath, Ernst Toller und Gustav Landauer," Munich, April 6, 1919, reprinted in Hans Lamm, *Von Juden in München: Ein Gendenkbuch* (Munich: Ner-Tamid-Verlag, 1958), 304.

revolution, but this language reinforced the dominant counterrevolutionary narrative about the Jewish revolution.

Public appeals also called on revolutionary leaders to take responsibility as Jews, not only for the damage done by the revolutions but also for the antisemitism that their activities had stirred up. In this debate over Jewish authorship of revolutionary agitation, the November 1918 Bavarian revolution proved to be particularly important because the USPD leader of the government, Eisner, was Jewish. Though Jews played important roles in the autumn revolutions elsewhere in Central Europe, most revolutionary heads of government were not Jewish, for instance non-Jews headed the provisional German government in Berlin and the Mihály Károlyi government in Hungary. The fact that Count Károlyi was not Jewish but rather was the head of one of Hungary's wealthiest, landowning aristocratic families, did not stop critics such as Tormay from portraying the National Council of the autumn revolution as Jewish. Indeed, there were Jews represented in the government, such as Oszkár Jászi, who served as minister for national minorities. However, Tormay polemically asked, "What is this obscure assembly after all? How dare it call itself the council of the nation? . . . Eleven Jews and eight bad Hungarians!"[84] Tormay went on to describe Károlyi's physical appearance in ways that for most readers would call up Jewish stereotypes:

I was brought back to earth by some unkempt vagabonds cheering Károlyi. And the living man there in the car seemed more like a corpse . . .. His long, bloodless body was thin and bent. His narrow head, with its artificial stern expression, lolled on his shoulder as if it were too heavy for his neck to support. His watery, squinting eyes shifted blankly from side to side.[85]

For Tormay, the government she hated and reviled found its natural and predictable leader in the decrepit Károlyi and its supporters among the "unkempt vagabonds."

In the autumn revolutions in Germany, some observers considered Eisner's leadership of the new "Freistaat Bayern" as a provocation. In 1918, the conservative *Bayerische Kurier* published two articles signed "Rahel Rabinowitz, a Jew." The first of the two, published on November 25, titled "Der Jude als Minister-präsident" (The Jew as prime minister)," suggested that Eisner's leadership should be viewed as an affront to self-respecting Germans. "I want to see the Germans with as much pride in themselves as I have in my own people, despite humiliations," she wrote.[86] This article and a second with the same signature on December 11, "Antisemitismus," caused an uproar in the press. The Jewish newspaper *Jüdische Echo* responded with strong criticism to Rabinowitz's argument. The author of this reply worried that Rabinowitz was

---

[84] Tormay, *Outlaw's Diary*, vol. 1, 6–7.   [85] Ibid., 71.

[86] *Bayerische Kurier,* November 25, 1918, "Der Jude als Minister-präsident."

actually justifying and promoting antisemitism and suggested that the articles had been commissioned by the right-wing *Bayerische Kurier* in order to have a Jewish writer voice the paper's own antisemitic ideas. In a letter to the editor published on December 27, 1918, Rabinowitz replied by denying that her articles were commissioned and defending her choice of outlet. In its rejoinder, the *Jüdische Echo* vehemently disputed what they called Rabinowitz's "poisonous slander," that Jews had no right to assume leadership roles in Germany.[87] The official Jewish community found itself in a difficult position as a result of these attacks. They needed to defend the community at large against antisemitic attacks and to repel arguments like those in the *Kurier* that would deny Jews the right to actively participate in German politics in the same way as all German citizens. The pursuit of these objectives forced Jewish communities to distance themselves from Jewish revolutionary leaders and revolutionary politics more generally. The cresting wave of antisemitism was, in effect, leading Jewish leaders to appeal directly to those revolutionaries, as Jews, to see how their political prominence was hurting the larger Jewish community and stirring up antisemitism.

Jewish community leaders across Central Europe attempted to fight against the crystallizing myth of a threatening Judeo-Bolshevism by trying to uncouple ethnic and religious identity from political associations. But, unintentionally, their protests compounded the politicization of religious identity. Appeals such as Sigmund Fraenkel's to individual Jewish politicians asked these men to avoid specific public political actions because of their ethnic or religious identity. Though the *Echo* opposed Rabinowitz's arguments and defended the rights of Jews to participate in German politics, it seemed to advocate that Jewish leaders, in trying to fight the Judeo-Bolshevik slander, needed to limit Jewish participation in revolutionary politics, bending their beliefs and loyalties in the interest of a larger religious or ethnic community. This defensive response to the Judeo-Bolshevik myth of the 1919 revolutions reinforced a conflation of race and politics that characterized interwar Central Europe.

The declaration of the first soviet government in Munich in April 1919 was met by a wave of antisemitic agitation that blamed Jews for the political crisis, the lost war, and revolution, especially for this new soviet revolution. But race, religion, and politics intersected in unpredictable ways. Prime Minister Eisner's assassin, Count Anton von Arco auf Valley, for example, was the son of a Jewish mother, leading some observers to attribute his right-wing political violence to his desire to prove his German nationalist credentials.[88] Following Eisner's assassination, Munich was filled with rumors of the declaration of a government of councils and antisemitic agitation. On April 6, 1919

---

[87] *Jüdische Echo*, November 29, 1918 and December 13, 1918.
[88] See this argument in Mitchell, *Revolution in Bavaria,* 237.

Sigmund Fraenkel, a prominent merchant and leader in Munich's Orthodox Jewish community, published an "Open Letter to Erich Mühsam, Dr. Wadler, Dr. Otto Neurath, Ernst Toller, and Gustav Landauer," the Jewish members of the first soviet government. In his letter, Fraenkel claimed that "We Jews of Munich have kept our quiet for all the difficult, painful weeks of the recent past ... because we were afraid of harming our religious community by chastising you in public, and because we hoped every day ... that you would realize the chaos of destruction and desolation in which your chosen [political] path must surely end."[89] Fraenkel felt himself compelled to write on "this day, on which thousands and thousands of inflammatory antisemitic pamphlets have been distributed on the streets of Munich." This experience of popular hatred had shown him clearly, "not only members of our religious community, but Judaism itself, [is] endangered if the mass of Munich's working population connects the tenets and beliefs of the Jewish religion with Bolshevik and communist heresies." Like many of Munich's burghers, Fraenkel accused the revolutionary leaders of preying on a population "worn out and confused by the four and a half years of war," and called upon them to look within themselves for the remnants of the "religion of their parents" and to end their revolutionary rule.[90]

As is demonstrated by period diarists, both antisemitic pamphleteering and rumors linking Jews with the revolutionary movements continued throughout the revolutionary period. The philologist Victor Klemperer noted an example in his diary on April 10, 1919. He remarked that airplanes had flown over Munich dropping leaflets published by the exiled SPD government in Bamberg as well as a flyer issued by the Munich Jewish community strongly opposing the anti-semitic hate campaign in the city.[91] Similarly, after the failed counterrevolution on Palm Sunday (April 13) in Munich, Thomas Mann wrote in his diary that people on the street cursed the "Saujuden," (Jewish swine) blaming the Jews for the disasters of revolution and for the shortages of coal and food in the besieged city.[92]

Employment of the myth of Judeo-Bolshevism to justify anti-Jewish violence was even more prominent in Hungary, where Jews made up a majority of the victims of the White Terror. The White Terror was directed in particular against Jews in the countryside in areas under the control of the counterrevolutionary National Army, but the specter of pogrom also hung over Budapest's large Jewish population. A poster displayed in late 1919 in Budapest gave visual representation to the idea of Jewish guilt for the revolutions and violence. Under the slogan "They wash their hands!," a caricatured Jew with a bloody knife between his teeth washes the red blood from his hands in the Danube in front of the Hungarian parliament building, which has red blood

---

[89] Reprinted in Lamm, *Von Juden in München*, 304.   [90] Ibid.   [91] Klemperer, 96.
[92] Mann, 214 (entry for April 28, 1919).

pouring from its windows.[93] This racialized visualization of the Judeo-Bolshevik myth also suggested that guilty Jews were washing their hands and hiding their guilt. It justified "unmasking" and "punishing" all Jews for the revolution, political violence, and national martyrdom, represented by the bleeding parliament building, a monument of Hungarian national pride from the 1890s millennium celebration.

As we saw in Chapter 3, the complaints office of the Pest Jewish community took sworn testimony in August and September about anti-Jewish violence in the White Terror across the country and then passed on the reports to government agencies in Hungary and published them abroad. Many of the witnesses were Jews who had fled to Budapest from their hometowns to escape anti-Jewish attacks. Others were residents of Budapest who had been traveling or visiting family and had therefore been witnesses to or victims of White violence. In a typical case, one Jewish resident of Budapest, Heinrich Buchsbaum, testified that he had left the city at the beginning of June 1919 "because of food riots" in the city.[94] He passed a week "undisturbed" in Dunaföldvár, visiting his parents and in-laws. When "a troop of about 35 officers, supposedly under the command of Baron Prónay" arrived in the town, his circumstance changed dramatically.[95] The officers assembled the local peasant population and began to agitate against the Jews. They also conducted what they called "summary justice," fining, for example, the two local Jewish booksellers tens of thousands of korona for selling the socialist *Népszava* newspaper, the main paper under the soviet government, which was still in power in Budapest.[96] Buchsbaum's brother-in-law, Eugen Kovács, was soon arrested at the hotel he owned. One of the White officers, First Lieutenant Német, ordered Kovács to pay a fine of 100,000 korona under threat of hanging. Extortion was a common feature of the antisemitic bullying and violence and this threat was all the more serious since White officers had already hanged the head of the local revolutionary judicial tribunal and his son in the market square that day. When Kovács managed to escape, White officers told the mob to find someone else to hang in his place. Although Kovács's wife and her sister were found and beaten, their lives were saved when the sister's husband appeared

---

[93] "Mosakodnak!" by Manno Militiades (Sopron: Röttig-Romwalter Nyomda, 1919), image can be viewed online from the Imperial War Museum, www.iwm.org.uk/collections/item/object/19290.

[94] Protocol reprinted in Krausz.

[95] Prónay was probably the most notorious of the officers of the White Terror and wrote about anti-Jewish violence in his memoirs: Pál Prónay, *A határban a Halál kaszál: Fejezetek Prónay Pál feljegyzéseiből*, edited and selected by Ágnes Szabó and Ervin Pamlényi (Budapest: Kossuth Kiadó, 1963), see chapter 3.

[96] As a comparison of the value of the fines of 10,000 and 30,000 korona, on July 10 one could acquire a pair of women's shoes or a used men's suit for about 1,000 korona "with connections and luck," according to János Komáromi, *A nagy háború anekdotái* (Budapest: Révai, 1936), 203.

and offered himself to the mob. After being beaten bloody with rifle butts, he was strung up from a tree branch that broke under his weight. Cut down and taken to the market square, he was hanged again, this time fatally. The terrified Buchsbaum fled back to Budapest. But as was true in many cases of Jews who were forced to flee from White violence, he did not feel safe even in the capital and eventually fled from Hungary. In Vienna, he joined the thousands of Hungarian refugees who escaped after the fall of the communist regime.

The events that Buchsbaum witnessed followed a similar pattern to those described by other witnesses to the White "officer brigades" elsewhere in Hungary (analyzed in Chapter 3).[97] Buchsbaum reported several instances where members of the local population or the local police authorities tried to step in to stop attacks. In his testimony, he reported that a district judge Frey attempted unsuccessfully to intervene with First Lieutenant Német on behalf of Kovács. The judge countered the Judeo-Bolshevik slander, attesting that the Jewish "Kovács was not a Red, rather was at least as White as the First Lieutenant and the district judge themselves."[98] But this heroic intervention failed to have any effect. The testimonies collected by the Pest Jewish community and forwarded to the government differentiated between the actions of local authorities, who often attempted to maintain order, and the White officer brigades, who acted lawlessly, and positioned the Jewish victims as allies of order, rather than agents of revolution.

The focus of these reports was on cases of anti-Jewish violence, and they made clear the nonpolitical and non-leftist credentials of the victims of White Terror they were describing. The April 1920 letter of the European head of the JDC, Julius Goldman, reported that, "Unfortunately, Jews of all classes both in Vienna and Budapest concede that the Jews themselves are greatly to blame for the change [in antisemitic attitudes] that has taken place." He went on to state, "concededly the Jews in Hungary were great profiteers and made great fortunes during the war" and then after the war, "the history of the communistic and Bolchevik [sic] outbreak in Hungary is well-known, the leaders of those outbreaks were almost exclusively Jews ... the[se] leaders are naturally held responsible for what took place."[99] On the copy of Goldman's letter in the JDC archives, this paragraph of agreement with the Judeo-Bolshevik myth is circled and marked "omit." But Goldman's assessment was widespread, and many of the affidavits of witnesses to anti-Jewish violence present a similar understanding. In

---

[97] The White militias were almost entirely made up of "officers," some were former officers of the Habsburg joint army or the Hungarian *Honvéd*, others seem to have received their rank from the militias, rather than in regular army service. In any case, it created a military anomaly of all-officer forces, and the militias were widely referred to as "officer brigades," since all the men had or claimed an officer's rank.

[98] Böhm.

[99] Letter, Julius Goldman to Felix Warburg, April 13, 1920, JDC-NY Collection 1919–1921, file # 148 [Hungary, General, 1919–20], p. 144.

defending the political innocence of specific victims, they represented a tacit acknowledgment that while Jewish *revolutionaries* might be expected to be targets of revenge and summary justice, broader anti-Jewish violence was almost always misdirected. Valid and invalid targets of political violence needed to be distinguished from the broad brush of antisemitism.

Even after the revolutions were defeated in both Munich and Budapest, rumors continued to circulate linking the threat of a new revolutionary cycle, with its likely destruction and privation for the general population, with the Jewish community. The prominent role of some Jewish counterrevolutionaries in both cities could not staunch the circulation of these potent antisemitic tropes. On the eve of the arrival of Horthy's National Army in Budapest in November 1919, the Budapest Jewish community sent an announcement to the local city newspapers to vociferously contradict what they saw as the slanderous information published the previous day in the paper *Az Est*.[100] In that article, Colonel Dobák, head of the police authority, had announced that his office had received word that "workers and Jews" were preparing disturbances for the period between the withdrawal of the Romanian forces and the arrival of the National Army. Jenő Polnay, newly elected president of the National Union of Hungarian Jews, wrote that the information must be either a mistake or the result of malicious denunciations.[101] "Our organization," he assured his fellow citizens, "can in good conscience take full responsibility that the portion of the population of the capital belonging to the Jewish religion awaits the arrival of the National Army with the same trust and anticipation as the Christian portion."[102] The letter ended with assurances of Jewish patriotism and commitment to upholding law and order.

Though in both Munich and Budapest Jews made many such attempts to differentiate themselves from revolutionary or foreign Jews who were "troublemakers," this effort to distinguish the patriotic and anti-revolutionary body of the Jewish community from the revolutionary minority was largely unsuccessful. As other examples of antisemitic scapegoating have shown, the strength of an association like Jew = Bolshevik lies in its simplicity, and the admission of "exceptions" to the rule would undermine its functionality. For most conservatives, the identification of some Jews with the revolutionary governments merely confirmed existing antisemitic sentiments. In fact, protests by leaders of the Jewish community that condemned certain "other Jews"

---

[100] *Pester Lloyd*, November 14, 1919, "Eine Erklärung des Bundes Ungarischer Juden," 3.

[101] From August 7 to 15, 1919, Polnay, a successful business executive, served as a minister in charge of national food distribution in the government of István Friedrich, one of the short-lived governments formed after the collapse of the revolutionary council government and the arrival of Romanian Entente troops and before the arrival in November 1919 of Horthy and the National Army.

[102] *Pester Lloyd*, November 14, 1919, "Eine Erklärung des Bundes Ungarischer Juden," 3.

may have had the unfortunate effect of strengthening the antisemitic tendency to blame the revolution on "the Jews" in general. In a confidential letter to Goldman, the American JDC representative to Romania, Alex Landesco, reported a troubling rumor that he had heard in March 1920 from the American military attaché in Bucharest. The attaché, Colonel Poillon, reported that he had heard from his sources in Budapest "that 12 men, among them 11 Jews, had been caught red-handed with poison needles with which they were going to assassinate the Admiral," meaning Hungary's regent, Admiral Horthy.[103] Landesco argued that although such a story "sounded fishy" and the thought of twelve men with armed with needles was "a very unlikely, ridiculous thing to imagine," he had "no doubt that the story of the 12 poison-needle conspiracy was duly forwarded to Washington." Every report, however fanciful, linking Jews to revolutionary activity played a role in the Hungarian government's defense of the anti-Jewish violence in Hungary.

Stories and news linking Jews to an ongoing Bolshevik threat were widespread in Central Europe in 1919 and the following years and were used as justifications both for authoritarian policies in general as well as for the imposition of antisemitic discrimination. As Landesco argued in his response to the poison-needle rumor, it "has done its part in creating the atmosphere of suspicion of and indifference to the fate of the Jews of Central and Eastern Europe which its statesmen now desire to bring about in order to be permitted by America to deal freely with the Jewish question in their respective lands."[104] Reports of Jewish crimes were a way to justify both official and unofficial persecution of Jews in the face of international criticism.

In understanding the role of the myth of Judeo-Bolshevism in interwar Central Europe, it is important to consider the political uses of this myth both internally and internationally to justify antisemitic measures. By equating Jews and communism, the Hungarian government could argue that anti-Jewish measures were not racist but rather measures to defend the government against a continuing revolutionary threat. Arrests or attacks on prominent Jews (such as the two *Népszava* editors in Budapest) could be portrayed as part of an ongoing political struggle, rather than racist lynchings. Portraying Jews as a dangerous political minority (Jew = Bolshevik) put them outside of the category of "national minority" groups, which had international protection under the Paris peace treaties and the rules of the League of Nations. Internally, the idea of Jews as linked to both international communism and the international protections of the League of Nations and minority treaties was used to stir opposition to the Paris peace system and to further the idea of a martyred

---

[103] Letter, Alex Landesco to Julius Goldman, March 5, 1920, JDC-NY Collection 1919–1921, file # 148 [Hungary, General, 1919–1920], p. 151.

[104] Ibid.

Hungarian nation, putting the Jews seemingly under the protection of the victors in Paris. International and national debates on Hungary's treatment of Jews relating to the Paris peace negotiations, the minority treaties, and Hungary's admission to the League of Nations were all moments when this myth (seemingly proposing an antagonism between "Hungarians" and an international "Jewry") was mobilized with popular resonance.[105] Fears of communism were manipulated to justify antisemitic politics and legislation as well as providing a ground for attacks on individual Jews.

Conclusion

These examples demonstrate how, across Central Europe, rumors and horror stories of the 1919 revolutions were used for political purposes, even entertainment. The dissemination of these stories went hand in hand with a belief in "Judeo-Bolshevism." Preexisting stereotypes linking Jews to revolutionary activity melded with narratives from revolutionary Russia and reports of the 1919 Central European revolutions. In each telling, the idea of Judeo-Bolshevism facilitated belief in horror stories and linked Jews to stories of violence and bloodshed. This was particularly true for the narratives of the 1919 Munich and Budapest revolutions, where prominent Jewish revolutionaries were the main protagonists. Numerous contemporaneous antisemitic publications make this point – one famous example with a very telling title is the 1921 French publication on the Hungarian 1919 revolution, *Quand Israël est roi* (When Israel is king).[106] Through this addition to the historic European revolutionary narrative, the myth of Judeo-Bolshevism, the 1919 Central European revolutions became stories not only about world revolution, but also about "world Jewry."

The myth of a Judeo-Bolshevik conspiracy in 1919 was more than just the reappearance of prerevolutionary stereotypes. It was an important piece of postwar Central European psychology. In 1919, the violence in Munich and Budapest that many on the political Right had predicted would come with the revolution finally came to pass but through their own actions. This pattern corresponds with that of a contemporaneous phenomenon that historian Richard Bessel analyzed: the dissemination during the interwar years of false memories of humiliation during demobilization. Bessel demonstrated that although soldiers later remembered being ignored or denigrated for their military service, in actuality the civilian population attempted to welcome its army home with celebrations, and that in fact many German soldiers had themselves been undisciplined in the demobilization at the end of the war,

---

[105] See Katzburg; on the minority treaties and the Jews, Carole Fink, *Defending the Rights of Others: The Great Powers, the Jews, and International Minority Protection, 1878–1938* (Cambridge: Cambridge University Press, 2004).
[106] Jérome and Jean Tharaud, *Quand Israël est roi* (Paris, 1921).

with large numbers deserting and breaking ranks.[107] Historian Jan Gross identified a similar pattern of violent dissociation in the memories of the mass murder of the Jewish residents of Jedwabne by their Polish neighbors in 1941. He argues "two conquests of this territory, by the Red Army in 1939 and the Wehrmacht in 1941 seem grafted upon each other in preserved narratives ... it appears that the local non-Jewish population projected its own attitude toward the Germans in 1941 ... onto an entrenched narrative about how the Jews allegedly behaved vis-à-vis the Soviets in 1939."[108] These cases are not only instances of a similar psychological phenomenon of transferring guilt to one's enemies or victims. Both are also Central European examples of the power of the same interwar narratives of Judeo-Bolshevism, and come broadly from the Central European anti-revolutionary and antisemitic world of the 1919 memoirists studied here. The right-wing memories contrasting an "ungrateful" home front with dutiful veterans and the Poles remembering their Jewish neighbors as Soviet supporters both echo and reinforce the counterrevolutionary narrative justifying violence.

Gender, along with race, often structured these narratives. In 1919, the actions of counterrevolutionaries, the violence of armed soldiers and militiamen against a largely unarmed population, were difficult to reconcile with traditional notions of soldiers' honor in warfare. Therefore, it was important that the citizenry be demonized in ways that disqualified it from honorable treatment. If women were in the crowds or among the victims, they must not have been proper women but were dangerous (mostly Jewish), defeminized women. If old men (mostly Jewish) were among the victims, then Jews needed to be understood as collectively dangerous. A similar transference of guilt occurred in both Munich and Budapest – Jews were the main victims of the counterrevolutionary violence, but they were remembered as its instigators. The far greater violence of the counterrevolution was understood as the result of the revolutionary violence. As Kaas and Lazarovics claimed, "It was the [Red] Terror Detachments, without which the Dictatorship of the Proletariat couldn't have existed, which generated the White Terror."[109] By examining memories of the revolutions, we are able to better understand the antisemitism that followed. It was not a direct reaction to the presence of Jews in the revolutionary governments but was a product of the need to reconcile the dishonorable and criminal behavior of the White Terror with existing societal norms.

---

[107] Richard Bessel, "The Great War in German Memory: The Soldier of the First World War, Demobilization and Weimar Political Culture," *German History* 6/1 (1988): 20–34.

[108] Jan Gross, *Neighbors: The Destruction of the Jewish Community in Jedwabne, Poland*, 2nd edition (New York: Penguin, 2002), 104.

[109] Kaas and Lazarovics, 315.

The creation and dissemination of rumors in revolutionary Munich and Budapest raised the level of terror and violence in these cities, and stoked antisemitism. Their wartime experiences made listeners inclined to distrust official information, so that even after the defeat of the revolution efforts to "set the record straight" lent further credence to rumors of Judeo-Bolshevik and other conspiracies. As the newspaper articles and pamphlets of 1919 became the memoirs and histories of the interwar period, these rumors were codified into a new revolutionary narrative. The narrative of the 1919 Central European revolutions reproduced, refined, and further distributed the scripts and stereotypes from which it was built. Their longevity and repetition added to their strength, reinforcing the same revolutionary archetypes and flavoring the European revolutionary narrative with the Central European leitmotif of the Judeo-Bolshevik conspiracy.

Gender analysis of the narrative deepens our understanding of the cultural context of interwar Central Europe. Analysis in particular of the portrayals of women's participation in the revolutions allows us to see how the revolutionary experience was instrumentalized in the service of a variety of nationalist and conservative ideologies. On both sides of the political divide women were seen to be symbolic representations of their community: either the nation or the workers' movement. The Right was more concerned with the dangerous women of the revolution, but both Left and Right considered women to be their most vulnerable members. They employed the rape and sexual mistreatment of women, or the danger of it, as the highest example of the barbarism of the other side. Rumors of licentious behavior by women members of revolutionary organizations became part and parcel of the myth of the revolution that continued to be described by the Right throughout the interwar years. Similarly, reports of sexual depravity and the mistreatment of women by the White officers' brigades became part of the myth of martyrdom on the Left. The intersections of racial and gender hierarchies and stereotypes reveal some of the mechanisms of postrevolutionary antisemitism and anti-Jewish violence.

6   Remembering the World Revolution

> To-day Russia is the only country where Bolshevism still exists – Hungary has drained the bitter cup – but the problem of Bolshevism has nevertheless become a world problem, since there is no State in which the social balance is as stable as of yore; antagonisms have grown sharper, discontent is more easily fanned and kindled, and everywhere propaganda is at work.
>
> Albert Kaas and Fedor de Lazarovics, *Bolshevism in Hungary*

With these words, Baron Albert Kaas began his English-language history of Bolshevism in Hungary, which was published in 1931. Kaas, a nobleman, a parliamentary representative, and a member of the interwar Hungarian establishment, addressed himself to the foreign reader and argued in effect that Hungary had battled the world revolution and beaten back international communism. In the preface, he explained how study of the Hungarian revolutionary episode remained important internationally even after "so protracted a period" as nine years. With the archaeological metaphor of a "fragment of pottery" from which "a whole era of development may be reconstructed," Kaas argued, "so the fragment of Bolshevism in Hungary gives us, in its circumscribed limits, a true picture of the entire policy of the Soviet, and its reign of a few months an uncompromising revelation of Moscow's governmental method."[1] Even in the context of 1930s Europe, Kaas considered the example of the Hungarian revolution undiminished in its relevance to politicians on the Right as they battled communists and socialists in their various countries.

A shard of pottery is a small piece but authentic; similarly, the Central European revolutions of 1918–19 were small and brief, but authors across the political spectrum wanted them to be remembered as real, authentic revolutions. For both the Left and the Right the events of 1919 became a founding myth, providing a foundation for a collective identity. For those on the Right, such as Kaas or Tormay, the violence and bloodthirstiness of the revolutionaries provided justification and legitimacy for the excesses of the White brigades. It also served as necessary justification for the continuation of many restrictive laws based on the postrevolutionary "state of emergency."

---

[1] Kaas and Lazarovics, 12.

206

Although many on the Left suffered from these harsh countermeasures, they too remembered the revolutions as "real," as having been a potentially permanent transformation of these societies. This formulation was also a way to justify the martyrdom of the revolutionaries who had died in defense of these regimes, had been arrested or executed, or had fled into exile. This interpretation of the importance of the 1919 revolutions also proved useful, in the wake of the defeats, in arousing the sympathy and support of radical politicians around the world. Although a defeated minority at home, the Hungarian and German communists could feel that they had not suffered in vain, nor made a revolution only in Budapest or Munich. Instead, they were part of an international struggle, the powerful revolutionary collective represented by international communism.

Though both the left- and the right-wing narratives of 1919 focused on the specific histories of each postwar revolution, the storylines on each side depended at their core on a store of preexisting stereotypes and myths. Accounts of the events of 1919, and especially the "lessons" drawn from those events, were based in broader turn-of-the-century cultural and political debates about society, modernization, and justice. The tales of 1919 were shared and disseminated in discursive and literal communities of memory, formed partly by more objective criteria such as "eyewitness," "participant," "worker," or "employer" but partly by shared worldview. They depended for their explanatory power on prewar cultures of protest or on various community understandings of politics, race, and historical progression. The polarized memories of these events make clear that they were products of the deep political chasms in pre–World War I Hungary and Germany, particularly divisions along class and economic fault lines. We have seen how the postrevolutionary trials, as well as the media coverage of these trials, acted as crucibles in which master narratives of revolutionary experiences were forged. In this chapter, we will examine the processes of remembering the revolutions, the individual and collective rituals and practices: memorialization of martyrs, newspaper editorials and feuilliton, memoirs, literature and political propaganda from the early interwar years; we will return to the centrality of race and gender in debates over meaning and the ways in which the uses of symbols and stereotypes became rooted in memories of the revolutionary events. Looking first at the dominant counterrevolutionary Right and then at the minority memory of the political Left, we observe the dialectical process in which the newly minted revolution narratives exerted influence over an existing stockpile of stereotypes and "myths" that were already available to all members of Central European society.[2]

---

[2] Burke; Thomas Butler, ed., *Memory: History, Culture and the Mind* (New York: Blackwell, 1989).

In 1925, the French sociologist Maurice Halbwachs argued that the memories of individuals are formed and recalled within a social milieu. Thus, he asserted, individual memories cannot be separated from this milieu: "we can understand each memory as it occurs in individual thought only if we locate each within the thought of the corresponding group."[3] This idea of socially shaped and determined memories, developed following the collective traumatic experience of the European "Great War," still has important implications for the way we interpret many common historical sources. Halbwachs observed that "just as people are members of many different groups at the same time, so the memory of the same fact can be placed within many frameworks, which result from distinct collective memories."[4] This idea of multiplicity not only of "memories," or versions of events, but also of communities of rememberers is one of the most important contributions of Halbwachs' theory as applied to the writing of history.

In the deeply divided political environment of interwar Central Europe, memories of the 1919 revolutions were fitted into preexisting cognitive frameworks of both political Left and Right. My focus is on certain "acts" of remembering, such as the writing of memoirs, the celebration and memorialization of the dead, and debates about the past. This chapter focuses on the two main political "communities of remembering" that developed in the postrevolutionary period in Bavaria and Hungary, the Right and the Left. It in some ways leaves aside the majority of the population, for whom the 1919 revolutions often were simply rolled into the story of the many horrors of the time: war, hunger, displacement, personal loss, inflation, and disease. Observers such as the novelist Thomas Mann or the philologist Victor Klemperer, who both experienced the 1918 and 1919 revolutions in Munich, wrote about the events in their diaries but moved on to other literary and academic concerns after the political upheavals had ended.

Perhaps partly because the events of 1919 were not universally viewed as pivotal, even at the time, and often were relegated to a minor role compared with the events of the world war, those with a strong political commitment on the Left or the Right fought not only for their interpretation but also for the historical significance of the revolutions. Like Kaas, they wrote and commemorated 1919 to keep it central to the debates of interwar politics. These were the groups who tried most determinedly to establish their versions of events within wider society. To adopt a metaphor Jay Winter and Emmanuel Sivan employed in their work on the memory of World War I, these are the groups who stood closest to the microphone in the choir of Central European interwar society.[5] In both Budapest and Munich, the memories of Left and Right almost entirely contradicted each other,

---

[3] Halbwachs, 53.   [4] Ibid., 52.

[5] Jay Winter and Emmanuel Sivan, eds., *War and Remembrance in the Twentieth Century* (Cambridge: Cambridge University Press, 1999), 28.

particularly in the attribution of morality to events. Because these competing constellations of memory were attached to popular movements that controlled independent media, they tended to drown out the more moderate voices in the choir. The creations of these communities of remembering, though their explanations were politically and morally opposed, were often quite similar in their strident form and tone. And they shared their contention of the centrality and importance of the 1919 revolutions to the debates of the present.

In the aftermath of war and revolution, many Central European city dwellers were in a state of ongoing agitation and conflict. The bourgeoisie were shocked by their experience of defeat, destruction, and violence, and as a result they were willing to tolerate greater levels violence in order to reestablish "law and order" during the counterrevolutions in 1919. Similarly, in the midst of an apparent world revolution, the working-class population had been ready to take up arms to defend its revolutionary victories against the reaction. But as time passed and the political and economic situation stabilized, most people were anxious for a return to normalcy and to avoid the political violence of the immediate postwar period. Activists fought against this complacency and forgetting, reminding their audiences of the drama and passion of the recent revolutionary struggles. Recalling the dangers and injustices of 1919 served to recruit new followers to their camp, consolidate their political communities and organizations, and justify their extreme beliefs and tactics.

The political Right often employed historical comparisons to justify its own aggression. This began with the counterrevolutionary violence in 1919 and continued through the interwar period to justify the actions of both state and nonstate actors against the Left, from arrest or internment for political crimes to assassinations by right-wing terrorists such as the Feme murders in Weimar Germany (1919–23). They also felt the need to lose themselves in a larger purpose, a broader national identity, and yet were terrified of the masses who had supported the revolution. The rough effort to balance these fears and the impulses of extreme nationalism were often expressed through highly gendered and sexual imagery and through an often equally graphic antisemitism.

The minority memory of the political Left, forged in a parallel but antithetical experience, found expression in the radical press and in historical writings and ceremonies that recalled the 1919 revolutions. Exiled from counterrevolutionary Hungary and forced into the criminalized margins of Weimar Germany, communists and former revolutionaries recalled their moment on the world stage in the face of continued threats and violence. But anti-communist laws were not the only material result of the dominant Right's interpretation of 1919. Postrevolutionary governments denied pensions to victims of the White violence in Bavaria, antisemitic *numerus clausus* legislation was passed in Hungary in 1920, and thousands of "Polish" or "Galician" Jews were rounded up and deported from both countries in the early 1920s.

The Left's preferred narrative of the 1919 revolutions was dusted off again after World War II to provide legitimacy to the new political situation in Central Europe. The state socialist regime in Hungary used the revolutionary heritage of 1919 to claim native legitimacy and local origins for a government popularly understood to be a Russian imposition. The Bavarian revolution of 1919 had a mixed role in the politics of postwar Germany. The German Democratic Republic, like socialist Hungary, found it convenient to attach its origins to the history of the German revolutions of 1918 and 1919 as a way to give some native legitimacy to its power. In preunification West Germany, however, the postwar government found little utility in tying itself to this history. The generation of 1968, however, turned to 1919 not only for native legitimacy for a German revolutionary tradition but also to learn "lessons" from this earlier, failed revolution. These postwar leftists connected the mistakes and failures of 1919 to the rise of fascism and Germany's crimes in World War II.

On the Right: Defense of Nation

The stereotypes and myths that people promoted and manipulated about the 1919 Central European revolutions followed explanatory narratives and patterns developed in the wake of earlier revolutions, such as the Paris Commune and the Russian Revolution as well as the foundational French Revolution and terror. Kaas and Lazarovics, for example, compared the October 1918 protests in Budapest with the storming of the Bastille in Paris in 1789 in his *Bolshevism in Hungary*.[6] In a 1921 article in the German communist daily *Rote Fahne*, Eugen Leviné's widow described how in the days before his execution Leviné was visited in his cell by a series of morbidly curious soldiers and bureaucrats, all wanting to see for themselves the "blood-thirsty Robespierre as he had been referred to in Munich."[7] Hundreds of newspaper articles and memoirs from Budapest and Munich denounced what they referred to as the "Russian Terror" of the 1919 Central European revolutions. Many writers on the Right strove to attach these historical references to the leading revolutionaries by assigning local figures the names "Lenin" or "Trotsky." This device indirectly asserted the unstated case that the crimes of the revolutionaries of 1919 were similar in scale and consequence to those of these major figures in the Russian Revolution.

An author in the Viennese *Neue Freie Presse* sifted through European history to explain metaphorically the bloody events of the *Geiselmord* in Munich that claimed ten lives.[8] He first made a long comparison with contemporary Russia, even criticizing the Munich revolutionaries as being "poor copies" of the real

---

[6] Kaas and Lazarovics, 35–41.   [7] *Die Rote Fahne* 251, June 5, 1921.
[8] "Die Ermordung der Geiseln in München: Nach dem russischen Beispiel," *Neue Freie Presse* 19648, June 5, 1919.

Bolsheviks. Looking further back in history he was able to find an allegory for Munich in the violent excesses of the Roman Emperor Caligula. In the end, like many contemporary observers in both Munich and Budapest, the Viennese author found his most fruitful comparison for the revolutionary events in Munich to be with the Paris Commune of 1871 at the end of the Franco-Prussian War. He compared the sieges of the two cities after defeat in war and the harsh justice served afterwards against the revolutionaries by the new national authorities. He found similarities, not only in the context of a lost war but also in the personalities of the revolutionary leaders, naming Raoul Rigault, the de facto head of the Commune's police force and the anticlerical radical held responsible for the killing of the archbishop of Paris, the "[Leviné-] Niessen of those times."[9] This article, published on the day of Leviné's execution, justified the use of the death penalty as a response to revolution through such historical parallels, although Leviné was not accused of a direct role in the murders unlike Rigault or Théophile Ferré, the communards in Paris who ordered the execution of the archbishop of Paris and five other hostages in 1871.

Some on the Right took a different tack, using the device of historical metaphor to argue instead that the 1919 revolutionaries were not "true" revolutionaries or idealists but rather mere criminals, unlike some of their historical forbearers. The Hungarian lawyer Oszkar Szőllősy, for example, emphasized this distinction in his article "The Criminals of the Dictatorship of the Proletariat."[10] He compared the Budapest revolutionaries unfavorably with the leaders of the late eighteenth-century French Revolution. "Every revolution," he wrote "has its idealistic champions, its enthusiasts who inflame the masses with a fiery passion and are themselves ready to endure all the suffering of Calvary in the service of the creed which they profess."[11] He claimed that one must admire certain of these idealists, such as the French revolutionary Camille Desmoulins, for their "unselfish enthusiasm." According to Szőllősy, the Hungarian revolutionaries, on the other hand, had attempted to flee rather than accept martyrdom for their beliefs because they were criminals not authentic revolutionaries motivated by idealism. Comparing him with Desmoulins or the famous Paris communard and anarchist Louise Michel, Szőllősy described Béla Kun as a small-time embezzler, frequenter of orgies, and a glutton, who even "during the 'lean' days of the Soviet regime . . . did not abstain from sumptuous banqueting."[12] This rhetorical strategy suggested that the 1919 revolutionaries were merely degenerate imitations of the French originals.

---

[9] Ibid.   [10] Reprinted in Tormay, *Outlaw's Diary*, vol. 2, appendix.
[11] Reprinted in ibid., 216.
[12] Ibid., 220. Historians have commented on both the actual appetites for luxury food and wine of certain communards, particularly Rigault, as well as the anti-Commune propaganda using these luxury appetites in a similarly critical way to Szőllősy here. See Merriman.

Nationalist Hungarian commentators such as Szőllősy and Kaas were also drawn to such international comparative historical arguments in order to contextualize the Hungarian experience for potentially sympathetic conservative audiences abroad. Szőllősy, for example, pointed out the international character of the Budapest revolution. Not only were counterrevolutionaries faced with native Hungarian radicals, but they were also forced to combat radical forces recruited from all over Europe, representatives of the "world revolution." "During the opening weeks of the Bolshevik regime [in Hungary]," Szőllősy claimed,

Budapest became the gathering-place of international adventurers flocking thither from all quarters of the globe, – "Spartacus" Germans, Russian Jews, Austrian, Rumanian, Bulgarian, and Italian communists hastened to thither in the hope of finding rich booty under the aegis of the Soviet Government. At a mass meeting held in the suburbs, speeches were delivered by demagogues in six different languages.[13]

This is an interesting complaint, since the multinational Hungarian kingdom, which most on the political Right were determined to preserve, had at least that many languages among its subject peoples. And many workers in the Budapest suburbs indeed came from these linguistic minorities, so while we do not know which "mass meeting held in the suburbs," Szőllősy was referring to, it can be imagined that political speeches may well have been held in multiple languages in the Hungarian capital in order to reach this ethnically diverse population of workers. But for the Hungarian Right in particular, the international dimension of their struggle was a source of encouragement and support for their cause. From this perspective, the Hungarian battle against international communism was a repetition of Hungary's historic role as a "bulwark of Christianity" in Europe during the Turkish wars of the sixteenth century.

The Right also mobilized rhetorical devices beyond historical and international allegories to understand and explain the revolutions. Medical science and psychiatry, among others, were marshaled to serve a similar purpose. By 1919, the language of psychology was very much a part of contemporary currents and usage, and it became susceptible to these political uses. Many contemporaries linked revolution with mental illness, and specifically the participation of women in revolutionary events tended to elicit the diagnosis of the particularly "feminine" mental illness, hysteria.

Both Budapest and Munich had been, pre–World War I, centers of psychiatric research and treatment. Toward the end of the war, in September 1918, Budapest had hosted a congress of the International Psychoanalytic Association. Because the war made travel impossible for many, the congress was only "international" in the sense of including participants drawn from the

---

[13] Reprinted in Tormay, *Outlaw's Diary,* vol. 2, 218.

territory of the Central Powers. According to one delegate, "everybody was in uniform, except Freud."[14] Among the many psychiatrists in uniform, two analysts who spent the war treating "war hysteria" were Emil Kraeplin and Eugen Kahn of the University of Munich. Following the war, these two German psychiatrists turned their attention to the psychology of revolution.[15] Towards the end of the nineteenth century Kraeplin had, in historian Paul Lerner's estimation, "revolutionized the psychiatric approach to illness by systematizing and standardizing its diagnoses .... His influence further sealed Germany's domination in psychiatric science."[16] Kraeplin's interest in personality as an object of psychiatric study as well as his research into the hereditary nature of many mental illnesses led him eventually to the eugenic movement and to the establishment of a research program in "racial hygiene."[17] He also played an important role in the way the Bavarian Revolution of 1919 became part of a medicalized political discourse in the early years of the Weimar Republic.

Kraeplin and other psychiatrists worried that during the war the mentally ill and physically degenerate were protected at home and in hospitals and institutions, while the strongest and best of "German masculinity" had perished at the front. In fact, some doctors working for the military had condemned the war as "reverse Darwinism," arguing that the war had culled the best men while inventing ways for the weakest to shirk their duty. In his examination of German psychiatrists' response to world-war-related trauma, Lerner demonstrated that, by 1918, many psychiatrists believed that the majority of their so-called hysterical patients were shirkers and liars who were merely trying to avoid military service.[18] The fact that so many of their wartime patients were men struggling with "hysterical" symptoms and hysteria before the war had been viewed largely as a "women's disorder" served to feminize these patients in further contrast to their fellow soldiers who were at the front.[19] After the November revolution, some of these same doctors asserted that the revolutionary ranks had been filled with former patients. In fact, in their view, the whole revolution could be attributed to mental illness: the psychopathology of the leaders and the "mass neurosis" of a war-exhausted population made more susceptible to revolutionary propaganda by the terrible experience of military defeat and political turmoil.

In fact, a whole host of Central European psychiatrists wrote on the relationship between war, revolution, and the psyche.[20] In trying to explain the 1919

---

[14] Sandór Radó, quoted in Lerner, 175.   [15] Ibid., 214–15.   [16] Ibid., 17.   [17] Ibid., 18, 22.
[18] Ibid.
[19] For this feminization, see also Heather R. Perry, *Recycling the Disabled: Army, Medicine, and Modernity in WWI Germany* (Manchester: Manchester University Press, 2014).
[20] H. Marx, "Ärztliche Gedanken zur Revolution." *Berliner klinische Wochenschrift* 12 (March 24, 1919): 279–80; Georg Stertz, "Verschrobene Fanatiker." *Berliner klinische Wochenschrift* 25 (June 28, 1919): 586–8; Paul Federn, *Zur Psychologie der Revolution: Die vaterlose Gesellschaft* (Leipzig and Vienna: Anzengruber Verlag Brüder Suschitzky, 1919);

revolutions in Munich and Budapest, some contemporary writers utilized the scientific prestige of psychiatry, and especially of the prominent Munich psychiatrists Kahn and Kraeplin, in several different ways. Medical and other professional journals published articles that provided psychiatric evaluations of individual revolutionaries (undertaken without actual examinations of the subjects) or of the mass of participants in the revolutions. There were few attempts by these authors to confront the many obvious methodological problems in this enterprise, instead they pushed ahead uncritically to harvest the political benefits of discovering that your enemies were debilitated or crazy.

These postwar and postrevolutionary publications demonstrate strikingly the conservative and nationalist transformation of the field of psychiatry during the war years that Lerner identified. But these psychological diagnoses of revolution, tainted though they might have been, did not only circulate within the professional community; they found resonance in society in several important ways. Most importantly, these "scientific" findings were used by the police and judiciary as they identified, assessed, and punished those associated with the two revolutionary episodes. Clippings of Kahn's diagnoses, which had been published in a medical journal, were pasted into the fact sheets in the police files and the diagnoses seem to have helped frame police investigations of all the major revolutionaries arrested in Munich. In many cases, officials highlighted their reliance on these highly speculative assessments with underlining and marginal notes on the clipped articles. In addition, the widespread employment of the nomenclature and analytical terms of psychiatry by the press as well as by the authors of anti-revolutionary books and memoirs broadly influenced public opinion, undermining whatever residual support for the Left survived. Rather than an opposing worldview, revolutionary ideas were an illness.

Because Munich had been an influential center of psychiatric research in prewar and wartime Germany, the application of psychiatric methods and terms to revolutions and revolutionaries by researchers such as Kahn and Kraeplin were immensely influential. The opinions of these scholars benefitted from their professional prestige but also from their credibility as firsthand witnesses to the 1919 revolutions in Bavaria. In August 1919, Kahn gave a lecture on the psychoses of revolution at the annual meeting of Bavarian psychiatrists in Munich. The well-received speech was then published in the German *Zeitschrift fuer die gesamte Neurologie und Psychiatrie* (Journal for neurology and psychiatry). In his exploration of the topic, Kahn applied thinly disguised names to the leaders of the Munich uprising and then explored their actions and biographies as case studies to illustrate a variety of mental illnesses.[21]

Jenő Udvary, "Psychológiai megfigyelések a harcztérről," *Hadtörtényelmi Közlemények* 22/1 (1921): 157–70.

[21] Eugen Kahn, "Psychopathen als revolutionäre Führer," *Zeitschrift fuer die gesamte Neurologie und Psychiatrie* 52 (1919): 90–116.

While Kahn diagnosed individual revolutionaries to suggest a revolutionary psychosis, his colleague and former professor, Kraeplin, examined the Munich revolution as a symptom of the general mental illness of postwar Germany.[22] Kraeplin published his speculative inquiry in an article published in the *Süddeutsche Monatshefte* in late 1919. Kraeplin had long held a particular interest in the mental health of the "nation" or "race." This interest had framed his wartime ideas about shellshock and led him to the field of eugenics. This perhaps explains why in the article, entitled "Psychiatrische Randbemerkungen zur Zeitgeschichte" (Psychiatric commentary on contemporary history)," Kraeplin analyzed the factors that he believed had chipped away at the "healthy psychological vigor of our people" during the war and which eventually led to defeat and revolution.[23] This article, appearing in a popular cultural monthly magazine rather than for a specialized audience of professionals, broadened the diagnosis of revolutionary hysteria – both by reaching a wider, non-medical-professional, educated reading public and by addressing the diagnosis not to individuals but to the whole revolutionary episode and therefore theoretically to all revolutionary participants.

In the article, Kraeplin argued for a sort of psychiatric version of the "stab in the back" myth of a military betrayed by the civilian government. He claimed that the mental health and will to fight of the German troops had been weakened during the war by the moral and psychological weakness of those on the home front, particularly women: "often it was women who were not up to the long deprivations of war and who tormented their fighting relatives with complaints and sometimes even grossly betrayed their trust."[24] The long war, physical deprivation, and hunger led inextricably to what he described as an epidemic of hysterical attacks in the German population. Kraeplin identified civilian protests for peace and food riots as wartime manifestations of mass hysteria. But more consequentially, he also explained the 1918 and 1919 revolutions as the result of racial and gender differences in psychological make-up and resilience. Women, according to Kraeplin, were less psychologically stable and therefore more susceptible to outbreaks of hysteria. According to him, research had proven that hysterical attacks function as an unconscious defense mechanism against perceived existential dangers. Hysteria was, in his words, "the last escape for the undeveloped, for those people less well equipped to deal with the problems of life, for children and youth, for women, and for the excitable, insecure, and weak-willed."[25] It was therefore the unnatural feminization of German society during the war that made it vulnerable to hysterical episodes, as mass conscription had removed young, healthy males from civilian life.

---

[22] Emil Kraeplin, "Psychiatrische Randbemerkungen zur Zeitgeschichte," *Süddeutsche Monatshefte* 16/2 (1919): 171–83.
[23] Ibid., 172.   [24] Ibid., 173.   [25] Ibid., 176.

Without the wartime disruption of normal social organization, the strong male element would presumably have prevented mass hysteria and revolution. As Kraeplin explained to his readers about hysteria, "In the mature man of inner strength these ancient defense mechanisms ... no longer play any role."[26] He therefore laid the blame for the revolutions on the home front, on women and also feminized home-front men front men vulnerable to hysteria.[27]

Among the males of the home front, Kraeplin singled out one group as especially susceptible to such hysterical attacks: Jews. His article thus offered a "scientific" and medicalized version of the common antisemetic stereotypes of a feminized Jewish male, who shared the female susceptibility to hysteria, the "last escape of the undeveloped."[28] It also dovetailed with the prominent German wartime myth of Jews as shirkers who did not perform their military duty. It was supposedly in response to popular complaints related to this belief that the Prussian War Minister Adolf Wild von Hohenborn ordered a wartime census of Jewish frontline military service in October 1916. Though the results disproved the antisemitic accusations, they were not widely publicized, and the fact that the government ordered a "Jew Count" left many Germans with the impression that Jews were either evading military service or serving in safe "desk jobs" on the home front.[29] Thus Kraeplin and his readers may have assumed that the German home front was both more female and more Jewish during the war. He saw it as no surprise that so many Jews were to be found at the head of the postwar revolutionary movements since, as he put it, "this could have been the result of the frequency of psychopathic tendencies among them."[30] The tendencies that he saw as particularly important among the Jews included "their skill at destructive criticism, their verbal and theatrical talents as well as their tenacity and ambition."[31] As he had for gender, Kraeplin offered his professional expertise as a basis for understanding race as a determinant of behavior and psychology.

Kraeplin's popular psychoanalysis of the revolution offered what he considered medical and biological "proof" that the trajectory of these revolutions was derived from the character of foreign and insidious leaders, who had misled an uneducated population made susceptible by the experience of the war. The language of psychiatry, as manipulated by Kraeplin, offered a useful

---

[26] Ibid.

[27] For an excellent exploration of home-front men, see Healy, *Vienna and the Fall of the Habsburg Empire*, especially chapter 6.

[28] Kraeplin, 176. See the classic studies of these stereotypes by Sander L. Gilman, *Difference and Pathology Stereotypes of Sexuality, Race, and Madness* (Ithaca, NY: Cornell University Press, 1985) and *The Jew's Body* (New York: Routledge, 1991).

[29] On the 1916 count (*Judenzählung*), see, among others, Werner T. Angress, "The German Army's 'Judenzählung' of 1916: Genesis-Consequences-Significance," *Leo Baeck Institute Yearbook* 23 (1978): 117–37; the catalog to the centenary exhibit at the Jewish Museum Munich: Ulrike Heikaus and Julia Köhne, eds., *Krieg! Juden zwischen den Fronten, 1914–1918* (Berlin: Hentrich & Hentrich Verlag, 2014).

[30] Kraeplin, 178.   [31] Ibid.

way to separate out the supposedly mentally degenerate leaders (identified as Jews or "Judaized" by their association with the home front) and to assign them full responsibility for the revolutions. Popular support for the revolutions (in the form of crowds and low-level followers) could then also be explained from a psychological perspective. The usually "healthy" body of the nation had been weakened and stressed by the war, and the feminized home front, with its crowds of women and children, was vulnerable to hysterical reactions and easy to mislead. Kraeplin provided a medical explanation for the treasonous activities of revolutionary crowds: the civilian population had also been suffering from mental illness. He argued that in this collective "case," the hysteria of revolution had been a manifestation of both the psychosis of the revolutionary leaders and of the primordial "escape of the undeveloped" from overwhelming problems, brought on by the war and economic deprivations. Thus, he presented the whole revolution as a mass psychotic episode.

The case of Eglhofer, the Red Army commander in Munich murdered by White troops, demonstrates how the language of psychiatry was used in 1919 to separate even non-Jews from the "healthy" body of the nation. Unlike Leviné and Toller who were Jewish and not from Bavaria, Eglhofer and all of the other men found responsible by the courts for the *Geiselmord* were undeniably Catholic and Bavarian. Eglhofer was born in 1896 in Munich into a Catholic craftsman's family. He served in the German navy during World War I and participated in one of the naval mutinies in the fall of 1918. A photo in his Bavarian police file showed him in a striped sailor's shirt, standing with a group of protesters holding posters of Rosa Luxemburg and Karl Liebknecht (Figure 6.1) After the war he returned to Munich and became one of the founders of the local communist party.[32] Despite his youth, and perhaps because of his experience as a revolutionary member of the military, Eglhofer served as the commander of the Red Army during the brief revolutionary regime. Because of this position, he was charged with murder for the order to hold and kill bourgeois hostages (which resulted in the *Geiselmord*). However, he never faced these charges in court because he was murdered by his guards while in police custody.

Kahn analyzed Eglhofer, under the barely disguised pseudonym "Robert Iglauer," as one of the case studies of revolutionaries already mentioned.[33] Kahn's medical assessment of Eglhofer was gleaned from his readings of police files and reports in the press rather than from clinical contact, as Kahn himself admitted in the article. After a brief synopsis of the twenty-three-year-old's life, Kahn described "Iglauer" as "brutal, hungry for power, vain, uneducated, of medium intelligence, with an athletic appearance." Psychologically, Kahn diagnosed him as an "antisocial psychopath" and "true criminal type."[34]

---

[32] StAM Pol. Dir. 10040, 23, "Rädelsführer zur Zeit der Räteregierung in München."
[33] Kahn.   [34] Ibid., 94.

Figure 6.1 Photograph of Eglhofer at a demonstration.
Staatsarchiv München, Polizei Direction 10040, 23.
Source: Bavarian State Archives.

In his general summary of the revolutionary participants in the introduction to his case studies, Kahn pointed out that "as is usual in psychological diagnosis, other symptoms are often present," these included a tendency to "hysterical reactions" noted for some revolutionaries. However, Kahn concluded, "it is [their] ethical inferiority which really marks them [the revolutionary leaders]. The driving force behind their actions was vanity and profit-seeking."[35] Once this account was published, police detectives then entered Kahn's psychiatric evaluation of Eglhofer into their own records, underling the author's characterization of the prisoner as an "antisocial psychopath" and a "true criminal type."[36]

[35] Ibid.   [36] StAM Pol. Dir. 10040 "Eglhofer, Rudolf," 144.

The publication of these highly speculative medical diagnoses of the revolutionaries led many contemporaries to believe that the experience of revolution was more a manifestation of mental illness than a mass movement that grew out of social injustice. In this dubious narrative, the violent ascent of the Right was therapeutic, not the bloody reestablishment of the old order. From this perspective, the revolutionary participation of a young, athletic Bavarian military veteran such as Eglhofer could be explained to readers in these medicalized terms. He was a "true criminal type" and the revolutionary government had been a criminal regime. This sort of diagnosis worked cognitively in two ways. By declaring revolutionary leaders to be psychopaths and biological criminals, the revolution could be portrayed as a "government of criminals," without evidence and without recourse to a legal process to demonstrate revolutionary crimes.

Introduced into the public sphere by this circle of conservative psychiatrists and lawyers, terms such as "hysterical," "nervous," "anti-social," and "psychopathic" were then widely employed by the press and even the courts to describe and criticize the revolutionaries. An article in the *Münchner Zeitung* on June 10, 1919, entitled "Jakobinertypen aus dem Luitpoldgymnasium" (Jakobin-types from the Luitpold Gymnasium), claimed to offer exclusive details about those responsible for the *Geiselmord*.[37] The author described Fritz Seidel, the commander at the gymnasium, as a "nervous type," who screamed at his soldiers and "got the greatest pleasure from locking people up." He was "quick to draw his gun over the smallest thing," and was very proud of his position, official car, and the servicemen assigned to him. The article claimed that Seidel and his wife had come to Munich after "taking part in the Berlin turmoil." Seidel's wife, who worked during the revolution at an infirmary on her street, was described as "similarly vain, coarse, and power-hungry." These characteristics, according to the *Münchner Zeitung*, were "traits [that] apparently served as a recommendation for someone to serve as infirmary matron under the soviet government."[38] This sarcastic assessment of revolutionary commitment (even nursing the wounded) as the result of bad character combined both psychological and moral traits.

Lawyers and court officials as well as the press generally found this asserted connection between revolutionary activities and mental illness useful in both Munich and Budapest. In the police file of Maria Lintner, a minor and an orphan arrested in Munich for robbery after the defeat of the revolutionary government, we can observe the way that politics and psychology were entwined into police work and procedures. Before her trial in juvenile court, Lintner was examined by Kraeplin's psychiatric clinic at the University of Munich. Psychiatrists there determined that she was "an unstable psychopath

---

[37] *Münchner Zeitung* 153, June 10, 1919.   [38] Ibid.

with hysterical tendencies," and she was apparently released until her trial for medical treatment. In a letter written to the police to complain about this decision, an officer of the juvenile court noted that "this sick young woman" had been released into the charge of a Dr. Schollenbruch, who, the writer claimed, "as was proven in court, was in the Red ambulance service during the soviet government, and is himself supposedly a psychopath."[39] The medical qualifications and mental health of Schollenbruch (as well as the decision to release a defendant to him for medical treatment) were challenged through claims of his political convictions; leftist politics served as symptoms of mental disease.

As Tormay's *Outlaw's Diary* made clear, the Right found it extremely useful to circulate through every possible medium this medicalized allegation that the objectives and behaviors of the Left resulted from a general sexual and psychological pathology. This rhetorical device, the depraved enemy, was given additional traction by the legal system's distinction between "political crimes" and "common criminals," a distinction asserted often in the trials of defeated revolutionaries. If political actors and revolutionaries could be shown to be pathological, "criminal types," then the courts were not required to provide them with the guarantees afforded political prisoners for their crimes of conscience.

Szőllősy, for example, reminded readers in his article "The Criminals of the Dictatorship of the Proletariat" that "In our moral judgment we distinguish between political and other criminals." "In cases where only the tendency or motive is of such [a political] character, while the means employed are base," a situation that he argued "is true of most revolutionary offences," then, he concluded, "we are confronted not with political, but with common crimes."[40] For Szőllősy and others, this understanding of the 1919 revolutions as criminal acts taken by pathological criminals simplified the historical narrative and decoupled the revolutions from the prior political history of Hungary and Germany and from the prewar politics of the working classes.

Szőllősy's article freely mixed legal definitions of criminality with biological and psychological ones produced by conservative psychiatrists and social scientists. According to him, the revolution threw off the rule of law that had served to keep "criminal and unhealthy instincts hitherto in check." This situation of lawlessness, then, attracted those "degenerate individuals who are criminally inclined."[41] In other words, the people who joined the revolutionaries did not do so because they shared their political goals but rather because they were criminals looking to exploit the lawlessness and chaos.

---

[39] Letter from Amtsgericht München, Jugendgericht, July 24, 1920; StAM Pol. Dir. 10147 Schollenbruch.

[40] Reprinted in Tormay, *Outlaw's Diary,* vol. 2, 217.   [41] Ibid., 218.

Though he was writing about Hungary and claiming expertise as a lawyer rather than a doctor, Szőllősy offered almost an identical explanation for the Hungarian revolutions as the one Kraeplin had offered for the German revolutions. Like Kraeplin, Szőllősy blamed the "terrible trials of four and a half years of war" and "its demoralizing effect" for preparing society for manipulation by outside agitators. Like Kraeplin, he discounted popular protests for revolution, even by soldiers themselves. For Szőllősy, the cause of what he described as "the exorbitant demands advanced by soldiers after the defeat" in the war (i.e., the mass protests for suffrage and representation) was the effect of war on certain soldiers, now "embittered by battle and grown accustomed to a distaste for a life of work." These damaged men were ripe for manipulation by the same groups Kraeplin had diagnosed in Germany as wartime shirkers and who Szőllősy labeled "a few educated persons of disordered intellect."[42]

Szőllősy illustrated what he interpreted as the connection between revolutionary recruitment and mental illness with the case of the Marxist philosopher and literary critic György Lukács, the people's commissar for public education.[43] Lukács was the son of a wealthy banker who, according to Szőllősy, had been "persuaded to join the Communists by the crack-brained daughter of an extremely rich Budapest solicitor." This woman had "assisted Béla Kun and his associates to counterfeit banknotes" and "finally . . . was thrashed publicly (in the street) with a hunting crop by an embittered 'bourgeois.'"[44] Szőllősy approvingly reported this whipping of a well-to-do young woman in public, certainly unchivalrous behavior for his political allies, as the reaffirmation of the healthy class and gender norms of society, which this supposedly mentally ill woman had upset through her behavior.

Not only did the Right use historical and psychological models to condemn the 1919 revolutions, they deployed preexisting prejudices about the city, the working class, and socialism as well. For conservatives, these revolutions had confirmed nearly all their worst fears about modern urban society. The violence and chaos that they had assumed would accompany democratization and socialism had for them come to pass in the two brief revolutions and in the counterrevolutions that followed. That the Whites were responsible for much

---

[42] Ibid., 219.
[43] Lukács was the most famous intellectual involved in the Hungarian revolutionary government. After its collapse he fled to Vienna and worked in Berlin and Moscow as well in the interwar period, during which time he wrote several important books of Marxist philosophy. His solid Marxist intellectual credentials make Szőllősy's description of how he joined the Communist Party even more ridiculous. It is possible that the woman described in the story is meant to be Gertrúd Bortstieber, Lukács' second wife and a fellow communist in 1919. For an intellectual biography see Lee Congdon, *The Young Lukács* (Chapel Hill: University of North Carolina Press, 1983).
[44] Ibid., 219.

of the violence themselves was ignored or dismissed as the inevitable result of the provocations of the Left.

Alongside gender and racial stereotypes, a key prewar prejudice that was applied to the 1919 revolutions was the general anti-urbanism of the Right, the roots of which lay in the nineteenth century. Despite a shared history of anti-urbanism, victorious counterrevolutionaries of Budapest and Munich viewed their cities differently. In the dominant narrative that developed in postrevolutionary Munich, the city was viewed as a victim of foreign agitators. In Budapest, on the other hand, the victorious Right considered the city itself to be foreign. The roots of these differences in the assessment of guilt in 1919 are in the different images that the cities had before the war. Budapest's German-speaking heritage and large Jewish population were loathed by Hungarian nationalists long before 1919. These nationalists rooted their idealized image of the nation in the agrarian estates of the countryside with their traditional social organization. While Munich was also a city of migrants in the nineteenth century, urban–rural conflicts had been mitigated by a large influx of peasants from the immediate hinterland and by the retention of the city's provincial character. This city, therefore, was viewed mostly as essentially Bavarian, not foreign.

In Budapest, anti-urban rhetoric was more vehement and persisted longer after the 1919 revolutions. In August 1920, a year after the collapse of the soviet government, the literary journal *Gondolat* published an article entitled "Bűnös Budapest" (an alliterative catchphrase in Hungarian, meaning guilty Budapest), in which the author, István Turcsányi, explained, "it should come as no surprise ... that the country holds its own capital city responsible for the fact that we [the nation] were driven to the edge of the grave." Turcsányi held Budapest responsible for the threefold suffering of the Hungarian nation (war, revolution, and the punitive peace treaty). He blamed the capital for these embarrassments, seeing it as non-Hungarian, having different and conflicting interests from those of the Hungarian people. He called Budapest, "this city which was estranged from the racial qualities and energies of Magyardom – and which damaged our national development more than all our enemies."[45] Hungarian anti-urbanism was able to survive because, unlike Munich, the Budapest middle class (much of it Jewish) was unable to assert itself in the face of the counterrevolutionary forces and because the prewar political regime of "old feudalism and old plutocracy," as Oszkár Jászi called it, was able to reestablish itself from its traditional power bases in the rural counties[46]

---

[45] Cited in Fischer, *Entwicklungsstufen des Antisemitismus in Ungarn*. "Bűnös Budapest" can be translated also as "sinful Budapest," the phrase Horthy used in his November 1919 arrival speech.
[46] Jászi, *Revolution and Counterrevolution*, 156–7.

During the preparation for the military attack on Red Munich and during the phase of acute violence in the first week of May 1919, there was also a great deal of anti-urbanism expressed in Bavaria by leaders of government forces and the *Freikorps*. They portrayed Munich as a "Red nest" and a "national shame." As late as the end of May, a report compiled by the military on the quality of new recruits to the army and the *Freikorps* complained about the "lack of fighting will" among urban young men who had recently enlisted. "In order to avoid the poisoning effects of the big city," the report recommended that troops should be moved from Munich into the countryside as soon as possible to avoid political contagion.[47] In Bavaria, this anti-urban version of events, which placed the blame for the revolution largely on the capital city, persisted among some military officers through the summer of 1919. It had much less traction among the general population. Once the revolutionary government was defeated, the urban middle classes organized themselves into the voluntary civic militia or *Einwohnerwehr*, and the elite of Munich, eclipsed during the brief revolutionary regime, was able to reestablish itself in public life.[48]

The urban militia served several important functions for conservatives in the city. Through it, the Munich middle class was able to assert itself as a counterweight to the formal military authorities who had organized the capture of the city. The *Einwohnerwehr* demonstrated that the city could "take care of its own safety," although that hadn't been the case in April when authorities were challenged by the armed Left. A recruitment poster for the *Einwohnerwehr* proclaimed, "Don't you support order and security?" above an image of Munich's cathedral, the Frauenkirche, engulfed in flames, even though this iconic building had survived both revolution and counterrevolution without any serious damage.[49] The *Einwohnerwehr* invariably claimed to meet recruitment goals and maintain orderly training, while the professional military assessed its competence and viability as much lower. On May 30, 1919, General Oven complained that "despite frequent advertisement in the papers, participation in the *Einwohnerwehr* is proceeding exceedingly slowly."[50] In their correspondence with the military command, the underlying assertion of independence by the urban militia leaders was clear as was their desire to relieve the government troops garrisoned in the city.

Enlistment in the *Einwohnerwehr* allowed the men of Munich's middle classes to escape identification as victims of the Red regime who needed to

---

[47] BHSA, Höhere Stäbe Bund 3/2, "Zur Lage in München," May 30, 1919, Generalkommando Oven.

[48] For more on the *Einwohnerwehr* in Bavaria, see David Clay Large, "The Politics of Law and Order: A History of the Bavarian Einwohnerwehr, 1918–1921," *Transactions of the American Philosophical Society* 70/2 (1980); for a survey of *Einwohnerwehren* and other paramilitary groups in Weimar Germany, see James Diehl, *Paramilitary Politics in Weimar Germany* (Bloomington: Indiana University Press, 1977).

[49] Poster in BHSA, Einwohnerwehr, Bund 13/2.   [50] BHSA, Höhere Stäbe Bund 3/2.

be rescued by the White forces and to establish new, active identities as combatants who were the instruments of defeating the Red menace. That this reassertion of agency was tied to anxieties about the overturning of traditional gender roles is evidenced by a popular "marching song" written by the humorist folksinger Weiß Ferdl.[51] Along with Karl Valentin, Weiß Ferdl was the most popular of the Munich folksingers in the first decades of the twentieth century.[52] Historian Robert Eben Sackett has demonstrated that Weiß Ferdl's performances became increasingly reactionary as he and his fans in the lower middle classes became more and more hostile to urban culture, Jews, and, after 1918, the Weimar Republic itself. Therefore, the mocking tone of the march "Einwohner Wehr" was one of friendly teasing from someone who shared an anti-revolutionary worldview, rather than dismissive political derision by an opponent. The first two verses championed the *Einwohnerwehr*'s restoration of order and praised the self-defense organized by men of property against "the dark characters" who had "plundered and stolen." The third verse, however, mockingly referred to the many "gray-haired men" who enlisted in the militia and proudly wore their blue/white armband, "that's a man, loyal German and true, who stands bravely for freedom and rights." The verse continued, "if (what horror) that man has a real mean wife at home, and if she's even a revolutionary and doesn't recognize him as master anymore," then, according to Weiß Ferdl, "there's only one thing that can help you, my dear man, join the *Einwohnerwehr*." In the same way the militia faced political dangers, it would also resist a potential revolution in the home according to Weiß Ferdl's song: "Join the *Einwohnerwehr*; only it will reestablish the old hierarchy." "When you stand before your wife with a rifle," claimed the song, "then she'll see you're a real man – she'll gladly agree that you alone are master."[53] In the final verse, Weiß Ferdl described the panic in the city caused by the target practice of the *Einwohnerwehr*, "oh God, what's going on in our city ... was the government overthrown again, will our rations be cut? ... No, it's just the *Einwohnerwehr*, each one testing his rifle, making sure his wife didn't stuff anything into the barrel."[54]

The perceived need to assert traditional masculine authority and overcome victimization, demonstrated by this Weiß Ferdl march, made the militias a vehicle for revenge and sometimes bloodlust. In his early memoir, *Wir sind Gefangene: Ein Bekenntnis*, Oskar Maria Graf described the transformation that occurred in Munich after government troops and *Freikorps* took over

---

[51] Text and music at BHSA, Einwohnerwehr, Bund 13/1, text by Weiß Ferdl, music by Adolf Dentl.

[52] For a history of Weiß Ferdl, Valentin, and Munich popular culture, see Robert Eben Sackett, *Popular Entertainment, Class, and Politics in Munich, 1900–1923* (Cambridge, MA: Harvard University Press, 1982).

[53] Text and music at BHSA, Einwohnerwehr, Bund 13/1, "Einwohner Wehr."   [54] Ibid.

Munich. He emphasized the leading role that Munich's middle class took in the arrests and denunciations after the defeat of the Red Army and Red Guard remnants. "No one was safe," he wrote, "a terrible wave of denunciation set in . . . .. Suddenly the burghers were back out of hiding, running eagerly after the troops with shouldered rifles and the blue/white civic guard armband." According to Graf, once they found a Red suspect, "they beat him, spit on him, howling and kicking as if they'd gone wild; then they would bring their half-dead prey to the soldiers."[55] In the aftermath of their liberation, many of the Munich burghers responded to this release of tension by acting out the violent fantasies that they had believed would be visited on them by the Reds. The terrible violence they had feared before 1919 came to pass, but they proved to be its agents not its victims.

After the defeat of the *Räterepublik* in May 1919, victorious conservative forces claimed that the Left retained the potential to launch a new, armed uprising as a justification for an armed civilian militia, such as the *Einwohnerwehr*. As has been well-documented, the majority of Germans persisted in locating the primary political danger as violence from the Left, not the Right, even after the military putsch by Wolfgang Kapp and his *Freikorps* followers in March 1920. The newsletter of the Munich Civic Council, published just three days after the failure of the Kapp putschists proclaimed, "Germany stands before the massive efforts of the communist movement to take over power."[56] The council went on to ask the burghers of Munich, "should they allow the times of April 1919 to return?" And then asserted, "If communism is victorious this time, there won't be anyone to save us!"[57] Despite the fact that the Kapp Putsch had so clearly demonstrated the Right's impatience with the Weimar federal government, the citizens of Munich were urged to organize for self-defense against the threat from the Left. They were also encouraged to defend the *Einwohnerwehr* against efforts to disarm it, despite the fact that disarmament of militias was obligatory as a condition of Germany's peace agreement.

For the Right, the specter of another revolution and particularly the example of the Munich "soviet terror" justified the creation of many of the paramilitary groups that flourished in the interwar period. In the April 1920 newsletter of the Munich *Einwohnerwehr*, it was reported that the finance ministry had complained that important work was not being done because of the time demands of *Einwohnerwehr* service. "It seems," the newsletter reported, "that it is not yet fully understood, that it is better to leave the non-pressing office work lying

---

[55] Graf, 498. [56] *Der Bürgerrat München* 1, March 19, 1920, "Wo stehen wir heute?"; BHSA, Einwohnerwehr, Bund 13/1.

[57] Ibid. The danger they referred to was the workers' guards, especially in the Ruhr, organized during a general strike to protect the republic from the right-wing putsch when the *Reichswehr* did not intervene to stop it. In this case, the army suppressed the Ruhr uprising with the assistance of *Freikorps* as in Munich 1919.

a few days, than end up with another *Räterepublik* and a repeat of the events of spring 1919." The article's author hoped that the *Einwohnerwehr* leadership would make it clear to the government that an employee's service in the *Einwohnerwehr* should not confront any obstacles (not even be debited from their vacation time). "Further," warned the newsletter in an assertion of middle-class pride against the upper classes, "if the directors can't get up the courage to take up arms in defense of their families, then they should at least not give their subordinates problems about the execution of their [*Einwohnerwehr*] duties."[58]

On the Left: Lessons and Sacrifices

For those on the political Left, the desire to remember the events of 1919 as "real revolutions" proved important as well. If these had been "real" revolutions (like the successful October revolution in Russia), they justified both individual actions as well as the resulting loss of life and destruction. The view that the revolutions in Budapest and Munich had been viable, and had been part of the world revolution, also served as a foundation for demonizing not only the Right but enemies within the Left as well. There were attempts to blame the failures on those on the Left who had given up too easily or whose excessive caution had hindered the progress of the revolution.[59] Most importantly, a heroic memory focused on the successful days of the revolutions in order to exalt the status of revolutionary "martyrs." In the months and years following the revolutions, the Left formally identified and memorialized its 1919 heroes and martyrs as both the Bavarian and Hungarian revolutions became central to the self-perception and sense of history of the international workers' movement.

As we have seen, the role of Munich in the German workers' movement was peripheral before autumn 1918 and the advent of the Eisner-led (USPD) regime that took over in November. Even later, after the Munich soviet revolution in April and its defeat in May, the memory of this revolution vied for prominence among German leftists with the failed Spartacus revolt in Berlin in January. Berlin was the center of the German workers' movement, and it was the barricades erected in the streets of Berlin by communists and the murdered leaders Rosa Luxemburg and Karl Liebknecht that came to symbolize heroic resistance and martyrdom on the Left. Even if it did not become the leading symbol of heroic action and mass resistance for the German Left, the memory

---

[58] BHSA IV, Kriegsarchiv, Einwohnerwehr, EW, Band 13, Atkt 3, April 23, 1920, "Bericht über die Erfahrungen anlässlich des Aufrufes der E.W. München, vom 13. – 22. März 1920," signed "Fuchs, für den Stadthauptmann."

[59] These critical perspectives of the German revolutionaries continued right up through to the generation of 1968 leftists who revived some of the early narratives of blame for the revolutions' failures.

of the Munich revolution and, especially, memories of the counterrevolutionary violence and White Terror, did have an important place in the symbolism of interwar Germany. Communist party member and political cartoonist George Grosz, for example, published many drawings in the early postwar years ridiculing the social democratic leadership and its apparent truce with the forces of the old order. The leftist Malik press published a collection of his drawings, *Das Gesicht der herrschenden Klasse* (*The Face of the Ruling Class*), in 1921. It included several images focused on the White Terror in Munich.[60] In the drawing "Postwar idyll," two aristocrats wearing hunting garb ride horses past a fat bourgeois smoking a cigar. In the background uniformed troops march by with guns and in the foreground three disabled veterans are seen begging. On the wall between a blind beggar and the cigar-smoking capitalist is a wanted poster offering 30,000 Marks for Levien's arrest.[61] For Grosz, the "postwar idyll" was only for the rich. As the rich enjoyed their leisure, a war continued against the poor and the communists.

In the drawing "Feierabend" or "end of the workday," Grosz again took the White Terror as his topic. He depicted a *Freikorps* soldier with a mustache leaning against a tree and smoking a cigarette. Behind him is the prominent feature of the Munich skyline, the twin towers of the city's cathedral, the Frauenkirche. At his feet, half sunk in the river, is the body of a beaten and bloodied worker.[62] The "workday" of the *Freikorps* was thus portrayed as the slaughter of the Munich working class. In "shot while trying to escape," Grosz went on to challenge the injustice of official reports about civilians killed in Munich during the White Terror. In this cartoon, a defenseless worker with his chin held high is tied to a post while an officer with a drawn sword and pistol and another soldier with a shovel aggressively charge towards him.[63] Grosz's political cartoons were immensely popular: the three editions of *Das Gesicht der herrschenden Klasse* together sold more than 25,000 copies, and his images were reproduced in the radical press as well as in his books, vastly increasing their distribution. Through these simple and graphic drawings, an image of the history of counterrevolution in Munich could be visualized by many on the German Left who had not experienced the events themselves.

Although hundreds of less prominent people lost their lives in the White Terror during the first week of May 1919, the judicial execution of the revolutionary leader Leviné became the symbol of both White Terror and class justice for the radical workers' parties in Munich. While a strike planned by the general workers' council in Berlin to protest his execution on June 5, 1919 was cancelled because organizers feared violence from government troops, workers' councils

---

[60] George Grosz, *The Face of the Ruling Class* (London: Allison & Busby, 1984), originally published as *Das Gesicht der herrschenden Klasse* (Berlin: Malik Verlag, 1921).
[61] Ibid., 15.   [62] Ibid., 46.   [63] Ibid., 37.

Figure 6.2 *"Gedenkblatt für Levine-Niessen"*
Staatsarchiv, Munich.
Source: Bavarian State Archives.

all over Germany assembled to sign petitions of protest against it. After his execution and unpublicized burial the following day in the new Jewish cemetery in Schwabing in Munich, his fellow communists and radical workers sought ways to honor Leviné. A week after his death, for example, police in Munich found copies of handbills and postcards that were being distributed as memorials for the "fallen Leviné." (Figure 6.2) One postcard showed a picture of a female figure of liberty with a hammer stepping away from a globe as a proletarian couple freed from their shackles looked lovingly at her and a caricatured capitalist cowered. On the card's reverse side, a memorial poem dedicated to Leviné was printed. The poem described his honorable appearance in the courtroom and the way the sun "fell on his dark hair and lit his pale face, where his hot dark eyes demonstrated his strength of will."[64] According to the poem, Leviné had not flinched before the sentencing and execution and had shown that his convictions "weren't built on sand." For those he left behind in the workers' movement, the poem consoled them with the promise, "even if Leviné's body was taken from us through the rawest despotism, his spirit remains alive and before our eyes. It will guide us in the coming struggles and difficult times until all men are brothers, until all are freed."[65]

The image of Leviné's martyrdom and his last words, "long live the world revolution!," were kept alive by the radical press and by demonstrations and

[64] StAM Pol. Dir. 10110, Levine-Niessen, 164, "Gedenkblatt für Levine-Niessen."   [65] Ibid.

memorials held in Munich throughout the years of the Weimar Republic. The first anniversary of Leviné's death in 1920 fell the day before elections. According to an article in the *Neue Zeitung*, the intervening year had been a terrible one for workers, "a year of horrors, of a class-biased legal system [*Klassenjustiz*], full of blood and death. The flag that inspires us disappeared; it was trampled in dirt and dust, ripped to shreds and spit on."[66] The communists had decided not to boycott the elections and the *Neue Zeitung* called on its readers to let the memory of Leviné's martyrdom transform the vote the following day into a "show of strength of all those willing to sacrifice themselves" for his cause.[67] In 1922, the anniversary of Leviné's death was the occasion for two public memorial services, as well as the publication of numerous memorial articles in the leftist press. According to a police report, at least 330 people attended a memorial service held on June 6 that year. The service featured a memorial speech about Leviné's life and work as well as poems by Toller, Mühsam, and Leviné. The program included revolutionary musical works performed by workers' choirs and Beethoven's "Eroica," performed by a professional pianist.[68] At this service and another held two days later in the offices of the radical newspaper *Neue Welt*, Leviné was eulogized as an idealist and held up as "an example for every revolutionary fighter."[69]

As the years passed, however, the police prevented these sorts of mass memorials and marches on the anniversary of Leviné's execution. In 1924, according to the liberal *Münchner Neuste Nachrichten*, a memorial party of around fifty communists were prevented from marching to lay a wreath at Leviné's grave. The police arrested the locksmith Karl Ganz, who was the leader of the procession and "who had earlier been sentenced to five years imprisonment for his part in the soviet government." According to the *Münchner Neuste Nachrichten*, his arrest "provided a signal for the crowd to attack the police in a failed attempt to free Ganz."[70] The police prevented similar marches and wreath-laying ceremonies in 1926 and 1928 as well.[71] In 1926, the watchman at the Jewish cemetery where Leviné was buried assisted the police in keeping out communist mourners by shutting the cemetery gates. The *Neue Zeitung,* in an article protesting the actions of the police, also addressed itself directly to the Munich Jewish community, asking if the closure of the "public cemetery" had occurred with their permission, "if not, would

[66] *Neue Zeitung* 433, June 5, 1920.   [67] Ibid.
[68] StAM Pol. Dir. 10110 Levine-Niessen, 201–2.
[69] *Die Rote Fahne* 262, June 8, 1922, "Die Levine-Gedenkfeier in der 'Neuen Welt'."
[70] *Münchner Neuste Nachrichten* 165, June 20, 1924, "Verhinderte Gedächtnisfeier für Leviné-Niessen."
[71] For 1926 see below; also, the conservative *Bayrischer Kurier* 156, June 4, 1928, "Verbot einer Demonstration des Rotfrontkämpferbundes in München," and the article by Frida Rubiner in the *Neue Zeitung* 129, June 5, 1927, "Eugen Leviné zum Gedächtnis. Zum achten Jahrestag seiner Ermordung."

they join us in protesting this terrible attack by the police?"[72] The ritualized conflicts between the police and communists on the anniversary of Leviné's death symbolized for both sides that the battle was a serious one, one that had not ended with the defeat of the revolutionary government in May 1919. Events in Munich were remembered as tragedies by the Left generally and by communists as their party's martyrdom at the hands of the majority Social Democratic Party in the government in Berlin.

The narrative of victimization of and within the Left in Hungary was quite different, largely because the Horthy regime was in power, as opposed to the center-left coalition in Germany, and because of the greater level of violence. Reprisals against revolutionaries in Hungary, especially in Budapest, had been harsher and lasted much longer than in Munich. The Horthy government placed severe restrictions on working-class organizations and meetings within Hungary, limiting the possibilities for memorializing the events and leaders of the revolutionary era. In the face of this repression, a larger number of revolutionary leaders accepted exile in the West and the Soviet Union, thus stripping the Left of its experienced leaders. These differences gave the leftist memories of the Budapest revolution a much different character from those cultivated in Munich. Most of the leaders of Kun's soviet government were able to flee to Vienna at the beginning of August just before the White triumph.[73] The Entente's representatives in Budapest had guaranteed the leaders safe passage in the negotiations to establish a moderate postrevolutionary government, and the Italian military mission guarded the train that took Kun and most of the other soviet leaders to Vienna. There, the local socialist government welcomed the fleeing Social Democrats, while many communists were arrested because it was feared they would incite revolution in Vienna. From Austria, the arrested communists were eventually sent to Moscow, where they joined many more exiles who had been traded to the Soviet Union by the Horthy regime in return for Hungarian prisoners of war. In his memoirs, published in Munich in 1924, Vilmos Böhm, a war minister during the Károlyi regime, and briefly Red Army commander under the soviet government, claimed that 100,000 people had fled Hungary during the White Terror or after Horthy's takeover.[74] This estimate, like the author's figure of 5,000 victims of the White Terror, was not based on reliable evidence and may be little more than the impression of an informed observer but, unfortunately, no more accurate figures exist. However,

---

[72] *Neue Zeitung* 128, June 8, 1926, "Am Grabe Eugen Levines. Schamloses Verhalten der Polizei. Der Friedhof verschlossen." Also, the state *Münchner Post* 127, June 7, 1926, "Verbotene Gedächtnisfeier."

[73] For an account of Lukács' escape, see Lee Congdon, *Exile and Social Thought: Hungarian Intellectuals in Germany and Austria, 1919–1933* (Princeton, NJ: Princeton University Press, 1991), 45–9.

[74] Böhm, 539.

it is certain that thousands of Hungarian refugees passed through Vienna and other Central European cities after the fall of the revolutionary governments in 1919.

Böhm and other political refugees from Horthy's Hungary were able to garner great international sympathy not only with communists or others the radical Left but among left-leaning intellectuals shocked by counterrevolutionary violence and supporters of the democratic 1918 revolution. Public figures in Austria and Germany wrote letters supporting asylum for famous Hungarian revolutionaries as well as for leftist academics like Lukács. The liberal philosopher Max Weber even sent a telegram to the Hungarian justice ministry warning that the government's international reputation would suffer if they prosecuted Lukács.[75] In 1920, the British Joint Labour Delegation, sent to Hungary to investigate the crimes of the White Terror and the "allegations of persecutions of the working classes in Hungary," reported many cases of intimidation, mishandling of leftist prisoners, and judicial murder.[76] The classification of the events of 1919 as "real" revolutions was important not only for the Left in Hungary but also internationally, as interventions on behalf of Hungarian émigrés and the commissioning of the British Labour report demonstrated, conferring international authentication for the suffering of the victims of the White Terror in Hungary.

The cases described in the British Labour report served as subject matter for a booklet of postcards made in exile in Vienna and printed in Buenos Aires by the socialist artist Mihály Biró.[77] During the soviet regime, Biró had created some of the most iconic posters in support of the Hungarian revolution, including the famous red hammer-wielding worker who became a symbol of the regime.[78] After fleeing the counterrevolution, he turned to documenting its horrors in his drawings. Like the work of the German artist George Grosz, Biró's political art publicized the horrors of counterrevolutionary violence and offered support to those who viewed the images in leftist publications. The cover of the packaging for Biró's postcard book displayed the name "Horthy," with the final "y" in the dictator's name made into a noose around the neck of an

---

[75] Congdon, *Exile and Social Thought*, 46. Weber was the founder of the liberal German Democratic Party (*Deutsche Demokratische Partei*, DDP) and an advisor to the Weimar Constitution. His political career was brief because he died of pneumonia in June 1920, during the influenza pandemic.
[76] British Joint Labour Delegation to Hungary.
[77] A set of postcards can be viewed at the Austrian National Library in Vienna. The drawings are included in an online exhibition, "Graphic Witness: Visual Arts and Social Commentary," at www.graphicwitness.org/contemp/biro.htm.
[78] Biró also created some famous prewar advertising images for iconic Hungarian brands such as Zwack's herbal liquor, Unicum. Biró's political and commercial posters were the subject of an exhibit at the Museum für angewandte Kunst (MAK) Vienna, and are reproduced in the catalog, Peter Noever, ed., *Mihály Biró: Pathos in Red*. MAK Studies 19 (Nürnberg: Verlag für Moderne Kunst, 2011).

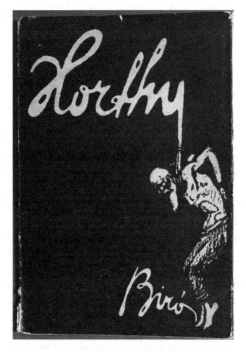

Figure 6.3 "Horthy!" Mihály Biró, 1920.
Source: 1946 reprint, Buenos Aires. Courtesy of Graphic Witness.

old and emaciated man. (Figure 6.3). Inside, in twenty images, Biró illustrated White officers throwing their victims into the Danube, chasing Jews from the schools, torturing prisoners, extorting the bourgeoisie, and hanging Jews. The twin images "Rape" and "The Beasts" were graphic renditions of the harrowing story of Mrs. Hamburger and her friend Neumann, related in the British Labour report.[79] Angered by the dissemination of these postcards, the Hungarian government put pressure on Austria to extradite Biró to face charges. Fearful for his safety, he fled to Argentina where he arranged for a second edition of the cards. Biró's postcards, like Grosz's drawings, presented a highly evocative narrative of events that emphasized the martyrdom of the Left, representing visually the suffering of the working class.

The main revolutionary leaders of Hungary and Bavaria took on quite different symbolic roles for their followers and detractors in the postrevolutionary period. In particular, conflicts over the correct interpretation of Kun's

---

[79] British Joint Labour Delegation to Hungary, 8–11. Hamburger's testimony is analyzed in detail in Chapter 3.

politics and actions became a cause of division among Hungarian communists. In exile in the Soviet Union since August 1920, Kun ultimately became a symbol of a wider division in the international communist movement. The origin of the controversy over Kun's legacy was at least partly personal, or based on perceived personal traits. The intellectuals of the Hungarian soviet often looked down on Kun, who was perceived to be rough and unintellectual. The Russian revolutionary Victor Serge remembered that Lukács viewed Kun as "a remarkably odious figure. He was the incarnation of intellectual inadequacy, uncertainty of will, and authoritarian corruption."[80] But beyond personal dislike, many of his opponents also held Kun responsible for the turn towards revolutionary elitism within the Communist International (Comintern).

In July 1920, the Second Congress of the Comintern adopted the "Twenty-One Conditions" to weed out all reformist or pacifist parties from revolutionary coalitions. The conditions required member parties to change their names to the Communist Party of their country, to expel socialist and reform politicians, and to shun any collaboration with socialist and social democratic parties and organizations. Already by the end of the year, the new rules supported the expulsion of centrist French communists and Italian reformers from the party. Since both the Bavarian and Hungarian revolutions had been declared by coalitions of socialist and communist politicians, and had been based on the idea of a unified "workers" political alliance, the failure of these revolutions, and what was viewed as the traitorous activity of socialists towards communists (especially the SPD in Germany), was the justification for this new centralization and exclusivity of the Comintern. David Cattell argued that the failure of the Hungarian revolution was used as justification for the decision to move towards revolutionary centralism under Soviet leadership.[81] Lenin and Gregori Zinoviev concluded from the Hungarian example that all collaboration with socialists was doomed to failure. Writing about the socialists, Zinoviev claimed that, after the events of 1919 in Central Europe, "The brand of Cain is now on the forehead of this party, it betrayed the proletariat, the revolution, the glorious party of the Hungarian Communists; it betrayed the International."[82] Similarly, Lenin cited the example of Hungary to both the French and Italian parties to explain the necessity of excluding moderate elements.[83] Several former members of the Hungarian soviet reinforced the views of Lenin and Zinoviev that the socialists were responsible for the failures in Budapest and that "the

---

[80] Victor Serge, *Memoirs of a Revolutionary, 1901–1941* (London: Oxford University Press, 1963), 187, quoted in Congdon, *Exile and Social Thought*, 49.

[81] David T. Cattell, "The Hungarian Revolution of 1919 and the Reorganization of the Comintern in 1920," *Journal of Central European Affairs* 11/1 (Jan.–Apr. 1951): 27–38.

[82] Zinoviev, "To the Proletariat of all the World," *Communist International* 4 (August 1919): 106, quoted in Cattell, 29.

[83] Cattell, 32–3.

continued toleration of Social Democratic elements within the International was suicide for the dictatorship of the proletariat."[84]

Not all communists supported the changes represented in the Comintern's 1920 conditions. There were many party members, from Hungary and other European nations, who resented this turn away from a commitment to a broader Marxist international revolution and towards the development of a narrower Soviet-dominated clique of parties. Lukács and Jenő Landler were among the many former colleagues of Kun in the soviet government in Budapest who came to blame him (rather than Lenin) for this change in the communist movement. From his exile in Moscow, Kun insisted that Hungarian communists stop paying trade union dues that supported the legal Social Democratic Party, the only legal political representation for the Hungarian working-class movement. His hard-line adherence to the Comintern's conditions led to a split with local Hungarian communist party leaders, who believed that the defeated and outlawed Communist Party depended on these legal, socialist-dominated institutions for its very existence.[85] In a book entitled *The Hungarian Plague in Moscow*, the Hungarian communist Henrik Ungar, a pseudonym of Heinrich Guttmann, wrote about the deleterious effect that Kun was having in the Soviet Union.[86] He dismissed Kun, who had been given great responsibility for the Central European communist parties, as "an adventurer and a pushy person." Ungar even accused Kun of stealing jewels and then using them to get better food while in prison in Hungary at a time when other communists who "couldn't buy their freedom died at the hands of Horthy's court-henchmen."[87] Ungar's claim that Kun stole jewels mirrored popular tales in Hungary at the time. Kosztolányi's novel *Anna Édes,* for example, opens with an imagined scene of gold jewelry falling from the sky as Kun fled to Vienna in an airplane.

Ungar's book, written, he claimed, in the service of the "defeated proletariat," offers a version of the old trope of the good king/bad advisors. Moderates within the communist movement like Guttmann (Ungar) were disappointed by the recent changes in Comintern policy that forbade collaboration with other socialist parties. Lenin and others had often used the example of Hungary as a warning about the perils of collaboration with social democratic parties, and Hungarian moderates came to blame this policy on the pernicious influence

---

[84] Eugene Varga, *Dictatorship of the Proletariat,* and Mattyás Rákósi, "Rapport du Parti Communiste Hongrois," quoted in ibid., 35.

[85] Congdon, *Exile and Social Thought,* 49.

[86] Henrik Ungar, *Die magyarische Pest in Moskau* (Leipzig: Veritas Verlag, 1921). Ungar is identified as the "old Hungarian Communist Heinrich Guttmann," by Richard Löwenthal, "The Hungarian Soviet and Internation Communism," in Andrew C. Janos and William B. Slottman, eds., *Revolution in Perspective: Essays on the Hungarian Soviet Republic of 1919* (Berkeley: University of California Press, 1971), 181.

[87] Ungar, 33. The references to getting better food also echo some of the right-wing slander about communist decadence discussed earlier in this chapter and in Chapter 5.

exerted by Kun once in exile in Moscow. Rather than blaming the Social Democrats for the failure of the Hungarian revolution they blamed Kun, and rather than blame Lenin for the new Comintern policies, they blamed Kun's influence. They believed Kun had unjustly shifted the blame away from his own poor leadership during the *tanácsköztársaság*, and now in Moscow he was seeking to focus attention on the supposedly traitorous participation of Social Democrats in the revolutionary government. Using this critical perspective, Ungar sought to absolve Lenin and the Russian communist leadership of any blame for the new anti-socialist Comintern policy. Leaders in Moscow had only Kun's biased representation of the reasons for the revolutionary debacle. Ungar argued that the Hungarians who were swaying the leaders of Soviet Russia to consider socialists as traitors were exactly those who were themselves guilty of treason against the working people: as in the old adage, Lenin was portrayed here like the "good king" and Kun as the "bad advisors."[88]

Within the international communist political leadership, competing factions participating in the ongoing debates utilized both the failed Hungarian revolution and the character and actions of Kun to support their factions and undermine the positions of their opponents. Kun's contested legacy was further complicated when Stalin turned on him and ordered his murder during the purges of the late 1930s. As a result, Kun's name and image were shunned by the post-1948 Stalinist communist regime in Hungary. The first leader of that government, Mátyás Rákosi, who himself had been Kun's fellow exile in Moscow, sought to purge his colleague's memory.[89]

As István Deák has pointed out, this had the absurd result that "an official 'History of the Hungarian Soviet Republic' published in 1949 achieved among its remarkable feats the complete omission of Kun's name."[90] Even after Stalin's death in 1953, Kun was mentioned sparingly in state socialist Hungary because of the awkward fact of his murder at the hands of the allied socialist power the Soviet Union. A statue of Kun was finally erected in Budapest in the late 1980s, during the period of Mikhail Gorbachev's glasnost in the USSR and as, even in Hungary, citizens began to explore the previously hidden history of 1919. The statue had only a short life in the public space of Budapest; after 1989, it was consigned along with other communist artifacts to the post-socialist "Statue Park" museum on the city's outskirts.

While Kun became a divisive symbol for Hungarian communists in exile and in death, quite the opposite happened with the Russian and Jewish Leviné. By

---

[88] Ibid., 35.

[89] In an additional irony, the postwar state socialist regimes in Eastern Europe were founded with "socialist unity" parties (i.e., just like the 1919 revolutions and against the 1920s Comintern policy that Kun advocated).

[90] István Deák, "Budapest and the Revolutions of 1918–19," *Slavonic and Eastern European Review* 46 (1968): 130.

the time of his martyrdom, Leviné had become a unifying figure for Bavarian communists. In later years, the memory of his death and his last words were adopted, even by noncommunist workers, as symbols of their defeat and suffering in 1919. Graf described an encounter he had with a worker in Munich's English Gardens after the fall of the revolution in 1919. The two had been imprisoned together for questioning after the revolution, and they exchanged information about their cellmates and the general political situation when they met. The worker began to cry, telling Graf about his personal tragedies.[91] His father had been shot, his wife had had a miscarriage that he blamed on the fighting, and he himself had been beaten while in custody. At first, the worker denied his political engagement along the lines taken by many revolutionary supporters who feared retribution with the Whites in charge: "I was on the front for four years . . .. Wounded three times . . .. I never wanted to have anything to do with Revolution . . .. I have tons of witnesses . . .. Everyone in the factory got a weapon . . .. I returned it on the 30th of April . . .. A few days later they hauled me out of bed . . .. I was beaten the whole way to the police station . . .. There is no God!!"[92] He claimed to be apolitical and only circumstantially involved in the revolution.

But, as the conversation continued, the worker's attitude shifted from self-defense and self-pity as he spoke about what he had heard of Leviné's heroic testimony before the court-martial. Even though he had just denied any active participation in the revolution, this worker told Graf that Leviné's testimony represented his own situation as well. The worker repeated a famous statement Leviné made in court, "We communists are just *Tote auf Urlaub* [dead men walking]." The worker then related this dramatic quote to his own situation, "He was right, Leviné . . .. We're too much for them . . .. We're just dead men walking." He raised his fist and proclaimed that "If it starts again, then I'll fight . . .. I'll fight 'til my end . . .. The hour is near!"[93] Leviné and his martyrdom, it seemed, had become a symbol for the commitment and resilience of workers in general.

This image of the beaten but defiant worker raising his fist and then disappearing into the darkness was one of the final vignettes in Graf's memoir of his years in Munich in the early twentieth century. He used the story of the worker to illustrate his own sense of political awakening after the Munich revolutions. As the worker vanished into the park, Graf described how his heart warmed:

I saw all the pictures again, which had formed my thoughts: the masses on the streets, the army of workers, the dark rows of the arrested, the bodies of the dead, and this *single* comrade. Everything became clearer and more permanent. And this man with raised fist became a legion. "The hour is near!" I cried instinctively. "It wasn't all for nothing!"

[91] Graf, 525.   [92] Ibid., 526.   [93] Ibid., 527.

I repeated deeply moved. My small circle exploded. I was more than just myself.
A feeling of happiness flooded my body.[94]

However, this feeling of losing oneself in the collective was described in the
memoirs of writers on both sides of the interwar political divide. While Graf
discovered his community with the oppressed working class of Munich and
Bavaria, we have seen that authors on the Right described similar feelings of
connection with the "nation." And in fact, this collective memory of 1919 was
a signal characteristic of interwar Central European culture across the political
spectrum.

Manifestations of Memory

The ideologically informed narratives that took hold in the political debates and
the popular imaginations of Germany and Hungary after the fall of the revolutionary governments emerged from court proceedings, press, propaganda,
works of literature and art, and even medicine. Once in place these views not
only had rhetorical and figurative importance, but often they also led to
practical and material consequences for residents of Munich and Budapest.
The dispute over Kurt Eisner's widow's pension provides an excellent
example. In 1919, the postrevolutionary but still majority SPD Bavarian
Landtag approved a pension for Eisner's wife, Elsa, and her two daughters,
as the widow and orphans of a government employee. He was, after all, prime
minister and was killed while still in office, though on his way to parliament to
offer his resignation. At a time of widespread remorse over Eisner's murder,
many of the SPD delegates had argued that civil service laws applied to the case
and thus Eisner's family should receive pensions. A disability pension was also
approved for the majority SPD leader Erhard Auer, who had been wounded in
the *Landtag* in the shootings that followed Eisner's assassination.

In 1921, as inflation increased, the *Landtag* raised Auer's pension to 24,000
Marks. Seeing the real value of her pension disappear, Elsa Eisner petitioned
for an increase to her pension as well. She received a reply that the government
did not recognize a legal obligation to pay her pension, which had been granted
only out of "propriety."[95] According to the *Neue Zeitung*, the pension was
nevertheless paid into 1923, when its value had been reduced by inflation to less
than the postage needed to mail it.[96] Then suddenly the pension was cut off
without notice. Elsa Eisner appealed to the government and eventually, in 1927,

---

[94] Ibid.
[95] "Bayerische Politik. Um die Pension der Witwe Eisners," *Münchner Zeitung* 93, April 3, 1928,
StAM Pol. Dir. 10041 – Eisner, Elsa. See also, "Der Rentenraub im Falle Eisner" *Neue Zeitung*
36, February 13, 1928; "Eisner und Auer," *Freiheit* 337, July 22, 1921.
[96] "Der Rentenraub im Falle Eisner," *Neue Zeitung* 36, February 13, 1928.

applied for legal aid to sue the state for the rectification of her and her daughters' pensions. The court proceedings in 1928 were postponed several times at the request of the Bavarian government. The case received a great deal of attention in the press and was covered by the full political spectrum of Munich's newspapers.

An article in the National Socialist *Völkischer Beobachter* drew its readers' attention to the names of the legal aid attorneys representing Elsa Eisner and her daughter Ruth (the other daughter was now too old to receive an orphan's pension). Following the names of the attorneys, Löwenfeld and Hirschberg, the author placed exclamation marks in case their readers might not notice that Jewish lawyers were representing Eisner's widow.[97] The article characterized the case as "unheard-of Jewish insolence," saying that

The Jew Kurt Eisner-Komanowsky made himself president of Bavaria through the most despicable act of treason in German history, the "November crime" of 1918 . . . now his wife and daughter outrageously demand a pension, a reward of sorts for the crimes of their husband and father! That the Bavarian government even bothers going to court with these women shows what wobbly legs the whole state stands on today! [98]

The *Völkischer Beobachter,* using the popular Nazi shorthand of "November crime," described the whole revolution, even the 1918 parliamentary regime led by Eisner, as a political crime. For its readers, characterizing all postwar German governments as illegitimate and criminal would have had the effect of excluding Eisner's dependents from consideration as heirs of government servants. The Nazi newspaper sought to further its own 1928 electoral agenda by using the Eisner pension case to attack the current conservative Bavarian government as standing on "wobbly legs," pulling away voters from an already right-wing and authoritarian government with the argument that it was "soft" in its dealings with Jewish "November criminals." Describing the revolution as a criminal rather than a political act implied that revolutionaries should be treated as criminals by the courts and the state pension denied.

The same Nazi journalist from the *Völkischer Beobachter*, August Bühl, argued in an article in *Das bayrische Vaterland* that the lawsuit represented "true Jewish insolence and cheek," describing Elsa Eisner as "a glorified East Galician and an arrogant Jewess." Eisner responded by suing Bühl for libel.[99] At the libel trial, her lawyer presented the court with evidence that Elsa Eisner, maiden name Belli, came from a Swiss Catholic family, and that Kurt Eisner himself was born in Berlin, the son of Emanuel Eisner, a military manufacturer with contracts to the imperial as well as several princely courts. Neither of Kurt

---

[97] "Eisners Witwe gegen den bayerischen Staat," *Völkischer Beobachter* 38, February 15, 1928.
[98] Ibid.
[99] "Gerichtssaal: Die Witwe Eisners als Klägerin," *Münchner Neuste Nachrichten* 111, April 23, 1928.

Eisner's parents had come from Galicia. Bühl protested that he had only repeated what had often been written in the press without correction. Had he known that she was not a Jew, he claimed, he would not have described her in these terms. The judge found him guilty of libel, calling the accusations in the articles "pure insults" and saying the "question of whether the widow Eisner is justified in pursuing the pension is a matter for the court to decide."[100] The court sentenced Bühl to an 800 Mark fine or ten days in prison and ordered him to publish the verdict of the case.[101] This was done in the April 26 issue of the *Völkischer Beobachter* under the headline "Die 'deutsche' Frau" (The "German" wife).[102] In it Bühl truculently admitted, "According to the court verdict, as we are faithfully reporting, the widow Eisner is not a Jewess." While complying with the court order in printing the libel case verdict, he continued, "we nonetheless repeat our question if Eisner's father didn't change his name and what he used to be called."[103] The court had forbidden the use of specific claims about Elsa Eisner, but Bühl continued the antisemitic implication that Eisner himself had a more "eastern" past, hidden behind his German-sounding name.

The conservative *Bayerischer Kurier*, while not resorting to the same sort of personal criticisms of the widow, could not resist inserting into its matter-of-fact reporting of the legal proceedings critical material such as: "The suit is based on the Bavarian civil service law, which it claims is also valid for Minister-President Eisner (elected by the Workers' and Soldiers' Council on the Theresienwiese!)."[104] The exclamation mark in the parenthetical comment about Eisner's election indicated the *Kurier*'s contempt for the idea that this body, the council, had any authority to elect state officials, when in fact in 1918 the councils shared authority within the various interim German governments. This use of an "editorial" exclamation mark in the *Kurier* article was not unusual in the contemporary press. However, unlike the papers of the far Right and Left, which were peppered with exclamation marks in this era, the *Kurier* had itself bemoaned the excessive "excitement" demonstrated by certain left-wing authors' punctuation.[105] But the Eisner case brought that same "excited" punctuation to the *Kurier* as well.

The left-wing papers, the *Neue Zeitung, Freiheit*, and *Die Fahne*, were just as adamant in expressing their views of the Eisner pension case. An article in the *Neue Zeitung* in April complained that the government's lawyer had "allowed himself the remark that, after all, the soldiers' widows receive far

[100] "Die Entschädigungsansprüche der Witwe Eisner," *Bayerische Staatszeitung* 93, April 23, 1928.

[101] Ibid.; "Gerichtssaal: Die Witwe Eisners als Klägerin," *Münchner Neuste Nachrichten* 111, April 23, 1928.

[102] "Die 'deutsche' Frau," *Völkischer Beobachter* 97, April 26, 1928.   [103] Ibid.

[104] "Die Klage der Witwe Eisners," *Bayerischer Kurier* 75, January 15, 1928.

[105] "Revolutionäre Frauen," *Bayerischer Kurier* 63, August 1, 1919, clipping in police file; StAM, Pol. Dir. 10.087.

less."[106] Outraged, the author continued, "He should have thought about the pensions of the officers, Kapp-putchists, and traitors of November 1923." The lawyer should have considered what sort of pension the widow of the current Minister President would get if he died in office, estimating "it would surely be more than a pathetic 100 Marks a month."[107] The leftist papers made many such comparisons between the situation of Elsa Eisner and that of other widows or pensioners. The far Left found the disability payments to the SPD politician Auer particularly galling. Auer, after all, was fully healed from the wounds he sustained after Eisner's assassination and, they claimed, he still worked and received a salary.[108] In an article written in 1921, after the upheavals of the failed Kapp Putsch had brought the right-wing Catholic BVP Gustav von Kahr to power in Bavaria, the communist *Freiheit* wrote, "We understand that the Kahr government values the contributions of our comrade Kurt Eisner differently than those of the right-socialist Auer, but we are quite uncertain if this different valuation is really all that flattering to Auer."[109] The acknowledgement of the legitimacy of the USPD-led Eisner regime through the pensions for his widow and children was incredibly important for the beleaguered German Left in the late 1920s, and the critical comparison of the relatively generous treatment of Auer (a majority SPD member) reinforced the post-1919 Comintern policy of total separation from mainstream socialists and social democrats.

The battles over pensions and government compensation for victims of post–World War I political violence were vehemently fought. In addition to the real needs of many victims' families in times of economic uncertainty, the payments carried important symbolic value. The payment of a pension implied legitimacy for the revolutionary government, and the decision to award compensation for loss of life implied that the postrevolutionary government took responsibility for the events that had brought it power or acknowledged that wrong had been done to the victim and their family by its supporters. Gumbel cited the lack of victims' compensation as a grave injustice, especially when compared with the generosity of the government to others who had taken up arms against established authority, such as the leaders of the Kapp Putsch of 1920.[110] Not only were these men not tried and sentenced like the revolutionaries of 1919 had been, but they also continued to receive their salaries, often retroactive to the time of their treasonous activity. Some even received salaries for the time they spent in hiding when their putsch failed.[111] Historian Ingo

[106] "Rentenschacher im Falle Eisner," *Neue Zeitung* 39, April 4, 1928.   [107] Ibid.   [108] Ibid.
[109] "Eisner und Auer," *Freiheit* 337, July 22, 1921.   [110] Gumbel, *Vier Jahre*, 95–108.
[111] L. Bendix, "Das Recht des Offiziers als amnestierten Hochverräters auf Pension," *Die Justiz* 2 (1926–7), example of the retroactive granting of his pension to General von Lüttwitz, Kapp's military leader, cited in Müller, 13–14. Lüttwitz was granted his salary even for the time he spent hiding illegally in Sweden on a false passport after the failure of the coup, having abandoned his troops to flee.

Müller contrasted the generous pensions awarded to the putsch leaders with the story of a police widow in Kiel whose husband had died fighting for the national government against the putschists; in her case, the Reich Pension Court ruled that his job as a policeman had been "to maintain public order" and so "any damage or loss caused by his death" was the policeman's own responsibility and risk, rather than a responsibility of the government he died defending.[112]

Dozens of families struggled for compensation for the loss of family members in the era of counterrevolutionary violence. Elsa Eisner's campaign for a pension as the widow of an assassinated government official was merely the most visible and perhaps politically contentious of these struggles. Throughout the 1920s, families in Munich fought to bring cases before the courts, to have the killers identified and tried, as well as to petition for much-needed financial compensation from the government. And because these decisions about pensions and victim compensation were made by the courts, they not only carried political symbolism but set legal precedent.

The case of the widow of Josef Sedlmaier in Munich offers an example of particularly bureaucratic illogic and injustice. Her husband, a worker, was arrested on May 2, 1919, the day after the fall of the revolutionary government. During the revolution, he had spent fourteen days on security patrol with the Workers' Brigade but had not served in the Red Army and had not participated in the fighting with White forces. He had turned in his weapon on April 27 but had not received a receipt. According to the arresting officer, his guilt was that "he couldn't prove that he had really turned in the weapon already on April 27." Sedlmaier and two neighbors who had been denounced as "dangerous Spartacists" were taken to a so-called court-martial commission, consisting only of a single Bavarian Army captain, and were sentenced to be executed by firing squad. As they were led into a courtyard where bodies from earlier executions lay, the three men panicked, attempted to flee, and were shot.[113] A review of Sedlmaier's case by the "committee on damages resulting from the unrest" decided that his execution had indeed been unjustified. None of the witnesses were able to provide incriminating evidence. The officer who had been in charge of the court-martial commission testified that "In the first days of May, I ordered so many arrests on the basis of information from the criminal police and trustworthy sources, that I cannot possibly remember the names of those arrested. I also cannot say whether Sedlmaier . . . was brought before me or if [he] was shot on the way to me as [he] tried to escape."[114] Because of the lack of incriminating evidence against Sedlmaier, his widow and two small

---

[112] *Entscheidungen des Reichsversorgungssgerichts* 4, 232, quoted in Müller, 14, n. 18.

[113] Case description from the Munich *Staatsanwaltschaftliche Akten* XIX 1254/19, quoted in Gumbel, *Vier Jahre*, 35.

[114] Gumbel, *Vier Jahre*, 35–6.

children were awarded a small pension by the damage commission. This decision was later overturned on appeal by the commissioner for damage reparations. In its 1925 verdict, the reasoning of the court was that "the damages are in no way the result of direct violence" on the part of the authorities. The pension court made an interesting distinction, claiming that "whatever the case may have been, the executing military authorities had intended to exercise their official authority. Even abuse or excesses of official authority cannot be seen as direct violence."[115] The goal of the damage commission had been to give reparations to bystanders killed in the fighting against the "Spartacists," but the court argued that at the point of his arrest, however unjustified, "Sedlmaier was actually withdrawn from the immediate circumstances of the battle against the Spartacists."[116] So, once falsely arrested, a person could at most be a victim of misplaced or miscarried justice but could not be considered the victim of the violence leading to the takeover. This decision was especially interesting since it gave a wide retroactive legitimacy to all sorts of "summary" actions of the military and militias.

This example and that of the widow Eisner highlight the ways in which contested memories of 1919 developed during the interwar years, leading to very real, personal and material consequences for many. The ways in which triumphant White and defeated Red survivors saw their experiences made compromise nearly impossible. Through the Eisner case we are also able to see how antisemitism merged with anti-Bolshevism, creating a complex of prejudice that meant, for the Right, merely calling someone a Jew was the same as proclaiming his or her guilt for the 1919 revolutions.

In Hungary, this connection between antisemitism and counterrevolution, the myth of Judeo-Bolshevism, was even stronger. The rhetorical power of the proclaimed "Christian and National" politics of the counterrevolutionary regime combined two powerful antisemitic libels. First, "Jewish Bolshevism" was blamed for the revolutions and even for the lost war, for having fatally weakened the home front. And second, "Jewish capitalism" was blamed for the inequities of prewar Hungarian society. Thus, the new regime was able to disguise the reestablishment of many hierarchical and unequal aspects of the old authoritarian society by scapegoating Jews and offering a populist program of "Christian renewal." This phrase was often used by conservative politicians who were calling for a kind of affirmative action for non-Jewish Hungarians who had previously been socially disadvantaged. Aside from the wave of anti-Jewish violence in the White Terror, the "Christian and National" agitation manifested itself in popular antisemitic protests, especially among university students, leading to the restriction of Jewish enrollment. It also manifested itself in what historian Victor Karády has called "minor anti-Jewish actions," such as difficulties placed in the way of Jewish proprietors who sought state

[115] Ibid., 36.   [116] Ibid.

business licenses or state contracts.[117] The postrevolutionary Horthy government's "mini land reform," as Karády called it, "disadvantaged newly purchased (mostly Jewish) landed properties."[118] The land reform, described by one historian as the "stingiest" of the new postwar states in Central Europe, distributed only about 8 percent of agricultural land and, most importantly, preserved the large landed estates of the rural Hungarian aristocracy into the post-monarchical era.[119] The prejudice in the reform towards maintaining traditional family estates meant that even this modest redistribution of economic resources protected the wealthy Hungarian "national" aristocratic wealth at the expense of "Jewish capital."

The main legislative manifestation of the Christian and National course in postrevolutionary Hungary was the *numerus clausus* law of 1920 that limited Jewish enrollment at institutions of higher learning to their approximate percentage of the population.[120] The wording of the law in fact made no mention of "Jews" but rather stated that, in addition to scholarly achievement and "political loyalty" (intended to prevent former revolutionary supporters from registering), "race and nationality" would be used as categories for determining admissions. But the anti-Jewish nature of the law was clear from the beginning of the legislative debates, which began in the summer of 1920 after antisemitic rioting by university students in the fall of 1919 had caused the universities to be closed. Since Jewish students had historically made up a large percentage of those in institutions of higher learning, as we saw earlier, the reduction of their admissions to 6 percent of the student population meant great personal hardship for many young people.[121]

This law had a permanent effect on the Hungarian Jewish community. Thousands of young Jewish Hungarians were either denied a university degree

---

[117] See Victor Karády, "Different Experiences of Modernization and the Rise of Antisemitism: Socio-Political Foundations of the *numerus clauses* (1920) and the 'Christian Course' in Post World War I Hungary," *Transversal* 2(2003): 31. Also Victor Karády and István Kemény, "Antisémitisme universitaire et concurrence de classe: La loi du *numerus clausus* en Hongrie entre les deux Guerres," *Actes de las Recherche en Sciences Sociales*, 34 (1980): 67–96.

[118] Karády, "Different Experiences," 31.

[119] The term is from Peter Kenez, *Hungary from the Nazis to the Soviets: The Establishment of the Communist Regime in Hungary, 1944–1948* (Cambridge: Cambridge University Press, 2006), 108.

[120] On the *numerus clausus* see Karády, "Different Experiences"; Karády and Kemény; as well as the excellent collection of essays edited by Victor Karády and Péter Tibor Nagy, *The Numerus Clausus in Hungary: Studies on the First Anti-Jewish Law and Academic Anti-Semitism in Modern Central Europe* (Budapest: Pasts Inc. Centre for Historical Research, 2012); also Katzburg, 60–79.

[121] At the time of the legislation, the government estimated the Jews to make up about 6 percent of the Hungarian population and so this is the figure that was applied to university admissions; Katzburg, 62. Karády, "Different Experiences," 27, argued that at some institutions (such as the medical schools in Pécs and Szeged) the law was "hardly enforced." His research demonstrates that Jewish admissions fell only to 7.8 percent between 1920 and 1924 but this reduction from an estimated 31.3–34.6 percent between 1895 and 1919 still represented a precipitous decline.

or forced to go abroad to study, if their families could afford it. While the numbers of Jewish refugees who fled the antisemitic violence in 1919 remains unknown aside from the estimates we have seen in Böhm's memoir and in the Jewish publication *Martyrium*, the number of Jewish refugees forced to leave Hungary by the *numerus clausus* law can be estimated from matriculation records of other Central European universities. The influx of Hungary's Jewish educational refugees at universities in neighboring countries was well-documented.[122] In 1921/22, 1,100 Hungarian Jewish students enrolled in universities in Prague and more than 800 in Vienna the following year.[123] Jewish students made up the overwhelming majority of Hungarians enrolled at universities in Weimar Germany, France, and even fascist Italy.[124] This educational exodus actually represented a massive, and what turned out to be permanent, Jewish emigration from interwar Hungary. Karády has demonstrated that of the thousands of Jewish students who studied abroad, only 164 of them submitted requests to have their foreign degree recognized in Hungary (*Nostrifikation*).[125] We must presume, then, that the vast majority remained abroad and built their lives and careers outside of Hungary.

The *numerus clausus* law of 1920 was the result of a number of political forces and must be understood in several contexts. Karády has argued that at the time of its promulgation in September, the law seemed "a mere compromise, a 'lesser evil' and – when all is said and done – a rather moderate concession to extremist claims backed up by violent anti-Jewish student mobilization and agitation."[126] Karády pointed out the even larger threat posed by those calling for extreme measures such as the confiscation of Jewish property through the legislation of economic "national parity."[127] The conservative leadership of the Christian and National government could not support such measures, which endangered private property and could lead to other communist-like calls for expropriation, even if along racial lines. But the removal of the traditional right to free admissions to the university attacked a different sort of Jewish capital, social rather than material; an attack on unrestricted Jewish access to future

---

[122] Much of the data about the effects of the *numerus clausus* law come from the petitions submitted to the League of Nations to protest it. See Katzburg, 64–9.

[123] Ibid., 64.

[124] See Michael L. Miller's fascinating case studies of *numerus clausus* exiles in Berlin and Vienna: "Numerus Clausus Exiles: Hungarian Jewish Students in Inter-War Berlin," in Karady and Nagy, *Numerus Clausus in Hungary*, 206–18; "From White Terror to Red Vienna: Hungarian Jewish Students in Interwar Austria," in Frank Stern and Barbara Eichinger, eds., *Wien und die jüdische Erfahrung 1900–1938: Akkulturation, Antisemitismus, Zionismus* (Vienna: Böhlau, 2009), 307–24. See also Karády, "Different Experiences," 32.

[125] In the entire period, "Hungarian academic authorities received between 1920 and 1934 only around 337 requests for recognition of foreign degrees, among them only one half (164) emanating from Jews." Karády, "Different Experiences," 32.

[126] Ibid., 27.   [127] Ibid., 28.

wealth based on professional status rather than on existing Jewish wealth was a way to respond to the popular calls for Jewish "expropriation" without disrupting existing property laws and relations.

The *numerus clausus* law was not only a populist gesture by an elitist government leadership. In post-Trianon ("rump") Hungary, the universities were in fact overcrowded. In addition to the thousands of refugees from the lost territories who came in particular to Budapest in 1919 and 1920, the postwar years continued to see a constant stream of educational refugees as young ethnic Hungarians from Czechoslovakia, Romania, and Yugoslavia "returned" to Hungary to complete their higher education in their native language. In the 1920/21 academic year, the first under the restrictions of the *numerus clausus* law, official estimates were that refugees made up around 40 percent of students at Budapest universities.[128]

There was further pressure on university admissions owing to the increasing number of female students, who had first been admitted to Hungarian universities in 1895. Mária Kovács has demonstrated that, in its initial legislative form in late 1919, the *numerus clausus* law was intended as a measure to revoke or limit the enrollment of women at Hungary's universities.[129] In "Ambiguities of Emancipation," Kovács argued that Hungary's ethnic politics, both before and after the world war, meant that anti-feminism and antisemitism were strongly linked in the minds of the country's political elite.[130] An initial suffrage reform effort in 1917 to give the vote to women with higher education was defeated in parliament after it was realized that "an astonishing 40 percent of the 260,000 women to be enfranchised by the bill belonged to what were, at the time, generally considered minority populations."[131] According to census categories, 26 percent of those to be potentially enfranchised were Jewish by religion and another 14 percent were native German-speakers, though the census results do not allow us to know how much overlap there was between these two categories.[132]

We have seen how, in the nineteenth century, suffrage restrictions in Hungary were closely tied to ethnic tensions and the resulting efforts by the elite to maintain Hungarian political domination in a multiethnic kingdom. The 1917 bill for women's suffrage failed because it connected the question of women's suffrage to a feared increase in the political strength of Jews and Germans relative to ethnic Magyars. Suffrage reform, especially when the still-limited

---

[128] For 1920/21, 37.5 percent of students overall were refugees but more than 40 percent of those in the medical and philosophical faculties. Their percentage had increased to more than 45 percent by the 1924/25 academic year; ibid.

[129] Mária M. Kovács, "The Politics of Emancipation in Hungary," CEU History Department Working Papers 1: *Women in History – Women's History: Central and Eastern European Perspectives* (1994): 83. See also, Mária M. Kovács, "Ambiguities of Emancipation: Women and the Ethnic Question in Hungary," *Women's History Review* 5/4 (1996): 487–95.

[130] Kovács, "Ambiguities of Emancipation."   [131] Ibid., 490.   [132] Ibid.

suffrage was tied to economic categories, such as level of taxes paid or a university degree, seemed to privilege these largely urban groups at the expense of the rural Hungarian peasant population. Ironically, the Jewish 26 percent of the women to be enfranchised, like their male coreligionists, would have mostly been Hungarian-speakers, who in the past were gladly accepted as "Hungarians" to pad the statistical strength of Magyars in the kingdom. Now, however, in smaller, post-Trianon "rump" Hungary, with Hungarian speakers an overwhelming majority, this was no longer necessary. In this brave new world, Jewish ethnicity trumped Hungarian language and individual identification with the Hungarian nation. Hungarian "nationality" was now effectively denied to Jews in the new "Christian and National" world of politics.

Therefore, not only male nationalists (many of whom were suspicious of women's suffrage to begin with) but also "Christian" women's organizations opposed the 1917 suffrage bill. Indeed, Edith Farkas, the leader of the Christian Socialist Association of Women, argued that the "concept of a restricted franchise based on educational qualifications is fatally flawed because it favors those noisy mademoiselles (who, in our society, are typically not Christian) over our true Hungarian women."[133] She demanded "that there either be no female vote" or only such suffrage legislation as would include "our Christian women with their sober mentality."[134] Beginning already in the suffrage debates during World War I, such conservative feminists offered arguments for women's rights that were predicated on the women's racial and ethnic identity and social role as Hungarian Christians, rather than on a broad emancipatory understanding of equality between the sexes.[135]

This linkage also meant that the feminist movement that emerged in Hungary after World War I was strongly nationalist and antisemitic. Conservative Hungarian feminists of this generation sought to separate their limited goal of access to education from a general emancipatory program that could have benefited Jews as well. Although the *numerus clausus* law did not limit women's enrollment at Hungarian universities, many institutions had already made their own rules barring female students in anticipation of such a law. For

---

[133] *Keresztény Nő* 7 (1918), quoted in ibid., 491. For more on Farkas and her organization, see Szapor, *Hungarian Women's Activism.*

[134] Kovács, "Ambiguities of Emancipation."

[135] This was, of course, not unique to Hungary, and many scholars have noted the tight links between women's organizations agitating for female suffrage and their ideologies of imperialism, nationalism, and colonial domination, especially in the case of the British Women's Social and Political Union and Christabel Pankhurst. See for example Nicoletta Gullace, "Christabel Pankhurst and the Smethwick Election: Right-wing Feminism, The Great War and The Ideology of Consumption." *Women's History Review* 33/3 (May 2014): 330–46; on Pankhurst's imperialist and racist politics, see Antoinette M. Burton, "The White Woman's Burden," in Nupur Chaudhuri and Margaret Strobel, eds., *Western Women and Imperialism* (Bloomington: Indiana University Press, 1992), 137–57.

example, women were banned from the country's largest university in Budapest for five years beginning in 1920.[136] Antisemitic women's leaders such as Tormay worked continuously in these years to influence lawmakers to intervene on behalf of "Hungarian women" and reopen higher education to "ethnically appropriate" women. This alliance of antisemitism with the conservative brand of Hungarian feminism represented, as Kovács' concluded, a "deal made by the second generation of women with mainstream illiberal politics."[137]

This "deal" was ironically almost a mirror image of that formed in the nineteenth century between members of the assimilating Jewish population and the same "illiberal" elites. As we saw earlier, in that case the Hungarian nobility offered social and political acceptance to wealthy assimilating Jews to keep suffrage limited and maintain Hungarian dominance over the so-called nationalities. In the postwar, linguistically homogenous, post-Trianon Hungary, Jews, who previously had been allies in the struggle for Hungarian-language domination, were suddenly considered a particularly threatening non-Magyar minority, and the emancipation of a different group (this time women) was now tied to the suppression of Jewish rights. With the *numerus clausus* law, Hungarian Jews suffered distinct material consequences from the prevailing understanding of "Jewish guilt" that attached to the dissolution of historic Hungary and particularly to the revolutionary upheavals of 1919.

In both Hungary and Bavaria, the group that suffered most from the effort to associate the revolutions with foreign and Jewish influence was the so-called Galician Jews or *Ostjuden*. The late nineteenth and early twentieth centuries had seen a mass emigration of Jews from the eastern provinces of Habsburg Galicia and Bukovina, as well as great numbers of Jews from the Polish provinces of the western Russian Empire.[138] Their numbers swelled during World War I as refugees from the Eastern Front and from anti-Jewish violence in areas occupied by the Russian Imperial Army fled to the urban centers of the monarchy.[139] While many wartime refugees had moved on or returned to their homes by the end of the war, many remained in their cities of refuge and joined the earlier generations of East European Jewish migrants living there without permanent legal status. Jews without Bavarian or Hungarian citizenship were deported in a series of actions from both countries in 1919 and the following

---

[136] Kovács, "Ambiguities of Emancipation," 493.   [137] Ibid., 494.

[138] The migrations had many causes, economic and social but also increasingly political. On the anti-Jewish violence that was a "push" factor in this migration, see Daniel Unowsky, *The Plunder: The 1898 Anti-Jewish Riots in Habsburg Galicia* (Stanford: Stanford University Press, 2018).

[139] On the wartime Jewish refugee crisis, see David Rechter, "Galicia in Vienna: Jewish Refugees in the First World War," *Austrian History Yearbook* 28 (1997): 113–30; on the situation in Hungary, Klein-Pejšová, "Between Refugees and the State" and "Budapest Jewish Community's Galician October."

years.[140] In many cases, the local-born Jewish population did not protest these deportations and in fact viewed the apparent focus on "foreign Jews" as an affirmation of their own patriotic stance and more secure place in the nation. A report by the JDC on whether their "repatriation committee" had aided in the roundup and deportation of Galician Jewish refugees in Budapest in 1919 relayed the widespread opinion among the Jewish leadership in Budapest that "no Hungarian Jew cares for a Galician Jew."[141] This statement was exaggerated, as Hungarian Jews had assisted wartime refugees immensely during the war, but it represents the pervasive nature of anti-Galician prejudice among native Jews as observed by American Jewish aid workers, who seem to have been taken aback by the attitude.[142]

In the wave of antisemitic agitation at the end of World War I, the strategy of separating native Bavarian or Hungarian Jews from the "foreign" Galician Jews or *Ostjuden* could pessimistically be said to have been a success. All over Central Europe there was antisemitic agitation, focused on Galician refugees, which subtly included all Jews in its dehumanizing rhetoric. In his 1922 bestseller *Die Stadt ohne Juden* (City without Jews), the Viennese Jewish novelist Hugo Bettauer imagined a radical expulsion of all Jews from postwar, "rump" Austria as the government gave in to this populist demand.[143] The silent-film version of the book, which appeared in 1924, includes poignant scenes of Jewish families rounded up with their belongings and deported in cattle cars.[144] The filmmaker Hans Karl Breslauer would not have had to stretch his imagination so far beyond the actual scenes of deportations of Jews considered to have Polish citizenship from Austria, Bavaria, and Hungary in the years that immediately preceded the film.

---

[140] On the Hungarian deportations, see Joseph Marcus, "Has JDC Money been Employed by the Hungarian Committee to Aid the Expulsion of Galician Jews?," report to the European Executive Council of the Joint Distribution Committee, Paris, France, JDC-NY Archives Collection 1919–1921, file #148, Localities: Hungary, General, 1919–1920. On the Bavarian expulsions: Dirk Walter, "Ungebetene Helfer – Denunziationen bei der Muenchener Polizei anlaesslich der Ostjuden-Ausweisungen 1919–1923/24," *Archiv fuer Polizeigeschichte* 18 (1996): 14–20; Reiner Pommerin, "Die Ausweisungen von "Ostjuden" aus Bayern 1923: Ein Beitrag zum Krisenjahr der Weimarer Republik," *Vierteljahrshefte fuer Zeitgeschichte* 34 (1986): 311–40; and Józef Adelson, "The Expulsion of Jews with Polish Citizenship from Bavaria in 1923," *Journal of Polish-Jewish Studies* 5 (1990): 57–73.

[141] See the report by Marcus, 15.

[142] Klein-Pejšová's work on the wartime assistance offered to refugees by the Hungarian Jewish community demonstrates that this statement was exaggerated for the Budapest Jewish community, but evidence of anti-Galician prejudice among Hungarian Jews is also widespread. David Rechter's research shows the same duality of sympathy and prejudice for the Galician refugees among Vienna's Jews, see chapter 2 in Rechter, *The Jews of Vienna and the First World War* (London: Littman Library of Jewish Civilization, 2001).

[143] Hugo Bettauer, *Die Stadt ohne Juden: Ein Roman von Übermorgen* (Vienna: Glorietta-Verlag, 1922).

[144] "Die Stadt ohne Juden," dir. Hans Karl Breslauer, 1924, rereleased 2000.

Bettauer's novel (and the film version) gave a biting satirical portrayal of the antisemites and showed with humor the dire consequences of the expulsion of the Jews for Austria, which, following contemporary stereotypes of Jewish power and influence, lost its ability to get loans internationally and became generally a backward, rural alpine country with no fashion or culture. The popular book and film not only poked fun at antisemitism by following it to its ridiculous logical conclusion but also had a love story of the Jewish hero, Leo Strakosch, and the daughter of an Austrian legislator a Viennese girl named Lotte, at its center. The reality of anti-Jewish agitation and violence in the postwar years was quite tragic, something masked in Bettauer's satire by a happy ending. Though neither Austria nor its neighbors voted to expel all Jews, mass deportations of noncitizens, mostly Jews, did occur, and Hungary's *numerus clausus* law drove thousands more young, educated Jews from the country. Bettauer himself was a prominent victim of anti-Jewish violence, assassinated in March 1925 by a former Austrian Nazi party member, gunned down in the center of Vienna.

Unlike in Bettauer's novel, where Jewish readers could enjoy the satirical portrayal of their antagonists, witnessing actual demonstrations calling for the deportation of Galician Jews must have been terrifying even for the native Jews of Munich and Budapest, who were ostensibly not the targeted population. In Bavaria, a public debate on the nature of the danger posed by Jews, especially the nominally foreign *Ostjuden*, had begun already under the regime of Kurt Eisner, after the revolution of November 1918. Because the independent socialist was a Jew and a radical, many Jews feared that the prominent role of Jews such as Eisner, Toller, and Leviné in the revolution would have terrible repercussions for their communities.[145] Concern that highly visible Jewish revolutionaries would call attention to Jews more broadly and bring political or physical retribution prompted some to try to remove external markers of Jewish difference. Historians Victor Karády and Peter Honigmann have documented the massive increase in Jewish conversions to Christianity during the revolutions of 1919 in Hungary and Germany, respectively. In Budapest, the monthly average for Jewish conversions jumped from one to three people a month before April 1919, to almost twenty a month from April to July, and thirteen per month from August to December 1919.[146] Examining trends in almost 200 years of conversion statistics for Berlin, Honigmann noticed several spikes of conversions around crisis events in German Jewish history, including around the post–World War I revolutions and counterrevolutions. Rather than

---

[145] See Jacob Reich, "Eine Episode aus der Geschichte der Ostjuden Münchens," in Hans Lamm, ed., *Vergangene Tage. Jüdische Kultur in München* (Munich: Langen Müller, 1982), 400–4.

[146] Peter Honigmann, "Jewish Conversions: A Measure of Assimilation? A Discussion of the Berlin Secession Statistics of 1770–1941," *Leo Baeck Institute Yearbook* (1989): 15; Honigmann employs Karády's research on conversions in Budapest to develop his theory about the reasons for conversion in the Berlin Jewish community.

the traditional view of Jewish conversions as a measure of assimilation, Honigmann argues that the spike in conversions in Berlin in 1919, like the one studied by Karády for Budapest, represented "an emotional response to the acutely felt antisemitic threat."[147]

Religious conversion was an understandable reaction by some Hungarian and German Jews to counterrevolutionary antisemitism and anti-Jewish activism, though it would be unlikely to protect such converts from the "Judeo-Bolshevik" slander. The convention of hyphenating "original" Jewish names was just one way that antisemites disregarded efforts like conversion or name-changing in their identification of "Jews," and often conversion was viewed as an attempt by Jews to disingenuously disguise themselves in order to fool or manipulate naive Christians. But just as we have seen with the reinforcement of other gender and racial stereotypes through their denial, those who changed their Jewish names also strengthened the negative associations with those names by seeming to hide them, and those who converted to prove their anti-revolutionary credentials similarly strengthened the identification of Judaism with revolution.

Conclusion

After the crises of revolution and counterrevolution passed, and a postrevolutionary status quo developed, narratives of the 1919 revolutions shaped interwar politics and culture. They were used to justify counterrevolutionary violence, raise militias, suppress leftist parties or politicians, deny state assistance to dependents of revolutionaries, deny access to education to Jews, and deport Jewish refugees. A set of different revolutionary narratives developed in the minority left-wing culture, where they were used by the victims of terror or postrevolutionary justice to vindicate their sacrifices as martyrs for the world revolution and by factions within the socialist and communist Left in debates over revolutionary tactics and leadership. Despite their diametrically opposite moral assessment of the 1919 revolutions, the sets of narratives on each side of interwar political culture presented the Hungarian and Bavarian revolutions as important moments in a world revolution, now defeated, at least temporarily. The brief and transitional nature of the Central European revolutions became more concrete through their connection to a larger, European historical narrative of revolution and particularly to its contemporary iteration in the twin stories of world revolution and "Judeo-Bolshevism." Kaas suggested that from the "shard of pottery" of the 1919 Hungarian revolution "a whole era of development may be reconstructed."[148] But just as in an archeological find a small shard might suggest the shape of a variety of vessels, in the interwar period witnesses and participants shaped the story of 1919 into different narratives supporting their worldviews, political programs, and actions.

[147] Ibid., 16–19.   [148] Kaas and Lazarovics, 12.

Conclusion

Many residents of Munich and Budapest experienced the events of 1919 as both political upheaval and personal trauma. The supporters and opponents of the various political movements, as well as the "innocent bystanders," witnessed the revolution and counterrevolution as violence and chaos, personal retribution, rumor, innuendo, denunciation, and misinformation. After the immediate crisis of counterrevolution, the interwar years were marked by account-taking, assessment of guilt, and searching for historical explanations, both on a personal and a societal level.

There were certainly many important similarities in the way the cities experienced the war and the revolutions. In addition to losing the war and suffering its massive casualties, Budapest and Munich had experienced some of the same social pressures and upheavals in the years leading up to the war. By the turn of the twentieth century, traditional elites in both places considered their political and social influence to be doubly threatened: by the emergence of socialism and mass politics more generally and by a vast upwardly mobile, educated (and what was disturbing for many, often Jewish) middle class in urban areas. This middle class itself was divided between a newer Christian and a more well-established Jewish bourgeois elite, particularly in Budapest, with its large Jewish population. The perception of an all-out economic and political struggle of the former against the later shaped the new post–World War I societies. Another similarity with important psychological consequences for nationalists in both countries was the phenomenon of lost territories and the refugees coming from these.

Though we have seen how the decades before World War I were filled with political, economic, and cultural conflicts and divisions in both Munich and Budapest, after the first year of war, and especially after the full four and a half years of fighting and the revolutions and upheavals that followed, the prewar years appeared in retrospect like a golden time of stability and prosperity. From their disrupted interwar lives, Central Europeans mourned the "world of security" that Stefan Zweig described in his classic memoir *Die Welt von Gestern* (World of yesterday).[1] In both the cities examined here, despite the onset of mass politics, the

---

[1] Stefan Zweig, *Die Welt von Gestern: Erinnerungen eines Europäers* (Stockholm: Bermann-Fischer Verlag, 1944). "Die Welt der Sicherheit" is the title of the first chapter.

figure at the head of government was a monarch (in Bavaria, actually a regent) whose long rule had lent stability to changing times.[2] Writing about modernism in Munich, historian Peter Jelavich reminds us that

one often reads that the Prinzregentenzeit was the "golden age" of Munich. To be sure the three decades that preceded the outbreak of World War I were certainly "golden" in comparison with events after August 1914, but the horrors of war and its aftermath should not blind one to the political and cultural conflicts ... it was not some ineffable gemütlich quality of Bavarian life that led to Munich's modernist fluorescence, but rather a myriad of tensions, uncertainties, and frustrations.[3]

The 1919 revolutions were often remembered as horrible caesurae in the history of comfortable class relations in Munich, but we have seen that the relationship between the revolutions and the social conflicts in the city was much more complex.

If this was true of the reign of the prince regent in Munich, then the long reign of Francis Joseph in Habsburg Hungary displays even more of the same characteristics of outward stability and inward chaos.[4] Francis Joseph reigned longer than any other European monarch, from 1848, in the midst of the revolutions, to his death during World War I in 1916.[5] Hungarian essayist Gyula Krúdy remembered in 1925 how the emperor's actual person had melded into the mass-produced images of him and the souvenir paraphernalia: "His facial features assumed the still permanence of a souvenir album bound in red leather, filled to the brim with memorabilia."[6] This glow of nostalgia was burnished because it was under the reign of Franz Joseph, during the era of the 1867 Settlement Agreement, that Hungary experienced what seemed to many its own "golden age," similar to that of Bavaria under Luitpold's regency.[7] Of course, Jelavich's warning about the sunny lens of hindsight is equally appropriate when considering pre–World War I Budapest and its cultural flowering. Yet, like in Munich, it was not the tranquility of the times which inspired these artists; rather they were involved in and were spurred on by the conflicts and contradictions of rapidly developing Budapest.

---

[2] The regency of Prince Luitpold, known by the wonderful German compound word, the *Prinzregentenzeit*, lasted a quarter century, from 1886 to 1912.

[3] Jelavich, 9.

[4] After the suppression of the Hungarian revolution in 1849, Francis Joseph presided over a period of national repression and absolutist rule in Hungary that was greatly resented. By the time of the Settlement of 1867 and his official coronation as king of Hungary, open hostility had cooled, but he was viewed at best ambiguously by most Hungarians.

[5] See Daniel Unowsky, *The Pomp and Politics of Patriotism: Imperial Celebrations in Habsburg Austria, 1848–1916* (West Lafayette, IN: Purdue University Press, 2005).

[6] "Francis Joseph I, the Foremost Gentleman in Europe" in Krúdy, *Krúdy's Chronicles*, 145.

[7] Those were the decades of poetry, art, and works by Endre Ady, Mihaly Babits, Gyula Krúdy, Dezső Kosztolányi, Ferenc Molnár, József Rippl-Rónai, Ödön Lechner, Béla Bartók, and many other important figures in modern literature, music, architecture, and the arts.

Because of the momentous violence and political dislocations of World War I and the struggles for control of the postwar governments of Germany and Hungary, the counterrevolutions in 1919 were most often understood as a reaction to immediate events. Revolutionary violence spawned counterrevolutionary violence; the participation of Jews in the revolutions was seized upon to justify an antisemitic reaction. But as the research in this book has demonstrated, counterrevolutionary violence, conflicts over gender roles, and antisemitism were all more than just a reaction to immediate revolutionary events. In particular, anxieties about the role of women and Jews in society and their political participation were the result of tensions and transformations that began well before World War I. The Right considered the revolutionary events of 1918 and 1919 the realization of their worst predictions about modern society. Yet, as we have seen, the violence and destruction of the "revolutionary interludes" was greatly enhanced by the actions of the counterrevolutionaries – thus, their "prophesies" about the destruction of revolution were fulfilled by their own violent and destructive activities. This has important implications for historians studying the interwar period in both Germany and Hungary. Rather than see the considerable participation of Jews in the 1919 revolutions as a cause of anti-semitic agitation in the years that followed, an explanation which right-wing terrorists and their apologists promoted at the time, we should look to the deeper causes of interwar antisemitism and put it in its broader context of what Shulamit Volkov called, for the German Empire, an "anti-emancipatory culture."[8]

By examining the 1919 revolutions and counterrevolutions from the per-spective of competing contemporary memories and narratives of the events, we have seen how many citizens of Munich and Budapest engaged in a nostalgic view of the pre–World War I years and whitewashed in their minds the terrible social, political, and economic divisions of the nineteenth century that would have been so important for explaining the outbreak of revolution. By referring to a harmonious prerevolutionary past, they were able to expel the revolutions from the so-called natural progression of Hungarian or Bavarian history. In order to justify the violence of the White Terror and to reaffirm prewar social structures, it was important for Hungarian and German elites to explain the 1919 revolutions as aberrations. They were blamed on foreigners and Jews, groups that were symbolic of the "cosmopolitan" modernity of the capital cities. This close association of Jews with blame for the revolution made it easy to claim that all revolutionaries were Jewish or "judaized" and all Jews were revolutionaries. The condemnation of the revolutions as unnatural also allowed for the exclusion of other progressive achievements seen as equally "foreign," including votes for women and working-class political activism (as in the councils).

---

[8] Volkov, "Antisemitism as Cultural Code."

In 1919, the revolutions in Munich and Budapest were part of a European experience of revolution following the end of the war. Contemporaries viewed the events in the context of the Russian Revolution and civil war, the breakup of empires, and the victories of socialists in democratic elections throughout Central Europe. Despite their shared past, subsequent political developments have uncoupled the histories of the soviet revolutions in Budapest and Munich. Events in each city have had a largely separate handling in the historiography and this has led to both their explanations and their consequences being imbedded in a very national historiography. While recognizing the unique character of each revolution, we have seen here that the revolutions tell us a different story when listened to together in their regional context.

In Hungary, the post–World War II socialist government put the 1919 events into an explanatory trajectory that tried to prove or disprove Hungary's readiness for revolution in 1919 and the "native" character of socialism and communism in Hungary. Counterrevolutionary terror in 1919 was linked to the criminalization of Horthy's regime and tied to Hungary's role in World War II and the Holocaust. Historians of the Holocaust and antisemitism in Hungary, such as Nathaniel Katzberg and Rolf Fischer, have made connections between the counterrevolutionary culture of 1919 and 1920 and the horrible events that came later, but the profound impact of 1919 on interwar culture (as opposed to its political effects) is only beginning to be explored.[9] Even in the 1980s in Hungary, there was a tendency to break with the communist hagiography of 1919, marked especially by the publication in 1979 of György Borsányi's critical biography of Béla Kun.[10] But the new willingness to criticize Kun and the early Soviet leaders led to unanticipated effect of "normalizing" the Horthy regime. The years since 1989 have seen the republication of many works about the 1919 revolutions written by important figures in the counterrevolutionary governments and their supporters.[11] The goal of this book is not to "recriminalize" Horthy or other interwar politicians, but rather to examine the crimes and excesses of the Hungarian counterrevolution of 1919 from a historical and cultural perspective and to evaluate the important role of counterrevolutionary ideologies for interwar Hungarian society. In doing this, it reinserts the 1919 revolution and its failure into the trajectory of Hungarian historiography that tends to focus more on the revolutions of 1848 and 1956 as keystones for understanding the history and mentality of the country and to see

---

[9] Katzburg; Fischer, *Entwicklungsstufen des Antisemitismus in Ungarn.*

[10] György Borsányi, *Kun Béla: Politikai életrajz* (Budapest: Kossuth Könyvkiadó, 1979). The book was soon banned from stores, and then reissued in 1988; it was published in English as *The Life of a Communist Revolutionary: Béla Kun*, translated by Mario D. Fenyo (Boulder, CO: Social Science Monographs, 1993).

[11] In particular, the reprinting of Váry's book, as well as Gratz, *A forradalmak kora*, and the work of Tormay.

1919 as either an aberration or as a predominantly political rather than popular phenomenon.

If the role of 1919 in Hungarian historiography has been shaped by the reality of the post–World War II socialist regime, the role of the 1919 revolution in Munich is inexorably tied up with its most infamous witness, Adolf Hitler. In his *Mein Kampf*, written in prison after the failed 1923 putsch attempt in Munich, Hitler himself made the connection between the 1919 revolution and his own political awakening. Historians of Germany have made not only the specifically Bavarian connection between the failed soviet revolution and the rise of Nazism (Munich's role as "birthplace of the movement") but also the larger connection between the "failed revolutions of 1918/1919" and the weakness of the Weimar Republic and the rise of political extremism. The research presented here explores the character of German democracy and civil society in the early twentieth century from both a local and a transnational perspective, allowing a comparison between the failed postwar revolutions in Germany and the reaction they inspired and the similar experiences in another Central European country, Hungary.

My research has demonstrated that, if anything, the experience of 1919 was even more divisive and certainly more violent in Hungary than in Germany. As we have seen in this book, Hungary had a wave of anti-Jewish violence in 1919–20 and one of the first legislative acts of the counterrevolutionary government was to pass the antisemitic *numerus clausus* law. If asked in 1920 or 1921 which country would see the dictatorship of an antisemitic party within a dozen years, most contemporaries would probably have answered Hungary. This comparison is of particular importance in the ongoing debate amongst German historians about Germany's exceptionalism. The shadow of the Third Reich is very long in German historiography and the crisis of 1919 is an important explanatory plank in the edifice. The comparison to Hungary is important in answering the call of David Blackbourn and Geoff Eley, among others, to put the idea of a German *Sonderweg* to the test of actual transnational comparisons. Here we see that the grounds for instability and political extremism caused by the failed 1919 revolutions in Germany were no greater than those in Hungary, where fascism was far less politically and popularly successful and where an antisemitic fascist party only took power during the German occupation in October 1944. The postwar "crisis of the bourgeoisie" remarked upon by scholars of German civil society was both broader than Germany alone and had its roots in phenomena that were remarkably similar all across nineteenth-century Europe.[12]

---

[12] While at the Center for the Comparative History of Europe and the Wissenschaftszentrum in Berlin, Germany, I was part of a group of scholars working under Jürgen Kocka on the development of civil society and the comparison of such developments across European regions and over time. I especially benefitted from discussions with Jörn Grünewald, whose book on

All history is shaped by the questions of the present. With comparative history this may be especially the case, since the choice of places or events to compare has an enormous influence on the resulting analysis. This book takes a comparison of two similar, contemporary events and uses their similarities to argue against both German and Hungarian "exceptionalism." Obviously every historical event is unique, and certainly the events of 1919 unfolded quite differently in Germany and Hungary. These differences can be studied in particular through the histories of the two revolutions that have been written from a largely political and national perspective. This work has instead focused on the similarities, since uniqueness does not preclude comparison. While I identify important differences between Budapest and Munich, in both the course of the revolutions and terror and the narratives that developed to explain them, the thrust of my argument has been to treat the two as sufficiently similar to allow for broader generalizations. By focusing on the parallel historical processes in both places, I have been able to use the 1919 events as part of an argument about a broader counterrevolutionary Central European culture. The progression in the two cities through defeat, revolution, terror, and counterrevolutionary government was remarkably comparable. And as this book has demonstrated, the memories of the revolutions were shaped by analogous forces and mobilized in similar ways in interwar Hungary and Germany.

The lost war and the political chaos across Central Europe gave impetus to further mass demonstrations against the monarchs, already ongoing since 1917, and then when these monarchs fell, to the formation of republics in autumn 1918. The main difference was that in Munich it was not clear that the Bavarian king had to fall, whereas in Habsburg Hungary it was clear that the empire was defunct and had to at least be reorganized (the declarations of independence by the various "minorities"). There was, however, a big difference in the leadership of this first democratic revolution, Mihály Károlyi compared to the more radical Kurt Eisner in Munich. Nonetheless, the scenes of mass demonstrations and proclamations of new governments were similar and similarly bloodless (except for the murder of István Tisza in Budapest).

In the ensuing phase of chaos and dissatisfaction, there were also many similarities between Bavaria and Hungary. The new governments (like the Provisional Government in Russia in 1917) found themselves under attack from both the Left and the Right. They also found themselves confronted by the Entente and the looming and very punitive peace settlements. Economic collapse followed the military collapse; the chaotic end of the war meant that hundreds of thousands of soldiers, many still with their issued weapons suddenly arrived in the cities, unemployed and with "front syndrome." In

workers' culture in early twentieth century Baku and Odessa raised a surprising number of similar conceptual challenges to my own comparison of the two 1919 revolutions.

Hungary, this situation was compounded by the arrival of thousands of refugees from the lost territories of old Hungary. In Munich, the turning point to further revolution was reached with the assassination of Eisner. In Budapest, it was with the announcement of the terms of the peace treaty and Hungary's territorial losses.

The demonstrations in the fall of 1918, which increasingly focused on the overthrow of the monarchy, raised the emotional anticipation that this overthrow would solve a variety of problems. Many of the most severe problems affecting the two societies at the end of the war, however, had little to do with the actual form of government or the existence of a monarch. The democratic revolution had raised great expectations (for a rosier world without the monarchs), which had not been fulfilled, and the agitation from the Left to make a "real" or better revolution coincided with agitation from the Right against the "illegitimate" new republican governments. The general feeling of the right-leaning but not political "Bürgertum" was that the situation was too precarious to hold.

In both cities, the crises in the spring of 1919 caused a nonviolent handover of power by the democratic government to a coalition of socialists and communists, who then declared a soviet republic. Here, the situations in Munich and Budapest began to differ widely, first, simply in the matter of time and chronology. While both soviet republics were declared fairly closely together in time (end of March and mid-April), the government in Budapest held out for 133 days; the government in Munich for one week, then the second *Räteregierung* was declared, which also lasted about a week. This meant that there was a great deal more time in Budapest for a real revolution to be felt in the day-to-day life of the city and its citizens, whereas in Munich the entire soviet period was experienced as a more transitional crisis. This didn't prevent the one major act of revolutionary terror, the *Geiselmord*, from being a major banner of justification for the counterrevolution.

The far more chaotic situation in Hungary led to the circumstance that the government only fled from Budapest in August (and Horthy only arrived in November), whereas in Munich the military defeat took only two days at the beginning of May. In Hungary, the ongoing military conflict with the neighboring states and the universal hatred of the terms of the peace treaty allowed the "Red Army" to gain significant support throughout the country in its battles to regain Hungarian territory. Even a large number of former Habsburg Army officers fought with this Red Army. Only after the military losses of the Red Army did the tables start to turn and the organizers of the counterrevolution really began to gather supporters.

Both cities endured a common experience of rumor, terror, and violence in the defeat of the revolutionary regimes. As the new counterrevolutionary authorities came to terms with the violence and chaos, the court verdicts in cases of revolutionary crimes, as we saw, were far harsher in Hungary and the courts had less sympathy for the idealist or economic motivations of revolutionary followers. The reason for this lay in the different roles that the two cities played in the nationalist discourse of the nineteenth century and in differences in their histories of ethnic and class conflict in the decades before World War I.

An examination of the revolutions that followed defeat in World War I in Hungary and Bavaria demonstrates several important components of a reforged idea of Judeo-Bolshevism, shaped by stories about 1919. This book makes three arguments for the pivotal place of the 1919 Central European revolutions in understanding the perceived relationship between Jews, cosmopolitanism, and nationalism. First, a majority of Central Europeans turned to preexisting antisemitic stereotypes to make sense of the revolutions in the fall of 1918 and the spring of 1919. Many contemporary observers read the revolutions as "Jewish," focusing attention on prominent Jewish leaders and presuming the revolutionary program as representing the interests of Jews. As this process developed, politics became racialized; Jews were understood to be the leaders and beneficiaries of revolution. Second, the 1919 events linked Central European Jews to a historical script that emphasized revolutionary violence. Indeed, both revolutionaries and counterrevolutionaries appropriated elements of the French Revolution, Paris Commune, and Russian Revolution (terror, hostages, soviet, etc.) to construct powerful narratives with the potential to motivate their followers. Because the Central European revolutions were also read as Jewish, Jews came to be associated with both the actual violence of 1919 and the historical archetypes of revolutionary violence itself.

Third, and most consequentially, while the highly visible participation of Jews in the revolutions is often viewed as the origin of the antisemitic violence so common in the counterrevolution, the causal relationship is actually stronger in the other direction. Not only was antisemitism used to justify anti-Jewish violence in the counterrevolution, but antisemitic ideology actually held the counterrevolution together. All the explanatory threads spun by contemporaries for understanding the revolutions of 1919 come back, at root, to the same basic antisemitic worldview. Psychological studies, gender fears, xenophobic worries about foreigners – in the myth of Judeo-Bolshevism all of these were woven together into a seemingly coherent political and historical narrative. This antisemitic understanding of the 1919 revolutions explains the prominent role that the narratives of these revolutions played in interwar politics despite the brevity of revolutionary rule and, with hindsight, the obvious unfeasibility of the revolutionary governments.

In this study of the way that the two revolutions were remembered and explained by contemporaries, I have used the intersection of gender and race to argue that the framework of gender hierarchy and symbols used in counterrevolutionary narratives helps us to better understand postrevolutionary antisemitism as much more than a reaction to the presence of Jews in the revolutionary leadership. Antisemitism was the language used to defend the entire conservative worldview that the revolutions had threatened. The challenge of the revolutions had been more than a challenge to political leadership and property; it had threatened to overturn the whole structure of society, and gender stereotypes were one way of describing this "world turned upside down." The phantoms of shorthaired revolutionary women and their Russian and Jewish companions haunted the fears and the writings of the counterrevolutionaries.

Both the left- and the right-wing narratives of the 1919 revolutions depended greatly on a store of preexisting stereotypes and myths within society for their explanatory power. They also depended on prewar cultures of protest or community understandings of politics. And surely the polarization of remembering is a product of the deep chasms in prewar Hungarian and German society, particularly along class and economic lines. In this way, images of women in the memories of 1919 are often the same contested images of the years before. These include images of women in crowds and food riots, the idea of women as being naturally apolitical or domestic, the stereotype of the radical "Russian" revolutionary student, and other antisemitic and class-based gender prejudices. The private became political, and the private lives of women became public and political statements. But also the events of an individual's life were remembered as having political significance, and in memoirs and retellings they were colored by the political nature of the 1919 events.

The memory of the 1919 revolutions as serious events and as part of the "world revolution" was important to both the political Left and Right and this memory had practical consequences in the way that the two societies were organized in the interwar years. This interpretation, which emphasized the world-political importance of local events, was not immediate but rather was formed through the process of understanding in the trials, the media, and historical writings. During the revolutions, we can discern a sort of double perception about these immediate and local events. Perceptions were shaped by rumors, by analogy to Russia or to historical events, and by the propaganda of competing ideologies. At the time, it seemed that people were able to see events one minute as tragedy and the next as farce; to refer to the revolutionaries as "charlatans" on the one hand and compare them to Lenin or Robespierre on the other. In general, events and threats were reported to the outside world as critical and serious at the same time that people were able to belittle the revolutions or joke about them. But through the process described in this book, a meaning was given to the 1919 revolutions and a narrative of cause and effect was established. The victorious political Right and the defeated Left naturally understood the events differently, but for each the revolutions of 1919 were central to their understanding of contemporary politics and society. This book has demonstrated that the memory of the 1919 revolutions as serious events and as part of the world revolution was important to both the political

Left and Right and that such beliefs led to acts of very real violence, even if the revolutions themselves seem in retrospect "minor" or "doomed." It has also shown the practical consequences of these memories in the way that the two societies were organized in the interwar years, with both the experience and the fantasies of political violence in 1919 continuing to justify further political extremism.

Bibliography

Archives and Library Collections

Berlin

Bundesarchiv (BA)
  Alte Reichskanzlei
  Deutsches Generalkonsulat für Ungarn
  Gestapo
  Informationsstelle der Reichsregierung
  Reichskommissar für Überwachung der öffentlichen Ordnung
  Vertretung der Reichsregierung in München
  Zentrales Staatsarchiv der DDR (ZStA Potsdam), Reichsministerium des Innern
Geheimes Staatsarchiv Preußischer Kulturbesitz Berlin
  Hauptabteilung Repositur 81, Gesandtschaft München nach 1807
Humbolt Universität zu Berlin
  Fachbereich Hungarologie: Zeitschriftensammlung
Jüdisches Museum
  Leo Baeck Institute Archives (memoir collection)

Budapest

Budapest Főváros Levéltára
  A büntetőbíráskodás
  Budapesti Királyi Ítélőtábla
Hadtörténelmi Levéltár
  Bűnügyi (1919–20)
  Hadtörténelmi minisztérium
  Hangulat és helyzet jelentések (1919–22)
Magyar Nemzeti Digitális Archívum ésFilmintézet
  Magyar Hiradók Gyűjteménye
Magyar Nemzeti Múzeum
  Történeti Fényképtár
Magyar Országos Levéltár (MOL)
  Belügyminisztérium Levéltár
  Igazságügyminisztériumi Levélár

VII.18.d. Budapesti Királyi Ügyészség büntető iratai, 1907–50
XVI.2. Budapesti Forradalmi Törvényszéki Fogház iratai, 1919
VII.102.a. Budapesti Királyi Büntetőtörvényszéki Fogház iratai
Koronaügyészség
Külügyminisztérium Levéltár
Minisztérelnökség
Politkatörténeti Intézet Levéltára (PTIL)
    Pártok: A Kommunisták Magyarországi Pártja és a Magyar kommunista emigráció
        iratainak gyűteménye
    Sajtó
    Szakszervezetek, munkás- és baloldali szervezetek, mozgalmak
    Személyi gyűtemények, visszaemlékezések
Széchényi Orzságos Könyvtár
    Kortörténeti Különgyűjtemény
    Koroda, Pál. "Szivárvány." (manuscript)
Országgyűlesi Könyvtár
    Nemzetgyűlésenek Naplója
    Tanácsok Országos Gyűlésének Naplója

                        Munich

Archiv der Münchener Arbeiterbewegung e.V.
Bayerische Staatsbibliothek
    Flugblätter
    Handschriftensammlung
Bayerisches Hauptstaatsarchiv (BHSA)
    Bamberger Akten
    Ministerium des Äussern
    Ministerium des Innern
    Ministerratsprotokolle
Bayerisches Hauptstaatsarchiv (BHSA) Abteilung IV: Kriegsarchiv
    Einwohnerwehr
    Freikorps
    Höhere Stäbe
    Reichswehrgruppenkommando 4: Nachrichtenabteilung
    Timmermann, Johannes. "Die Entstehung der Freikorpsbewegung 1919 in
        Memmingen und im Unterallgäu." Manuscript in Kriegsarchiv library. Munich,
        1996.
Fotomuseum
Graphik- und Plakatsammlung
Staatsarchiv München (StAM)
    Polizeidirektion
    Staatsanwaltschaft München I
Stadtarchiv München/Oberbayern (StadtAMü)
    Flugblätter
    Polizeidirektion

Stadtchronik
Münchener Stadtmuseum

United States

American Jewish Joint Distribution Committee (JDC) Archives, New York
Collection 1919–21
Hoover Institute, Stanford, CA
Hoover Archives
Hoover Library
Leo Baeck Institute New York (microfilm collection also at the Jewish Museum in Berlin)

Vienna

Österreichische Nationalbibliothek
Bildarchiv und Grafiksammlung

Periodicals

Bayerische Staatszeitung
Bayrischer Kurier
Érdekes Újság
Freiheit
Leipziger Neueste Nachrichten
Literary Digest
London Times
Münchener Post
Münchner Neueste Nachrichten
Münchner Zeitung
Népszava
Neue Freie Presse
Neue Zeitung
New York Times
Pester Lloyd
Pesti Hírlap
Rote Fahne
Völkischer Beobachter
Vörös Újság
Zeitschrift fuer die gesamte Neurologie und Psychiatrie

Printed Primary Sources

Aktenstücke aus dem Archiv ungarischer Gerichtshöfe über die Prozesse einiger Kommunisten, 1919–1920 Budapest:Königl. Ung. Staatsdrukerei, 1920.

Ay, Karl-Ludwig. *Appelle einer Revolution. Das Ende der Monarchie. Das revolutionäre Interregnum. Die Rätezeit. Dokumente aus Bayern zum Jahr 1918/1919. Zusammenstellung und historische Einführung*. Munich: Süddeutscher Verlag, 1968.

Bauer, Franz J., ed. *Die Regierung Eisner 1918/19: Ministerratsprotokolle und Dokumente*. Vol. 10: *Quellen zur Geschichte des Parlimentarismus und der politischen Parteien*. Düsseldorf: Droste Verlag, 1987.

Biró, Mihály. *Horthy: The White Terror in Hungary during the Regime Horthy*. Set of postcards. These can be viewed at the Austrian National Library in Vienna and are included in an online exhibition, "Graphic Witness: Visual Arts and Social Commentary," at www.graphicwitness.org/contemp/biro.htm.

British Joint Labour Delegation to Hungary. *The White Terror in Hungary: Report of the British Joint Labour Delegation to Hungary*. London: Trade Union Congress & The Labour Party, May 1920.

Deuerlein, Ernst, ed. *Der Hitler Putsch: Bayerische Dokumente zum 8./9. November 1923*. Quellen und Darstellungen zur Zeitgeschichte, vol. 9. Stuttgart: Deutsche Verlags-Anstalt, 1962.

Deutsche Liga für Menschenrechte. *Das Zuchthaus als politische Waffe*. Berlin: Deutsche Liga für Menschenrechte, 1927.

Eisele, Hans. *Bilder aus dem kommunistischen Ungarn*. Innsbruck: Tyrolia, 1920.

Freiwilliges Landesjägerkorps. *Entwurf einer Vorschrift für die Unterdrückung innerer Unruhen*. Weimar: Rudolf Borkmann, 1919.

Friedel, Helmut, ed. *Süddeutsche Freiheit: Kunst der Revolution in München 1919*. Catalog to the exhibit at Lenbachhaus, Munich, November 10, 1993–January 9, 1994. Munich: VG Bild-Kunst, 1993.

Halle, Felix. *Deutsche Sondergerichtsbarkeit, 1918–1921*. Berlin: Franke Verlag, 1922.

Heikaus, Ulrike and Julia Köhne, eds. *Krieg! Juden zwischen den Fronten, 1914–1918*. Catalog to the centenary exhibit at the Jewish Museum, Munich. Berlin: Hentrich & Hentrich Verlag, 2014.

Hubert, Viktor and Gusztáv Müller. *Perbeszedek gyüjteménye*. Pécs: Dunántúl egyetemi nyomdája, 1928.

Krausz, Jakob, ed. *Martyrium: Ein jüdisches Jahrbuch*, 59–66. Vienna, 1922.

Kriegsgeschichtliche Forschungsanstalt des Heeres, ed. *Darstellungen aus den Nachkriegskämpfen deutscher Truppen und Freikorps*. Vol. 4: *Die Niederwerfung der Räteherrschaft in Bayern 1919*. Berlin: F. S. Mittler, 1939.

Krúdy, Gyula. *Krúdy's Chronicles: Turn-of-the-Century Hungary in Gyula Krudy's Journalism*. Edited and translated by John Bátki. Budapest: Central European University Press, 2000.

Kun, Béla . *Brüder, zur Sonne, zur Freiheit! Ausgewählte Reden und Artikel zur Zeit der ungarischen Räterepublik 1919*. Selected by Tibor Hajdú. Budapest: Corvina Press, 1977.

Lenin, V. I. *Collected Works*, vol. 29. 4th edition. Moscow: Progress Publishers, 1972.

Siklós, András. *Ungarn 1918/1919: Ereignisse/Bilder/Dokumente*. Budapest: Corvina, 1979.

Szatmari, Eugen [Jenő]. *Im Roten Budapest*. Beiträge zur den Problemen der Zeit 10 Berlin: Kulturliga, 1919.

Ujváry, Dezső and Francis Deak, eds. *Papers and Documents Relating to the Foreign Relations of Hungary*. Vol. 1: *1919–1920*. Budapest: Royal Hungarian Ministry for Foreign Affairs, 1939.

Michaelis, Herbert, Ernst Schraepler, and Günter Scheel. *Ursachen und Folgen: Vom deutschen Zusammenbruch 1918 und 1945 bis zur staatlichen Neuordnung Deutschlands in der Gegenwart. Eine Urkunden- und Dokumentensammlung zur Zeitgeschichte*. Vol. 3: *Der Weg in der Weimarer Republik*. Berlin: Dokumenten-Verlag Dr. Herbert Wendler & Co., 1960.

Memoirs

Ansky, S. [pseudonym for Shloyme Zanvl Rappoport]. "The Destruction of Galicia: Excerpts from a Diary, 1914–17." In David Roskies, ed., *The Dybbuk and Other Writings*, 169–208. New Haven, CT: Yale University Press, 2002.

The Enemy at His Pleasure: A Journey through the Jewish Pale of Settlement during World War I. Translated by Joachim Neugroschel. New York: Metropolitan Books, 2002.

Bonn, M. J. [Moritz Julius]. *So macht man Geschichte? Bilanz eines Lebens*. Munich: Paul List Verlag, 1953.

Dietz, Károly. *Oktobertól – augusztusig: Emlékirataim*. Bupapest: Vilmos Rácz Kiadó, 1920.

Dwinger, Edwin Erich. *Sibirisches Tagebuch: Armee hinter Stacheldraht und Zwischen Weiß und Rot*. Velbert und Kettwig: Blick + Bild Verlag, 1965. First published 1929 and 1930 by Eugen Diederichs Verlag.

Erwemweig, W. [pseudonym for Anton Gyömörey]. *Düstere Wolken über Komorn . . . Ein Erlebnis in Ungarn im Jahre 1921*. 1954.

Gál, Imre. *A polgár a viharban: Napló a vörös diktaturáról*. Budapest: Duna Könyvkiadó, 1937.

Graf, Oskar Maria. *Wir sind Gefangene: Ein Bekenntnis*. Munich: Deutscher Taschenbuch Verlag, 1981. First published 1927.

Hitler, Adolf. *Mein Kampf*. Translated by Ralph Manheim. Boston: Houghton Mifflin, 1971.

Hofmiller, Josef. *Revolutionstagebuch 1918/19: Aus den Tagen der Münchner Revolution*. Edited by Hulda Hofmiller. Leipzig: Karl Rauch Verlag, 1938.

Horthy, Miklós. *Memoirs*. New York: Robert Speller, 1957.

Karl, Josef. *Die Schreckensherrschaft in München und Spartakus in bayerischen Oberland. Tagebuchblätter und Ereignisse aus der Zeit der "bayr. Räterepublik" und der Münchner Kommune im Frühjahr 1919 nach amtlichen Quellen*. Munich: Hochschulverlag, 1919.

Károlyi, Michael [Mihály]. *Memoirs of Michael Károlyi: Faith without Illusion*. Translated by Catherine Károlyi. New York: E. P. Dutton, 1957.

Kiss, Ferenc. *Ecce homo: Emlékirataim a forradalom és diktatúra idejéből*. Budapest: Athenaeum, 1920.

Klemperer, Victor. *Leben sammeln, nicht fragen wozu und warum: Tagebücher 1918–1924*. Edited by Walter Nowojski. Berlin: Aufbau Verlag, 1996.

Lehár, Anton. *Erinnerungen: Gegenrevolution und Restaurationsversuche in Ungarn,*
1918–1921. Edited by Peter Broucek. Munich: R. Oldenbourg Verlag, 1973.

Leviné, Rosa. *Aus der Münchener Rätezeit.* Berlin: Vereinigung Internationaler Verlags-
Anstalten, 1925.

Leviné-Meyer, Rosa. *Leviné: The Life of a Revolutionary.* Introduction by
E. J. Hobsbawm. Glasgow: Saxon House, 1973.

Mann, Thomas. *Tagebücher 1918–1921.* Edited by Peter de Mendelssohn. Frankfurt
a.M.: S. Fischer Verlag, 1979.

Müller-Meiningen, Ernst. *Aus Bayerns schwersten Tagen: Erinnerungen und*
Betrachtungen aus der Revolutionszeit. Berlin: Walter de Gruyter, 1924.

Niekisch, Ernst. Gewagtes Leben: Begegnungen und Begebnisse. Köln and Berlin:
Kiepenheuer & Witsch, 1958.

Noske, Gustav. *Erlebtes aus Aufstieg und Niedergang einer Demokratie.* Offenbach:
Bollwerk Verlag, 1947.

Teglas, Csaba. *Budapest Exit: A Memoir of Fascism, Communism and Freedom.*
College Station: Texas A&M University Press, 1998.

Toller, Ernst. *Eine Jugend in Deutschland. Hamburg:* Rowohlt Taschenbuch
Verlag,1988. First published 1933 by Querido Verlag.

Tormay, Cecile. *An Outlaw's Diary.* Vol. 1: *Revolution.* Vol. 2: *The Commune.* Foreword
by the Duke of Northumberland. London: Philip Allan & Co., 1923. Originally
published 1925 as *Le Livre Proscrit.*

Wollenberg, Erich. *Als Rotarmist vor München.* Reprint edition. Hamburg:
Internationale Sozialistische Publikationen, 1972. First published 1929 in Berlin.

Zweig, Stefan. *Die Welt von Gestern: Erinnerungen eines Europäers.* Stockholm:
Bermann-Fischer Verlag, 1944.

Novels and Dramas

Árva, Imre. "Édesanyám alakára ráborult a bánat: Hazafias színjáték." With music by
Kálmán Murgács. Budapest: Kovács és Szegedi, 1939.

Berend, Miklósné. *Boszorkánytánc: 1918–1926.* 2nd edition. Budapest: Pantheon,1932.

Bettauer, Hugo. *Die Stadt ohne Juden: Ein Roman von Übermorgen.* Vienna: Glorietta-
Verlag, 1922.

Csikós, Jenő. *Vihar a levelet . . . Regény.* Budapest: Tér Könyvkiadó, 1940.

Czikle, Valéria. *Három világ: Regény három részben: békében, világháborúban,*
forradalmakban. Budapest: Országos Gárdonyi Géza Irodalmi Társaság, 1931.

Döblin, Alfred. *November 1918: Eine deutsche Revolution.* 3 vols. Olten: Walter Verlag,
1991. Based on the original 1950 edition.

Eszterhás, István. *Forradalom a Kígyó utcában: Regény.* Budapest: Stádium, 1944.

Feith, Jenő. *A vörös ochrana: Regény.* Debrecen: Szerző, 1934.

Gebrian, Istvánné. *Rabságunk kezdetén. Regény.* Budapest: Pallas, 1922.

Halassy, V. *A fehér lobogó: Népszínmű.* Budapest: Pallas, 1922.

Horváth, Ödön von. *Der ewige Spießer: Erbaulicher Roman in drei Teilen.* Frankfurt a.
M.: Suhrkamp Verlag, 1977. First published 1930.

Sechsunddreizig Stunden: Die Geschichte vom Fräulein Pollinger. Frankfurt a.M.:
Suhrkamp Verlag, 1979.

Koroda, Pál. *Színpadok mákvirágai.* Budapest: Nemzeti Irodalmi Társ, 1920.

Kosztolányi, Dezső. *Anna Édes*. Translated by George Szirtes. New York: New Directions, 1991. Originally published 1926 in Hungarian.

Lázár, István. *A vörös számum: Regény*. Budapest: Légrády Testvérek Kiadása, 1920.

Malvin, Bokor S. "Éva föl jegyzéseiből: Kis regény." *Érdekes Újság* 41 (1919).

Pál, P. *Eszterke problémája: Ifjúsági regény*. Budapest: Korda, 1937.

Roth, Joseph. *The Emperor's Tomb*. Translated by John Hoare. New York: Overlook Press, 2002. Originally published 1938 as *Die Kapuzinergruft*.

The Radetzky March. Translated by Eva Tucker. Woodstock, NY: Overlook Press, 1974.

Somogyvári, Gyula. *És Mihály harcolt . . . Regény*. 2 vols. Budapest: Singer-Wolfner, 1940.

Surányi, Miklós. *A csodavárók: Regény*. 2 vols. Budapest: Singer-Wolfner, 1930.

Szabó, Dezső. *Az elsodort falu: Regény három kötetben*. Budapest: Genius Kiadás, 1919.

Szitnyai, Zoltán. *Nincs feltámadás: Regény*. Budapest: Athenaeum, 1932.

Tábor, István. *Forradalom a fekete városban: Kis regény*. Budapest: Könyv- és Lapkiadó Rt., 1943.

Tormay, Cecile. *The Stonecrop: A Novel*. New York: R. M. McBride & Co., 1923.

Vécsey, Zoltán. *A siró város: (Kassa) Regény*. Budapest: Genius, 1936.

Contemporary Secondary Sources

Árky, József. *Igy folytatódott! . . . [Regény]*. 2 vols. Budapest: Stephaneum, 1936.

Bartha, Ábel. *Az ellenforradalomtól a nemzet újjáébredéséig*. Budapest: Fehér és Glatler, 1926.

Benz, Wolfgang, ed. *Politik in Bayern, 1919–1933: Berichte des württemburgischen Gesandten Carl Moser von Filseck*. Stuttgart: Deutsche Verlags-Anstalt, 1971.

Bethlen, Count Stephen. "Hungary in the New Europe." *Foreign Affairs* 3/1 (1925): 445–58.

Bird, Charles. "The Influence of the Press upon the Accuracy of Report." *Journal of Abnormal and Social Psychology* 22 (1927): 123–9.

Birinyi, Louis K. *The Tragedy of Hungary: An Appeal for World Peace*. Cleveland, OH: self-published, 1924.

Bizony, Ladislaus. *133 Tage ungarischer Bolschewismus: Die Herrschaft Bela Kuns und Tibor Szamuelys*. Leipzig: Waldheim Eberle, 1920.

Böhm, Wilhelm [Vilmos]. *Im Kreuzfeuer zweier Revolutionen*. Munich: Verlag für Kulturpolitik, 1924.

Brammer, Karl. *Verfassungsgrundlagen und Hochverrat*. Berlin: Verlag für Politik und Wirtschaft, 1922.

Buday, László. *Megcsonkított Magyarország*. Budapest: Pantheon Irodalmi Részvénytársaság, 1921.

Cady, Helen Mary. "On the Psychology of Testimony." *American Journal of Psychology* 35 (1924): 110–12.

Deutsch, Helene. "Psychologie des Weibes in den Funktionen der Fortpflanzung." *Internationale Zeitschrift zur Psychoanalyse* 11/1 (1925): 40–53.

Erneszt, Sándor. *A keresztény nemzeti politika egy éve*. Budapest: Stephaneum Nyomda, 1921.

Federn, Paul. *Zur Psychologie der Revolution: Die vaterlose Gesellschaft*. Leipzig: Anzengruber Verlag Brüder Suschitzky, 1919.

Gratz, Gusztáv, ed. *A bolsevizmus Magyarországon*. Budapest: Franklin Tarsulat, 1921. *A forradalmak kora: Magyarország története, 1918–1920*. Budapest: Akadémiai Kiadó, 1992. First published 1935 by Magyar Szemle Társaság.

Grosz, George. *The Face of the Ruling Class*. Introduction and notes by Frank Whitford. London: Allison & Busby, 1984. Originally published 1921 as *Das Gesicht der herrschenden Klasse*.

Guckenheimer, Eduard. *Der Begriff der ehrlosen Gesinnung im Strafrecht. Ein Beitrag zur strafrechtlichen Beurteilung politischer Verbrecher*. Hamburg: W. Gente, 1921.

Gumbel, Emil. *Verschwörer. Beiträge zur Geschichte und Soziologie der deutschen nationalistischen Geheimbünde seit 1918*. Berlin: Der Malik Verlag, 1924. *Vier Jahre politischer Mord*. Heidelberg: Verlag Das Wunderhorn, 1980. First published 1922 by Verlag der neuen Gesellschaft.

Horthy, Miklós. *Titkos iratai*. Edited by Miklós Szinai and László Szűcs. Budapest: Kossuth Könyvkiadó, 1962.

Huszár, Karl [Károly], ed. *Die Proletarierdiktatur in Ungarn: Wahrheitsgetreue Darstellung der bolschewistischen Schreckensherrschaft*. Regensburg: Verlag Jos. Koesel, 1920.

Jászi, Oscar [Oszkár]. "Dismembered Hungary and Peace in Central Europe." *Foreign Affairs* 2/2 (1923): 270–81. *The Dissolution of the Habsburg Monarchy*. Chicago: University of Chicago Press, 1929. "Feudal Agrarianism in Hungary." *Foreign Affairs* 16/4 (1938): 714–18. *Homage to Danubia: Writings in English by Oscar Jaszi, 1923–1957*. Edited by György Litván. Lanham, MD: Rowman & Littlefield, 1995. "Kossuth and the Treaty of Trianon."*Foreign Affairs* 12/1 (1933): 86–97. *Mi a radikalizmus?* Budapest: Az Országos Polgári Radikális Párt kiadása, 1918. "Neglected Aspect of the Danubian Drama." *Slavonic and East European Review* 14/28 (1934): 492–506. *Revolution and Counter-Revolution in Hungary*. Introduction by R. W. Seton-Watson. New York: Howard Fertig, 1969. .

Kaas, Albert and Fedor de Lazarovics. *Bolshevism in Hungary: The Béla Kun Period*. London: Grant Richards, 1931.

Kahn, Eugen. "Psychopathen als revolutionäre Führer." *Zeitschrift fuer die gesasmte Neurologie und Psychiatrie* 52 (1919): 90–106.

Károlyi, Michael [Mihály]. *Fighting the World: The Struggle for Peace*. Translated by E. W. Dickes. New York: Albert & Charles Boni, 1925.

Kelemen, Béla. *Adatok a szegedi ellenforradalom és a szegedi kormány történetéhez (1919): Naplójegyzetek és Okiratok*. Szeged: self-published, 1923.

Kolosváry-Borcsa, Mihály. *A zsidókérdés magyarországi irodalma: A zsidság szerepe a magyar szellemi életben, a zsidó származású írók névsorával*. Budapest: Stádium Sajtóvállalat Részvénytársaság, 1941.

Komáromi, János. *A nagy háború anekdotái*. Budapest: Révai, 1936.

Kozma, Miklós. *Az összeomlás, 1918–1919*. Budapest: Kárpátia Stúdió, 2019. First published 1933.

Kraeplin, Emil. "Psychiatrische Randbemerkungen zur Zeitgeschichte." *Süddeutsche Monatshefte* 16/2 (1919): 171–83.

Loewenfeld, Philipp. *Das Strafrecht als politische Waffe*. Berlin: Dietz, 1933.

Luzsénszky, Alfonz. *Történetek: 1879–1919*. Budapest: Szerző, 1944.

A zsidó nép bűnei: Történelmi tanulmány. Budapest: Szerző, 1941.

Mahovits, Gyula. *A kis hős: Történet a vörös-oláh harcok idejéből*. Törökszentmiklós: Szerző, 1938.

Mályusz, Elemér. *The Fugitive Bolsheviks*. London: G. Richards, 1931.

Marx, H. "Ärztliche Gedanken zur Revolution." *Berliner klinische Wochenschrift* 12 (March 24, 1919): 279–80.

Der Münchener Bluttag. Berlin: Wilhelm Wagner, 1919.

Der Münchener Geiselmord: Wer trägt die Schuld? Berlin: Der Firn, 1919.

Nemeny, Wilhelm. *133 Tage Bolschewistenherrschaft*. Berlin: Kulturliga, 1920.

Nyári, Andor. *János kálváriája*. Budapest: Táltos, 1926.

Padányi, Viktor. *Összeomlás: 1918–19*. Szeged: Szerző, 1942.

Vörös vihar: Regény a magyar nemzet nehéz idejéből. Budapest: Stádium, n.d.

Pogány, Josef [József]. *Der Weiße Terror in Ungarn*. Vienna: Verlagsgenossenschaft Neue Welt, 1920.

Prónay, Pál. *A határban a Halál kaszál: Fejezetek a Prónay Pál feljegyzéseiből*. Edited and selected by Ágnes Szabó and Ervin Pamlényi. Budapest: Kossuth Kiadó, 1963.

Rathenau, Walther. *Kritik der dreifachen Revolution*. Berlin: 1919.

Sándor, Ernszt. *A keresztény nemzeti politika egy éve*. Budapest: Stephaneum Nyomda, 1921.

Schachtel, Ernest G. "On Memory and Childhood Amnesia." *Psychiatry* 10 (1946): 1–26.

Schickert, Klaus. *Die Judenfrage in Ungarn: Jüdische Assimilation und antisemitische Bewegung im 19. und 20. Jahrhundert*. 2nd, expanded edition. Essen: Essener Verlagesanstalt, 1937.

Schmitt, Carl. *The Concept of the Political*. Translated by George Schwab. New Brunswick, NJ: Rutgers University Press, 1976

Schweder, Paul. *Der Münchner Geiselmord vor Gericht: Vorgeschichte, ausführlicher Verhandlungsbericht und Urteil*. Munich: Hochschulverlag, 1919.

Sebottendorf, Rudolf von. *Bevor Hitler kam: Urkundliches aus der Frühzeit der nationalsozialistischen Bewegung*. Munich: Deukula Verlag Graffinger, 1933.

Segall, Jakob. "Die Entwicklung der Juden in München von 1875 bis 1905: Eine Bevölkerungsstatistische Studie." Dissertation, Ludwig Maximilians University, 1908.

Shepard, Walter James. "The New Government in Germany," *American Political Science Review* 13/3 (1919): 361–78.

Siegert, Max. *Aus Münchens schwerster Zeit: Erinnerungen aus dem Münchener Hauptbahnhof während der Revolutions- und Rätezeit*. Munich: Manz, 1928.

Stern, William. "Abstracts of Lectures on the Psychology of Testimony and on the Study of Individuality." *American Journal of Psychology* 21 (1910): 270–82.

Stertz, Georg. "Verschrobene Fanatiker." *Berliner klinische Wochenschrift* 25 (June 28, 1919): 586–8.

Die Sünden der Revolution: Blitzlichter aus deutschen und österreichischen Zeitungen, Nürnberg: Nürnberger Bücherei- und Verlags-Gesellschaft, Döllinger & Co., 1919.

Sulyok, Dezső. *A magyar tragédia I: A Trianoni Béke és következményei*. Newark, NJ: Szerző kiadása, 1954.

Szántó, Béla. *Klassenkämpfe und die Dictatur des Proletariats in Ungarn*. Vienna: Neue Erde, 1920.

Szatmáry, Ernst. *Im Roten Budapest*. Berlin: Verlag der Kulturliga, 1919.

Szekfű, Gyula. *Der Staat Ungarn: Eine Geschichtsstudie*. Stuttgart: Deutsche Verlags-Anstalt, 1918.

Tarján, Vilmos. *A Terror*. Foreword by László Fényes. Budapest, 1919.

Tharaud, Jerome and Jean Tharaud. *When Israel is King*. Translated by Lady Whitehead. New York: Robert McBride, 1924. Originally published 1921 as *Quand Israël est roi*.

Thoma, Ludwig, Dietrich Eckart, and Klaus Eck. *So ein Saustall! Altbairisches aus den finstersten Zeiten des Systems*. Munich: Karl-Köhrig-Verlag, 1938.

Toller, Ernst. *Justiz-Erlebnisse*. Berlin: E. Laubsche Verlagsbuchhandlung, 1927.

Udvary, Jenő. "Psychológiai megfigyelések a harcztérről." *Hadtörtényelmi Közlemények* 22/1 (1921): 157–70.

Ungar, Henrik. *Die magyarische Pest in Moskau*. Leipzig: Veritas Verlag, 1921.

Vámbéry, Arminius. *Hungary: The Story of the Nations*. New York: G. P. Putnam's Sons, 1898.

Vargha, Zoltán. *Az új urak: Rajz a kommunizmus korából*. Mezőtur: Törökny, 1938.

Váry, Albert. *A vörös uralom áldozatai Magyarországon: Hivatalos jelentések és bírói ítéletek alapján írta és kiadja*. 3rd edition. Szeged: Szegedi Nyomda, 1993.

Vécsey, Zoltán. *Visszaemlékezések 1919-ről*. Budapest: Gondolat, 1989.

Wadleigh, Henry Rawle. *Munich: History, Monuments, and Art*. London: T. Fisher Unwin, 1910.

Secondary Sources

Ablovatski, Eliza. "The 1919 Central European Revolutions and the Myth of Judeo-Bolshevism." In Michael L. Miller and Scott Ury, eds., *Cosmopolitanism, Nationalism and the Jews of East Central Europe*, 137–54. New York: Routledge, 2014.

Adelson, József. "The Expulsion of Jews with Polish Citizenship from Bavaria in 1923." *Journal of Polish-Jewish Studies* 5 (1990): 57–73.

Albertini, Béla. *A Magyar szociofotó története a kezdetektől a második világháború végéig*. Budapest: Magyar Fotográfiai Múzeum, 1997.

Albrecht, Willy. *Landtag und Regierung in Bayern am Vorabend der Revolution von 1918*. Berlin: Duncker & Humblot, 1968.

Allen, William Sheridan. *The Nazi Seizure of Power: The Experience of a Single German Town, 1922–1945*. New York: F. Watts, 1984.

Anderson, Margaret Lavinia. *Practicing Democracy: Elections and Political Culture in Imperial Germany*. Princeton: Princeton University Press, 2000.

Windthorst: A Political Biography. Oxford: Clarendon Press, 1981.

Angermund, Ralph. *Deutsche Richterschaft, 1919–1945: Krisenerfahrung, Illusion, politische Rechtsprechung*. Frankfurt a.M.: Fischer, 1990.

Angress, Werner T. "The German Army's 'Judenzählung' of 1916: Genesis-Consequences-Significance." *Leo Baeck Institute Yearbook* 23 (1978): 117–37.

Aschheim, Steven. *Brothers and Strangers: The East European Jew in German and German Jewish Consciousness, 1800–1923.* Madison, WI: University of Wisconsin Press, 1982.

Ash, Timothy Garton. *The Uses of Adversity: Essays on the Fate of Central Europe.* New York: Vintage, 1990.

Assmann, Aleida. *Erinnerungsräume: Formen und Wandel des kulturellen Gedächtnisses.* Munich: C. H. Beck, 1999.

Assmann, Jan and John Czaplicka. "Collective Memory and Cultural Identity." *New German Critique* 65 (Spring/Summer 1995): 125–33.

Auerbach, Hellmuth. "Hitlers politische Lehrjahre und die Münchener Gesellschaft 1919–1923." *Vierteljahrshefte fuer Zeitgeschichte* 25 (1977): 1–45.

Austensen, Roy A. "Austria and the 'Struggle for Supremacy in Germany,' 1848–1864." *Journal of Modern History* 52/2 (June 1980): 195–225.

Ay, Karl-Ludwig. *Die Entstehung einer Revolution: Die Volksstimmung in Bayern während des Ersten Weltkrieges.* Berlin: Duncker & Humblot, 1968.

Balog, Ivan. "Anti-Semitism Demythologized?" *Budapest Review of Books* 3/1 (1993): 23–8.

Balogh, Sándor. "A bethleni konszolidáció és a magyar 'neonacionalizmus.'" *Történelmi Szemle* 5/3–4 (1962): 426–48.

Banac, Ivo. *The Effects of World War I: The Class War after the Great War: The Rise of Communist Parties in East Central Europe, 1918–1921.* Boulder, CO: East European Monographs, 1983.

Barany, George. "Magyar Jew or Jewish Magyar? To the Question of Jewish Assimilation in Hungary." *Canadian-American Slavic Studies* 8 (1974): 1–44.

Barkai, Avraham, Paul Mendes-Flohr, and Steven M. Lowenstein. *Aufbruch und Zerstörung, 1918–1945.* Munich: C. H. Beck Verlag, 1997.

Barkey, Karen and Mark von Hagen, eds. *After Empire: Multiethnic Societies and Nation-Building. The Soviet Union and the Russian, Ottoman, and Habsburg Empires.* Boulder, CO: Westview Press, 1997.

Baron, Salo W. "Newer Approaches to Jewish Assimilation." *Diogenes* 29 (1960): 56–81.

Batkay, William M. *Authoritarian Politics in a Transitional State: István Bethlen and the Unified Party in Hungary, 1921–26.* Boulder, CO: East European Monographs, 1982.

Bauer, Franz J. "Ein fragwürdiges Erbe der Revolution: Volksgerichte und Standgerichte in Bayern 1918–1924." *Unser Bayern* 43/5 (1994): 37–8.

Becker, Josef. *Liberaler Staat und Kirche in der Ära von Reichsgründung und Kulturkampf. Geschichte und Strukturen ihres Verhältnisses in Baden, 1860–1876.* Mainz: Matthias-Grünewald-Verlag, 1973.

Bender, Thomas and Carl E. Schorske, eds. *Budapest and New York: Studies in Metropolitan Transformation, 1870–1930.* New York: Russell Sage Foundation, 1994.

Berend, Iván T. "Alternatives to Class Revolution: Central and Eastern Europe after the First World War." In Pat Thane, Geoffrey Crossick, and Roderick Floud, eds., *The Power of the Past: Essays for Eric Hobsbawm,* 251–82. Cambridge: Cambridge University Press, 1984.

Decades of Crisis: Central and Eastern Europe before World War II. Berkeley: University of California Press, 1998.

Berghahn, Volker. *Germany and the Approach of War in 1914.* New York: St. Martin's Press, 1973.

Imperial Germany, 1871–1914: Economy, Society, Culture and Politics. Providence, RI: Berghahn Books, 1994.

Modern Germany: Society, Economy and Politics in the Twentieth Century. Cambridge: Cambridge University Press, 1982.

Bergmann, Klaus. *Agrarromantik und Großstadtfeindschaft*. Meisenheim am Glan: 1970.

Bering, Dietz. *The Stigma of Names: Antisemitism in German Daily Life, 1812–1933*. Translated by Neville Plaice. Ann Arbor: University of Michigan Press, 1992.

Berkley, George E. *Vienna and its Jews: The Tragedy of Success, 1880s–1980s*. Cambridge, MA: Abt Books and Madison Books, 1988.

Bessel, Richard. "Eine nicht allzu grosse Beunruhigung des Arbeitsmarktes: Frauenarbeit und Demobilmachung in Deutschland nach dem Ersten Weltkrieg." *Geschichte und Gesellschaft* 9 (1983): 211–29.

Germany after the First World War. Oxford: Clarendon Press, 1993.

"The Great War in German Memory: The Soldiers of the First World War, Demobilization and Weimar Political Culture." *German History* 6/1 (1988): 20–34.

"Policing, Professionalisation and Politics in Weimar Germany." In Clive Emsley and Barbara Weinberger, eds., *Policing Western Europe: Politics, Professionalism, and Public Order, 1850–1940*, 187–218. New York: Greenwood Press, 1991.

Betts, Paul. "The Twilight of the Idols: East German Memory and Material Culture." *Journal of Modern History* 72/3 (Sept. 2000): 731–65.

Beyer, Hans. *Von der Novemberrevolution zur Räterepublik in München*. Schriftenreihe des Instituts für deutsche Geschichte an der Karl-Marx-Universität Leipzig. Berlin: Rütten & Loening, 1957.

Bialas, Wolfgang and Georg G. Iggers, eds. *Intellektuelle in der Weimarer Republik*. Frankfurt/Main: Peter Lang, 1996.

Blackbourn, David. *Class, Religion and Local Politics in Wilhemine Germany: The Centre Party in Würtemberg before 1914*. New Haven, CT: Yale University Press, 1980.

History of Germany, 1780–1918: The Long Nineteenth Century. 2nd edition. Oxford: Blackwell Publishing, 2002.

"The Political Alignment of the Centre Party in Wilhelmine Germany: A Study of the Party's Emergence in Nineteenth-Century Wurttemberg." *Historical Journal* 18/4 (1975): 821–50.

"Progress and Piety: Liberalism, Catholicism and the State in Imperial Germany." *History Workshop Journal* 26 (1988): 57–78.

Blackbourn, David and Geoff Eley, eds. *The Peculiarities of German History: Bourgeois Society and Politics in Nineteenth-Century Germany*. Oxford: Oxford University Press, 1984.

Blessing, Werner K. "The Cult of Monarchy, Political Loyalty and the Workers' Movement in Imperial Germany." *Journal of Contemporary History* 13/2 (April 1978): 357–75.

Staat und Kirche in der Gesellschaft: Institutionelle Autorität und mentaler Wandel in Bayern während des 19. Jahrhunderts. Göttingen: Vandenhoeck & Ruprecht, 1982.

Blom, Ida, Karen Hagemann, and Catherine Hall, eds. *Gendered Nations: Nationalisms and Gender Order in the Long Nineteenth Century.* London: Berg, 2000.

Bodó, Béla. "Favorites or Pariahs? The Fate of the Right-Wing Militia Men in Interwar Hungary." *Austrian History Yearbook* 46 (2015): 327–59.

"Hungarian Aristocracy and the White Terror." *Journal of Contemporary History* 45/4 (Oct. 2010): 703–24.

"Iván Hejjás: The Life of a Counter-Revolutionary." *East Central Europe* 37/2–3 (2010): 247–79.

"Militia Violence and State Power in Hungary, 1919–1922." *Hungarian Studies Review* 33 (2006): 121–67.

Pál Prónay: Paramilitary Violence and Anti-Semitism in Hungary, 1919–1921. Pittsburgh, PA: Center for Russian and East European Studies, 2011.

"Paramilitary Violence in Hungary after the First World War." *East European Quarterly* 38/2 (2004): 129–72.

The White Terror: Antisemitic and Political Violence in Hungary, 1919–1921. New York: Routledge, 2019.

"The White Terror in Hungary 1919–1921: The Social Worlds of Paramilitary Groups." *Austrian History Yearbook* 42 (2011): 133–63.

Boemeke, Manfred F., Roger Chickering, and Stig Förster, eds. *Anticipating Total War: The German and American Experiences, 1871–1914.* Cambridge: Cambridge University Press, 1999.

Böhler, Jochen, Wlodzimierz Borodziej, and Joachim von Puttkamer, eds. *Legacies of Violence: Eastern Europe's First World War* Munich: De Gruyter Oldenbourg, 2014.

Borbándi, Gyula. *Der ungarische Populismus.* Mainz: v. Hase & Koehler, 1976.

Borsányi, György. *The Life of a Communist Revolutionary: Béla Kun.* Translated by Mario D. Fenyo. Boulder, CO: Social Science Monographs, 1993. Originally published 1979 in Budapest as *Kun Béla: Politikai életrajz.*

Bosl, Karl, ed. *Bayern im Umbruch: Die Revolution von 1918, ihre Voraussetzungen, ihr Verlauf und ihre Folgen.* Munich: Oldenbourg, 1969.

"Gesellschaft und Politik in Bayern vor dem Ende der Monarchie: Beiträge zu einer sozialen und politischen Strukturanalyse." *Zeitschrift für Bayerische Landesgeschichte* 38 (1965): 1–31.

"Heinrich Held: Journalist – Partiepolitiker – Staatsmann." *Zeitschrift fuer bayerische Landesgeschichte* 31/3 (1968): 747–67.

"München 'Deutschlands heimliche Hauptstadt': Historische Bemerkungen zur Strukturanalyse des modernen Hauptstadt- und Großstadttypus in Deutschland." *Zeitschrift für Bayerische Landesgeschichte* 30 (1967): 298–313.

"Typen der Stadt in Bayern: Der soziale und wirtschaftliche Aufstieg der Städte und des Bürgertums in bayerischen Landen." *Zeitschrift für Bayerische Landesgeschichte* 32 (1969): 1–23.

Botz, Gerhard. "Die Kommunistischen Putschversuche 1918/19 in Wien." *Österreich in Geschichte und Literatur* (1970): 13–23.

Boyer, John. "Power, Partisanship, and the Grid of Democratic Politics: 1907 as the Pivot Point of Modern Austrian History." *Austrian History Yearbook* 44 (2013): 148–74.

Braham, Randolph L. *The Politics of Genocide: The Holocaust in Hungary*, vol. 1. New York: Columbia University Press, 1981.

Braham, Randolph and Béla Vago, eds. *The Holocaust in Hungary Forty Years Later.* Boulder, CO: Social Science Monographs, 1985.

Brandmüller, Walter. "Die Publikation des 1. Vatikanischen Konzils: Aus den Anfängen des Bayerischen Kulturkampfes" (Part 1). *Zeitschrift für Bayerische Landesgeschichte* 31 (1968): 197–258.

Breuer, Stefan. *Anatomie der konservativen Revolution.* Darmstadt: Wissenschaftliche Buchgesellschaft, 1993.

Brix, Emil. *Die Umgangssprachen in Altösterreich zwischen Agitation und Assimilation: Die Sprachenstatistik in den zisleithanischen Volkszählungen, 1880 bis 1910.* Vienna: Böhlau, 1982.

Brown, Malcolm and Shirley Seaton. *Christmas Truce.* London: Secker and Warburg, 1984.

Brozsat, Martin. "Faschismus und Kollaboration zwischen den Weltkriegen," *Vierteljahreshefte für Zeitgeschichte* 14 (1966): 225–51.

Bryan, G. McLeod. *These Few Also Paid a Price: Southern Whites Who Fought for Civil Rights.* Macon, GA: Mercer University Press, 2001.

Burke, Peter. *Varieties of Cultural History.* Ithaca: Cornell University Press, 1997.

Burton, Antoinette M. "The White Woman's Burden." In Nupur Chaudhuri and Margaret Strobel, eds., *Western Women and Imperialism*,137–57. Bloomington: Indiana University Press, 1992.

Butler, Thomas, ed. *Memory: History, Culture and the Mind.* New York: Basil Blackwell, 1989.

Buzinkay, Geza. "The Budapest Joke and Comic Weeklies as Mirrors of Cultural Assimilation." In Thomas Bender and Carl Schorske, eds., *Budapest and New York: Studies in Metropolitan Transformation, 1870–1930*, 224–48. New York: Russell Sage Foundation, 1994.

Cahnman, Werner J. *German Jewry: Its History and Sociology.* Edited by Joseph B. Maier, Judith Marcus, and Zoltán Tarr. New Brunswick, NJ: Transaction Publishers, 1989.

Canetti, Elias. *Crowds and Power.* Translated by Carol Stewart. New York: Noonday, 1962.

Canning, Kathleen. "Gender and the Imaginary of Revolution in Germany." In Klaus Weinhauer, Anthony McElligott, and Kirsten Heinsohn, eds., *In Search of Revolution: Germany and its European* Context, *1916–1923*, 103–26. Berlin: Transit Verlag, 2015.

_. "Gender Order/Disorder and New Political Subjects in the Weimar Republic." In Gabriele Metzler and Dirk Schumann, eds., *Geschlechterordnung und Politik in der Weimarer Republik*,59–80. Heidelberg: Friedrich-Ebert-Stiftung, 2016.

"War, Citizenship and Rhetorics of Sexual Crisis: Reflections on States of Exception in Germany, 1914–1920." In Geoff Eley, Jennifer Jenkins, and Tracie Matysik, eds., *German Modernities from Wilhelm to Weimar: A Contest of Futures*,235–57. London: Bloomsbury Academic Press, 2016.

Canning, Kathleen, Kerstin Barndt, and Kristen McGuire, eds. *Weimar Publics/Weimar Subjects: Rethinking the Political Culture of Germany in the 1920s.* New York: Berghahn Books, 2010.

Carevali, Ralph C. "The False French Alarm: Revolutionary Panic in Baden, 1848," *Central European History* 18 (1985): 119–42.

Carsten, F. L. *The Reichswehr and Politics: 1918–1933*. Oxford: Clarendon, 1966.
Revolution in Central Europe, *1918–1919*. London: Temple Smith, 1972.
Cassirer, Ernst. *Language and Myth*. Translated by Susanne K. Langer. Unabridged reprint of 1946 edition. New York: Dover, 1953.
Cattell, David T. "The Hungarian Revolution of 1919 and the Reorganization of the Comintern in 1920." *Journal of Central European Affairs* 11/1 (Jan.–Apr. 1951): 27–38.
Chickering, Roger and Sig Förster, eds. *Great War, Total War: Combat and Mobilization on the Western Front, 1914–1918*. Cambridge: Cambridge University Press, 2000.
Childers, Thomas. *The Nazi Voter: The Social Foundations of Fascism in Germany, 1919–1933*. Chapel Hill: University of North Carolina Press, 1983.
"The Social Language of Politics in Germany: The Sociology of Political Discourse in the Weimar Republic." *American Historical Review* 95/2 (April 1990): 331–58.
Chirot, Daniel, ed. *The Origins of Backwardness in Eastern Europe: Economics and Politics from the Middle Ages until the Early Twentieth Century*. Berkeley: University of California Press, 1989.
Clark, Christopher and Wolfram Kaiser, eds. *Culture Wars: Secular-Catholic Conflict in Nineteenth-Century Europe*. Cambridge: Cambridge University Press, 2003.
Congdon, Lee. *Exile and Social Thought: Hungarian Intellectuals in Germany and Austria, 1919–1933*. Princeton, NJ: Princeton University Press, 1991.
The Young Lukács. Chapel Hill: University of North Carolina Press, 1983.
Connelly, John. "The Uses of *Volksgemeinschaft*: Letters to the NSDAP Kreisleitung Eisenach, 1939–1940." *Journal of Modern History* 68/4 (Dec. 1996): 899–930.
Cornwall, Mark. *The Undermining of Austria-Hungary: The Battle for Hearts and Minds*. New York: Palgrave Macmillan, 2000.
Cornwell, John. *Hitler's Pope: The Secret History of Pius XII*. New York: Penguin Putnam, 1999.
Crane, Susan. "Writing the Individual Back into Collective Memory." *American Historical Review* 102/5 (1997): 1372–85.
Crenshaw, Martha, ed. *Terrorism, Legitimacy, and Power: The Consequences of Political Violence*. Middletown, CT: Wesleyan University Press, 1983.
Csizmadia, Andor. *A magyar állam és egyházak jogi kapcsolatainak kialakulása és gyakorlata a Horthy-korszakban*. Budapest: Akadémiai Kiadó, 1966.
Csizmadia, Andor and Kálmán Kovács, eds. *Die Entwicklung des Zivilrechts in Mitteleuropa: 1848–1944*. Budapest: Akadémiai Kiadó, 1970.
Csizmadia, Andor, Kálmán Kovács, and László Asztalos. *Magyar állam- és jogtörténet*. Budapest: Tankönyvkiadó, 1972.
Daniel, Ute. "The Politics of Rationing versus the Politics of Subsistence: Working-Class Women in Germany, 1914–1918." In Roger Fletcher, ed., *From Bernstein to Brandt: A Short History of German Social Democracy*, 89–95. London: E. Arnold, 1987.
The War from Within: German Working-Class Women in the First World War. Translated by Margaret Ries. Oxford: Berg Publishers, 1997.
Davies, Norman. *White Eagle, Red Star: The Polish–Soviet War, 1919–1920*. New York: St. Martin's Press, 1972.
Davis, Belinda J. "Food Scarcity and the Empowerment of the Female Consumer in World War I Berlin." In Victoria DeGrazia and Ellen Furlough, eds., *The Sex of*

Things: Gender and Consumption in Historical Perspective, 287–300. Oakland, CA: University of California Press, 1996.

Home Fires Burning: Food, Politics, and Everyday Life in World War I Berlin. Chapel Hill: University of North Carolina Press, 2000.

Deák, István. "Budapest and the Hungarian Revolutions of 1918–19." *Slavonic and Eastern European Review* 46 (1968): 129–40.

"Hungary." InHans Rogger and Eugen Weber, eds., *The European Right: A Historical Profile*, 364–408. Berkeley: University of California Press, 1965.

"Hungary from 1918–1945." *Occasional Papers of the Institute on East Central Europe* 19 (1988).

"Jewish Soldiers in Austro-Hungarian Society." Leo Baeck Memorial Lecture 34. New York: Leo Baeck Institute, 1990.

"The Social and Pychological Consequences of the Disintegration of Austria-Hungary in 1918." *Oesterreichische Osthefte Jahrgang* 22 (1980): 22–31.

"Survivor in a Sea of Barbarism." Review of *Hungary's Admiral on Horseback: Miklós Horthy, 1918–1944* by Thomas Sakmyster. *New York Review of Books*, April 8, 1999, 53–6.

Diehl, James M. *Paramilitary Politics in Weimar Germany.* Bloomington: Indiana University Press, 1977.

Diner, Dan. *Das Jahrhundert verstehen: Eine universalhistorische Deutung.* Munich: Luchterhand, 1999.

Doblhoff, Lily Báró. *Horthy Miklós.* Budapest: Antheneum Kiadása, n.d.

Donson, Andrew. *Youth in the Fatherless Land: War Pedagogy, Nationalism, and Authority in Germany, 1914–1918.* Cambridge, MA: Harvard University Press, 2010.

Dorondo, D.R. *Bavaria and German Federalism: Reich to Republic, 1918–1933, 1945–49.* New York: St. Martin's Press, 1992.

Dorst, Tankred and Helmut Neubauer, eds. *Die Münchner Räterepublik. Zeugnisse und Kommentar.* Frankfurt a.M.: Suhrkamp Verlag, 1966.

Douglas, Donald M. "The Parent Cell: Some Computer Notes on the Composition of the First Nazi Party Group in Munich, 1919–1921." *Central European History* 10 (1977): 55–72.

Downs, Laura Lee. *Manufacturing Inequality: Gender Division in the French and British Metalworking Industries, 1914–1939.* Ithaca, NY: Cornell University Press, 1995.

Drabek, Anna M., Richard G. Plaschka, and Helmut Rumpler, eds. *Das Parteiwesen Oesterreichs und Ungarns in der Zwischenkriegszeit.* Vienna: Verlag der Oesterreichischen Akademie der Wissenschaften, 1990.

Dupeux, Louis. "'Kulturpessimismus', Konservative Revolution und Modernität." In Manfred Gangl and Gérard Raulet, eds., *Intellektuellendiskurs in der Weimarer Republik*, 287–300. Frankfurt a.M: Campus, 1994.

Eksteins, Modris. *Rites of Spring: The Great War and the Birth of the Modern Age.* New York: Houghton Mifflin, 1989.

Eley, Geoff. "Remapping the Nation: War, Revolutionary Upheaval and State Formation in Eastern Europe, 1914–1923." InPeter J. Poichnyj and Howard Astor, eds., *Ukrainian–Jewish Relations in Historical Perspective*,

205–46 Edmonton: Canadian Institute of Ukrainian Studies, University of Alberta, 1988.

Reshaping the German Right: Radical Nationalism and Political Change after Bismarck. Series: *Social History, Popular Culture, and Politics in Germany.* Ann Arbor: University of Michigan Press, 1980.

, ed. *Society, Culture and the State in Germany, 1870–1930.* Ann Arbor: University of Michigan Press, 1997.

Erdei, Ferenc. "A magyar társadalom a két világháború között" I–II. *Valóság* 4/5 (1976): 23–53.

Evans, Richard J. *Death in Hamburg: Society and Politics in the Cholera Years, 1830–1910.* Oxford: Clarendon Press, 1987.

"Epidemics and Revolution: Cholera in Nineteenth-Century Europe." *Past and Present* 120 (1988): 123–46.

, ed. *The German Underworld: Deviants and Outcasts in German History.* London: Routledge, 1988.

, ed. *The German Working Class, 1888–1933: The Politics of Everyday Life.* London: Croom Helm and Barnes & Noble Books, 1982.

Rituals of Retribution: Capital Punishment in Germany, 1600–1987. New York: Oxford University Press, 1996.

Farkas, József, ed. *Räterepublik und Kultur Ungarn 1919.* Budapest: Corvina Kiadó, 1979.

Feldman, Gerald. "Economic and Social Problems of the German Demobilization, 1918–1919." *Journal of Modern History* 47/1 (1975): 1–23.

"War Economy and Controlled Economy: The Discrediting of 'Socialism' in Germany during World War I." In H.-J. Schroeder, ed., *Confrontation and Cooperation: Germany and the United States in the Era of World War I, 1900–1932.* Providence, RI: Berg, 1993.

Fink, Carole. *Defending the Rights of Others: The Great Powers, the Jews, and International Minority Protection, 1878–1938.* Cambridge: Cambridge University Press, 2004.

Fischer, Fritz. *Griff nach der Weltmacht: Die Kriegsziele des kaiserlichen Deutschland 1914/18.* Düsseldorf: Droste Verlag, 1961.

War of Illusions: German Policies from 1911–1914. Translated by Marian Jackson. Foreword by Alan Bullock. New York: Norton, 1975.

Fischer, Holger. *Eine kleine Geschichte Ungarns.* Frankfurt: Suhrkamp, 1999.

"Neuere Entwicklungen in der ungarischen Sozialgeschichtsforschung." *Archiv für Sozialgeschichte* 34 (1994): 131–56.

Oszkár Jászi und Mihály Károlyi: Ein Beitrag zur Nationalitätenpolitik der bürgerlich-demokratischen Opposition in Ungarn von 1900 bis 1918 und ihre Verwirklichung in der bürgerlich-demokratischen Regierung von 1918 bis 1919. Munich: Dr. Rudolf Trofenik, 1978.

Fischer, Rolf. *Entwicklungsstufen des Antisemitismus in Ungarn, 1867–1939: Die Zerstörung der magyarisch-jüdischen Symbiose.* Munich: Oldenbourg, 1988.

Fitzpatrick, Sheila. "How the Mice Buried the Cat: Scenes from the Great Purges of 1937 in the Russian Provinces." *Russian Review* 52/3 (July 1993): 299–320.

"Signals from Below: Soviet Letters of Denunciation of the 1930s." *Journal of Modern History* 68/4 (Dec. 1996): 831–66.

"Supplicants and Citizens: Public Letter-Writing in Soviet Russia in the 1930s." *Slavic Review* 55/1 (Spring 1996): 78–105.

Fitzpatrick, Sheila and Robert Gellately, eds. "Practices of Denunciation in Modern European History, 1789–1989." Special issue, *Journal of Modern History* 68/4 (Dec. 1996).

Forgacs, Eva. "Avant-Garde and Conservatism in the Budapest Art World: 1910–1932." In Thomas Bender and Carl E. Schorske, eds. *Budapest and New York: Studies in Metropolitan Transformation, 1870–1930*, 309–32. New York: Russell Sage Foundation, 1994.

Franz, Georg. "Munich: Birthplace and Center of the National Socialist German Workers' Party." *Journal of Modern History* 29/4 (December 1957), 319–34.

Franz-Willing, Georg. *Die Hitlerbewegung: Der Ursprung, 1919–1922*. Hamburg: R.v. Deckers Verlag, 1962.

Freifeld, Alice. *Nationalism and the Crowd in Liberal Hungary, 1848–1914*. Washington, DC: Woodrow Wilson Center Press and Johns Hopkins University Press, 2000.

Frigyesi, Judit. "Jews and Hungarians in Modern Hungarian Musical Culture." In Ezra Mendelsohn, ed., *Modern Jews and their Musical Agendas*, 40–60. New York: Oxford University Press, 1993.

Fritz, Wolfgang. *Der Kopf des Asiaten Breitner: Politik und Oekonomie im Roten Wien*. Vienna: Loecker Verlag, 2000.

Fritzsche, Peter. "The Case of Modern Memory." *Journal of Modern History* 73/3 (2001): 87–117.

Fromm, Erich. *The Working Class in Weimar Germany: A Psychological and Sociological Study*. Translated by Barbara Weinberger. Edited by Wolfgang Bonss. Cambridge, MA: Harvard University Press, 1984.

Fuller, William C., Jr. *The Foe Within: Fantasies of Treason and the End of Imperial Russia*. Ithaca, NY: Cornell University Press, 2006.

Fussell, Paul. *The Great War and Modern Memory*. New York: Oxford University Press, 2000. First published in 1975.

Galántai, József. *Hungary in the First World War*. Translated by Éva Grusz and Judit Pokoly. Budapest: Akadémiai Kiadó, 1989.

Garnett, Robert S. *Lion, Eagle, and Swastika: Bavarian Monarchism in Weimar Germany, 1918–1933*. New York: Garland, 1991.

Gatens, Rosanna M. "Turnips and War Memorials: E. J. Gumbel's Critique of German Militarism, 1919–1932." *International Social Science Review* 83, no. 1/2 (2008): 27–46.

Geertz, Clifford. "Ideology as a Cultural System." In David Apter, ed., *Ideology and Discontent*,47–76. London: Free Press, 1964.

Geiger, Theodor. *On Social Order and Mass Society: Selected Papers*. Translated by Robert E. Peck. Edited by Renate Mayntz. Chicago: University of Chicago Press, 1969.

Gellately, Robert. "Situating the 'SS State' in a Social-Historical Context: Recent Histories of the SS, the Police, and the Courts in the Third Reich." *Journal of Modern History* 64/2 (June 1992): 338–65.

Gerencsér, Miklós, ed. *Vörös Könyv 1919*. Lakitelek: Antológia Kiadó, 1993.

Gergely, Jenő. "Gömbös Gyula: As ellenforradalom vezáralakja." *História* 22 (2000): 17–22.

Gergely, Jenő and Pál Pritz, *A trianoni Magyarország, 1918–1945*. Budapest: Vince Kiadó, 1998.

Gerő, András. *Modern Hungarian Society in the Making: The Unfinished Experience*. Budapest: Central European University Press, 1995.

Gerő, András and János Poór, eds. *Budapest: A History from Its Beginnings to 1998*. Boulder, CO: Social Science Monographs, 1997.

Gersdorff, Ursula von. "Frauenarbeit und Frauenemanzipation im Ersten Weltkrieg." *Francia* 2 (1974): 502–23.

Gerstenberg, Guenther. *Freiheit! Sozialdemokratischer Selbstschutz in München der 20er und 30er Jahre*. 2 vols. Catalog to the exhibit of the same title in Münchener Glashalle, 1998. Andechs-Erling: Ulenspiegel, 1997.

Gerwarth, Robert. "The Central European Counter-Revolution: Paramilitary Violence in Germany, Austria and Hungary after the Great War." *Past and Present* 200 (2008): 175–209.

The Vanquished: Why the First World War Failed to End. New York: Farrar, Straus and Giroux, 2016.

Gerwarth, Robert and John Horne, eds. *War in Peace: Paramilitary Violence in Europe after the Great War*. Oxford: Oxford University Press, 2012.

Geyer, Martin. "Formen der Radikalisierung in der Münchener Revolution, 1918–1919." In H. Konrad and K. M. Schmidlechner, eds., *Revoutionäres Potential in Europa am Ende des Ersten Weltkrieges*, 63–87. Vienna: Böhlau, 1991.

"Munich in Turmoil: Social Protest and the Revolutionary Movement, 1918–1919." In Chris Wrigley, ed.,*Challenges of Labour: Central and Western* Europe, *1917–1920*, 51–71. London: Routledge, 1993.

"Recht, Gerechtigkeit und Gesetze." *Zeitschrift fuer neuere Rechtsgeschichte* 16 (1994): 349–72.

"Teuerungsprotest, Konsumentenpolitik und soziale Gerechtigkeit während der Inflation: München 1920–1923." *Archiv für Sozialgeschichte* 30 (1990): 181–215.

Verkehrte Welt: Weltkrieg, Revolution und Inflation in München. Göttingen: Vandenhoeck & Ruprecht, 1998.

Geyer, Michael. "The Stigma of Violence, Nationalism, and War in Twentieth-Century Germany." *German Studies Review* 5 (Winter 1992): 75–110.

Gilbert, Martin. *First World War*. London: Weidenfeld and Nicolson, 1994.

Gilman, Sander L. *Difference and Pathology Stereotypes of Sexuality, Race, and Madness*. Ithaca, NY: Cornell University Press, 1985.

The Jew's Body. New York: Routledge, 1991.

Gioielli, Emily R. "Enemy at the Door: Revolutionary Struggle in the Hungarian Domestic Sphere, 1918–1926." *Zeitschrift für Ostmitteleuropa Forschung* 60/4 (Dec. 2011): 519–38.

"'Home is Home No Longer': Political Struggle in the Domestic Sphere in Post-Armistice Hungary, 1919–1922." *Aspasia: The International Yearbook of Central, Eastern, and Southeastern European Women's and Gender History* 11 (March 2017): 54–70.

Glatz, Ferenc. "Klebelsberg tudománypolitikai programja és a magyar történettudomány." *Századok* 5/6 (1969): 1176–200.

Gluck, Mary. *Georg Lukacs and his Generation, 1900–1918*. Cambridge, MA: Harvard University Press, 1985.

"A Problem Seeking a Frame: An Aesthetic Reading of the "Jewish Question" in Turn-of-the-Century Hungary." *Austrian History Yearbook* 23 (1992): 91–110.

"Toward a Historical Definition of Modernism: Georg Lukacs and the Avant-Garde." *Journal of Modern History* 58/4 (1986): 845–82.

Gordon, Michael R. "Domestic Conflict and the Origins of the First World War: The British and the German Cases." *Journal of Modern History* 46/2 (June 1974): 191–226.

Gosztonyi, Péter. *A Magyar Golgota: A politikai megtorlások vázlatos története Magyarországon, 1849–1963 és egyéb korrajzi történetek*. Budapest: Heltai Gáspár, 1997.

Grau, Bernhard. *Kurt Eisner 1867–1919: Eine Biographie*. Munich: C. H. Beck, 2001.

Grayzel, Susan R. *Women and the First World War*. New York: Routledge, 2002.

Women's Identities at War: Gender, Motherhood, and Politics in Britain and France during the First World War. Chapel Hill: University of North Carolina Press, 1999.

Grayzel, Susan and Tammy Proctor, eds. *Gender and the Great War*. New York: Oxford University Press, 2017.

Gross, Jan T. *Neighbors: The Destruction of the Jewish Community in Jedwabne, Poland*. 2nd edition. New York: Penguin, 2002.

"A Note on the Nature of Soviet Totalitarianism." *Soviet Studies* 34/3 (July 1982): 367–76.

Gruber, Helmut. *Red Vienna: Experiment in Working-Class Culture, 1919–1934*. New York: Oxford University Press, 1991.

Grunberger, Richard. *Red Rising in Bavaria*. London: Arthur Barker, Ltd., 1973.

Gullace, Nicoletta. *The Blood of Our Sons: Men, Women, and the Renegotiation of British Citizenship During the Great War*. New York: Palgrave Macmillan, 2002.

"Christabel Pankhurst and the Smethwick Election: Right-wing Feminism, the Great War and the Ideology of Consumption." *Women's History Review* 33/3 (May 2014): 330–46.

Gullickson, Gay L. *Unruly Women of Paris: Images of the Commune*. Ithaca, NY: Cornell University Press, 1996.

Gunst, Péter. "Agricultural Exports in Hungary (1850–1914)." *Acta Historica Academiae Scientiarum Hungaricae* 35, no. 1/4 (1989): 61–90.

Haffner, Sebastian. *Failure of a Revolution: Germany 1918–19*. Translated by Georg Rapp. New York: Library Press, 1973.

Hagemann, Karen. "Men's Demonstrations and Women's Protests." *Gender and History* 5/1 (1993): 101–9.

Hajdu, Tibor. *The Hungarian Soviet Republic*. Budapest: Akadémiai Kiadó, 1979.

Közép-Európa forradalma, 1917–1921. Budapest: Gondolat, 1989.

"A Tanácsköztársaság a történetírásban." *História* 21/4 (1999): 13–15.

"Választójog 1918–1919-ben." *História* 5/6 (1985): 49–51.

Halbwachs, Maurice. *On Collective Memory*. Edited and translated by Lewis A. Coser. Chicago: University of Chicago Press, 1992.

Hämmerle, Christa, Oswald Überegger, and Birgitta Bader-Zaar, eds. *Gender and the First World War*. New York: Palgrave Macmillan, 2014.

Hanák, Péter. *The Garden and the Workshop: Essays on the Cultural History of Vienna and Budapest*. Foreword by Carl E. Schorske. Princeton, NJ: Princeton University Press, 1998.

"Problems of Jewish Assimilation in Austria-Hungary in the Nineteenth and Twentieth Centuries." In Pat Thane, Geoffrey Crossick, and Roderick Floud, eds., *The Power of the Past: Essays for Eric Hobsbawm*, 235–50. Cambridge: Cambridge University Press, 1984.

Ungarn in der Donaumonarchie: Probleme der bürgerlichen Umgestaltung eines Vielvölkerstaate. Vienna: Verlag für Geschichte und Politik, 1984.

, ed. *Zsidókérdés, asszimiláció, antiszemitizmus*. Budapest: Gondolat, 1984.

Handler, Andrew, ed. and trans. *The Holocaust in Hungary: An Anthology of Jewish Response*. Tuscaloosa, AL: University of Alabama Press, 1982.

Hanebrink, Paul. *A Specter Haunting Europe: The Myth of Judeo-Bolshevism*. Cambridge, MA: Harvard University Press, 2018.

In Defense of Christian Hungary: Religion, Nationalism and Antisemitism in Inter-War Hungary, 1890–1944. Ithaca, NY: Cornell University Press, 2006.

"Transnational Culture War: Christianity, Nation, and the Judeo-Bolshevik Myth in Hungary, 1890–1920." *Journal of Modern History* 80/1 (2008): 55–80.

Hannover, Heinrich and Elisabeth Hannover-Drück. *Politische Justiz, 1918–1933*. Frankfurt a.M.: Fischer Bücherei, 1966.

Harman, Chris. *The Lost Revolution: Germany 1918 to 1923*. London: Bookmarks, 1982.

Harris, James F. *The People Speak! Anti-Semitism and Emancipation in Nineteenth-Century Bavaria*. Social History, Popular Culture, and Politics in Germany. Ann Arbor: University of Michigan Press, 1994.

Hart, Mitchell. *Social Science and the Politics of Modern Jewish Identity*. Stanford, CA: Stanford University Press, 2000.

Hauszmann, János. *Bürgerlicher Radikalismus und demokratisches Denken im Ungarn des 20. Jahrhunderts: Der Jászi-Kreis um "Huszadik Század" (1900–1949)*. Frankfurt, Bern: Peter Lang, 1988.

Hautmann, Hans. "Vienna: A City in the Years of Radical Change, 1917–20." In Chris Wrigley, ed.,*Challenges of Labour: Central and Western* Europe, *1917–1920*, 87–104. London: Routledge, 1993.

Healy, Maureen. "Becoming Austrian: Women, the State and Citizenship in World War I." *Central European History* 35/1 (2002): 1–35

"Denunziation und Patriotismus: Briefe an die Wiener Polizei im Ersten Weltkrieg." *Sozialwissenschaftliche Informationen (Sowi)* 27/2 (1998): 106–12.

Vienna and the Fall of the Habsburg Empire: Total War and Everyday Life in World War I. Cambridge: Cambridge University Press, 2004.

Heller, Agnes. "Cultural Memory, Identity and Civil Society." *Internationale Politik und Gesellschaft* 2 (2001): 139–41.

Herz, Rudolf and Dirk Halfbrodt. *Revolution und Fotographie: München 1918/19*. Berlin: Verlag Dirk Nishen and Münchner Stadtmuseum, 1988.

Herzog, Dagmar. *Intimacy and Exclusion: Religious Politics in Pre-revolutionary Baden*. Princeton: Princeton University Press, 1996.

Hillmayr, Heinrich. *Roter und Weißer Terror in Bayern nach 1918: Ursachen, Erscheinungsformen und Folgen der Gewalttätigkeiten im Verlauf der revolutionären Ereignisse nach dem Ende des Ersten Weltkrieges*. Munich: Nusser Verlag, 1974.

Hirschfeld, Gerhard and Wolfgang J. Mommsen, eds. *Social Protest, Violence and Terror in Nineteenth- and Twentieth-Century Europe*. New York: St. Martin's Press, 1982.

Hobsbawm, Eric. *Age of Extremes: The Short Twentieth Century, 1914–1991*. New York: Penguin, 1994.

Hoegner, Wilhelm. *Die verratene Republik: Geschichte der deutschen Gegenrevolution*. Munich: Isar Verlag, 1958.

Hoensch, Jörg K. *A History of Modern Hungary, 1867–1994*. Translated by Kim Traynor. 2nd edition. London: Longman, 1996.

Hoffmann, Eva. "Life Stories East and West." *Yale Review* 88/1 (Jan. 2000): 1–19.

Hohorst, Gerd, Jürgen Kocka, and Gerhard Ritter, eds. *Sozialgeschichtliches Arbeitsbuch: Materialien zur Statistik des Kaiserreichs 1870–1914*. Vol. 2. Munich: C. H. Beck, 1975.

Höller, Ralf. *Der Anfang, der ein Ende war: Die Revolution in Bayern 1918/19*. Berlin: Aufbau Taschenverlag, 1999.

Holquist, Peter. "'Conduct Merciless Mass Terror.' Decossackization on the Don, 1919." *Cahiers du Monde Russe* 38/1–2 (Jan.–June 1997): 127–62.

"'Information is the Alpha and Omega of Our Work': Bolshevik Surveillance in its Pan-European Perspective." *Journal of Modern History* 69/3 (1997): 415–50.

Honigmann, Peter. "Jewish Conversions: A Measure of Assimilation? A Discussion of the Berlin Secession Statistics of 1770–1941." *Leo Baeck Institute Yearbook* 34 (1989): 3–45.

Horváth, Zoltán. *Die Jahrhundertwende in Ungarn: Geschichte der zweiten Reformgeneration (1896–1914)*. Berlin: Luchterhand, 1966.

Hoser, Paul. *Die politischen, wirtschaftlichen und sozialen Hintergründe der Münchner Tagespresse zwischen 1914 und 1934*. 2 vols. Frankfurt am Main: Peter Lang, 1990.

Houze, Rebecca. *Textiles, Fashion, and Design Reform before the First World War: Principles of Dress*. Burlington, VT: Ashgate, 2015.

Hsia, Ke-Chin. "'War Victims': Concepts of Victimhood and the Austrian Identity after the Habsburgs." *Contemporary Austrian Studies* 27 (2018): 245–52.

Huettl, Ludwig. "Die Stellungnahme der Katholischen Kirche und Publizistik zur Revolution in Bayern 1918/1919." *Zeitschrift fuer bayerische Landesgeschichte* 34/2 (1971): 652–95.

Hümmert, Ludwig. *Bayern: Vom Königreich zur Diktatur, 1900–1933*. Pfaffenhofen: Verlag W. Ludwig, 1979.

Hupchick, Dennis P. and R. William Weisberger, eds. *Hungary's Historical Legacies: Studies in Honor of Steven Béla Várdy*. Boulder, CO: East European Monographs, 2000.

Hurten, Heinz, ed. *Zwischen Revolution und Kapp-Putsch: Militär und Innenpolitik 1918–1920*. Vol. 2: *Quellen zur Geschichte des Parlimentarismus und der politischen Parteien*. Düsseldorf, Droste Verlag, 1977.

Illényi, Balázs. "Számolni nehéz: A Tanácsköztársaság áldozatai." *HVG* [formerly *Heti Világgazdaság*] (July 31, 1999): 86–8.

Ingrisch, Doris. *Die Revolutionierung des Alltags: Zur intellektuellen Kultur von Frauen im Wien der Zwischenkriegszeit.* Vienna: Österreichischer Kunst- und Kulturverlag, 1999.

Janos, Andrew C. *The Politics of Backwardness in Hungary, 1825–1945.* Princeton, NJ: Princeton University Press, 1982.

Janos, Andrew C. and William B. Slottman, eds. *Revolution in Perspective: Essays on the Hungarian Soviet Republic of 1919.* Berkeley: University of California Press, 1971.

Jedlicka, L. "Die Anfänge des Rechtsradikalismus in Österreich (1919–1925)." *Wissenschaft und Weltbild* 24(1971): 96–110.

Jelavich, Peter. *Munich and Theatrical Modernism: Politics, Playwriting and Performance, 1890–1914.* Cambridge, MA: Harvard University Press, 1985.

Jochmann, Werner. "Structure and Functions of German Anti-Semitism, 1878–1914." In Herbert A. Strauss, ed., *Hostages of Modernization: Studies on Modern Antisemitism, 1870–1933/39,* 41–61. Berlin: Walter de Gruyter, 1993.

Joll, James. *The Origins of the First World War.* London: Longman, 1984.

Judson, Pieter. *The Habsburg Empire: A New History.* Cambridge, MA: Belknap Press of Harvard University Press, 2016.

Kaeble, Hartmut. *Der historische Vergleich: Eine Einführung zum 19. und 20. Jahrhundert.* Frankfurt: Campus Verlag, 1999.

Kaiser, David E. "Germany and the Origins of the First World War." *Journal of Modern History* 55/3 (Sept. 1983): 442–74.

Kann, Robert A. *A History of the Habsburg Empire, 1526–1918.* Berkeley: University of California Press, 1974.

Kann, Robert A., Béla Király, and Paula Fichtner, eds. *The Habsburg Empire in World War I: Essays on the Intellectual, Military, Political and Economic Aspects of the Habsburg War Effort.* Boulder, CO: East European Monographs, 1977.

Karády, Victor. "Different Experiences of Modernization and the Rise of Antisemitism: Socio-political Foundations of the *numerus clausus* (1920) and the 'Christian Course' in Post World War I Hungary." *Transversal* 2 (2003): 3–34.

"Symbolic Nation-Building in a Multi-Ethnic Society: The Case of Surname Nationalization in Hungary." *Tel Aviver Jahrbuch für deutsche Geschichte* 30 (2002): 81–103.

Karády, Victor and István Kemény. "Antisémitisme universitaire et concurrence de classe. La loi du *numerus clauses* en Hongrie entre les deux Guerres." *Actes de las Recherche en Sciences Sociales* 34 (1980): 67–96.

Karády, Victor and Péter Tibor Nagy, eds. *The Numerus Clausus in Hungary: Studies on the First Anti-Jewish Law and Academic Anti-Semitism in Modern Central Europe.* Budapest: Pasts Inc. Centre for Historical Research, 2012.

Katzburg, Nathaniel. *Hungary and the Jews: Policy and Legislation, 1920–1943.* Ramat-Gan: Bar-Ilan University Press, 1981.

Katzenstein, Peter. *Disjoined Partners: Austria and Germany since 1815.* Berkeley: University of California Press, 1976.

Kelly, Alfred, ed. *The German Worker: Working-Class Autobiographies from the Age of Industrialization.* Translated and introduced by Alfred Kelly. Berkeley: University of California Press, 1987.

Kende, Tamas. "The Language of Blood Libels in Central and East European History." CEU History Department Working Papers Series, 2: *Pride and Prejudice: National Stereotypes in 19th and 20th Century Europe East to West* (1995): 91–104.

Kenez, Peter. *Hungary from the Nazis to the Soviets: The Establishment of the Communist Regime in Hungary, 1944–1948*. Cambridge: Cambridge University Press, 2006.

Kershaw, Ian. "Ideology, Propaganda and the Rise of the Nazi Party." In Peter D. Stachura, ed., *The Nazi Machtergreifung*, 162–81. London: George Allen & Unwin, 1983.

Király, Béla and Nándor F. Dreisziger, eds. *East Central European Society in World War I*. Boulder, CO: Social Science Monographs, 1985.

Király, Béla and Stephen Fischer-Galati, eds. *Essays on War and Society in East Central Europe*. Boulder, CO: East European Monographs, 1987.

Király, Béla and Ignác Romsics, eds. *Geopolitics in the Danube Region: Hungarian Reconciliation Efforts, 1848–1998*. Budapest: Central European University Press, 1999.

Király, Béla and László Veszprémy, eds. *Trianon and East Central Europe: Antecedents and Repercussions*. Boulder, CO: Social Science Monographs, 1995.

Kirchheimer, Otto. *Political Justice: The Use of Legal Procedure for Political Ends*. Princeton, NJ: Princeton University Press, 1961.

Kirschenbaum, Lisa. "Gender, Memory, and National Myths: Ol'ga Berggol'ts and the Siege of Leningrad." *Nationalities Papers* 28/3 (Sept. 2000): 551–64.

Klein-Pejšová, Rebekah. "Between Refugees and the State: Hungarian Jewry and the Wartime Refugee Crisis in Austria-Hungary." In Peter Gatrell and Liubov Zhvanko, eds., *Europe on the Move: Refugees in the Era of the Great War*, 156–76. Oxford: Oxford University Press, 2017.

"The Budapest Jewish Community's Galician October." In Marsha L. Rozenblit and Jonathan Karp, eds.,*World War I and the Jews: Conflict and Transformation in Europe, the Middle East, and America*, 112–30. New York: Berghahn Books, 2017.

Klimó, Árpád von. *Nation, Konfession, Geschichte: Zur nationalen Geschichtskultur Ungarns im europäischen Kontext*. Munich: Oldenbourg, 2003.

Klimó, Árpád von and Jurgen Danyel. "Die ungarische Nachkriegsgeschichtsschreibung: neuere Trends und Tendenzen." *Zeitschrift für Geschichtswissenschaft* 47/10 (1999): 869–73.

Koch, H. W. *In the Name of the Volk: Political Justice in Hitler's Germany*. New York: St. Martin's Press, 1989.

Volksgerichtshof: Politische Justiz im 3. Reich. Munich: Universitas, 1988.

Koenker, Diane P., William G. Rosenberg, and Ronald Grigor Suny, eds. *Party, State and Society in the Russian Civil War: Explorations in Social History*. Bloomington: Indiana University Press, 1989.

Kolb, Eberhard, ed. *Vom Kaiserreich zur Weimarer Republik*. Cologne: Kiepenhauer & Witsch, 1972.

Komlos, John. "Austria and European Economic Development: What Has Been Learned?" In Charles W. Ingrao, ed., *State and Society in Early Modern Austria*, 215–28. West Lafayette, IN: Purdue University Press, 1994.

Kormendy, Lajos, Istvan Majoros, Laszlo Miklosi, and Paul Gradvohl, "Identité nationale et histoire en Hongrie: L'impact des mutations politiques récentes." *Historiens et Geographes* 90/366 (1999): 219–28.

Kontler, László. *A History of Hungary: Millennium in Central Europe.* London: Palgrave Macmillan, 2002.

Konrád, George [György]. *The Melancholy of Rebirth: Essays from Post-Communist Central Europe, 1989–1994.* New York: Harcourt Brace, 1995.

Kopelew, Lew and Gerd Koenen, eds. *Deutschland und die Russische Revolution, 1917–1924.* Munich: Wilhelm Fink Verlag, 1998.

Kosa, John. "Hungarian Society in the Time of the Regency (1920–1944)." *Journal of Central European Affairs* 16 (1956/7): 253–65.

Kovács, Mária M. "Ambiguities of Emancipation: Women and the Ethnic Question in Hungary." *Women's History Review* 5/4 (1996): 487–95.

Liberal Professions and Illiberal Politics: Hungary from the Habsburgs to the Holocaust. New York and Washington, DC: Woodrow Wilson Center Press and Oxford University Press, 1994.

"The Politics of Emancipation in Hungary." CEU History Department Working Papers no. 1: *Women in History – Women's History: Central and Eastern European Perspectives* (1994): 81–8.

Kovacs-Bertrand, Aniko. *Der ungarische Revisionismus nach dem Ersten Weltkrieg: Der publizistische Kampf gegen den Friedensvertrag von Trianon (1918–1931).* Munich: Oldenbourg, 1997.

Kovrig, Béla. *Hungarian Social Policies 1920–1945.* New York: Committee for Culture and Education of the Hungarian National Council, 1954.

Kovrig, Bennett. *Communism in Hungary: From Kun to Kádár.* Stanford, CA: Hoover Institution Press, 1979.

Kritzer, Peter. *Die bayerische Sozialdemokratie und die bayerische Politik in den Jahren 1918 bis 1923.* Munich: Dissertationsdruck-Schön, 1969.

Kučera, Rudolf. *Rationed Life: Science, Everyday Life, and Working-Class Politics in the Bohemian Lands, 1914–1918.* New York: Berghahn Books, 2016.

Kurimay, Anita. "Interrogating the Historical Revisionism of the Hungarian Right: The Queer Case of Cécile Tormay." *East European Politics and Societies* 30/1 (Feb. 2016): 10–33.

Lamm, Hans, ed. *Von Juden in München: Ein Gedenkbuch.* Munich: Ner-Tamid-Verlag, 1958.

Landauer, Carl. "The Bavarian Problem in the Weimar Republic: Part I." *Journal of Modern History* 16/2 (June 1944): 93–115.

"The Bavarian Problem in the Weimar Republic: Part II." *Journal of Modern History* 16/3 (Sept. 1944): 205–23.

Lapp, Benjamin. *Revolution from the Right: Politics, Class, and the Rise of Nazism in Saxony, 1919–1933* Studies in Central European Histories. Atlantic Highlands, NJ: Humanities Press International, 1997.

Large, David Clay. "The Politics of Law and Order: A History of the Bavarian Einwohnerwehr, 1918–1921." *Transactions of the American Philosophical Society* 70/2 (1980).

Where Ghosts Walked: Munich's Road to the Third Reich. New York: W. W. Norton, 1997.

Laszlo, Leslie. "Hungary: From Cooperation to Resistance, 1919–1945." In Richard J. Wolff and Jörg K. Hoensch, eds., *Catholics, the State, and the European Radical Right, 1919–1945,* 119–36. Boulder, CO: Social Science Monographs, 1987.

Lazaroms, Ilse Josepha. "Humanitarian Encounters: Charity and Gender in Post–World War I Jewish Budapest." *Jewish History* 33 (2020): 115–32.

Lees, Andrew. *Cities, Sin and Social Reform in Imperial Germany.* Ann Arbor: University of Michigan Press, 2002.

Lehnert, Detlef. "Propaganda des Buergerkrieges? Politische Feindbilder in der Novemberrevolution als mentale Destabilisierung de Weimarer Republik." In Detlef Lehnert and Klaus Megerle, eds., *Politische Teilkulturen zwischen Integration und Polarisierung. Zur politische Kultur in der Weimarer Republik,* 61–101. Wiesbaden: VS Verlag für Sozialwissenschaften, 1990.

Leidinger, Hannes and Verena Moritz. *Gefangenschaft, Revolution, Heimkehr: Die Bedeutung der Kriegsgefangenenproblematik für die Geschichte des Kommunismus in Mittel- und Osteuropa 1917–1920.* Vienna: Böhlau Verlag, 2003.

Lendvai, Paul. *The Hungarians: A Thousand Years of Victory in Defeat.* Translated by Ann Major. Princeton, NJ: Princeton University Press, 2003.

Lerner, Paul. *Hysterical Men: War, Psychiatry, and the Politics of Trauma in Germany, 1890–1930.* Ithaca, NY: Cornell University Press, 2003.

Lerner, Paul and Mark S. Micale. "Trauma, Psychiatry and History: A Conceptual and Historigraphical Introduction." In *Traumatic Pasts: History, Psychiatry and Trauma in the Modern Age, 1870–1930,*1–27. Cambridge: Cambridge University Press, 2001.

Levitt, Cyril. "The Prosecution of Antisemites by the Courts in the Weimar Republic: Was Justice Served?" *Leo Baeck Institute Yearbook* 36 (1991): 151–67.

Lidtke, Vernon L. *The Outlawed Party; Social Democracy in Germany, 1878–1890.* Princeton, NJ: Princeton University Press, 1966.

Liedtke, Rainer and David Rechter, eds. *Towards Normality? Acculturation and Modern German Jewry.* London: Leo Baeck Institute Mohr Siebeck, 2003.

Liulevicius, Vejas Gabriel. *War Land on the Eastern Front: Culture, National Identity, and German Occupation in World War I.* Cambridge: Cambridge University Press, 2000.

Loftus, Elizabeth F., Mahzarin R. Banaji, and Rachel A. Foster. "Who Remembers What? Gender Differences in Memory." *Michigan Quarterly Review* 26/1 (1987): 64–85.

Low, Alfred D. "Austria between East and West: Budapest and Berlin, 1918–1919." *Austrian History Yearbook* 4–5 (1968–9): 44–62.

"The First Austrian Republic and Soviet Hungary." *Journal of Central European Affairs* 20 (1960): 174–203.

"The Soviet Hungarian Republic and the Paris Peace Conference." *Transactions of the American Philosophical Society* 53/10 (1963): 1–91.

Lukacs, John. *Budapest 1900: A Historical Portrait of a City and Its Culture.* New York: Grove Weidenfeld, 1988.

McCagg, William O., Jr. "Hungary's 'Feudalized' Bourgeoisie." *Journal of Modern History* 44/1 (March 1972): 65–78.

"Jewish Conversion in Hungary in Modern Times." In Todd M. Endelman, ed., *Jewish Apostasy in the Modern World,* 142–64. New York: Holmes and Meier, 1987.

Jewish Nobles and Geniuses in Modern Hungary. New York: Columbia University Press, 1971.

"Jews in Revolutions: The Hungarian Experience." *Journal of Social History* 6/1 (Fall 1972): 78–105.

Mack, Karlheinz, ed. *Revolutionen in Ostmitteleuropa 1789–1989: Schwerpunkt Ungarn*. Munich: Oldenbourg, 1995.

Maderthaner, Wolfgang. *Die Anarchie der Vorstadt: Das andere Wien um 1900*. Frankfurt: Campus Verlag, 1999.

Marin, Irina. *Peasant Violence and Antisemitism in Early Twentieth-Century Eastern Europe*. Cham, Switzerland: Palgrave Macmillan, 2018.

Mayer, Arno. *Dynamics of Counterrevolution in Europe, 1870–1956: An Analytic Framework*. New York: Harper & Row, 1971.

Politics and Diplomacy of Peacemaking: Containment and Counterrevolution at Versailles, 1918–1919. New York: Knopf, 1967.

McNeal, Robert H. "Women in the Russian Radical Movement." *Journal of Social History* 5/2 (Winter 1971–2): 143–63.

Mehringer, Hartmut, Anton Großmann, and Klaus Schönhoven, *Die Parteien KPD, SPD, BVP in Verfolgung und Widerstand*. Vol. 5 of *Bayern in der NS-Zeit*, edited by Martin Brozsat and Hartmut Mehringer. Munich: Oldenbourg, 1983.

Melin, Gerhard. "'Red' and 'Catholic' Social Integration and Exclusion: Municipal Welfare Policy and Social Reality in Vienna (1918–1938)." *Central European University Working Paper Series 3: Urban Space and Identity in the European City 1890–1930s* (1995): 55–72.

Melinz, Gerhard and Susan Zimmermann, eds. *Wien, Prag, Budapest: Blütezeit der Habsburgermetropolen. Urbanisierung, Kommunalpolitik, gesellschaftliche Konflikte, 1867–1918*. Vienna: Promedia, 1996.

Menczer, Bela. "Bela Kun and the Hungarian Revolution of 1919." *History Today* 19 (1969): 299–309.

"The Habsburg Restoration: Hungary in 1921." *History Today* 22 (1972): 128–35.

Mérei, Gyula. *A Magyar Októberi Forradalom és polgári pártok*. Budapest, Akadémiai Kiadó, 1969.

Merriman, John. *Massacre: The Life and Death of the Paris Commune*. New York: Basic Books, 2014.

Meyer, Michael A., ed. *German-Jewish History in Modern Times*. Vol. 3: *Integration in Dispute, 1871–1918*; Vol. 4: *Renewal and Destruction, 1918–1945*. New York: Columbia University Press, 1997–8.

Miller, Michael L. "From White Terror to Red Vienna: Hungarian Jewish Students in Interwar Austria." In Frank Stern and Barbara Eichinger, eds. *Wien und die jüdische Erfahrung 1900–1938: Akkulturation, Antisemitismus, Zionismus*,307–24. Vienna: Böhlau, 2009.

Mitchell, Alan F. *Revolution in Bavaria, 1918–1919: The Eisner Regime and the Soviet Republic*. Princeton, NJ: Princeton University Press, 1965.

Mitchell, B. R. ed. *International Historical Statistics: Europe, 1750–2005*. 6th edition. New York: Palgrave Macmillan, 2007.

Möckl, Karl. *Die Prinzregentenzeit: Gesellschaft und Politik während der Ära des Prinzregenten Luitpold im Bayern*. Munich: Oldenbourg, 1972.

Mócsy, István. *The Effects of World War I. The Uprooted: Hungarian Refugees and their Impact on Hungary's Domestic Politics, 1918–1921.* Boulder, CO: Brooklyn College Press, 1983.

Moeller, Robert G. "Dimensions of Social Conflict in the Great War: A View from the Countryside." *Central European History* 14/2 (1981): 142–68.

Molnár, Miklós. *A Concise History of Hungary.* Translated by Anna Magyar. Cambridge: Cambridge University Press, 2001.

    From Béla Kun to János Kádár: Seventy Years of Hungarian Communism. Translated by Arnold J. Pomerans. New York: Berg Publishers, 1990.

Mommsen, Wolfgang. "The German Revolution, 1918–1920." In Richard Bessel and E. J. Feuchtwanger, eds., *Social Change and Political Development in Weimar Germany,* 21–54. London: Croom Helm, 1981.

Moore, Barrington, Jr. *Injustice: The Social Bases of Obedience and Revolt.* New York: M. E. Sharpe, 1978.

Morenz, Ludwig, ed. *Revolution und Räteherrschaft in München: Aus der Stadtchronik 1918/1919.* Munich: Albert Langen – Georg Mueller Verlag, 1968.

Mosse, George. *Fallen Soldiers: Reshaping the Memory of the World Wars.* New York: Oxford University Press, 1990.

Mosse, Werner E., ed. *Deutsches Judentum in Krieg und Revolution, 1916–1923: Ein Sammelband.* Tübingen: J. C. B. Mohr, 1971.

Müller, Ingo. *Hitler's Justice: The Courts of the Third Reich.* Translated by Deborah Lucas Schneider. Cambridge, MA: Harvard University Press, 1991.

Müller, Klaus-Jürgen and Eckhardt Opitz, eds. *Miltär und Militärismus in der Weimarer Republik.* Düsseldorf: Droste, 1978.

Müller, Wolfgang. *"Ein Ewig Raetsel bleiben will Ich": Wittelsbacher Schicksale, Ludwig II., Otto I. und Sisi.* Munich: Koehler & Amelang, 1999.

Nadkarni, Maya. "The Death of Socialism and the Afterlife of its Monuments: Making and Marketing the Past in Budapest's Statue Park Museum." In Katharine Hodgkin and Susannah Radstone, eds., *Contested Pasts: The Politics of Memory,* 193–207. New York: Routledge, 2003.

Nagy, Zsolt. *Great Expectations and Interwar Realities: Cultural Diplomacy in Horthy's Hungary.* Budapest: Central European University Press, 2017.

Nagy, Zsuzsa L. "Budapest and the Revolutions of 1918 and 1919." In Chris Wrigley, ed., *Challenges of Labour: Central and Western Europe, 1917–1920,* 72–86. London: Routledge, 1993.

    Forradalom és ellenforradalom a Dunántúlon, 1919. Budapest: Kossuth Kiadó, 1961.

    "Fővárosi választások a két háború között," *Historia* 5/6 (1985): 56–8.

    The Liberal Opposition in Hungary, 1919–1945. Budapest: Adamémiai Kiadó, 1983.

    "Transformations in the City Politics of Budapest: 1873–1941." In Thomas Bender and Carl E. Schorske, eds.,*Budapest and New York: Studies in Metropolitan Transformation, 1870–1930,* 35–55. New York: Russell Sage Foundation, 1994.

Nagy-Talavera, Nicholas M. *The Green Shirts and Others: A History of Fascism in Hungary and Romania.* Iaşi: Center for Romanian Studies, 2001.

Nemes, Dezső. *Az ellenforradalom hatalomrajutása és rémuralma Magyarországon, 1919–1921.* Budapest: Szikra, 1953.

    Az ellenforradalom története Magyarországon, 1919–1921. Budapest: Akadémiai Kiadó, 1962.

Nemes, Robert. *The Once and Future Budapest*. DeKalb, IL: Northern Illinois University Press, 2005.

Neubauer, Helmut. *München und Moskau 1918/1919: Zur Geschichte der Rätebewegung in Bayern*. Munich: Isar Verlag, 1958.

Niewyk, Donald L. "Jews and the Courts in Weimar Germany." *Jewish Social Studies* 37 (1975): 99–113.

Noever, Peter. *Mihály Biró: Pathos in Red*. MAK Studies 19 Nürnberg: Verlag für Moderne Kunst, 2011.

Nusser, Horst. "Militärischer Druck auf die Landesregierung Johannes Hoffmannvom Mai 1919 bis zum Kapputsch." *Zeitschrift für bayerische Landesgeschichte* 33/2 (1970): 818–50.

Oişteanu, Andrei. *Inventing the Jew: Antisemitic Stereotypes in Romanian and Other Central East-European Cultures*. Lincoln: University of Nebraska Press, 2009.

Ophir, Baruch and Falk Wiesemann, eds. *Die jüdischen Gemeinden in Bayern, 1918–1945. Geschichte und Zerstörung*. Munich: Oldenbourg, 1979.

Ormos, Mária and Béla Király, eds. *Hungary: Governments and Politics, 1848–2000*. Translated by Nóra Arató. Boulder, CO: Social Science Monographs, 2001.

Ostler, Fritz. *Der deutsche Rechtsanwalt: Das Werden des Standes seit der Reichsgründung*. Karlsruhe: C. F. Müller, 1963.

Paál, Vince. *A politika és a publicisztika vonzásában: Gratz Gusztáv pályafutása*. Budapest: Wolters Kluwer, 2018.

Paces, Cynthia. "*Gender and the Battle for Prague's Old Town Square*." In Elena Gapova, ed., *Gendernye istorii Vostochnoi Evropy* [Gendered (hi)stories from Eastern Europe], 124–31. Minsk: European Humanities University Press, 2002.

Pach, Zsigmond Pál. "Az ellenforradalmi történelemszemlélet kialakulása Szekfű Gyula Három nemzedékében." *Történelmi Szemle* 5 (1962): 387–425.

Pastor, Peter. *Hungary between Wilson and Lenin: The Hungarian Revolution of 1918–1919 and the Big Three*. Boulder, CO: East European Monographs, 1976.

"Recent Hungarian Publications on Bela Kun." *Slavic Review* 48/1 (Spring 1989): 89–96.

, ed. *Revolutions and Interventions in Hungary and its Neighbor States, 1918–1919*. Boulder, CO: Social Science Monographs, 1988.

"The Vix Mission in Hungary, 1918–1919: A Re-examination." *Slavic Review* 29/3 (1970): 481–98.

Pásztor, Mihály. *A Fehérterror néhány jelensége. Pest megye 1919–1920*. Budapest: Pest Megyei Levéltár, 1985.

Perry, Heather R. *Recycling the Disabled: Army, Medicine, and Modernity in WWI Germany*. Manchester: Manchester University Press, 2014.

Pető, Andrea. "'As He Saw Her': Gender Politics in Secret Party Reports in Hungary during the 1950s." *CEU History Department Working Paper Series* 1: *Women in History – Women's History: Central and Eastern European Perspectives* (1994): 107–17.

"As the Storm Approached. The Last Years of the Hungarian Women's Societies before the Stalinist Takeover." *CEU History Department Yearbook* (1994–5): 181–206.

"Constructions of Emotions in the Hungarian Underground Communist Movement." Institut für die Wissenschaften vom Menschen Junior Fellows Conferences, *Ideas in Transit* 5 (1998): 108–19.

Pethő, T. "Contradictory Trends in Policies of the Horthy Era." *New Hungarian Quarterly* 4/12 (1963): 115–31.

Peukert, Detlev J.K. *The Weimar Republic: The Crisis of Classical Modernity.* Translated by Richard Deveson. New York: Hill and Wang, 1989.

Phelps, Reginald. "'Before Hitler Came': Thule Society and Germanen Orden." *Journal of Modern History* 35/3 (1963): 245–61.

Pohl, Karl Heinrich. *Die Münchener Arbeiterbewegung: Sozialdemokratische Partei, Freie Gewerkschaften, Staat und Gesellschaft in München, 1890–1914.* Munich: K. G. Saur, 1992.

"Power in the City: Liberalism and Local Politics in Dresden and Munich." In James Retallack, ed., *Saxony in German History: Culture, Society and Politics, 1830–1933*, 289–308. Ann Arbor: University of Michigan Press, 2000.

Pölöskei, Ferenc. *Hungary after Two Revolutions (1919–1922).* Budapest: Akadémiai Kiadó, 1980.

A rejtélyes Tisza-gyilkosság. Budapest: Helikon, 1988.

"Választójog, parlamentarizmus 1919 után." *História* 5/6 (1985): 54–6.

Pommerin, Reiner. "Die Ausweisungen von "Ostjuden" aus Bayern 1923: Ein Beitrag zum Krisenjahr der Weimarer Republik." *Vierteljahrshefte für Zeitgeschichte* 34 (1986): 311–40.

Prinz, Friedrich and Marita Krauss, eds. *München – Musenstadt mit Hinterhöfen: Die Prinzregentenzeit, 1886–1912.* Munich: C. H. Beck, 1988.

Puhle, Hans-Jürgen and Hans-Ulrich Wehler, eds. *Preußen im Rückblick.* Göttingen: Vandenhoeck & Ruprecht, 1980.

Pulzer, Peter. *The Rise of Political Anti-Semitism in Germany and Austria.* Revised edition. Cambridge, MA: Harvard University Press, 1988.

"Why Was There a Jewish Question in Imperial Germany?" *Leo Baeck Institute Yearbook* 25 (1980): 133–46.

Rachamimov, Iris. *POWs and the Great War: Captivity on the Eastern Front.* The Legacy of the Great War. Oxford: Berg, 2002.

Ránki, György. "A Clerk-misszió történetéhez." *Történelmi Szemle* 10/2 (1967): 156–87.

"Gondolatok az ellenforradalmi rendszer társadalmi bázisának kérdésehez az 1920-as évek elején." *Történelmi Szemle* 3–4 (1962): 353–69.

Ránki, György and Attila Pók, eds. *Hungary and European Civilization.* Budapest: Adamémiai Kiadó, 1989.

Rauchensteiner, Manfried. *Der Tod des Doppeladlers: Österreich-Ungarn und der Erste Weltkrieg.* Graz: Styria Verlag, 1993.

Rechter, David. "Galicia in Vienna: Jewish Refugees in the First World War." *Austrian History Yearbook* 28 (1997): 113–30.

The Jews of Vienna and the First World War. London: Littman Library of Jewish Civilization, 2001.

Reich, Jacob. "Eine Episode aus der Geschichte der Ostjuden Münchens." In Hans Lamm, ed., *Vergangene Tage: Jüdische Kultur in München*, 400–4 (Munich: Langen Müller, 1982).

Reichardt, Sven. *Faschistische Kampfbünde: Gewalt und Gemeinschaft im italienischen Squadrismus und in der deutschen SA*. Cologne: Böhlau-Verlag, 2009.

"Formen faschistischer Gewalt. Faschistische Kampfbuende in Italien und Deutschland nach dem Ersten Weltkrieg. Eine typologische Deutung ihrer Gewaltpropaganda während der Bewegungsphase des Faschismus." *Sociologus* 51/1–2 (2001): 49–88.

Reinke, Herbert. "'Armed as if for a War': The State, the Military and the Professionalisation of the Prussian Police in Imperial Germany." In Clive Emsley and Barbara Weinberger, eds., *Policing Western Europe: Politics, Professionalism, and Public Order, 1850–1940*, 55–73. Westport, CN: Greenwood Press, 1991.

Rév, Erika. *A Népbiztosok Pere*. Budapest: Kossuth Kiadó, 1969.

Richarz, Monika. "Demographic Developments." In Michael A. Meyer, ed., *German-Jewish History in Modern Times*. Vol. 3: *Integration in Dispute, 1871–1918*, 7–34. New York: Columbia University Press, 1997.

Ritter, Gerhard A. "Worker's Culture in Imperial Germany: Problems and Points of Departure for Research." Special issue, *Journal of Contemporary History* 13/2. (April 1978): 165–89.

Rogger, Hans and Eugen Weber, eds. *The European Right: A Historical Profile*. Berkley, CA: University of California Press, 1965.

Romsics, Ignác. *The Dismantling of Historic Hungary: The Peace Treaty of Trianon, 1920*. Translated by Mario D. Fenyo. Boulder, CO: Social Science Monographs, 2002.

Ellenforradalom és konszolidació: A Horthy-rendszer elsö tíz eve. Budapest: Gondolat, 1982.

István Bethlen: A Great Conservative Statesman of Hungary, 1874–1946. Translated by Mario D. Fenyo. Boulder, CO: East European Monographs, 1995.

"The Hungarian Peasantry and the Revolutions of 1918–19." In Chris Wrigley, ed., *Challenges of Labour: Central and Western Europe, 1917–1920*, 196–214. London: Routledge, 1993.

"Nation and State in Modern Hungarian History." *Hungarian Quarterly* 42/164 (2001): 37–60.

"Nemzeti traumánk: Trianon." *Magyar Tudomány* 3 (1996): 272–81.

"The Peasantry and the Age of Revolutions: Hungary 1918–1919." *Acta Historica Academiae Scientiarum Hungaricae* 35/ 1–4 (1989): 113–33.

Roos, Walter. *Die Rote Armee der Bayerischen Räterepublik in München 1919*. Heidelberg: Verlag Rhein-Neckar Zeitung, 1998.

Rozenblit, Marsha L. "The Jews of the Dual Monarchy." *Austrian History Yearbook* 23 (1992): 160–80.

Reconstructing a National Identity: The Jews of Habsburg Austria during World War I. New York: Oxford University Press, 2001.

Rürup, Reinhard. *Emanzipation und Antisemitismus: Studien zur 'Judenfrage' der bürgerlichen Gesellschaft*. Göttingen: Vandenhoeck & Ruprecht, 1975.

"'Parvenu Polis' and 'Human Workshop': Reflections on the History of the City of Berlin." *German History* 6/3 (1988): 233–49.

Probleme der Revolution in Deutschland 1918/19. Wiesbaden: Franz Steiner Verlag, 1968.

Sabrow, Martin. *Die verdrängte Verschwörung. Der Rathenau-Mord und die deutsche Gegenrevolution.* Frankfurt: Fischer Taschenbuch-Verlag, 1999.

Sackett, Robert Eben. *Popular Entertainment, Class, and Politics in Munich, 1900–1923.* Cambridge, MA: Harvard University Press, 1982.

Sakmyster, Thomas. *A Communist Odyssey: The Life of József Pogány/John Pepper.* Budapest: Central European University Press, 2012.

Hungary's Admiral on Horseback: Miklós Horthy, 1918–1944. Boulder, CO: East European Monographs, 1994.

Sammartino, Annemarie H. *The Impossible Border: Germany and the East, 1914–1922.* Ithaca, NY: Cornell University Press, 2010.

Sármány-Parsons, Ilona. "Ungarns Millenniumsjahr 1896." In Emil Brix and Hannes Stekl, eds., *Der Kampf um das Gedächtnis: Öffentliche Gedenktage in Mitteleuropa,* 273–91. Vienna: Böhlau, 1997.

Schachter, Daniel L., ed. *Memory Distortion: How Minds, Brains, and Societies Reconstruct the Past.* Cambridge, MA: Harvard University Press, 1995.

Scheck, Raffael. *Mothers of the Nation: Right-Wing Women in Weimar Germany.* New York: Berg Publishers, 2003.

Schmidt, Ernst and Franz Bauer. "Die bayerischen Volksgerichte 1918–1924. Das Problem ihrer Vereinbarkeit mit der Weimarer Verfassung." *Zeitschrift fuer Bayerische Landesgeschichte* 48 (1985): 449–78.

Schmolze, Gerhard. "'Ganz neue Menschen werden kommen': Vor 75 Jahren wurde Gustav Landauer in Muenchen erschossen." *Unser Bayern* 43/5 (1994): 35–6.

Schmolze, Gerhard, ed. *Revolution und Räterepublik in München 1918/19 in Augenzeugenberichten.* Foreword by Eberhard Kolb. Düsseldorf: Karl Rauch Verlag, 1969.

Schneider, Ludwig M. *Die populäre Kritik an Staat und Gesellschaft in München, 1886–1914: Ein Beitrag zur Vorgeschichte der Münchner Revolution von 1918/19.* Munich: Neue Schriftenreihe des Stadtarchivs München, 1975.

Schorske, Carl E. *Fin-de-Siècle Vienna: Politics and Culture.* New York: Vintage, 1981. First published 1961.

German Social Democracy, 1905–1917: The Development of the Great Schism. Cambridge, MA: Harvard University Press, 1983.

Schulze, Hagen. *Weimar Deutschland, 1917–1933.* Berlin: Siedler Verlag, 1994.

Schumann, Dirk. *Politische Gewalt in der Weimarer Republik: Kampf um die Strasse und Furcht von dem Bürgerkrieg.* Essen: Klartext Verlag, 2001.

Schuster, Frank M. *Zwischen allen Fronten: Osteuropäische Juden während des Ersten Weltkriegs (1914–1919).* Cologne: Böhlau, 2004.

Schwarze, Johannes. *Die bayerische Polizei und ihre historische Funktion bei der Aufrechterhaltung der öffentlichen Sicherheit in Bayern von 1919–1933.* Munich: Kommissionsbuchhandlung Wölfle, 1977.

Schwend, Karl. *Bayern zwischen Monarchie und Diktatur: Beiträge zur Bayeriscen Frage in der Zeit von 1918 bis 1933.* Munich: Richard Pflaum Verlag, 1954.

Scott, Joan Wallach. *Gender and the Politics of History.* Revised edition. New York: Columbia University Press, 1999.

Seipp, Adam R. *The Ordeal of Peace: Demobilization and the Urban Experience in Britain and Germany, 1917–1921.* Farnham: Ashgate Publishing, 2009.

Seligmann, Michael. *Aufstand der Räte: Die erste bayerische Räterepublik vom 7. April 1919*. Grafenau: Trotzdem Verlag, 1989.

Seton-Watson, Hugh. *Eastern Europe between the Wars, 1918–1941*. Hamden, CT: Archon Books, 1962.

Sharp, Alan. *The Versailles Settlement: Peacemaking in Paris, 1919*. The Making of the 20th Century. New York: St. Martin's Press, 1991.

Siklós, András. *Revolution in Hungary and the Dissolution of the Multinational State, 1918*. Budapest: Akadémiai Kiadó, 1988.

Ungarn 1918/1919. Ereignisse/Bilder/Dokumente. Budapest: Corvina, 1979.

Silagi, Denis. "Die Juden in Ungarn in der Zwischenkriegszeit (1919–1939)." *Ungarn-Jahrbuch* 5 (1973): 198–214.

Silber, Michael K. "The Historical Experience of German Jewry and its Impact on Haskalah and Reform in Hungary." In Jacob Katz, ed., *Toward Modernity: The European Jewish Model*, 107–57. New Brunswick, NJ: Transaction Books, 1987.

Sinkó, Katalin. "Zur Entstehung der staatlichen und nationalen Feiertage in Ungarn, 1850–1991." In Emil Brix and Hannes Stekl, eds., *Der Kampf um das Gedächtnis: Öffentliche Gedenktage in Mitteleuropa*, 251–71. Vienna: Böhlau, 1997.

Sked, Alan. *The Decline and Fall of the Habsburg Empire, 1815–1918*. London: Longman, 1989.

Slezkine, Yuri. *The Jewish Century*. Princeton, NJ: Princeton University Press, 2004.

Smith, Helmut Walser. *The Butcher's Tale: Murder and Anti-Semitism in a German Town*. New York: Norton, 2003.

The Continuities of German History: Nation, Religion, and Race across the Long Nineteenth Century. New York: Cambridge University Press, 2008.

German Nationalism and Religious Conflict: Culture, Ideology, Politics, 1870–1914. Princeton, NJ: Princeton University Press, 1995.

Sneeringer, Julia. *Winning Women's Votes: Propaganda and Politics in Weimar Germany*. Chapel Hill, NC: University of North Carolina Press, 2002.

Sorkin, David. "Emancipation and Assimilation: Two Concepts and their Application to German-Jewish History." *Leo Baeck Institute Yearbook* 35 (1990): 17–33.

Sperber, Jonathan. *The Kaiser's Voters: Electors and Elections In Imperial Germany*. Cambridge: Cambridge University Press, 1997.

Popular Catholicism in Nineteenth-Century Germany. Princeton, NJ: Princeton University Press, 1984.

Spindler, Max, ed. *Bayerische Geschichte im 19. und 20. Jahrhundert, 1800–1970*. Vol. 1: *Staat und Politik*. Vol. 2: *Innere Entwicklung, Land, Gesellschaft, Wirtschaft, Kirche, geistiges Leben*. Munich: C. H. Beck, 1978.

Handbook der bayerischen Geschichte. 4 vols. Munich: C.H. Beck, 1967–75.

Steinmetz, Willibald, ed. *Private Law and Social Inequality in the Industrial Age: Comparing Legal Cultures in Britain, France, Germany and the United States*. London: Oxford University Press for the German Historical Institute, 2000.

Stern, Fritz. "Death in Weimar." *Yale Review* 87/4 (Oct. 1999): 1–20.

The Politics of Cultural Despair. Berkeley: University of California Press, 1961.

Sternsdorf-Hauck, Christiane. *Brotmarken und rote Fahnen: Frauen in der bayrischen Revolution und Räterepublik 1918/1919*. Frankfurt/Main: isp-Verlag, 1989.

Steward, Jill. "'Gruss aus Wien': Urban Tourism in Austria-Hungary before the First World War." In Malcolm Gee, Tim Kirk, and Jill Steward, eds., *The City in Central*

Europe: Culture and Society from 1800 to the Present, 123–44. Brookfield, VT: Ashgate, 1999.

Stockdale, Melissa K. "My Death for the Motherland is Happiness": Women, Patriotism, and Soldiering in Russia's Great War, 1914–1917." *American Historical Review* 109/1 (February 2004): 78–116.

Stolleis, Michael and Dieter Simon, eds. *Rechtsgeschichte im Nationalsozialismus: Beiträge zur Geschichte einer Disziplin*. Tübingen: J. C. B. Mohr, 1989.

Streubel, Christiane. *Radikale Nationalistinnen: Agitation und Programmatik rechter Frauen in der Weimarer Republik*. Frankfurt: Campus Verlag, 2006.

Strong, George V. *Seedtime for Fascism: The Disintegration of Austrian Political Culture, 1867–1918*. New York: M. E. Sharpe, 1998.

Sugar, Peter F. , Péter Hanák, and Tibor Frank, eds. *A History of Hungary*. Bloomington: Indiana University Press, 1990.

Swett, Pamela. *Neighbors and Enemies: The Culture of Radicalism in Berlin, 1929–1933*. New York: Cambridge University Press, 2004. "Political Violence, *Gesinnung*, and the Courts in Late Weimar Berlin." In Mark Roseman, Frank Biess, and Hanna Schissler, eds., *Conflict, Catastrophe and Continuity: Essays on Modern German History*, 60–79. New York: Berghahn Books, 2007.

Sweet, William. "The Volksgerichtshof." *Journal of Modern History* 46/2 (June 1974): 314–29.

Szabó, Ágnes. "A Kommunisták Magyarországi Pártja az ellenforradalmi rendszer társadalmi viszonyairól (1919–1933)." *Történelmi Szemle* 5/3–4 (1962): 370–85.

Szalai, Erzsébet. "Refeudalization," *Corvinus Journal of Sociology and Social Policy* 8/2 (2017): 3–24.

Szapor, Judith. *Hungarian Women's Activism in the Wake of the First World War: From Rights to Revanche*. London: Bloomsbury, 2017.

Szapor, Judith and Agatha Schwartz, eds. "Gender and Nation." Special issue, *Hungarian Studies Review* 41/1–2 (Spring–Fall 2014).

Szarka, Laszlo. "Alternativen der ungarischen Nationalitaetenpolitik 1918–1920." *Acta historica Academiae Scientiarum Hungaricae* 35/1–4 (1989): 135–48.

Szilassy, Sándor. *Revolutionary Hungary, 1918–1921*. Astor Park, FL: University of Tampa and the Danubian Press, 1971.

Tasca, Angelo. *The Rise of Italian Fascism, 1918–1922*. Translated by Peter and Dorothy Waite. New York: H. Fertig, 1966.

Teter, Magda. *Blood Libel: On the Trail of an Antisemitic Myth*. Cambridge, MA: Harvard University Press, 2020.

Tezla, Albert. *Hungarian Authors: A Bibliographical Handbook*. Cambridge, MA: Belknap Press of Harvard University Press, 1970.

Theweleit, Klaus. *Männerphantasien*. Vol. 1: *Frauen, Fluten, Körper, Geschichte*. Vol. 2: *Männerkörper – zur Psychoanalyse des weißen Terrors*. Paperback edition with new epilogue by the author. Munich: Piper, 2000. First published 1977–8 by Verlag Roter Stern/Stroemfeld.

Thom, Deborah. *Nice Girls and Rude Girls: Women Workers in World War I*. London: I. B. Taurus, 1998.

Thoss, Bruno. *Der Ludendorff-Kreis 1919–1923*. Munich: Kommissionsbuchhandlung R. Woelfle, 1978.

Tilkovszky, L. *Pál Teleki (1879–1941), A Biographical Sketch*. Translated by D. Székely. Budapest: Akadémiai Kiadó, 1974.

Tökés, Rudolf L. *Béla Kun and the Hungarian Soviet Republic: The Origins and Role of the Communist Party of Hungary in the Revolutions of 1918–1919*. New York: Praeger, 1967.

Tokody, Gyula. *Deutschland und die ungarische Räterepublik*. Budapest: Akadémiai Kiadó, 1982.

Toth, Agnes. *Migrationen in Ungarn 1945–1948: Vertreibung der Ungarndeutschen, Binnenwanderungen und slowakisch-ungarischer Bevölkerungsaustausch*. Munich: Oldenbourg, 2001.

Trory, Ernie. *Hungary 1919 and 1956: The Anatomy of Counter-Revolution*. Hove, Sussex: Crabtree Press, 1981.

Unowsky, Daniel. *The Plunder: The 1898 Anti-Jewish Riots in Habsburg Galicia*. Stanford, CA: Stanford University Press, 2018.

The Pomp and Politics of Patriotism: Imperial Celebrations in Habsburg Austria, 1848–1916. West Lafayette, IN: Purdue University Press, 2005.

Unowsky, Daniel and Laurence Cole, eds. *The Limits of Loyalty: Imperial Symbolism, Popular Allegiances, and State Patriotism in the Late Habsburg Monarchy*. New York: Berghahn Books, 2007.

Unowsky, Daniel and Robert Nemes, eds. *Sites of European Antisemitism in the Age of Mass Politics, 1880–1918*. Waltham, MA: Brandeis University Press, 2014.

Vago, Bela, ed. *Jewish Assimilation in Modern Times*. Boulder, CO: Westview Press, 1981.

Vago, Bela and George L. Mosse, eds. *Jews and Non-Jews in Eastern Europe, 1918–1945*. New York: Wiley, 1974.

Valiani, Leo. *The End of Austria-Hungary*. Translated by Eric Mosbacher. New York: Knopf, 1973.

Varga, F. János. "Schönwald Pál: A Károlyi-per." *Társadalmi Szemle* 40/7 (1985): 104–6.

Vasari, Emilio. *Ein Königsdrama im Schatten Hitlers: Die Versuche des Reichsverwesers Horthy zur Gründung einer Dynastie*. Vienna: Verlag Herold, 1968.

Verhey, Jeffrey. *The Spirit Of 1914: Militarism, Myth and Mobilization in Germany*. Studies in the Cultural History of Modern Warfare. Cambridge: Cambridge University Press, 2000.

Vermes, Gábor. *István Tisza: The Liberal Vision and Conservative Statecraft of a Magyar Nationalist*. Boulder, CO: East European Monographs, 1985.

Völgyes, Iván. *The Hungarian Soviet Republic, 1919: An Evaluation and a Bibliography*. Stanford, CA: Hoover Institution Press, 1970.

, ed. *Hungary in Revolution, 1918–1919: Nine Essays*. Lincoln: University of Nebraska Press, 1971.

Volkov, Shulamit. "Antisemitism as Cultural Code: Reflections on the History and Historiography of Antisemitism in Imperial Germany." *Leo Baeck Yearbook* 23 (1978): 25–46.

"The Social and Political Functions of Late 19th Century Anti-Semitism: The Case of the Small Handicraft-Masters." In Herbart A. Strauss, ed.,*Hostages of Modernization: Studies on Modern Antisemitism, 1870–1933/39*, 62–79. Berlin: Walter de Gruyter, 1993.

Vondung, Klaus. "Deutsche Apokalypse 1914." In *Das Wilhelminische Bildungsbürgertum. Zur Sozialgeschichte seiner Ideen*. Göttingen: Vandenhoeck & Ruprecht, 1976.

Wachsmann, Nikolaus. *Hitler's Prisons: Legal Terror in Nazi Germany*. New Haven: Yale University Press, 2004.

Waite, Robert G. L. *The Vanguard of Nazism: The Free Corps Movement in Post-War Germany, 1918–1923*. New York: Norton, 1970. First published 1952.

Walter, Dirk. *Antisemitische Kriminalität und Gewalt: Judenfeindschaft in der Weimarer Republik*. Bonn: Verlag J. H. W. Dietz Nachfolger, 1999.

"Ungebetene Helfer – Denunziationen bei der Münchener Polizei anlässlich der Ostjuden-Ausweisungen 1919–1923/24." *Archiv für Polizeigeschichte* 18 (1996): 14–20.

Wasserstein, Bernard. *The Secret Lives of Trebitsch Lincoln*. New Haven, CT: Yale University Press, 1988.

Weckerlein, Friedrich, ed. *Freistaat! Die Anfänge des demokratischen Bayern 1918/19*. Munich: Piper, 1994.

Wehler, Hans-Ulrich. *Das deutsche Kaiserreich, 1871–1918*. Göttingen: Vandenhoeck & Ruprecht, 1973.

Weisbrod, Bernd. "Gewalt in der Politik: Zur politischen Kultur in Deutschland zwischen den beiden Weltkriegen." *Geschichte in Wissenschaft und Unterricht* 43/7 (July 1992): 391–404.

Werle, Gerhard. *Justiz-Strafrecht und polizeiliche Verbrechensbekämpfung im Dritten Reich*. Berlin: Walter de Gruyter, 1989.

Werner, George S. *Bavaria in the German Confederation, 1820–1848*. Rutherford, NJ: Fairleigh Dickinson University Press, 1977.

Wetzel, Richard F. *Inventing the Criminal: A History of German Criminology, 1880–1945*. Chapel Hill: University of North Carolina Press, 2000.

Wilson, Keith, ed. *Forging the Collective Memory: Government and International Historians through Two World Wars*. Providence: Berghahn Books, 1996.

Wingfield, Nancy M. *The World of Prostitution in Late Imperial Austria*. Oxford: Oxford University Press, 2017.

Wingfield, Nancy M. and Maria Bucur, eds., *Gender and War in Twentieth Century Eastern Europe*. Bloomington: Indiana University Press, 2006.

Winter, Jay. "Catastrophe and Culture: Recent Trends in the Historiography of the First World War." *Journal of Modern History* 64/3 (1992): 525–32.

Sites of Memory, Sites of Mourning: The Great War in European Cultural History. Cambridge: Cambridge University Press, 1998.

Winter, Jay and Geoffrey Parker. *The Great War and the Twentieth Century*. New Haven, CT: Yale University Press, 2000.

Winter, Jay and Jean-Louis Robert, eds. *Capital Cities at War: London, Paris, Berlin, 1914–1919*. Cambridge: Cambridge University Press, 1997.

Winter, Jay and Emmanuel Sivan, eds. *War and Remembrance in the Twentieth Century*. Cambridge: Cambridge University Press, 1999.

Wirsching, Andreas. *Vom Weltkrieg zum Bürgerkrieg? Politischer Extremismus in Deutschland und Frankreich, 1918–1933/39*. Munich: De Gruyter Oldenbourg, 1999.

Wood, Roger. *The Conservative Revolution in the Weimar Republic*. New York: St. Martin's Press, 1996.

Wrigley, Chris, ed. *Challenges of Labor: Central and Western Europe, 1917–1920*. New York: Routledge, 1993.

Wróbel, Piotr. "The Kaddish Years: Anti-Jewish Violence in East-Central Europe, 1918–1921." *Jahrbuch des Simon-Dubnow-Instituts* 4 (2005): 211–36.

Wüllenweber, Hans. *Sondergerichte im Dritten Reich: Vergessene Verbrechen der Justiz*. Frankfurt a.M.: Luchterhand, 1990.

Yitshaki, Shlomo. "Ha-yehudim be-mahapehot hungariya, 1918–1919." *Moreshet* 11 (1969): 113–34.

Zamoyski, Adam. *Phantom Terror: Political Paranoia and the Creation of the Modern State, 1789–1848*. New York: Basic Books, 2014.

Zeidler, Miklós. "Irredentism in Everyday Life in Hungary during the Inter-war Period." *REGIO: Minorities, Politics, Society* 12 (2002): 71–88.

Zeman, Z. A. B. *The Break-up of the Habsburg Empire, 1914–1918: A Study in National and Social Revolution*. London: Oxford University Press, 1961.

Ziemann, Benjamin . *War Experiences in Rural Germany, 1914–1923*. Translated by Alex Skinner. Oxford: Berg Publishers, 2007.

Zimmermann, Susan. *Die bessere Hälfte? Frauenbewegungen und Frauenbestrebungen im Ungarn der Habsburgermonarchie 1848 bis 1918*. Budapest: Promedia-Napvilág Kiadó, 1999.

"'Making a Living from Disgrace': The Politics of Prostitution, Female Poverty and Urban Gender Codes in Budapest and Vienna, 1866–1920." In Malcolm Gee, Tim Kirk, and Jill Steward, eds., *The City in Central Europe: Culture and Society from 1800 to the Present*, 175–95. Brookfield, VT: Ashgate, 1999.

Prächtige Armut: Fürsorge, Kinderschutz und Sozialreform in Budapest: Das sozialpolitische Laboratorium der Doppelmonarchie im Vergleich zu Wien 1873–1914. Sigmaringen: Thorbecke, 1997.

Zimmerman, Werner Gabriel. *Bayern und das Reich, 1918–1923: Der bayerische Föderalismus zwischen Revolution und Reaktion*. Munich: Richard Pflaum Verlag, 1953.

Zorn, Wolfgang. *Bayerns Geschichte im 20. Jahrhundert: Von der Monarchie zum Bundesland*. Munich: Verlag C.H. Beck, 1986.

Zwicker, Lisa Fetheringill. "Antisemitism, the Limits of Antisemitic Rhetoric, and a Movement against Russian Students at German Universities, 1908–1914." *Leo Baeck Institute Year Book* 55/1 (2010): 193–203.

Dissertations

Brenner, Arthur David. "Radical Pacifist, Refractory Professor: A Political and Intellectual Biography of Emil J. Gumbel (1891–1966)." Dissertation, Columbia University, 1993.

Gioielli, Emily. "White Misrule: Terror and Political Violence during Hungary's Long World War I." PhD Dissertation, Central European University, 2015.

Lange, Thomas. "Bayern im Ausnahmezustand 1919–1923: Zur politischen Funktion des bayerischen Ausnahmerechts in den ersten Jahren der Weimarer Republik." Dissertation, Ludwig Maximilians University, Munich, 1989.

Motyl, Katherina. "Bodies that Shimmer: An Embodied History of Vienna's New Woman, 1893–1931." Dissertation, University of Chicago, 2017.

Rape, L. "Die österreichische Heimwehr und ihre Beziehungen zur bayerischen Rechten zwischen 1920 und 1923." Dissertation, University of Vienna, 1968.

Index

Printed by Printforce, the Netherlands